A GUIDE TO
THE MAKERS OF
AMERICAN WOODEN PLANES

THIRD EDITION

EMIL AND MARTYL POLLAK

D1709767

THE ASTRAGAL PRESS   MENDHAM, NEW JERSEY

Published by
The Astragal Press
P.O. Box 239
Mendham, NJ 07945-0239

Library of Congress Catalogue Card Number 94-72304
ISBN 1-879335-51-4

Third Edition

To Herman Freedman, for his stead-
fast and valuable support

and

To the many plane collectors and
dedicated researchers, who were kind
enough to share their knowledge with
us and thus made this book possible.

CONTENTS

ACKNOWLEDGMENTS

This book was made possible through the efforts of many people. Some of the material we have used has been previously published in a variety of sources; much has been generously contributed by individual collectors from their personal research. Our primary role has been that of organizer, interpreter, illustrator, and editor.

We owe a great debt to Ken and Jane Roberts, who pioneered in this field and whose research has stood the test of time. With the Roberts' kind permission, we made extensive use of *Wooden Planes in 19th Century America, Volumes I and II,* and *Planemakers in New York State.*

Our thanks also go. . .

- to Herman Freedman, friend and mentor, who did yeoman service in rounding up plane rubbings and who provided the biographical articles on I. Day, Charles Dupee, Levi Little, L. Sampson, John and Moses Sleeper, Timothy Tileston, the Waltons, father and sons, and T. Waterman.
- to Elliot Sayward, who created and edited *Plane Talk* during its first nine years as a quarterly clearing house of information, and who allowed us full use of this material.
- to James I. Garvin, Curator of the New Hampshire Historical Society, for his help on the planemakers of that state.
- to Austin Heicher, who shared with us the work he had done on wedge outlines.
- to Larry Brundage, whose insatiable love for research helped solve many puzzles for us.
- to Don and Anne Wing, who shared both their collection and their store of information with us, and who provided invaluable information in their series of articles on major New England planemakers that appeared in *Plane Talk.*
- to Ed Ingraham for his generosity in making available to us his research on early New England planemakers.
- to Bud Steere for his time-consuming review of his own extensive collection in order to provide us with many rubbings and descriptive material.
- to Dick Hay, whose excellent *Directory of Baltimore Plane & Edge Tool Makers* was of great help to us and who gave additional help on the Baltimore area planes.
- to Dom Micalizzi for cheerfully tracking down New York City planemakers whenever asked.
- to Paul Kebabian for making his fine collection available to us and patiently answering our many questions.
- Jack Kebabian for the use of his pioneering work on the Nicholsons, Cesar Chelor, and other important early makers.
- to Bill Hilton, who provided us with much valuable information on the Boston and eastern Massachusetts makers and dealers.
- to Carl Bopp for making available his original research on the Whites and other early Philadelphia planemakers.
- to Alex Farnham, who gave us access to information on the New Jersey planemakers included in his fine book *Early Tools of New Jersey and the Men Who Made Them.*
- to Charles Ewing for making available to us his extensive research on the planemakers of Kentucky, Indiana, Michigan, and Illinois.
- to Gil and Mary Gandenberger for information on the Cincinnati planemakers, provided by them in their monograph *Cincinnati Plane, Edgetool Makers, and Dealers 1819-1851 (revised).*
- to Michael Humphrey for the use of the material appearing in his *Catalog of American Wooden Planes,* a quarterly that he edits and publishes continuing the work of *Plane Talk.*

1

- to John Tannehill and William Warner for making available their extensive research on the Carpenter family, and providing a substantial portion of the biographical material shown.
- to Chuck Prine for his original research on the early Pittsburgh planemakers.
- to Sara Holmes for her work on New Orleans hardware dealers.
- to Bob Graham, another pioneer whose work has stood the test of time.
- to Ben Blumenberg for all of his extensive research.

We would also like to thank for their help:

Donald Achenberg
Bill Ackroyd
Roger G. Alexander
Hank Allen
Charles Alley
Robert L. Allinger
Glenn Anderson
Donald A. Armistead
Mo Arnold
Bill Baader
Milton Bachelor
Wendell E. Badger
James S. Baird
Willis Barschied, Jr.
Jim Bassett
Kendall Bassett
Alan Bates
Milton Bachelder
Ray Beauduy
Frank Beck
Dale R. Beeks
Merc Beitler
Rick Benze
Robert Bernard
Jeff Biddle
Russell Bigelow
Bill Bilancio
Jerold Billings
Jack Birky
Dan Blackhurst
Clarence Blanchard
Jim Blower
Bill Boltz
B.J. Bond, Jr.
Len Borkowski
Gordon Bradford
Bruce Bradley
George Braun
Ray Brody
Bud Brown

Douglas V. Brown
James Brown
Seth Burchard
Kenneth Butler
Dale Butterworth
Richard Cammauf, Jr.
Thomas O. Carlsen
Dale Carpenter
Joe Casilli
Sherwood Chamberlain
Richard Chapman
Joe Clarkin
Jack Clouser
Brian Coe
Rodney Cole
Victor Cole
Dan Comerford
James A. Conrad
James Cooley
Bill Corsetti
Fred Courser
J.B. Cox
Talbot Crane
Dick Croteau
Bill Curtis
Richard De Avila
Andy D'Elia
Charles W. Darling, Sr.
Ron Davis
Thomas J. Davis
Ed Delaney
Andrew Delans
Emmet De Lay
Gordon Deming
John Dempsey
Barry Deutchmann
L G. De Wolf
Malcolm Dick
Dick Dickerson
George Dodge

Lee Donnelly
Martin J. Donnelly
Roger Draheim
Ralph Drew
Rick Ducey
Michael Dunbar
Stanley Duvall
Joe Dzaidul
Tony Eckert
Robert Elliot
Thomas Lee Elliott
Dave Englund
Jim Erdman
Bill Eviston
Charles and Cherie Fisk
Frank Flynn
Norman Forgit
Allan Foster
Gene Fox
Leonard France
Charles L. Frank
Jim Frederick
John Freeman
Rod Galstep
E.G. Gannicott
Rev. Dan Gatti, S.J.
James F. Gauntlett
James H. Gettle
John Gillis
Edward M. Gipson
Howard Godfrey
Jerold Goolsby
Robert Gordon
John C. Goss
Ronald Grabowski
Chuck Granick
Joe Grasso
Jack Grossman
Peter Habicht
Robert Haffner

John Haltmeyer
Dale Hanchett
Edward Harbulak
Joe Hauck
Don Hawkins
Jack S. Hays
Dave Heckel
Ted Heicher
Don Henschel
Oliver L. Herrick
John W. Hess
Carson Hicks
John Higdon
Ray and Jim Hill
Richard Holland
Sara J. Holmes
Ken Hopfel
Doug Houser
Dick Howe
Jack Howe
Charles F. Hummel
Doug James
Michael Jenkins
Eugene D. Johnson
Forrest B. Johnson
Frank D. Johnson
Jake Johnson
Frank E. Jones IV
Robert S. Jones
John Kahn
Ray Kauffman
Steve Kayser
Herb Kean
Steve Kean
John Kesterson
Arthur B. Kevorkian
Gene Kijowski
Ted Kinsey
Gerald R. Kline
Andrew Knapp
Tom Kohanski
Frank Kosmerl
Alan Lane
Patrick Lasswell
Harvey Lauer
James Lea
Pat Leach
Jim Leamy
Robert M. Leary

Glenn Leathersich
Robert G. Leckie, Jr.
David Lefkowith
Charles Leverone
Michael H. Lewis
R. Lewis
Ted Lindquist
Joe Link
Bill Linstromberg
George M. Little
Jeff Lock
Carol and Mary Lou Lomax
Phil Lothrop
Dan Ludwig
Harry Ludwig
John R. Mansavage
Ernie Martin
Walter J. Marx
Bill McCoy
James McCue
Tom McGill
Malcolm McGregor
Barton McGuire
Larry McKee
Michael B. McKee
Larry McManus
David Mello
John Meloney
William Melton
Charles Miecznikowski
Robert Mindek
Ed Mohler
Frank Moody
Cort Moore
Robert W. Moore
Ross Morcomb
Joe Morton
Ron Mossing
Ronald E. Mower
Jim Mulder
Tony Murland
Donald K. Myers
H. Nelke
Bob Nelson
Bill Neyer
Bob Nichols
Bob Ochenas
Robert Oehman
E.A. Olsen

Eric C. Olson
Steve Orbine
Robert Palm
Charles S. Parsons
Don Paschall
Roy Paulson
Ron Pearson
Rich Peiffer
David G. Perch
Francis Pfrank
Melvin Phaff
Bill Philips
Robert Pratt
Don Prowant
Hal Prucha
Bernard Prue
Jim Puckett
Mark and Jane Rees
Robert M. Reilly
Tom Relihan
E.J. Renier
H.R. Richardson
Max Richardson
Lee Richmond
Floyd Ridley
Bill Rigler
J.D. Riley
Gary Roberts
Warren Roberts
Joe Robichau
John M. Ross
Ray Sager
Robert Sand
George Sawyer
Erv Schaffer
Edna and Merrill Schmidt
Louis Schmidt
Richard Schusler
Art Scipione
David Scofield
Steve Scruggs
Gary Seekings
Dan Semel
Al Seymour
Bruce Shaughnessy
Tom Silberg
Eric Skopec
Rick Slaney
Frank Sleeper

Roger Smith
Edward Sorilla
Robert M. Soule
Richard Souza
Dave Spang
Richard Spurgeon
Richard Stair
Joe Stakes
David Stanley
John H. Stanley, Jr.
Philip Stanley
Richard Starr
Charles Staude
Harold Stiffler
Von Stoffer
Neil R. Stoll
Christopher Storb
Daniel P. Taber
Mike Tabor
Tony Tafel
Chris Tahk
John Tallis
Don Taylor
Terry Thackery
A.R. Thompson
David Thompson
Neil B. Todd
Laurent Torno, Jr.
Ray Townsend
Wayne Treadway
Paul Troutman
Dave Truesdale
Richard Turpen
William R. Velich
Darrell M. Vogt
Henry Voigt
Gene Walbridge
Philip Walker
John Walter
Tom Ward
Vern Ward
James Wareham
Bill Watkins
Merle Webb
Michael Weichbrod
Paul Weidenschilling
Dave Weinbaum
Dan Weinstock
Greg Welsh

Ron Wessels
Bob Westley
Karl West
Bob Wheeler
John Whelan
Paul Whitehouse
Philip Whitby
Bill Wilkins
Hampton Williams
James E. Wilson
John H. Wilson
David Wingo
Ray Wisnieski
Dick Wood
Don Wood
Dan Woodford
Parker Worley
Charles R. Wright
Robin Wyllie
Cliff Yaun
Bob Zarich
Gale Zerkle
Jack Zimmerman
John Zimmers
Steve Zluky

INTRODUCTION

The purpose of *A Guide to the Makers of American Wooden Planes* is to bring together in a concise and convenient form the significant information now available. We have tried to make the book useful and accessible to both the beginning and the advanced collector, to historians and genealogists, and to all others with an interest in the subject. We have included background information on the major types of planes and molding profiles, as well as a glossary explaining the terms used, and an extensive bibliography for those seeking additional information. Since value and how to determine it is an important element in collecting, we include a chapter on "What's A Plane Worth." We also provide a geographic directory that lists planemakers and dealers alphabetically under the states and cities in which they were known to work.

The heart of the guide however is the directory of planemakers and dealers. There are some 2000 biographical entries, supplemented by 2200 imprint illustrations, 1500 of which are rated for relative rarity, and almost 900 wedge outlines to help with identification.

The first planes used in this country were brought from England and the Continent by immigrant artisans. We have documentation of this dating back to the early 17th century. These early examples were probably for the most part bench planes, grooving planes, and rabbets, used for preparing the wood surface and for joinery. Molding planes appeared in listings toward the end of the 17th century: hollows and rounds, beads and reeds, together with some ovolos and ogees. The first recorded English planemaker (i.e., a man who made planes for sale and not just for his own use) was Thomas Granford who made planes in London, probably before 1700. John Davenport is believed to be a contemporary, as were possibly others still awaiting documentation. One of Granford's apprentices was Robert Wooding, who worked in London 1710-28. His planes exist in some number in England and have been found in this country in circumstances indicating their having been brought here by users.

The first recorded American planemaker, Francis Nicholson of Wrentham, Massachusetts, began his planemaking not long after Wooding; his working years were probably sometime between 1728 and 1753. But imported English planes predominated, certainly in the major seaport cities of Boston, New York, and Philadelphia, where mercantile connections, tradition, and the relative ease and economy of sea transportation compared with costly overland shipping, favored the English makers.

The appearance of the first professional planemakers coincided with the change in architectural and furniture styles and the use of more ornamental moldings. The wood used in fine furniture evolved from oak (so difficult to shape ornamentally) to walnut and mahogany. Shipping improved, trade expanded, and a whole new prosperous middle class developed, both in England and the colonies, anxious to acquire fine homes and furniture as symbols of its success.

The English retained their reputation for superior workmanship well into the 19th century. In addition to planes, plane irons were imported in large numbers from Sheffield and Birmingham.

The earliest colonial planemaking developed in the area between Boston and Providence, beginning in Wrentham, MA, and spreading outward: the Nicholsons, father and son, and Cesar Chelor in Wrentham, Jonathan Ballou and Jo. Fuller in Providence, RI, Samuel Doggett in Dedham, MA, Henry Wetherel in Norton, MA, John Walton and his sons in Reading, MA.

The planes made by these New Englanders differed from those of the English and their countrymen to the south in several ways. They made their early planes out of yellow birch, rather than the beech used by the others. Their plow planes had a distinctive style and, not surprisingly, are called Yankee plows. They were longer (10" vs. 7"-8½"), their fence arms were square, not rounded, and were set into the skate which was the same length as the stock. (See chapter on types of planes).

The New Englanders also tended to lag the English and the colonies to the south in reducing the size of their molding planes to the final standard length of 9½". We find many of their early planes still measuring 9⅞" to 10" right up to and through the Revolutionary War.

By the 1750's and 1760's planemakers also began to appear in the mid-Atlantic area. These are shadowy figures: Thomas Grant in New York City, Samuel Caruthers and Benjamin Armitage in Philadelphia. But Philadelphia and New York City still apparently looked to England for most of their planes until after the Revolution.

That war, and the economic distress that followed it, created a hiatus in the economy that lasted for a decade, until the adoption of the new constitution and the election of Washington as president. In the 1790's the new country recovered its prosperity and growth resumed. This reflected itself in planemaking and, for the first time, American makers began to produce planes in quantity.

The important names of this period, 1790-1810, include: New Englanders Jo. Fuller and John Lindenberger of Providence, RI, Aaron Smith of Rehoboth, MA, John Sleeper of Newburyport, MA, Nicholas Taber of New Bedford, MA, William Raymond of Beverly, MA, Levi Little of Boston and Henry Wetherell of Chatham, CT. John Stiles was active in Kingston, NY. In Philadelphia there was a large group: Thomas Napier, William Brooks, Thomas Goldsmith, John Butler, Amos Wheaton, and William Martin, all producing planes in the English style.

Further to the west in Lancaster, PA, Dietrich Heiss and his son Jacob were active and further south in Maryland, William Vance and John Keller began the tradition of the Baltimore makers.

Only New York City, among the major cities, lacked an active maker during this period. Perhaps this was because it was primarily a trading port and, unlike Philadelphia and Baltimore, was not a center of fine furniture making. Perhaps also an 1801 advertisement of Gerrit Van Wagenen, a merchant and importer, gives a clue: ". . .a handsome assortment of Carpenters' and Cabinetmakers' planes of Stothert's make all of which he will sell on reasonable terms." Stothert of Bath was an important English maker (-1785-1841) whose planes are often found in the greater New York area. English imports remained competitive, especially in New York.

During the early years of the 19th century, the country moved westward, first to western Pennsylvania and the newly important town of Pittsburgh, then into the Ohio territories and beyond. Cincinnati became an important planemaking center, and later St. Louis. The number of planemakers proliferated. Their various business endeavors prospered and failed as the country was periodically racked with panics and war. By the second quarter of the 19th century, the wooden plane had reached its zenith. The introduction of machines, the use of water and steam power, and the great improvements in transportation and communication led to the formation of larger companies, the use of convict labor, and the development of distribution systems that reached far beyond the place where the planes were made. This period also saw the beginnings of the metal plane, which would soon supersede the wooden one. By the 1880's the end was in sight. Though wooden planes continued to be offered into the 20th century, it was to a shrinking market made up largely of those who would not accept the change.

The *Guide*, then, is a reference to an important period in our economic and cultural history. It provides an insight into a group of men and the tools they made; tools that helped build the houses, the furniture, the ships, the coaches and wagons, the barrels; the many items vital to everyday life. To hold these tools in your hand is to touch and feel history.

The major portion of the *Guide* is an alphabetically arranged biographical directory of plane-makers and dealers. This is supplemented by a geographical directory listing makers and dealers by the states and cities in which they worked. This can be helpful in identifying a maker when only the location portion of an imprint is readable.

The maker or dealer is listed as his name appears on his imprint. The imprint is almost always found near the top of the toe (front) of the plane.

We have used a system of stars to indicate the relative rarity of a majority of the imprints that are illustrated. In determining rarity we have considered examples already known and those likely to be discovered.

RARITY RATINGS

★★★★★ (unique or almost unique) denotes fewer than 10 examples
★★★★ (extremely rare) denotes between 10 and 50 examples
★★★ (very rare) denotes between 50 and 100 examples
★★ (rare) denotes between 100 and 250 examples
★ (uncommon) denotes between 250 and 500 examples
FF (found freqently) denotes over 500 examples

WE WISH TO EMPHASIZE STRONGLY THAT WHAT WE ARE OFFERING IS ONLY AN EDUCATED GUESS AND A ROUGH GUIDE TO RELATIVE RARITY. We are not setting values. Our judgments are based on dealers' price lists and catalogs and listed auctions over the past seven or eight years; on discussions with dealers and collectors; on seemingly endless visits to antique shows, dealers' shops, tool society meetings, flea markets, and exposure to literally hundreds of plane collections. Still, we reiterate, what we offer is only our opinion and is subject to error.

We wish to list a few other caveats:

Regarding the FF (found frequently) category, we would like to point out that there are important qualifications that should be borne in mind. For instance, while Sandusky Tool Co. was a prolific manufacturer, whose planes are common (most designated FF), one of the highest priced wooden planes ever sold at auction was a Sandusky center-wheel plow. Also, though some Jo. Fuller planes are rated FF, they are eagerly sought after as classic examples of late 18th century, early 19th century, American wooden planemaking, and sell for significant prices. On the other hand, many early 19th century planes, whose makers' imprints are quite rare, sell for less. The point is that relative rarity of the planemaker's imprint is only one of the many factors that determine price. IN SUMMARY, THOUGH THE STAR SYSTEM MAY BE USEFUL AS AN INDICATION OF RARITY, RARITY IS ONLY ONE OF THE CRITERIA THAT DETERMINE VALUE. PLEASE SEE "WHAT'S A PLANE WORTH?" FOR A MORE COMPLETE DISCUSSION OF VALUE.

Not all known makers' imprints have been rated. In most of these cases, we simply don't have enough information to make a judgment.

We have tried to be conservative in establishing our relative rarity evaluations. We would prefer that should time prove us wrong, the imprint would be found rarer than our estimate rather than the reverse.

All imprint reproductions are actual size. Here too we want to qualify. The imprints were taken from rubbings of actual planes. Some of these planes are over 200 years old. Many have been much used and abused. Wood has shrunk and expanded, cracked, suffered from rot, insects and rodents. Planes were dropped, hammered on, or used as a hammer. Imprints were struck unevenly or overstruck. Imprint dies were damaged or worn down. In order to make the imprint clear and usable, we enlarged and retouched the rubbings before returning them to actual size. The result, we believe, is useful, authentic, and reasonably accurate, but that's all.

Wedge outlines are shown at 55% of actual size and represent that portion of the wedge that appears above the body of the plane.

In the 18th century and early 19th century, "I" was used for "J" (e.g., I. IONES for J. JONES) and a long "f"" was used for "s". We have alphabetized as the letters appear on the imprint. We would also like to point out that spelling in the 18th and 19th centuries was rather haphazard. Chelor could very quickly become Shaylor, or Hide become Hyde. The custom of naming sons after fathers for generation after generation, and the son dropping the Jr. on the death of the father, and his son in turn adopting it, can easily lead to confusion. As for geographical locations, towns and villages have frequently been renamed over the years and boundary lines have been moved.

We have included tool dealers and hardware dealers when their marks appear on a plane. In some cases they made planes as well as distributed them. In many cases we don't know.

The geographic directory lists states and then cities alphabetically: under them the planemakers who worked there. These directories should prove helpful in identifying partially illegible imprints, and in providing a checklist for regional collecting and research.

Please note that the letter "P" in parentheses indicates that this is a probable location for the planemaker involved.

WHAT'S A PLANE WORTH?

Recently sold at auction:
- A Francis Nicholson crown molder - $10,000.
- An Israel White patented three-arm plow plane - $8,500.
- A Sandusky Tool Co. handled boxwood center-wheel plow plane with ivory tips - $8,000.

These of course are the exceptional prices. It is still possible to buy common but good, usable planes for as little as $10. However, rare 18th century planes, as well as choice 19th century ones, frequently sell for $500 and more and it's seldom that an 18th century plane by a known maker, in good condition, will sell for less than $100. This has not always been the case. Rather it is something that has occurred quite recently. So let's examine what has happened to affect the value of planes and what may happen in the future.

In a free market, such as that for antique tools, price is set by supply and demand. The supply side of tools is, by definition, finite. Hidden hoards will undoubtedly continue to be found in barns and attics and higher prices will tend to bring additional material onto the market. But most planemakers, the early ones in particular, made planes over relatively short periods of time and supplied small market areas. If we estimate that an average maker could produce three or four planes a day and therefore probably no more than a 1000 a year working full time (assuming a demand for that many), and then consider the daily wear and tear and the many hazards the planes were exposed to over the past 150 to 250 years, it's remarkable that so many examples survive. Several serious efforts have been made to determine what has survived of some of the early makers' work. The authors undertook such a census of the planes of Francis and John Nicholson and Cesar Chelor in 1985 (*The Chronicle*, June 1985). 3500 census forms were distributed to every collector believed to own examples. Eighty-nine respondents reported owning 248 planes: 106 by Francis Nicholson, 51 by John Nicholson, and 91 by Cesar Chelor. Because of our work on the *Guide* and exposure to collectors and collections, we were reasonably satisfied that we had identified most planes found to date. This, then, is what has survived (except for examples that may still be found) of the work of three early, active, planemakers who produced over a number of years.

Alan Bates did a similar census of Thomas Napier (*Thomas Napier, The Scottish Connection*, 1986), another active 18th century Philadelphia planemaker, who worked for 10 to 20 years. Only 46 examples were reported.

So on the supply side we have a limited number of planes made by documented 18th century makers; perhaps a total of 25,000 to 50,000, when we include the more prolific makers such as Jo. Fuller, John Sleeper, Aaron Smith, and Henry Wetherell. As for the 19th century, particularly the middle and later periods, when machine production became dominant, tremendous numbers of planes were produced, and a great many still remain. Nevertheless, certain types of planes and certain makers from this period are quite rare.

On the demand side of the equation, there are several points to be considered. First, there has been a great revival of interest in our historical heritage, in particular economic and technological history, the study of how the average person lived and supported himself. We see it expressed in increased attendance at museums and historical parks, in the restoration of old houses and even entire sections of our cities. Combined with this renewal is a rising interest in the collection and study of artifacts and memorabilia, the proliferation of antique shows, craft fairs, and flea markets. The tremendous price increase in early American furniture and art is another manifestation, as is the growth in the circulation of magazines such as "Fine Woodworking" and various antique journals, and the success of companies such as Woodcraft and Garrett Wade in retailing quality hand tools for the user. There is an increasing appreciation of things handcrafted and a growing number of young artisans entering fields previously thought to be dying. It is as if people are trying to find individuality and roots in an increasingly impersonal and highly technological society.

This trend has had a profound effect on the demand for antique tools and signed wooden planes in particular. Some of this demand comes from the artisan-user who finds such tools better made and/or cheaper than their modern counterparts. Sometimes they are otherwise unavailable, and to many restorationists, using antique tools is the only authentic way to work.

There is an even greater demand from collectors, with a growing recognition that these planes are among this country's oldest signed artifacts. These were the tools used to make the fine furniture now exhibited in museums and to decorate the historic buildings we so admire. At the very least they were good honest working tools, patinated by long hard use. They played an important role in the lives of their owners and in the economic development of our country. And in the case of the finest examples, made of exotic woods and trimmed with brass and ivory and other ornamentation, they are an expression of the maker's pride of workmanship and truly works of art.

How large is this demand from collectors? The various American antique tool clubs and societies probably have at present a total membership of 10,000 to 15,000. Non-member collectors may be several times that number; a grand total of perhaps 50,000 overall, probably double that of ten years ago, and growing. Certainly a very small number compared to those who collect stamps, or coins, or even baseball cards. Not only are the numbers of tool collectors tiny compared with those in other fields, but, not surprisingly, no tool has ever even approached the auction price of the Brasher doubloon, or the 24¢ U.S. inverted airmail. The total realization of the most successful two-day tool auction has been less than the price of a single Winslow Homer or a George Bellows painting.

Our conclusion therefore is that the supply, particularly of the early planes is quite limited, and that the number of collectors (the demand side) has been growing, and is likely to grow much more, though it is still relatively small by most standards.

Let us now turn our attention to the criteria the market seems to apply in valuing planes.

TYPE OF PLANE

A cornice plane will typically sell for 25 times, or more, the price of a hollow or round by the same maker. Why? Partly, perhaps, because of visual appeal - the simple little round versus the dramatic large crown molder with its complex profile, large iron, wedge and tote. But mostly, we believe, it's a question of supply. A study made by Anne and Donald Wing of the production records of the Greenfield Tool Co. for November 1854 illustrates the point. Of a total of 11,900 planes made in that month, 4600 or 38% were bench planes. 4300 or 37% were molding planes. 1300 (11%) were match planes, 700(6%) were rabbets and 262 (2%) were plow planes, and 700 (6%) were others. Of the 4300 molding planes, 2400 were hollows and rounds, 1100 were beads, 795 were complex molding planes, and only 15 were wide, handled planes - which presumably included cornice planes.

An ordinary, unhandled plow plane will sell for at least four or five times the price of a hollow or round. Again, the Greenfield production records show that in 1853 a total of 1843 plows were made, an average of only 150 per month. Plows represented only 2% of the total production for November 1854, vs. 20% for the hollows and rounds.

Though we recognize that we may be over-simplifying a complicated subject, we would offer as a rough rule of thumb the following list, showing relative rarity by type of plane in ascending order.

- hollow and rounds
- rabbets
- beads
- ordinary moldings
- dadoes, filletsters, sash planes
- complex molding planes
- unhandled plow planes
- handled plow planes
- panel raisers
- cornice planes/crown molders

Bench planes made after the first quarter of the 19th century are fairly common. Earlier, particularly with 18th century makers' imprints, they are quite rare, perhaps because users at that time tended to make their own and save money; or perhaps because bench planes got harder use and, being easier to replace, were simply used up and discarded.

MATERIAL USED

Returning again to the Greenfield Tool Co., we find that of the 1843 plow planes produced during 1853, 1227 were made of beech, 356 of boxwood, 182 of rosewood, and 78 of ebony. Only two of the boxwood and two of the ebony planes were ivory tipped. The 1872 Greenfield catalog priced handled beech plows at $7, rosewood or boxwood at $9, ebony at $12, rosewood trimmed with ivory at $13.50 to $18.20, and ebony trimmed with ivory at $16.55 to $20.20, a very high price in terms of 1872 wages. Rarity based on the material used, again as a rough rule of thumb, begins with beech, then boxwood, rosewood, and, the most rare, ebony. Ivory trim or parts adds another magnitude of rarity to each category, as does exotica such as German silver trim.

Lignum, rosewood and ebony are sometimes found in bench planes, particularly those from coastal areas, where these materials were most readily available.

Cherry and fruitwoods such as apple were also used occasionally, sometimes by the 18th century makers. Sun planes were often made of these woods. Bench planes, particularly jointers, are found made of apple, maple or mahogany, and were usually owner-made. The unusual woods, particularly when they enhance the appearance of a plane, add significantly to its value.

REGIONAL PREFERENCES

There is at present a strong tendency to collect planemakers by region. Partly this may be chauvinism; more likely it has a practical basis, the fact that, for example, the planes made by a Massachusetts maker will most often be found in Massachusetts and thus will be more available to Massachusetts collectors. Also research can more readily be done in one's own locality. At any rate, there is frequently little appreciation of the rarity of one region's planemakers in another region. While premium prices may be paid at a New Hampshire auction when two determined local collectors want a plane made by a New Hampshire maker, the same plane might arouse little interest in Pennsylvania. This tendency is changing, but it is still a reality of the marketplace.

There has been much greater interest in 18th century New England planes by New Englanders than that shown by mid-Atlantic collectors in comparable New York and Pennsylvania planemakers.

For example, Caruthers, a very rare mid-18th century Philadelphia maker has generally sold for much less than the similarly rare and early Dedham, MA, maker, S. Dean. This seems to be changing as collectors outside of New England become interested in their local planes and recognize the relative values.

AESTHETICS

Some planemakers have attracted collectors because of the great variety of planes they made, the high quality of their workmanship, or their unusual styling. They may command a market premium although they are not that uncommon. Some examples would be J.R. Tolman, Israel White, and E.W. Carpenter.

CHARISMA OF THE MAKER

Planes by Cesar Chelor and Francis Nicholson are not as rare as those of John Nicholson, yet they most often sell for more. Chelor was a black slave owned by Francis Nicholson and freed on his master's death. Planes signed by him, therefore, were made after 1753. Yet despite this later date, his planes, on a comparable basis, will tend to sell for more than those of his master, Francis Nicholson, who is considered our first documented planemaker, and may have signed planes as early as 1728. John Nicholson, son of Francis, probably worked as early as the 1730's. His planes are the rarest of the three. He signed planes before Cesar Chelor, yet he often runs a poor third in prices realized. So the charisma of being a freed black slave or being the first planemaker offsets the fact of greater rarity. At the other extreme of charisma are the imprints of tool and hardware stores that suffer from collector disinterest. Some are very rare, indeed, and most have interesting stories to tell.

CONDITION

The determination and description of condition is still in the formative stage. Several dealers have attempted to establish a uniform grading system which has received some acceptance. Condition undoubtedly affects price, but in elusive ways. For some collectors a mint appearance will command a premium; for others a rich, patinated look, achieved from years of use and careful maintenance will be the most desireable. For some a re-shaped plane, perhaps a round remodeled into a molding plane, will have a special interest; yet for others it will devalue the plane. How much should a carefully made repair affect the price? How much cleaning or refinishing should a plane have, and how does that influence its value? If a plane was used over an owner's lifetime, isn't it perfectly reasonable to expect that the plane iron is no longer the original one or that the wedge has perhaps been replaced? Under the best of circumstances, much about condition will remain subjective and judgmental and a will-o'-the-wisp in establishing price.

Having said this, there are still certain factors of condition which seem to affect price:
 • A weak, overstruck, or partial maker imprint can signficantly reduce the value of a plane, particularly where the imprint is the major attraction in an otherwise undistinguished piece.
 • Worm holes: a few are acceptable; a great many are not.

- Dry rot: often not fully visible, it can render a plane virtually valueless. Watch out for planes that seem too light. That may be your clue.
- Cracks: usually not too serious unless life-threatening.
- Screw holes: usually from the attachment of a temporary fence. Not considered serious.
- A hanging hole: we don't mind them. They seem to be a part of the owner's presence, much like the patina.
- Missing wedge: a missing wedge most definitely detracts from the value of a plane.
- A deformed wedge: planes were dropped, wedge finials were struck and over time the effect was cumulative. Moderate deformity comes under the heading of honest use; beyond that point it really detracts. We can't deny that a crisp, well-formed wedge is a delight and collectors will pay more for it.
- An improper wedge: this should be considered the same as a missing wedge.
- Missing boxing: again a question of degree.
- A missing plane iron or improper iron (really the same thing): serious if you're planning to use; less serious for the collector. Much as the original owner may have had to replace the iron, so we believe it acceptable for the present owner to adapt an iron contemporary to the plane.
- A sole profile recut: the usual result is an ill-proportioned plane body, a widened mouth, cut down boxing and a plane that just looks wrong. Our ancestors were of necessity frugal and often had to improvise. If you can accept the tool in that spirit, fine. Otherwise, unless very rare, it's best to avoid.
- Plane shortened (or shot): really bad news. A barbaric practice committed mainly on older planes over the $9\frac{1}{2}$" standard length adopted in the 19th century. If done to the toe, it's really terrible, since the maker's imprint will have been removed. If done to the heel, the imprint will have been saved, but the shortened plane will seem out of proportion.
- Stains: there's a difference between surface grime and a true stain. Stains are a problem and a badly stained plane is best avoided.
- The driftwood look: the plane may look awful, but if there's no rot you can usually bring back the wood and re-create the appropriate finish.
- Stripped threads on screw-arm planes: seriously damaged threads reduce value significantly.

Some other factors that affect value:
- Sets of planes, such as a complete matched set of hollows and rounds, or a graded set of beads or a matched set of complex moldings, will add value. The sum is usually worth more than its parts in this instance.
- A matched pair of plank planes often tends to be under-valued because of its bulk, the space it consumes, and because it doesn't show well on the shelf. This is also true of the larger bench planes.
- A toted (handled) plow plane is more valuable than an untoted one.
- Always check owners' names that may be imprinted on the plane. Occasionally marks of recognized cabinetmakers, clockmakers, or joiners are found, adding greatly to the interest and value of the piece.
- Sandusky, Greenfield, and Auburn are very common imprints, yet some of the types of planes they made are very rare. Planes of any one of these companies would make a very interesting specialized collection, particularly since reprints of their old trade catalogs are available for guidance.

This discussion on value is meant only as a guide. The subject is a complex one. The market for American wooden planes is still thin and relatively inefficient. Price, however, cannot be ignored. It will undoubtedly receive increasing attention. As always, knowledge is power. Caveat emptor!!

Price information on American wooden planes is offered in two books published by The Astragal Press. *A Price Guide to Antique Tools* illustrates 350 of the more common maker imprints and gives price ranges for these by type of plane and condition. *Prices Realized on Rare Imprinted American Wooden Planes* lists 2000 recent transactions by planemaker, imprint, and condition. (See the Bibliography).

TYPES OF PLANES

This is a brief review of the more common types of planes, the ones most likely to be encountered. There are many variations of these, many other specialized planes, and many designed for specific industries, e.g., coopers', coachmakers', and shipwrights' planes. Readers who are interested in a more detailed description of these, and other kinds of planes, are urged to refer to John Whelan's book *The Wooden Plane: Its History, Form and Function* (see Bibliography).

PLANES USED TO PREPARE OR FINISH THE WOOD SURFACE

BENCH PLANES A series of (usually) four planes commonly found on the workbench. All have a flat sole, an iron held at a 45° - 50° angle to the stock, and no side throat opening, but instead, a wide opening at the top of the plane for the escape of shavings.

SMOOTH PLANE $6\frac{1}{2}$" to $10\frac{1}{2}$" long and used to do the final finishing and smoothing on the surface of the wood.

JACK PLANE 14" to 16" long and the most widely used of all the bench planes. It is used for planing off the most amount of wood in the least amount of time, i.e., for the rough work.

FORE PLANE 18" to 22" long. Less common than jack planes and used to smooth off the work after using a jack. However, in many cases, a fore plane was not owned at all and the workman went from the jack plane to the smoother or jointer.

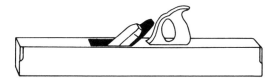

JOINTER PLANE 22" to 32" long, used to make the finishing passes on the long straight edges of the wood pieces preparatory to joining them. A plane of this type longer than 36" is usually called a floor plane.

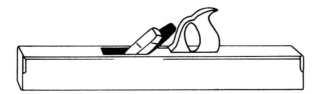

CIRCULAR OR COMPASS PLANE Similar to the smoother in appearance and use, except that the sole is convex from front to back, enabling the plane to be used on curved surfaces.

MITER PLANE (sometimes called "block" plane) Looks similar to the smooth plane except that the iron is set at a 35° (or lower) angle to the stock rather than the 45° of the smoother. It has a very narrow mouth opening and because the blade angle is so low, the blade is often reversed so that the bevel is up. Used to trim the end grain of wood. Since it can be held in one hand, it is also used for a wide variety of other finishing and fitting work.

TOOTHING PLANE Much the same size and shape as the smoother, except that the iron is almost vertical to the stock and is serrated. Used to ridge the wood prior to glueing veneer, or to level difficult grain.

PLANES USED TO SHAPE WOOD FOR A FUNCTIONAL PURPOSE

SASH PLANE For making window frames; using either a single iron consisting of two distinct sections or, most commonly, two irons, a rabbet and a molding blade, so that both the groove for the glass and the decorative inside molding are cut at the same time. A very similar plane is the DOOR PLANE, which cuts the groove for the door panel and the molding at the same time.

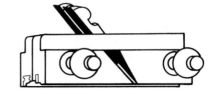

COPING PLANE   Sold with sash planes and having a blade configured exactly the reverse of the sash plane's, since the molding had to fit into the coping cut.

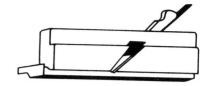

PUMP PLANE   A jack-sized plane with an astragal-like shaped sole, making one half of a hollow pipe that was used with a chain pump. It was ususually made by the user or adapted by him from an old jack plane.

NOSING PLANE   For making the rounded front edge of a stair tread. The cutting edge of the iron is a hollow semi-circle. It can also be found with two irons, each making a half of the cut.

RAISING PLANE OR PANEL RAISER   Used to cut out a flat area around the edges of a panel (as in door panels) so that the center of the panel stands out in relief and the edges are narrow enough to fit into the side grooves. Usually about 14" to 16" long and 2" to 4" wide, with a skewed iron.

SPAR OR MAST PLANE   Generally the size of a smoother and shallowly concave from side to side so it can follow the shape of a mast or spar. Used by shipwrights (and usually made by them) and frequently of lignum or other exotic wood.

TABLE PLANES   Used in pairs for making a drop-leaf table; one cut the rounded edge of the table, the other cut the hollow edge of the leaf that fitted over it.

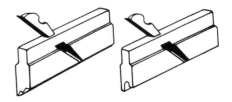

PLANES USED FOR JOINING WOOD

JOINTER   See bench planes.

RABBET (in England "rebate"). Used to cut away a step (called a rabbet) along the edge of the wood that will accommodate another piece of wood, as in an overlapping joint or as on the back of a picture frame to receive the glass. The plane is usually flat-bottomed with the iron extending the full width of the sole and slightly beyond. The iron is set straight or skewed. A distinguishing feature of the the rabbet and the dado is the gracefully curved open throat for shavings escape.

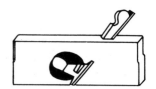

DADO PLANE The purpose of the dado is similar to that of the plow, but the dado is designed to cut a groove across the grain without tearing the wood. To accomplish this the iron is skewed so that the wood fibers may be peeled back. It is preceded by a vertical iron sharpened with two knife-like spurs, to sever the fibers.

SIDE RABBET The cutting edge of this plane extends up the side of the plane body (stock) rather than along the bottom, and the iron is almost vertical to the stock. The plane is used to clean and widen the sides of the rabbet or dado and was sold in pairs for a right- and left-hand cut.

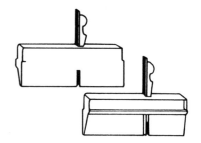

FILLETSTER (in England "fillister"). The filletster is used for the same purpose as the rabbet, except that the filletster has a fence to control the width of the rabbet cut and usually a depth stop to control the depth. The filletster is also distinguished by a small throat opening like that of a molding plane, rather than the wide curve of the rabbet plane. Filletsters with adjustable fences are called "moving filletsters."

HALVING PLANE This is a fixed filletster which cuts a rabbet as deep as it is wide, used for making half-lap joints.

PLOW PLANE This plane is used to cut a groove, with the grain, parallel to the edge of the wood. The plow consists of two major sections: the plane stock (usually 8 - 9" long) which came with a set of irons of varying widths; and the fence, whose attached arms fit through the stock and are fixed in place by wedges or by screw nuts. (Continental European plows, conversely, have the arms attached to the stock and fitting through the fence). The fence regulates the distance of the groove from the edge of the wood and, usually the plow is fitted also with a depth stop, to control the depth of the groove.

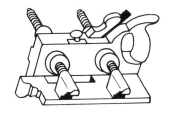

Handled screw-arm plow
ca.1850.

The standard plow plane derives from the English style. The Yankee plow plane was developed and used in New England during the 18th and very early 19th centuries, after which it was superseded by the standard plow. The Yankee plow tended to be longer (usually 10"), the fence did not extend beyond the stock, the arms were square and mortised into the fence. The arms were most often secured by thumb-screws, sometimes with wedges, and occasionally with both.

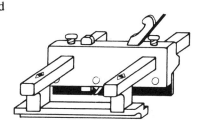

Yankee plow, ca. 1800.

MATCH PLANES (TONGUE AND GROOVE) A set of two planes, one of which cuts a tongue in the center of the edge of a board and the other of which cuts a corresponding groove in another board. These planes were often found combined in a single stock as shown in the illustration, the tongue plane on one side, the grooving plane on the other, facing in opposite directions. They may be found in sets with adjustable fences mounted on arms as in a plow: these are usually the longer (13" - 14") sets called plank planes.

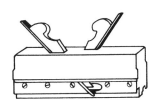

PLANES USED TO DECORATE WOOD

In the following illustrations the hatched areas are the profiles cut by the molding planes and the darker lines represent the shape of each molding plane.

CHAMFER PLANE Used to cut away the sharp right angle edges of a piece of wood to form a bevel, or chamfer, usually 45°. The common form has a sole deeply V-grooved, so it can fit over the right-angle edge. The iron protrudes into this groove far enough to cut the desired width of chamfer, and a sliding box is moved down in front of it to form the mouth.

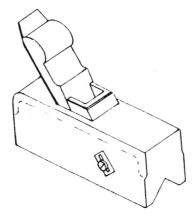

HOLLOW AND ROUND PLANES These are the most common molding planes, sold in pairs and usually available in 24 sizes from 1/16" to 2" wide in the U.S, and 18 sizes in England. The hollow has a shallow concave iron and so cuts a convex shape, while the round has a shallow convex iron and so makes a concave cut. The planes were usually used together to form more elaborate shapes.

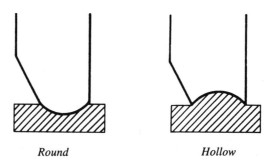

Round   *Hollow*

QUARTER ROUND This plane makes the common convex molding that consists of a quarter of a circle.

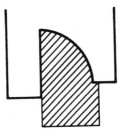

Quarter Round with fence

20

COVE A plane that cuts a reverse of the quarter round, i.e. a concave quarter circle. Elliptical forms are also seen.

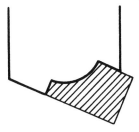

BEADING PLANES A bead is a small, convex, half circle molding, and beading planes make several kinds including:

CENTER BEAD Makes a bead in the center of the wood.

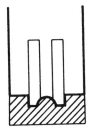

SIDE BEAD Makes a bead along the edge of the wood.

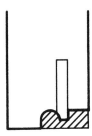

ASTRAGAL Makes a bead set in from the edge of the wood.

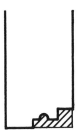

REEDING PLANE   Makes two or more beads, side by side.

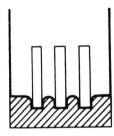

FLUTING PLANE   Reverse of a bead: cuts a holow groove of semi-circular shape. Multiple fluting planes cut two or more flutes, side by side.

SNIPE BILLS   Planes used to clean and widen the cuts made by other molding planes. They were sold in right- and left-hand pairs.

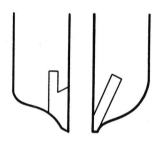

OGEE   A plane that cuts an S-shaped molding. A Roman ogee joins a circular hollow and a round, while a Grecian ogee joins elliptical curves and almost always ends in a quirk. A regular ogee has the hollow near the edge of the board; a reverse ogee places the round section there.

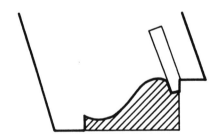

OVOLO   A plane that cuts a convex curve. A quarter round may be called a "square" or Roman ovolo, while one of elliptical shape, usually ending in a quirk, is a Grecian ovolo.

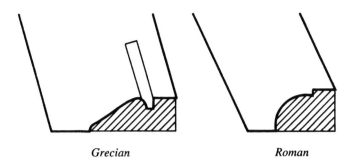

Grecian   *Roman*

COMPLEX MOLDERS   Molding planes cutting combinations of some of the simpler forms described above are usually lumped together under this designation. Common forms are Grecian ogee with bevel, or with bead, or with astragal; and Grecian ovolo with similar additions.

CORNICE PLANE OR CROWN MOLDER   A wide plane cutting a large complex molding, often equipped with handles or hole for thongs in front for pulling as well as pushing. The molding is cut in a board which is then mounted at an angle at the juncture of wall and ceiling to form the "crown molding." The king of the molding planes, it is much prized by collectors. The largest known cornice plane is in the collection of the North Andover, Ma., Historical Society. Made by William Raymond, it is 9" wide.

For a complete description of all the planes, plus the various molding profiles, along with illustrations, refer to *The American Wooden Plane* by John Whelan (see Bibliography).

W.F. ACHENBACH

Achenbach patent (No. 310163, Jan. 6, 1885) consisted of two ½" wide steel wear strips set into the sole of the plane, one in front of the mouth, the second toward the rear. The two examples reported, one a jack, the other a smoothinng plane, were manufactured under the Ogontz Tool Co. name (w.s.). ★★★★★

ACUSHNET

Several bench planes have been reported. Two smoothing planes have have carried the numbers " 21" and " 93" respectively. The town of Acushnet is near New Bedford, MA. Possibly a trade name used by Lamb & Brownell or The Taber Plane Co. (w.s.) each of whom made planes for hardware dealers.

A  B

A. ADAMS

A. Adams was probably a late 18c planemaker, whose style would indicate a southeastern New England location. A large crown molder, with offset handle, a Yankee-style plow plane, and several 10" molding planes, all made of yellow birch, have been reported. The plow plane is similar in style to that of Jo. Fuller. ★★★★★

H. ADAMS

Listed in an 1856 directory as a Hopkinton, MA, planemaker. No example of his work has been reported. (see William Adams)

H. ADAMS & CO.

There is no record of an H. Adams & Co. in the NYC directories. There was however a J.H. ADAMS & CO. listed as a hardware dealer 1841-70, after which time it became Joseph H. Adams & Son until 1873. The cove molding plane whose imprint is illustrated below is also imprinted "156" on its heel. This is the style number for a cove in the Auburn Tool Co. (w.s.) 1869 price list.   ★★★

M. ADAMS

Several examples have been reported, including a cornice plane and a complex molder. Possibly from the Holliston area of MA. Appearance is early 19c. A Moses Adams was listed in the 1850 census as a carpenter, age 69, in Holliston and was also listed in the Federal census from 1810 to 1840.

WILLIAM ADAMS

Listed in an 1856 directory as a Hopkinton, MA, planemaker. No example of his work has been reported. (see H. Adams)

ADAMS HARDWARE & PAINT CO.

A Lowell, MA, hardware company whose imprint was reported on an 8" long smoothing plane.

C.W. ADDIS

This name was listed as a planemaker in the 1850 New Haven, CT, directory. (see Beacher & Addis)

WM. ADGER

The 1850 Federal census listed William Adger as a 32-year old merchant, born in South Carolina and owning realty worth $20,000. A probable hardware dealer.   ★★★

T. AIKMAN

Probably Thomas Aikman, a cabinetmaker/planemaker who lived in the city of Burlington, NJ, just across the Delaware River from Philadelphia. Thomas Aikman was born in Scotland ca.1780 and became part of the Scottish migration to America, although the date of his arrival here is not known. He married his first wife, Jane Lazilere,on October 7, 1802; his second wife, Franklina Elizabeth on April 24, 1821. They lived on Pearl Street in Burlington, where he had a house, barn and shop. Aikman was listed as actively working as a cabinetmaker in Burlington, ca.1800, and died from "debility" in 1850 according to the *New Jersey 1850 Mortality*. Part of his inventory reads "lumber in shop" and "tools, saws, planes, etc."

Aikman planes are rare; nearly all have just the T. AIKMAN (A) imprint, omitting a location. Perhaps he spent only a brief time working in Philadelphia, just across the rive, or perhaps he felt, at some time, that a Philadelphia location stamp was more prestigious than a Burlington one.   A: ★★★   A1: ★★★★

A   A1   A

ALBANY TOOL CO.

Thought to be a hardware dealer. One example appears on a boxwood, screw-arm handled plow with M. Crannell (w.s.) style nuts and fence profile; two others a skew rabbet marked "181", which was the Auburn Tool Co. style number for skew rabbets, and a #14 round marked "180", the Auburn style number for hollows and rounds.   ★★★

GEORGE ALBERT

Listed as a planemaker in Madison, IN, in the 1850 federal census, age 20, born in Kentucky. No example has been reported.

H. ALBERT & CO.

Henry Albert was listed as a planemaker in the 1808 and 1818 Philadelphia, PA, directories.   ★★★

A. ALBERTSON & CO.

The EAIA *Directory of American Toolmakers* lists A. Albertson & Co. as a maker of drawknives and edge tools in Poughkeepsie, NY, 1850-70. Two jack planes with the A. Albertson & Co. imprint have been reported.

ALFORD

Consider Alford, one of the earliest New York City planemakers, worked 1812-17 at 15 Catherine Street. An advertisement in the *Connecticut Courant* of June 29, 1819, offering a reward of $20 for a runaway apprentice, is signed Consider Alford, blind-maker, No. 15 Catherine Street, New York. Alford married Lucy Fitch Kennedy, the sister of Leonard Kennedy (w.s.) and the aunt of Samuel Kennedy (w.s.) in 1800 in Windham, CT. Samuel Kennedy was making planes by 1817 at Alford's former New York City address. ★★

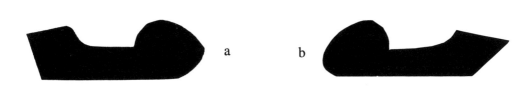

a   b

ALFRED ALFORD PLANE CO.
Alfred and Arba Alford were the principals, making planes from 1849 to 1853 in the old Hitchcock Chair factory in Riverton, CT, (then called Hitchcockville). The firm was succeeded by the Phoenix Co. (w.s.).

J.M. ALLARD
James Madison Allard was the youngest son of Samuel Haven Allard (1784 - 1878) and Judith Fall Allard. He was born April 9, 1819, in that part of Eaton, NH, that is now Madison; and died in North Conway, NH, March 24, 1888, aged 69. He learned the carpenter's trade and later settled in Conway, where he owned and cultivated a farm and also worked at his trade. He was elected constable and also selectman. Examples reported include a 17" razeed closed handle jack, and a 9⅜" long molding plane with round chamfers.

C. ALLEN
Caleb Allen (b. Providence, RI, 1777 - d. 1854) appeared on an 1814 jury list as a "tool cutter" and was listed in the 1850 Federal census as a carpenter in Lansingburgh, NY, age 73. Lansingburgh, which was founded ca.1770, became part of Troy, NY, in 1791, although the original name has continued to be used. Allen came to Lansingburgh in 1787. His molding planes are made of beech, and range in length from 9⅜" to 9¾" . The shorter planes have rounded chamfers; the longer, flat chamfers. One example has an iron made by Green (Sheffield 1774-1824—). The variations in length and style would suggest that Allen made planes over a long period, though probably not in large quantities. Both his wedge shape and the incised imprint are very similar to those of S.E. Jones (w.s.), also of Lansingburgh, who preceded Allen, and to whom Allen may have been apprenticed.   A: ★★★★   A1: ★★   *(see next page)*

A   A   A1

J.S. ALLEN

James S. Allen, who was listed in the 1850 census of Vernon, OH, as a cabinet- and toolmaker, age 41, was born in Massachusetts and came to Ohio sometime before 1835. In the 1860 census he was listed as a joiner.A plow plane with his imprint and location stamp has been reported.

T.C.G. ALLEN

Thomas C.G. Allen was listed in the Milwaukee, WI, directories 1851-57 as a planemaker, and in the 1850 census as a carpenter, age 31, and born in Scotland. No example has been reported.

ALLEN & CO.

Benjamin Allen & Co. advertised in the Dec. 2, 1829 *Providence Daily Advertiser* woodworking tools including bench planes and also an assortment of molding tools of Smith's make (probably Ezekiel Smith, w.s.). A coping plane and an adjustable sash made by J.R. Gale (w.s.) have been reported overstruck by the Allen & Co. mark. Allen's shop at 4 Broad Street was about a block away from Gale's.

ALLEN & ELDRIDGE

This company was listed in the 1850 Products of Industry census as a planemaker in Williamstown, MA, employing nine hands and producing 14,000 planes worth $4000. If these figures were correct, the output probably included unfinished parts for others, since examples are seldom found. The principals, who were also listed as merchants, were Squire S. Allen, age 34, born in NY, and James A. Eldridge (w.s.), age 29, born in Massachusetts. ★★

ALLEN & NOBLE

Boston, MA, hardware dealer —1855—. ★

ALLEN & STORM

Probably a hardware dealer. This imprint has been reported on the toe of an Edward Carter (C imprint) reverse ogee and on an E. & C. Carter/Troy N.Y. astragal.

Wm. ALLYN

Allyn has been reported several times. Appearance is ca.1840. One example, a 9½" beech hollow has a W. Butcher iron, while another, a 1" boxed bead, has three different owners' stamps.

AMERICAN PLANE CO.

Probably a private brand. Appearance is mid-19c. ★★★

AMHERST TOOL CO.

Planes reported include a 7⅞" coffin-shaped smoother and a 16" jack, both with an Auburn Tool Co. Thistle Brand double iron. Appearance is ca.1870.   A & B: ★★★

A
 B

D. AMSDEN

Downing Amsden was a planemaker and joiner, who worked in Lebanon, NH, 1807-28. His planes are made of beech. The earlier imprint (A) appears on molding planes with Sleeper-type wedges. Chamfers are rounded on planes from both periods.   A: ★★★ B: ★★   *(continued next page)*

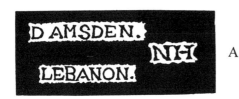 A

 B

29

 A

 B

ANCHOR PLANE CO.
This name appears on a 16" jack plane with a Buck Bros. double iron, and on a 22" razeed beech fore plane. Possibly a brand name.

ANDERSON & LAING
A hardware dealer in Wheeling, VA (now WV), 1839-52. Examples reported include a pair of screw arm plank planes and a boxwood plow plane with ivory tips. (Also see Greer & Laing)

 A

 B

ANDRUSS
This imprint was used on planes manufactured by two brothers, David T. Andruss (1803-32) and George W. Andruss (1806-1860), who were sons of J. Andruss (w.s.). Working dates were —1821-1841—. The firm advertised "wholesale and retail plane manufacturing" as well as "coachmaking tools of every description." Imprints were often carelessly applied and the name is sometimes inverted.   A, A1 & B: ★

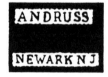

A

A1

B

J. ANDRUSS
Jonathan Andruss (1766-1843), father of David T. and George W. (see Andruss), and probably the earliest of the Newark, NJ, planemakers. He most likely worked before 1821.   ★★

O. ANDRUS
Obed Andrus, a Glastonbury, CT, planemaker, who probably worked from the early 1840s to 1871. In the 1850 census he was listed as a planemaker, age 40, born in CT, with real estate worth $700; and in the 1860 census as a toolmaker with real estate worth $1000.   A, B, & C: ★★   D & E: ★   *(see next page)*

A

B

C

D

E

J. ANGERMYER

Several examples have been reported. Appearance is ca.1830; probable location is western PA. ★★★★

J.J. ANGERMYER

Possibly a variant of J. Angermyer or another family member. The style of the imprint is very similar; the wedge outline quite different. The name appears on a 9½" long round with ⅜" round chamfers, and was found in Columbiana County, Ohio, on the Pennsylvania border. ★★★★

ANTARCTIC CO.

This name has been reported on a round plane, along with a location stamp NEW YORK. Appearance is late 19c. ★★★★

C.T. ANTHONY

This imprint appears on a molding plane with a location stamp MEDINA, N.Y. An 1854 gazeteer describes Medina as "a thriving post-office county, about 36 miles northeast of Buffalo on the Erie Canal and the Rochester, Lockport and Niagara Falls Railroad; population 3000-4000."

THOS. L. APPLETON

Thomas L. Appleton, was a prolific Boston (or more properly, Chelsea, just north of Boston), MA, plane manufacturer, producing under his own name from 1878-92. (see also Gladwin & Appleton and Tucker & Appleton)   A: FF   B: ★

A   B   A

B. ARMITAGE

Benjamin Armitage Jr. was an early Philadelphia, PA, planemaker. His working dates are thought to be ca.1760- 72. He was an apprentice to Samuel Caruthers (w.s.), who was perhaps Philadelphia's earliest planemaker. Molding planes that have been reported are 10" long. Armitage died in 1781.
A: ★★★★   B: ★★★★

A
B

WILLIAM ARMSTRONG

A hardware dealer in New Orleans and a native of St. Martinville, LA, who first appears in the city directories in 1838. He was listed in the 1850 Federal census as a merchant, aged 40, born in Louisiana and living in New Orleans. His firm was in business at several locations in the Vieux Carré (the French Quarter) until his death in 1872.   A, B, & C: ★★★

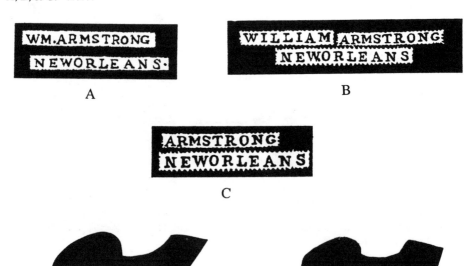

A

B

C

A   B

ARNOLD & CROUCH

Planemakers of Northampton, MA, ca.1850-60. Charles S. Crouch was listed in the 1850 census as a toolmaker in Williamsburg, MA, age 24, born in MA, and living with Ansell Strong, a carpenter. In 1853 he was employed by the Greenfield Tool Co. (w.s.). He was probably the Crouch of both Arnold & Crouch and Peck & Crouch (w.s.). Arnold may have been W.F. Arnold, who was a hardware dealer in Northampton at that time. The eagle imprint shown below is also found on the planes of H. Wells, Peck & Crouch, and J.D. Kellogg, all of Northampton (all w.s.). The imprint shown is incuse. ★

ARNOLD & FIELD

Several examples have been reported: a 10" birch sash plane and a 10" molder with fluting on the toe and heel and a relieved wedge. Field may be the Richard M. Field of Fuller & Field (w.s.). ★★★★

ARROWMAMMETT

The trade name used by the Baldwin Tool Co. for planes produced by their Arrowmammett Works in Middletown, CT. The Baldwin Tool Co. was established in Middletown in 1841 by Austin Baldwin, who made planes earlier in New York City as A. & E. Baldwin (w.s.). A plank tongue plane and a molding plane have been reported with an A. & E. BALDWIN/NEW YORK imprint and a subsequent overprint ARROWMAMMETT WORKS/MIDDLETOWN. Arrowmammett offered an extensive line of planes, as shown in its 1857 catalog (see Bibliography), and also produced a variety of plane irons in the Baldwin Tool Co. name. In the 1850 census it reported production of 40,000 planes worth $25,000. Around 1860 Arrowmammett was taken over by the Globe Mfg. Co., a maker of plane irons. Imprint C is incuse.   A, B & C: FF

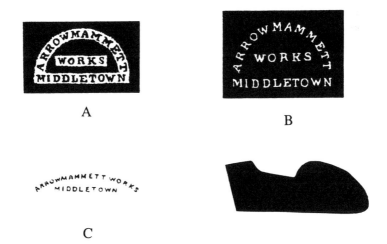

A

B

C

CHAS ASHLEY

Charles Ashley, of Ogdensburg, NY, was a hardware dealer ca.1860. The imprint shown appears on the heel of a Benson & Crannell complex molder. ★★

G. ASHLEY

George Ashley was a Little Falls and Binghamton, NY, hardware dealer, 1845-70. An astragal with the B imprint has been reported with "102" imprinted on its heel, the Auburn Tool Co. inventory number for an astragal. A: ★   B: ★★★

A   B

L.C. ASHLEY

Lewis C. Ashley of Troy, NY, received patent no. 14436 dated March 18, 1856. Ashley apparently jumped the gun in ordering his stamp die. The patent utilized a metallic throat piece to adjust the mouth of a bench plane as the sole wore down.   ★★★★★

L.C. Ashley
Patented Feb
1856

ASTEN & THROCKMORTON

This imprint, together with a 224 FULTON AVENUE location stamp, has been reported on a handled boxwood plow plane made by Lamb & Brownell (w.s.). A probable hardware dealer.

ATKINSON

John Atkinson, a Baltimore, MD, planemaker, used this imprint 1829-35 and 1840-42. (see Atkinson & Co. and Atkinson & Chapin)   ★★

34

T. ATKINSON

Thomas Atkinson was listed in the Louisville, KY, city directories in 1832, 1841-52, and again 1865-66, as a plane manufacturer. In 1838-39 he was a partner in Littel & Atkinson (w.s.). The 1850 census listed him as a planemaker in Louisville, age 44, born in England, with real estate worth $3000.   A & B: ★★

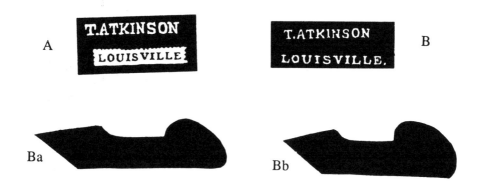

ATKINSON & CO.

John Atkinson, a Baltimore, MD, planemaker used this imprint in 1837. (see Atkinson and Atkinson & Chapin) ★★★

ATKINSON & CHAPIN

John Atkinson and Philip C. Chapin appeared as planemakers in an 1836 Baltimore directory but no example of their imprint is known. (see P. Chapin, Atkinson, Atkinson & Co.)

AUBURN TOOL CO.

A major manufacturer of wooden planes, located in Auburn, NY. As a successor to Casey, Clark & Co. (w.s.) it operated under the Auburn name from 1864 to 1893, when it merged with with the Ohio Tool Co. It owned and used a number of brand names including New York Tool Co., Owasco Tool Co., Genesee Tool Co., Ensenore (all w.s.), Thistle Brand, and Star. During 1864-65 and 1874-77, the company used prison labor at the Auburn Prison. The 1865 NY State census reported that 50 men were employed, producing 35,000 planes worth $35,000, 25,000 dozen plane irons worth $12,000 and 30,000 pairs of ice skates worth $45,000, utilizing steam power. An 1884 report listed the company's annual plane production at 300,000, nearly half of which were toy planes for children. (See the Bibliography for the reprint of its 1869 price list). Imprint B is incuse.   A, B, C: FF A1: ★   (continued on next page)

A

A1

AUBURN TOOL C°
AUBURN N Y   B

AUBURN TOOL C°
AUBURN,N.Y   C

ADAM AULT

Best known as an early Hanover, PA, organ builder, Adam Ault was born in Prussia, landed in Philadelphia in 1785. After a short stay in Bethlehem, PA, he migrated to Lititz, PA, in Lancaster County. Here he lived for 10 years, was a machinist by trade and a member of the Moravian church. He learned organ building during his years in Lititz in the factory of David Tannelberger. He moved to Hanover, PA, and built a two-story brick building at the corner of York Street and Middle Street.

He built 25 pipe organs. His first one was purchased by the Lutheran and Reformed Congregation, known as the Stone Church in Codones Twp. It was used for half a century and then replaced.

He also built parts for David Tannelberger in Lititz. In 1805 the organ installed in Emmanuel Reformed Church in Hanover, that was made by Adam Ault, bore the name of Bachman, a successor to David Tannelberger.

Adam Ault died August 1848 at the age of 83. In addition to organs, he is credited with building a threshing machine for grain harvesting; he drilled and bored rifle barrels by hand; made gun stocks and shoe lasts and, apparently, woodworking planes.   A & B: ★★★

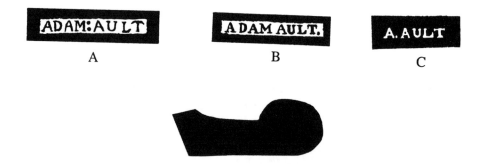

ADAM:AULT   A DAM AULT.   A. AULT
A   B   C

SAMUEL AUXER

A Lancaster, PA, planemaker (1834-1909) whose working dates were —1860-1880—. Some of his bench planes use the double wedge patented by E.W. Carpenter (w.s.), and a self-adjusting screw-arm sash plane using the E.W. Carpenter Improved Arm patent has been reported. On his trade card he described himself as formerly of Kieffer & Auxer (w.s.) and successor to E.W. Carpenter and said that he made "planes, gauges, yardsticks & etc." (see Auxer & Remley)   ★★

SAMUEL AUXER
LANCASTER. PA

AUXER & REMLEY

Lancaster, PA, planemakers, ca.1860-70. The partnership consisted of Samuel Auxer and Reuben J. Remley. (see Samuel Auxer and Kieffer & Auxer) ★★★

J. AVERY

A probable planemaker and/or dealer. A plow plane and several hollows and rounds 9½" long have been reported. Appearance is second quarter of the 19c. A dado plane has been reported stamped both J. KELLOGG AMHERST MASS. (w.s.) and J. AVERY.

G. AXE

George Axe (1800-1884) made planes in Buffalo, NY, 1855-80. The B imprint was struck on the inside of both halves of a sash plane imprinted M. LANG (w.s.), a Buffalo hardware dealer. A: ★★★★

A

B

AYERS & CO.

B. and Francis Ayers were hardware dealers in Jacksonville, IL, 1831-60—.

J.M. BABBIT
James M. Babbit was listed in the 1850 census as a planemaker, age 38, working in Turtle Creek (Lebanon), Warren County, Ohio, the same town in which H.B. Miller and P. Probasco (both w.s.) had worked earlier. He was also listed as a planemaker in a ca.1856 Mason, Ohio, directory. Mason is just north of Cincinnati and the Kentucky state line and close to Louisville, where Babbit apparently also operated, based on the imprint shown.

BABCOCK BROTHERS
An Evansville, IN, hardware dealer comprising three brothers, Elisha, Henry, and Charles Babcock, who were in business 1837-51. Charles and Edward O. Babcock appear as hardware dealers and woodworkers in the 1870-71 directory.   ★★

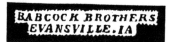

J. R. BACHELDER
A probable North Danville, VT, planemaker, b.1826. Bachelder worked with his father as a carpenter and in 1850 operated a carriage and furniture shop in Peacham, VT. In 1863 he was recorded as selling a shop and sawmill with tools in North Danville, VT, and in that year was employed by E. & T. Fairbanks Co. as an ornamental and sign painter. In 1887 he was listed as retired.   ★★★

R. BACON
A number of examples have been reported. The molding planes are 10" long, birch, with flat chamfers. Wedges vary, some of the Nicholson style (A), others more relieved (B). Probable location is southeastern New England, date ca.1800.   ★★★   *(continued next page)*

a   b

J. BAGLEY

Several examples of molding planes have been reported; all about 9½" long with narrow flat chamfers. Appearance is ca.1800.

R. C. BAILEY

R.C. Bailey was listed as a planemaker in Ogdensburg, NY, in the 1850 NY State business directory. The 1850 Federal census listed a Roswell C. Bailey as a millwright, age 37, born in NY state and working in Oswegatchie, St. Lawrence County, the same county in which Ogdensburg is located. Bailey's imprint R.C. BAILEY/OGDENSBURGH used the old spelling of the town. The H was dropped in 1868 when Ogdensburg became a city.   A & B: ★★★

A   B

BAILEY & RICHARDSON

Stephen A. Bailey and William Richardson were St. Louis, MO, hardware dealers, 1866-86. Planes bearing the 608 MARKET ST address were probably imprinted during 1867-82 when the firm occupied that address. ★★★

BAKER & GAMWELL

There was probably a relationship to Webb & Baker and Webb & Gamwell (both w.s.)   ★★★

A. & E. BALDWIN

New York City planemakers, Austin Baldwin (1807-1886), born in Connecticut, and his half-brother, Elbridge Gerry Baldwin (1810-1864), made planes under this name from 1830 to 1841. The firm was the successor to E. Baldwin (w.s.; Enos Baldwin, their father). In 1841 Austin Baldwin moved to Middletown, CT, where he founded the Baldwin Tool Co. (w.s.). Austin was active in the early opposition to the use of prison labor, a sore point for many years between those planemakers who used prison contract labor and those who did not. After selling out his interest in the Baldwin Tool Co. in 1857, he formed Austin Baldwin & Co. (NYC) that carried on a foreign exchange and express business. In 1872 he also took charge of the newly formed State Steamship Line. He was Speaker of the Connecticut House in 1855 and was twice nominated for Governor by the Know-Nothing party. The C imprint is incuse. (see also Arrowmammett and E. Baldwin). The C imprint has been reported overprinted by an Arrowmammett Works B imprint.   A, B, C, D: FF   D1: ★★★

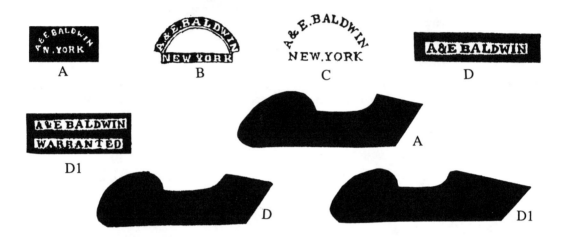

A   B   C   D

D1

A

D   D1

E. BALDWIN

Enos Baldwin was born in Cavendish, VT, June 28, 1783, and died in NYC in 1829. He was the father of Austin and Elbridge Gerry Baldwin, to whom he taught planemaking and who succeeded him as A. & E. Baldwin (w.s.). Enos made planes in Albany, NY, 1807—, and in New York City ca.1816-29. He had moved to Newburgh, NY, in 1815 and remained there for an undetermined time. An advertisement in *The Statesman*, published in NYC April 23, 1824, illustrated a fore plane and a molder by "ENOS BALDWIN, Planemaker, No. 90 Elizabeth-Street New York" and offered a general assortment of carpenters', joiners', coopers', cabinet- and coachmakers' planes. Elbridge Gerry Baldwin continued under the name E. Baldwin (1842-50) after A. & E. Baldwin ceased operations in 1841, using the same E. Baldwin stamp as his father..   A: ★   A1 & B: FF

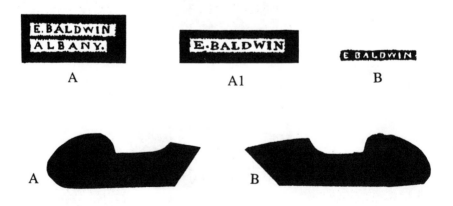

A   A1   B

A   B

BALDWIN TOOL CO.

Founded in Middletown, CT, in 1841 by Austin Baldwin (see A. & E. Baldwin). The company manufactured planes from 1841 to 1857. The factory was located on the Arrowmammett River and was called the Arrowmammett Works (see Arrowmammett). In 1850 the company employed 30 hands and produced 40,000 planes. Austin Baldwin resigned as president in 1857 and sold his stock to the Globe Manufacturing Co. which continued making plane irons only.

GEORGE BALL

Longworth's *City Directory* for 1827 listed George Ball as a planemaker at 109 Mercer St., New York City. He was also listed in the 1842-60 directories as a planemaker "colored." No example of his work has been reported.

ION BALLOU

Jonathan Ballou was one of the earliest American planemakers and probably the first to make planes in Providence. He was born in 1723 in Lincoln, RI, and married Elizabeth West in 1768, but had no children. He was admitted as a freeman in Providence in 1751 and in a 1752 land transfer was referred to as a shop-joiner. He died in 1770, leaving a modest estate that included his interest in a paper mill and "a large number of tooles (sic) of all kinds, new and old with some stock." His widow advertised for sale, a month after his death, "a parcel of carpenters' and joiners' tools and sundry other things." ★★★

BALTIMORE PLANE CO.

Probably an imprint of Carlin & Fulton, hardware dealers in Baltimore, MD, around 1890.

G.P. BANCROFT

This imprint has been reported on a plow, a panel raiser, and on several molding planes, all of early 19c appearance. The location stamp GRANVILLE, may be Granville, Ohio, Licking County, just east of Columbus.
A: ★★   B: ★★★

A   B   A

BARBER & ROSS

A probable mid- to late 19c Washington, DC, hardware dealer. A 9½" long skewed rabbet has been reported with the (A) imprint on its toe and the (B) imprint on its heel.

 A    B

JOHN BARCLAY

John Barclay was listed as a planemaker in the 1815 directory published in Pittsburgh, PA, with an address on the south side of Diamond Alley between Wood and Smithfield. He was not listed in the 1819 directory or subsequently. No example with this imprint has been reported.

F. BARINGER

A number of examples have been reported, including several molding planes, a crown molder, and a door check plane. Probable location is eastern Pennsylvania. Probable working period is early 19c.

BARKER & BALDWIN

? Barker and Lovewell H. Baldwin (born NY state, ca.1830) were Auburn, NY, hardware merchants ca.1850-57, and may have been the successors to Watrous & Osborne (w.s.) which had occupied the same premises previously. The imprint shown is incuse.   ★★★

BARKER&BALDWIN
AUBURN
N-Y

Jno. M. BARKLEY

John M. Barkley, was a Baltimore, MD, planemaker, during the period 1816-24.   A: ★★   B & C: ★★★

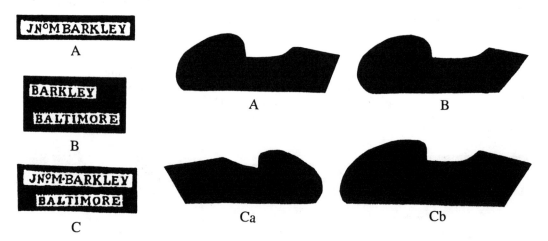

BARKLEY & HUGHES

Baltimore, MD, but dates and principals are not known. (see Jno. M. Barkley)   ★★★

BARNARD

This name has been reported on two 9¼" long beech molding planes with rounded chamfers; and on a jack plane. The imprint is very similar to the "BARNARD" in A. BARNARD (w.s.).

A. BARNARD

A number of examples have been reported. A jack and a jointer were imprinted with the date 1835.
A: ★★   B: ★★★★

 A

 B

JULIUS BARNARD

(b.1769) In 1792 he advertised in the Northampton, MA, *Gazette* that he made and had for sale a variety of items, "Desks, bookcases. . .bench planes and moulding tools." No examples of his imprint have been reported.

A. BARNES

Amory Barnes (1806-1893) was the son of R. Barnes (w.s.), from whom he probably learned planemaking. He was listed as engaged in manufacturing in the 1840 census for Orange, MA, and some of his planes have the location imprint S. ORANGE, MASS.   A: ★   B: ★★★   C:★★

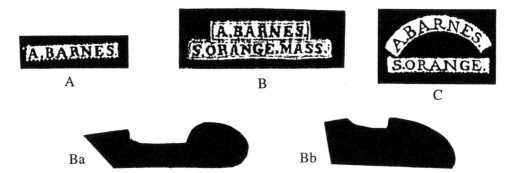

R. BARNES

Russell Barnes, father of A. Barnes (w.s.), was born in Cambridge, MA, in 1774 and died in Orange, MA, in 1853. He was listed as "plainmaker" in Orange town records and was shown in the 1840 census for Orange as being engaged in manufacturing. His wife had the memorable name of Submit. One of his planes is date-stamped 1823. An impressive example of his work is illustrated on p.187 of Sellens' *Woodworking Planes*, a 4" cornice plane with two irons.   A & A1: ★★   B: ★★★

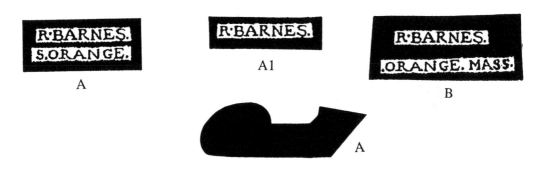

T.P. BARNES
The imprint has appeared on a W.G. Lamb (w.s.) 8" smoother.

M. BARR & CO.
Matthew Barr was a Nashua, NH, hardware dealer ca.1865, whose planes may have been supplied by C. Warren (w.s.). ★★★

L.M. BARROWS
This imprint appears on a 9" long compassed smoother. The location VASS. was Vasselborough, Maine, on the east bank of the Kennebec River, 14 miles northeast of Augusta, with a population of 3000 in 1850.

H. BARRUS & CO.
A Goshen, MA, planemaking firm working 1854-59 and consisting of Hiram Barrus (1828-1883), Theron Levi Barrus (1829-1906) and Loren Barrus (1825-1899), all brothers, and sons of N.L. Barrus (w.s.). ★

BARRUS & BIGELOW   see Bigelow and Barrus

N.L. BARRUS
Nathan L. Barrus, a 19c planemaker in Warren, RI. Father of Hiram, Theron Levi, and Loren Barrus (see H. Barrus & Co.) and brother-in-law of Leonard B. Bigelow (see L.B. Bigelow). He was listed in an 1845 Warren directory as a planemaker, and in the 1850 census as a housewright. (also see Bigelow and Barrus)   ★★

WILLIAM A. BARRUS

A Cummington, MA, planemaker whose working dates were 1877—. He was the son of Hiram Barrus. (see H. Barrus & Co.)

BARRY   see Barry & Co.

S. S. BARRY

Samuel S. Barry was a planemaker in New York City (1827-41), a hardware dealer with various partners (1841-47), and again a planemaker (1848-50). (see also Kennedy, Barry & Way; Barry & Way; and Barry, Way, & Sherman)   ★

BARRY & CO.

A Samuel Barry was listed as a planemaker in the 1817, 1818, 1830-31 and 1833 Philadelphia directories. The Barry imprint B has a straight edge after the "Y", suggesting that it was cut down from the BARRY & CO. A imprint. (see Parrish & Barry)   A & B: ★★★

BARRY & WAY

A partnership composed of Samuel S. Barry and William Way, dealers in hardware in New York City, 1842-47. Successor to Kennedy, Barry & Way, and predecessor to Barry, Way & Sherman (both w.s.).   FF

BARRY, WAY, & SHERMAN

A partnership composed of Samuel S. Barry, William Way and Byron Sherman, hardware dealers in New York City in 1847 only. Successor to Barry & Way (w.s.).

A.C. BARTLETT'S OHIO PLANES

An imprint used by the Sandusky Tool Co. (w.s.) on planes manufactured for Hibbard, Spencer, Bartlett & Co. (w.s.), a large Chicago hardware firm, from 1890 into the 1920s.   A & B: FF

A

B

C. BARTLETT

Various examples have been reported from several sources. These include a rabbet, dado, molding plane, jointer, and jack. Appearance is early 19c.

S.B. BARTLETT

This imprint has been reported on an unusual type of plane, a combination hollow and round. The two irons face in opposite directions, the same as with a combination tongue and groove. A Samuel B. Bartlett, age 22, born in England, was listed in the 1850 census as living in Watertown, NY, and a toolmaker.   ★★

D.R. BARTON   see D.R. Barton & Co.

D.R. BARTON & CO.

A major Rochester, NY, edge tool and plane manufacturing company founded by David R. Barton (1805-1875) in 1832 and continuing to 1874 when the business was taken over by William R. and Royal L. Mack (already partners in the firm), who renamed it Mack & Co. after the death of David R. Barton in 1875. They retained the trade name D.R. Barton & Co. and used it until 1923. Examples also exist of planes with a partially removed Greenfield Tool Co. imprint overstruck with the D.R. Barton oval stamp (imprint E). The firm made a wide variety of tools besides planes and plane irons, including coopers' tools, draw knives, axes, saws and chisels. The 1850 census reported 85 employees and the 1870 census, 193. Care should be taken not to confuse the "1832" in the trademark as the date of the tool; it was the founding date of the firm. A reprint of the D.R. Barton 1873 illustrated catalog is listed in the Bibliography. We believe that the A, B, and C imprints were used during the period before 1865. Imprints D through G cover the period from 1865 through 1923 when the Macks came into the business, first as partners and then as sole owners in 1874. Imprint D was probably the earliest of this group. The circular imprints E and F were used by D.R. Barton Tool Co. (w.s.) in 1874 but were apparently discontinued in 1875 and then revived by the Macks when they absorbed D.R. Barton Tool Co. into D.R. Barton & Co. in 1879. The (D), (E) and (G) imprints are incuse. (see D.R. Barton Tool Co., Barton & Babcock, Barton & Belden, Barton & Milliner, and Barton & Smith)   A through H: all FF   *(see next page)*

46

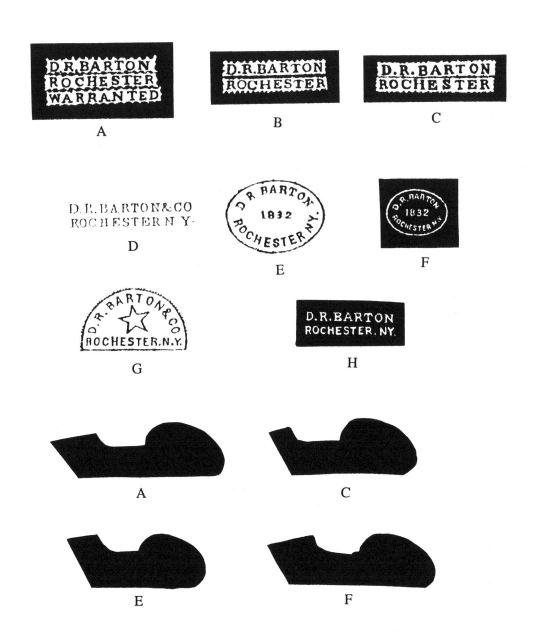

D.R. BARTON TOOL CO.

Formed in Rochester, NY, in 1874 by David R. Barton and his sons, Charles and Edward. It advertised planes, edge tools and axes. David died in 1875 and the company continued until 1879 when it went into receivership. It was then taken over by Mack & Co., which had previously acquired D.R. Barton & Co. Therefore, for several years two Rochester firms were turning out products using the D.R. Barton trade name: D.R. Barton & Co. (w.s.) and D.R. Barton Tool Co. Advertisements placed in the 1874 and 1875 Rochester City Directory by the D.R. Barton Tool Co. state "Goods stamped D.R. Barton & Co. are not made by us. For GENUINE D.R. Barton Edge Tools, Planes, Axes &c be sure to address D.R. Barton Tool Co. and not D.R. Barton & Co." The D.R. BARTON

1832 trademark label is clearly shown in the 1874 advertisement, but was dropped in the 1875 catalog (see D.R. Barton & Co.)

W.J. BARTON
Various planes carrying this imprint have now been reported, including a screw arm tongue and groove, a gutter plane, and two smoothing planes. They all have a PHILA (Philadelphia) location stamp. Appearance would suggest an 1830-40 time period. A Barton was listed in the 1837 and 1840 Philadelphia directories as a cabinetmaker. On one plane the Barton imprint overstamped another imprint that was rendered illegible except for the "warranted," suggesting that Barton may also have been a dealer.   ★★★★

BARTON & BABCOCK
A partnership of David R. Barton, who previously had been in nail manufacturing, and John H. Babcock, a blacksmith, who in 1832 began an edge tool business, continuing at least until 1834. There is no indication that planes were made, nor have any examples of such an imprint been reported. The year 1832 however was subsequently used by D.R. Barton & Co. as the beginning date of the firm. Later, in 1849, Babcock worked as a blacksmith for D.R. Barton & Co. (w.s.).

BARTON & BELDEN
A Rochester, NY, partnership consisting of David R. Barton and Ira Belden, a hardware merchant. The partnership seems to have lasted only a short time around the mid-1840s. The 1844 directory lists the firm as edge tool makers. No example of this imprint has been reported. (see D.R. Barton & Co.)

BARTON & MILLINER
A partnership formed in 1863 between David R. Barton and Joel P. Milliner in Rochester, NY. The partnership apparently lasted only one year and no examples of the imprint have been reported. Milliner was in the edge tool business earlier in Kingston, Ontario, Canada. His plane imprint at that time was J.P. Milliner & Co. and a number of examples are known. (see also D.R. Barton & Co.)

BARTON & SMITH
A Rochester, NY, partnership consisting of David R. Barton and probably Albert H. Smith, a hardware merchant, which operated around 1842.   A: ★★   B: ★★★

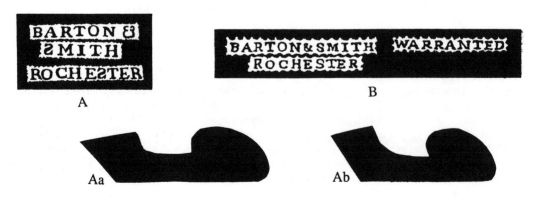

48

D. BASSETT

This imprint has been reported separately on a jack, a fore plane and a plow. Appearance is early 19c.

E. BASSETT

Examples reported are molding planes, 10" long, made of beech, some with maple boxing, one with lignum. Appearance is late 18c. Possibly Elijah Bassett, son of John Basset (w.s.), who was born in Norton, MA, in 1754, and was noted as a laborer in Taunton, MA, in 1786 and a yeoman in 1797. He died in Taunton in 1803. The wedge style is very similar to the (B) wedge of John Basset. ★★★★

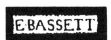

J. BASSET

Several examples have been reported, made of yellow birch, with flat chamfers, chamfered wedge slot, and fluting. Appearance is late 18c, southeastern New England. (also see John Basset)

IOHN BASSET

Two birch molding planes, 9⅞" long, have been reported, with the additional location imprint OF NORTON. Two other molding planes also 9⅞" long, but made of beech with ⅜" flat chamfers and relieved wedges identical with those of E. Bassett (w.s.) have also been reported. Their maker is possibly John Basset, born in Norton, MA, 1725, noted as a joiner in Taunton, MA, in 1757, and a shop joiner in Norton in 1749 and 1761 (also see J. Basset). The interesting double imprint (C) appears on a 10" long rabbet with ⅜" wide flat chamfers. The bottom imprint is the (B) imprint of this early maker. The upper mark with the modern "J" in John and two "t's" in Bassett may be a later stamp of the planemaker or simply a different John. A: ★★★★★ B: ★★★★
C: ★★★★★

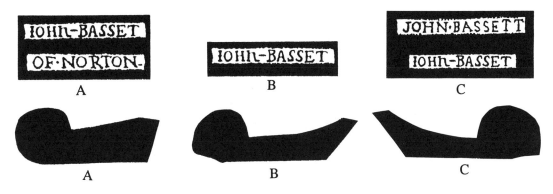

J.E. BASSETT & CO.

A hardware dealer in New Haven, CT. The firm was founded in 1784 by Titus Street. In 1792 it became Street & Hughes, in 1821 S. Hughes & Son, in 1838 E.B.M. Hughes, and in 1855 J.E. (John E.) Bassett & Co. It continued in business until 1967. A label inscribed "Made for and sold by J.E. Bassett & Co. Importers of Hardware, No. 150 Chapel Street, New Haven Conn" was affixed to the side of a hollow made by W.H. Pond (w.s.). Two UNION FACTORY/H. CHAPIN (w.s.) hollows exist, labeled "Sold by/J.E. Bassett & Co./Dealers in/Hardware/ No. 236 Chapel Street/New Haven Conn." The W.H. Pond label is green, the Chapin yellow. The "236 Chapel Street" label has also been reported in green on an H.L. Narramore (w.s.) hollow. Bassett apparently bought from a number of planemakers and used a variety of labels.   A & B: ★★

 A

 B

I.S. BATTEY

Isaac S. Battey, planemaker of Providence, RI, —1841-55, who was listed in the 1850 census as a planemaker, age 33, born in RI. He was married to Clarissa A. Child, sister of J.E. Child (w.s.)   ★

BATTEY & EDDY

A partnership founded in April 1841 between Isaac S. Battey and James A. Eddy, hardware merchants and plane manufacturers in Providence, RI. The partnership was short-lived and was dissolved in September of the same year. (see I.S. Battey and also James A. Eddy)   ★★★

J.F. BAUDER

Jacob Frederick Bauder (1817-1893) was born in Philadelphia, PA, and died in Palmyra, NJ (across the river from Philadelphia). There are records indicating he made planes in Lancaster City, PA, —1841—, and in Manheim, PA, 1843-52. He then returned to Philadelphia where he continued as a planemaker until his retirement. It is also probable that he made planes in Philadelphia prior to Lancaster City and Manheim, using the (B) imprint, since two examples have been reported with the (A) imprint overprinting the (B). His planemaking style, particularly his wedges, bears a striking resemblance to that of E.W. Carpenter (w.s.), for whom he may have worked.   A: ★★   B: ★★★★

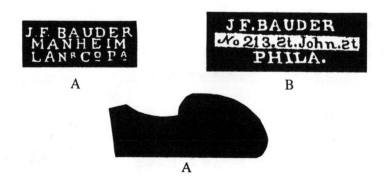

A   B

A

50

W. BAUM & CO.

William Baum, a Cincinnati, OH, planemaker, 1850-52, who earlier (in 1841) was listed as a plane manufacturer in Louisville, KY, and in 1853 was a foreman at Schaeffer & Cobb (w.s.). (also see W. Baum/J. Harrison)   ★★

W. BAUM & CO./J. HARRISON & CO.

This imprint appeared on a howel. W. Baum was a Cincinnati, OH, planemaker 1850-52. John Harrison was listed as a Zanesville, OH, planemaker in the 1850 census. (see W. Baum & Co. and also J. Harrison & Co.)

EZ. BAXTER

A number of planes have been reported, made of birch, with a relieved wedge, and the general characteristics of Aaron Smith's work. Appearance of the planes is ca.1800. (see Aaron Smith)   ★★★★

BAY STATE WORKS

Examples have been reported on two smooth planes, a plow, and two hollows. Appearance is ca.1850-75.

J. BAYLEY

A half dozen examples have been reported from four different sources. Planes are made of beech, molders are 9⅜" long; appearance is early 19c. Location seems to be New England.

BEACHER & ADDIS

Baldwin Beecher and Charles W. Addis, who were planemakers in New Haven, CT, 1850-53. Baldwin Beacher (or Beecher) was listed as a joiner, at 122 George St. in Patten's 1840 New Haven directory; as a joiner, age 40, in the 1850 census; and as a carpenter in 1860. Charles Addis was listed as a planemaker in the 1850 census, age 21, and living with Nathan Fenn, age 40, a joiner (see Joel Fenn). Both men were born in Connecticut. ★★

BEAK & LANG

This imprint appears on a fore plane with a Buffalo location mark (see M. Lang and Lang & Co.)

CLARENCE A. BEARSE

Listed as a planemaker in the New Bedford, MA, directories 1867-72. No example of an imprint has been reported. There may be a relationship with Bodman & Bearse and Bodman, Bearse & Hussey (w.s.; see also J.M. Taber).

ISRAEL O. BEATTIE

A wide complex molder has been reported with the imprint I.O. BEATTIE double struck (B) and obliterating an earlier stamp. It's likely that I.O. Beattie was Israel O. Beattie, a hardware dealer in Middletown, NY, —1861-72—. A: ★★   B: ★★★★

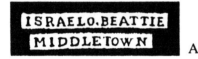
A

B

JONATHAN BEILEY

A Milwaukee, WI, sash and plane maker; listed in the 1859 city directory. No example has been reported.

W.B. BELCH

William B. Belch was a hardware dealer and planemaker in New York City, 1831-64. The 1850 census listed him as a "plainmaker" employing seven men to make 7000 "plains" selling for $9000. A 9⅜" beech rabbet with a Mottram (Sheffield 1800-33) iron and a 14" grooving plane have been reported, both with a VT imprint. The wedge pattern of the rabbet is very similar to that of W.B. Belch, NY, indicating they may be the same maker, with Vermont likely his earlier location.   A, A1, & B: ★★   C: ★★★★   *(continued on next page)*

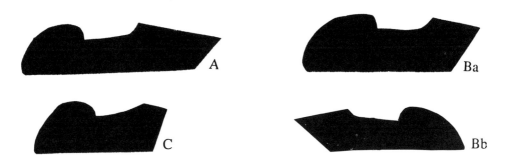

BELCHER BROS.

A hardware company located in Providence, RI. It was founded in 1826 by Joseph Belcher and was continued by his sons, Joseph H. and Leander C. Belcher. The name was Belcher Bros. from 1857 until 1884 when Edward A. Loomis became a partner and the name was changed to Belcher and Loomis.   ★★

JOHN BELL

A prolific Philadelphia planemaker whose working period was 1829-51. He was listed in the 1850 census as a planemaker, age 50, born in Pennsylvania and living with Henry Bibighaus, age 72, a Lutheran minister. He was succeeded in 1852 by Samuel H. Bibighaus. An example has been reported of a Spayd & Bell imprinted plane with the JOHN BELL portion of the (A) imprint overprinting the SPAYD & BELL, suggesting that John Bell succeeded the partnership. (see S.H. Bibighaus and also Spayd & Bell)   A, B, C: FF

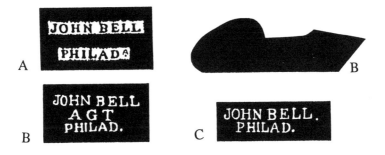

DAVID BENSEN

An Albany, NY, planemaker (1802-1853) who made planes under his name or that of five different partnerships between 1827 and 1850. (see Bensen & M'Call, Benson & Mockridge, Bensen & Munsell, Bensen & Parry, and Randall & Bensen)   A, B, C: FF   D: ★

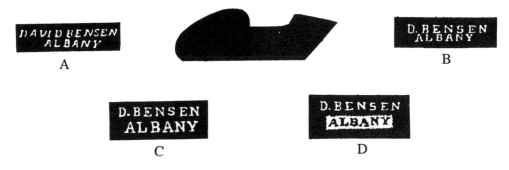

BENSEN & CRANNELL

One of the most frequently found imprints among Albany-made planes. A partnership of Nicholas Bensen (1810- 1862, b. NY), probably a relation of David Bensen (w.s.), and Matthew Crannell Jr. They made planes over the period 1844-62 and in 1851 added a "Mechanics Tool Store" to their shop. In 1855 they employed 15 hands and produced $10,000 worth of planes and tools. The 1860 census listed them having five employees producing 6000 planes worth $4000.   FF

BENSEN & M'CALL

David Bensen and Thomas J. McCall made planes in Albany, NY, 1842. (see David Bensen and also Thomas J. McCall)   ★★

BENSEN & MUNSELL

A partnership consisting of David Bensen and Noel Munsell, in Albany, NY, 1849-50. Munsell was a printer and publisher and probably provided capital for the firm. (see David Bensen)   ★★

BENSEN & PARRY

Planemaking partnership of David Bensen and John S. Parry, in Albany, NY, 1838-39. (see David Bensen; Parry)   ★★

J. BENSON

A number of examples have been reported. Many seem to have been found in the Hudson Valley (NY). All have been made of beech, the molding planes ranging between $9\frac{3}{8}$" and 10", with round chamfers. One plane was dated "1818."   *(continued on next page)*

54

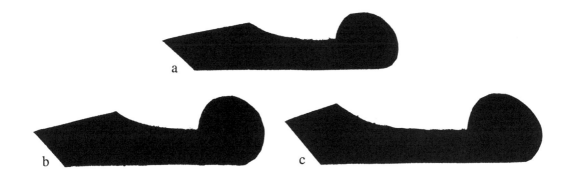

a

b   c

SAMUEL L. BENSON

Listed in the 1850 census as living in Lowell, MA, a 45-year old carpenter, born in Vermont. He employed five hands, making $5000 worth of sash, blinds, and planes. No example has been reported.

BENSON & MOCKRIDGE

A partnership of Abraham Mockridge and David Bensen, successor to Randall & Bensen. It operated in Albany, NY, 1830-31. This is the only instance where Bensen is spelled BENSON. Abraham Mockridge moved to Newark in 1833. (see A. Mockridge, Mockridge & Francis, Mockridge & Son, David Bensen) ★★

BENSON &
MOCKRIDGE

Aa   Ab

G.A. BENTON

George A. Benton, who made planes in Chelsea, MA (but stamped them Boston), 1856-68. In the 1850 census he was listed as a planemaker, age 34, born in Connecticut, and living next door to A. Cumings (w.s.). In the 1840 census he was shown in manufacturing or trade, living in Glastonbury, CT, with three members of his household also in manufacturing or trade.   A: ★★   B & C: ★★★

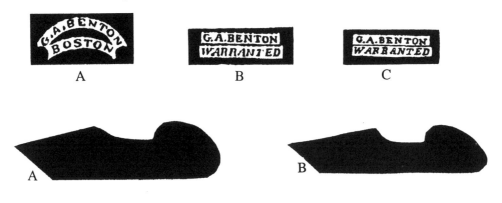

G.A. BENTON
BOSTON
A

G.A. BENTON
WARRANTED
B

G.A. BENTON
WARRANTED
C

A   B

BENTON, EVANS & CO.

A Rochester, NY, planemaking partnership of James S. Benton (1805-1863, b.in CT) and John Evans, during the period 1834-38. Evans was employed as a blacksmith by D.R. Barton (w.s.) in 1849. Benton was agent for Leonard Kennedy Jr. in Utica in 1833. (see Kennedy). Between 1838 and 1855 he worked mainly for D.R. Barton in Rochester. He was listed as a planemaker in the 1850 census.   ★★

B.F. BERRY

Benjamin F. Berry made planes under his own imprint in Watertown, NY, ca.1840. Lorenzo Case worked for him as a planemaker in 1840. Earlier, in 1834-35, Berry was listed as a planemaker in the Utica directory but was probably a bench hand. He was listed in the 1850 census as a toolmaker in Pamelia (a few miles north of Watertown), age 41, and born in Massachusetts. (see L. Case)   A, B & C: ★

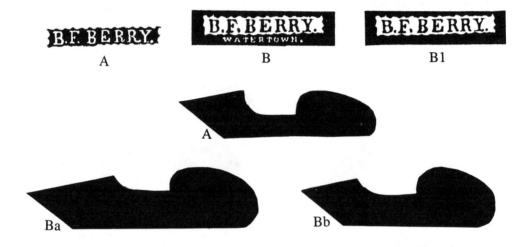

A   B   B1

A

Ba   Bb

E. BERRY

Ebenezer Berry (1788-1839) of Beverley, MA, is believed to have been the stepson of William Raymond from whom he probably learned planemaking. (see W. Raymond)   A: ★★   B ★★★

A   B

E. BERRY & CO.

Reported on a 9¾" long rabbet with flat chamfers. The imprint appears to be related to the E. Berry (A) imprint.

JOHN L. BERRY

A Springfield, Ohio, cabinetmaker —1825-52— who advertised in 1830: "CARPENTER & CABINET-MAKER'S TOOLS - The Subscriber has now on hand and will keep constantly for sale at his cabinet shop on South Street a general assortment of carpenter and cabinetmaker's tools, which will be disposed of at the Cincinnati prices."

BERRY & VANNAMER

This imprint has appeared on a 9½" boxed bead with round chamfers and on a 9⅜" two-iron boxed molding plane. Appearance is mid-19c.

BEWLEY

A New York City planemaking firm that operated 1822-32 and consisted of Edmund, who is listed in the directories for the years 1822-30, and Thomas, for the years 1831-32. There was apparently no connection with the English firm, Robert Bewley, which made planes from 1798 to 1847 under the imprint BEWLEY/LEEDS. A, A1, & B: ★

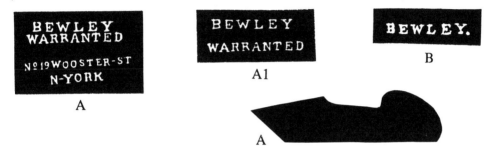

S.H. BIBIGHAUS

Samuel H. Bibighaus (b.1820 in PA) was a prolific planemaker and dealer in Philadelphia, PA, and was the successor to John Bell (w.s.) in 1852. He was listed as a planemaker in the 1853, 1856-57, and 1860 Philadelphia directories and as a hardware dealer in the 1840, 1844, and 1849 directories and in the 1850 census.

A & D: ★   B, C, & E: ★★

BIDDLE & CO.

Hardware distributors and wholesalers in Philadelphia, PA, sometime after 1862. (see R. & W.C. Biddle & Co.)   ★★★

R. & W.C. BIDDLE & CO.

Robert and William C. Biddle, Philadelphia, PA, were listed as hardware merchants in the 1840, 1854, and 1862 Philadelphia directories, and were the predecessors of Biddle & Co. (w.s.).   ★★

A.F. BIDWELL

Reported in the 1850 census as a 26-year old merchant in Coldwater, Michigan, born in New York state (see G.L. Bidwell)   ★★★

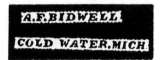

G.L. BIDWELL

Reported in the 1850 census as a 33-year old hardware merchant in Adrian, Michigan, and born in New York state (see A.F. Bidwell and L.F. Bidwell)   ★★★

L.B. BIDWELL

Leonard B. Bidwell was a Hartford, CT, planemaker, 1844-48. He was listed as living in East Hartford in the 1830 and 1840 censuses. The 1840 census showed seven members of his household engaged in manufacturing and trade. He lived five houses away from Peter Brooks (see P. Brooks & Co.; also see Bidwell & Hale).   ★★

L.F. BIDWELL

This name has been reported on a screw-arm match plane with the additional location imprint COLDWATER MICH. A probable hardware dealer.

BIDWELL & BICKFORD

A hardware store founded in 1854 in Valparaiso, IN, which became H. (Henry) Bickford in December of that year. It was succeeded by Carpenter & Parke in 1859.   ★★★

58

BIDWELL & HALE

A partnership in Newark, Wirt County, Virginia (near the Ohio line) believed to have consisted of Leonard B. Bidwell (see L.B. Bidwell) and Joseph Hale. A price broadside of the firm from ca.1860 describes them as "Manufacturers of Planes and bench, hand, or clamp screws of all sizes" and proceeds to list a wide variety of plane types and offers a "liberal discount to wholesale purchasers." No example of an imprint has been reported.

L.B. BIGELOW

Leonard Bacon Bigelow (1809-1865), born in Connecticut, was a Providence, RI, planemaker, 1831-53, first as a partner and future brother-in-law of Nathan L. Barrus (N.L. Barrus) in Bigelow and Barrus w.s.). By 1854 he was listed as a machinist employed by the Providence Machine Co.   ★★

BIGELOW & BARRUS

A partnership between Nathan L. Barrus (w.s.) and Leonard B. Bigelow (w.s.) which was announced in a newspaper notice dated Nov. 1, 1836, at a location at 7 Weybosset St., Providence, RI, recently vacated by Jonas R. Gale (J.R. Gale, w.s.). The partnership possibly ended some seven weeks later as the result of a fire No examples have been reported. Though planes are marked Bigelow and Barrus some contemporary records listed the firm as Barrus & Bigelow.   ★★★

L. BIGLOW

Possibly Levi Biglow (1794-1874) born in Fitzwilliam, NH, and died in Randolph, VT. He was listed as a mechanic on his death certificate. Several planes have been reported, a 10" beech quarter round, a 10" beech round, a grecian ovolo and an ogee.   ★★★

ROBERT BINGHAM

Listed as a planemaker working for himself in Buffalo, NY, 1864-65. Earlier, from 1854-63, he worked for L. & I.J. White (w.s.) as a planemaker and before that for D.R. Barton (w.s.). No examples of his imprint have been reported.

BLAIR & CO.   see W. Blair & Co.

W. BLAIR & CO.

A Chicago, IL, hardware company, which appeared in the city directories 1853-88.   A & B: ★

A   B

C. BLASDELL

Various examples have been reported, including a round and a molding plane. They are 9¾" long, are made of beech, have flat chamfers and a Sleeper-type wedge. Appearance is ca.1800.   ★★★

I. BLOSSOM

Examples reported appear to have been made ca.1800.   ★★★

W.H. BLYE

William H. Blye of De Ruyter (a town south of Cazenovia, NY) received U.S. patent no. 6304 on April 10, 1849, for a hinged plane fence that was used for chamfering. The (A) imprint shown below appears on a plane that was made by Hayden (w.s.) who was licensed by Blye. Blye was listed in the 1850 census as a carpenter, age 43, born in New York. The Blye-patented wooden fences have also been reported on planes made by M.B. Tidey and E.C. Ring (both w.s.). A handled rabbet has been reported which is imprinted by William H. Blye and has the patented fence with an adjustable tie rod attached. The (B) imprint we show is from a ¾" boxed bead, 9½" long, with a W. Field iron and with no evidence of a fence or any other attachment, suggesting that Blye also made conventional planes. The (C) imprint was reported on an 11¾" long closed-handle grooving plane also imprinted HAYDEN/SYRACUSE. There is an M. HART imprint on the plane iron.   A & B: ★★★★

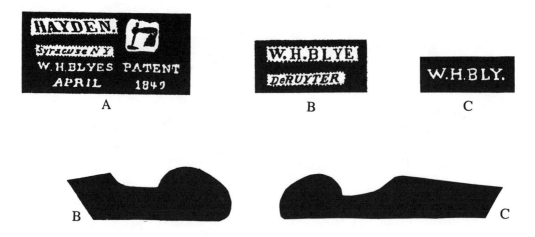

BODMAN & BEARSE

This name appears on a 16" razeed bench plane with the additional location imprint PAWTUCKET. (see J.M. Taber, Clarence A. Bearse, Bodman Bearse & Hussey, and Bodman & Hussey)

BODMAN, BEARSE & HUSSEY

A probable Pawtucket, RI, planemaker. Several planes have been reported whose appearance is mid-19c. (see J.M. Taber, Bodman & Bearse, Clarence A. Bearse, and Bodman & Hussey)   ★★★

BODMAN & HUSSEY

Planemakers in Pawtucket, RI, ca.1870. (see J.M. Taber)   ★★

JOHN BOERNHOEFT

Listed as a planemaker in New York City for one year only, 1850. In the years preceding and following he was a piano maker. No example of his imprint has been reported.

J. BOGERT

John B. Bogert, was a New York City hardware dealer, 1842-70-.   A & B: ★★★

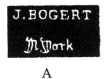  

A   B   A

WILLIAM K. BOGGES

Listed as a planemaker in the 1850 St. Louis, MO, directory. No examples of his imprint have been reported. (see William K. Boggus, a possible misspelling)

WILLIAM K. BOGGUS

Listed as a planemaker in Cincinnati, Ohio, 1839-40. (see William K. Bogges, a possible misspelling)

BOGMAN & VINAL

Boston, MA, hardware dealers, 1867-85.

G. BOHN

A possible maker. Appearance is ca.1800; probable location is eastern PA.

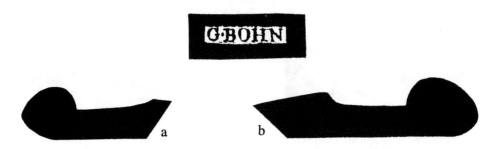

BOND & SARGEANT

Advertised themselves as "General Dealers in Hardware" in the 1836 Buffalo, NY, city directory.   ★★

CHRISTOPHER BONNELL

Listed in an 1851 directory as a planemaker on Zanes Island near Wheeling, VA, (now WV). No planes bearing this imprint have been reported.

BEBEE BOOTH

Listed as a merchant in the Terre Haute, IN, 1850 census. One example has been reported.

R.W. BOOTH

A wholesale hardware dealer in Cincinnati, OH, 1849-52, and earlier, in 1846, partner in Clark & Booth. An example has been reported with the (A) imprint on the toe end of the plane and the (C) imprint on the heel. (see R.W. Booth & Co.)   A & C: ★★   B: ★★★

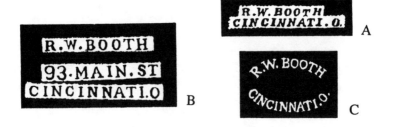

R.W. BOOTH & CO.

Hardware dealers, jobbers, and importers in Cincinnati, OH, 1853-79. (see R.W. Booth)

RUDOLPH BORN

Chicago, IL hardware dealer. ★★★

P. BOSSART

This imprint has been reported on a number of planes that appear to have been professionally made in the second quarter of the 19c. ★★★

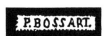 

BOSTON FACTORY

This imprint has appeared on various planes. Appearance is ca.1850. ★★★

H.E. BOUCHER MFG. CO.

This imprint appears on a 3¾" miniature smoothing plane and runs vertically on the toe.

H.E. BOUCHER MFG. CO. N.Y.

T.J. BOWDEN & SON

A low angle coffin-shaped smoother, 11½" long and steel soled, has been reported bearing this imprint. It has an A.L. WHITING & CO./WORCESTER MASS. iron. Appearance is mid-19c.

J. E. BOWKER & CO.

A Boston, MA, hardware dealer —1872— (John E. Bowker). ★★ *(see next page)*

J.J. BOWLES
John J. Bowles, an East Hartford, CT, planemaker, —1838-43. He advertised during this period that he could offer 48 different types of planes. (see Brooks & Bowles) ★★★

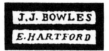

JOHN BOYD
A number of planes have been reported with this imprint.

N.J. BOYD
A probable New York City hardware dealer. The imprint appears on a J. & W. Webb (w.s.) molding plane.

J. BRACELIN
James Bracelin was listed in the 1850 census as an edge tool maker, age 34, living in Dayton, OH, and born in New York. In the 1860 census and in an 1869 Dayton city directory he was still listed as an edge tool maker. His planes are seldom seen, so planemaking may have been a sideline or an earlier occupation. A & B: ★★

 A  B

J. BRADFORD
Joseph Bradford (b. 1808 in Turner, ME) made coopers', carpenters' and ship joiners' tools in Portland, ME, from about 1837 until 1884. The 1860 census reported he had one employee, and produced $1000 worth of coopers' tools, $200 worth of joiners' tools and $100 in repairs. A: ★★ B & B1: ★ *(continued next page)*

 A  B

B1

B

F.S. BRADLEY & CO.

A New Haven, CT, hardware dealer, 1866-91.   ★★

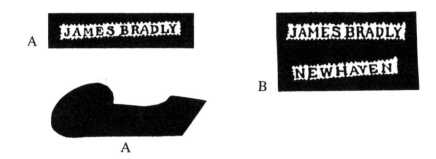

JAMES BRADLY

A Connecticut planemaker who probably worked ca.1800.   A & B: ★★★

A

B

A

BRAGAW & BLAKE

Isaac Bragaw and Howard P. Blake manufactured planes and were hardware dealers in Hartford, CT, 1847-50.

S. BRANCH

Six planes have been reported, all birch; five are molding planes, four of them 9⅞" long, one 8", all with flat chamfers; one is a Yankee plow plane. Appearance is 18c southern New England. A Stephen Branch (1762-1828) was a joiner in Lisbon, CT.   ★★★★

a

b

BRAZER

Probably Benjamin Brazer (or Brasier) listed in the Lowell, MA, directory of 1832 as a toolmaker and in 1833-35 as a planemaker. He appeared in the 1850 census as a carpenter in Boston, MA, age 47. (see Gardner & Brazer)   ★★★

G. BREMERMAN

Gerd Bremerman, a St. Louis hardware merchant. The name was spelled with two N's in the directories from 1853 on. He operated under this imprint 1848-54—. (see also Bremermann Raschoe & Co. and G. Bremermann & Co.) ★★

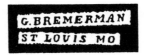

G. BREMERMANN & CO.

Gerd Bremermann and ?, hardware merchants in St. Louis, MO, 1864-67. No examples of this imprint have been reported. (see G. Bremerman)

BREMERMANN RASCHOE & CO.

Gerd Bremermann and ? Raschoe, hardware merchants in St. Louis, MO, 1857-60. No examples of this imprint have been reported. (see G. Bremerman)

BRIDGE

Joseph P. Bridge was a planemaker in Washington, DC, —1855-64. ★★★

BRIDGE TOOL CO.

This imprint appears on a transitional style 26" long fore plane with a lever cap and the additional location imprint ST. LOUIS MO. It is a brand name used by Shapleigh Hardware Co., St. Louis, MO, for second quality iron- and wood-bottomed planes during the 20th c.

E. BRIGGS

Thought to be Elisha Briggs (ca.1738-1803), who came to Keene, NH, in 1763; or Eliphalet (1713-1780), father of Elisha, who came to Keene in 1767 or earlier; or Elisha's brother, Captain Eliphalet (1735-1776), who came to Keene in 1768 or earlier. All came from Norton, MA, where H. Wetherel made planes during that period, using a similar IN NORTON imprint. Elisha Briggs was a joiner, millwright and housebuilder, and was married in Wrentham in 1758. ★★★★★

N. BRIGGS

Thought to be Nathaniel Briggs (1744-1777), who lived in Norton, MA, and moved to Keene, NH, in 1773. He was the second cousin of Elisha and Eliphalet Briggs, Jr. (see E. Briggs). His brother, Rufus, who remained in Massachusetts, married a Margaret Wetherel. Nathaniel Briggs died of wounds received at the battle in Bennington, VT, and though his estate included planes and other woodworking tools, there is no record as to his trade. His father and brothers were woodworkers. Several examples of N. Briggs' work have been reported, including a 10⅛" birch tongue plane with 1/4" flat chamfers. 18c in appearance. ★★★★

S. BRIGGS

There have been several reports of planes bearing this imprint. Most are made of birch and have late 18c characteristics. A skewed rabbet that has been reported has a relieved wedge.

W.A. BRIGGS   see Pond & Briggs

A. BRIGHT & J. CHAPPELL

Listed in the 1837 Pittsburgh, PA, business directory as planemakers. The B imprint omits the ampersand and includes a date. (also see J. Chappell)   A & B: ★★★

 A    B

BRIGHT & CO.

A probable hardware dealer in Pottsville, PA; mid- to late 19c.

A.F. BROMBACHER & CO.

This NYC dealer, which claimed to have been established in 1760, carried tools for both coopers and gaugers, and issued a catalog as late as 1922. Its line included howels and crozes, head floats, sun planes, and coopers' jointers, made by both D.R. BARTON and I. & I.J. WHITE. ★   *(see next page)*

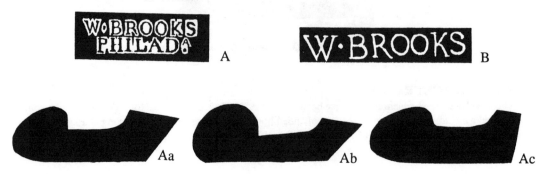

D. BROOKS

A gutter plane with offset tote has been reported, with the additional location stamp PHILA.

P. BROOKS   see P. Brooks & Co.

P. BROOKS & CO.

Probably Peter Brooks, who made planes ca.1850 in Williamstown, So. Williamstown, Westfield and Pittsfield, MA, and East Hartford, CT. The 1840 census showed him in East Hartford, CT, with five members of his household in manufacturing, living next door to Harvey Crane (see H. Crane). Truman Nutting (see T. Nutting) invoiced Brooks for 450 jointer and 410 jack plane handles in 1847. The 1850 census listed him as a toolmaker in Westfield, MA, age 47, with real estate worth $2000. A combination tongue and groove plane has been reported with the imprint P. BROOKS/PATENT. There is, however, no record of a patent having been issued. (see Brooks & Bowles)   A & B: ★★★   C: FF

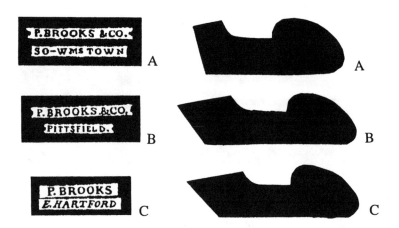

W. BROOKS

William Brooks was one of the important 18c Philadelphia, PA, planemakers who worked from 1791 or earlier to 1807.   A: ★★   B: ★★★★

BROOKS & BOWLES
This imprint appears on a 28" razeed jointer. Appearance is ca.1850. (see P. Brooks & Co. and John J. Bowles) ★★★

C.P. BROWN
A New Haven, CT, planemaker, whose planes appear to have been made ca.1840-50. A Charles Brown of New Haven is listed in the 1840 census as being in manufacturing or trade and in the 1850 census as a manufacturer, age 49. ★★★

J.G. & F.H. BROWN
A W.H. Pond (w.s.) T-rabbet has been reported with the imprint "Made for J.G. & F.H. Brown/New Haven." The imprint shown appears on a 7" long carriagemakers' coffin smoother.

J.S. BROWN
A Baltimore, MD, planemaker who worked —1842.

J.T. BROWN
A plane and edge tool maker in Baltimore, MD, during the period —1824-43—. ★

BROWN BROTHERS
Most probably a hardware firm. The imprint appears on a plank match tongue.

BROWN & PIKE

Reported on a 16" open handled jack. Possibly a Boston hardware dealer

BROWN TOOL CO.

Various planes have been reported both bench and molding, with Sandusky and Auburn Tool style numbers. Possibly a hardware dealer or a brand name.

BROWN & WOOD

This imprint appears on the heel of a J.F. & G.M. LINDSEY side rabbet. Probably a hardware dealer.

H. BROWNING

Horace Browning of Rowe, MA, whose working dates were —1850-55. He was listed in the 1850 census as age 40 and a manufacturer of joiners' tools, employing three hands and producing bench and molding planes worth $2000. He died in 1866.   ★

BRUFF BROTHER & SEAVER

A hardware dealer listed the New York City directory for 1859-60 and comprising Charles Bruff and George A. Seaver.   ★★★

BRUMLEY

Joseph Brumley, a planemaker who advertised in Washington DC newspapers in 1800 as a cabinetmaker, but also kept ironmongery, including a large assortment of planes. He stated that any kind of plane could be supplied on shortest notice and that "Orders for planes from merchants will be speedily executed." The case for a walnut tall-case clock made in Mt. Holly, NJ, in 1785 was signed by Joseph Brumley. In 1798 he advertised as a cabinetmaker in Trenton, NJ, and then moved on to Georgetown, Washington DC, in 1800.   ★★★

a   b

BRUNNER
Made wooden spill planes in Bethlehem, PA.

W.W. BRYAN
William W. Bryan (b. 1811 in NY) was a Rochester, NY, hardware merchant 1836-48, and edge tool maker 1850-55. Some time after 1847 he was located adjacent to D.R. Barton (w.s.-also see Bush & Bryan).   ★★★

W. BRYCE & CO.
William Bryce operated a hardware store in New York City 1846-73.   ★★★

BUCKEYE PLANE CO.
The imprint appears on two 16" beech jack planes. Their irons are stamped Buckeye Plane Co./Ohio. There is a #13 on each plane's toe. The Ohio Tool Co., Sandusky Tool Co., and Greenfield Tool Co. all used #13 for jack planes. The imprint is also reported on a filletster with OHIO imprinted on the toe. The brand name "Buckeye" was used by the Buckeye Manufacturing and Foundry Co. 1904-23 for its iron bench planes. Possibly another Ohio Tool Co. brand name.

BUFFALO TOOL CO.
Location and dates are unknown, though quite possibly a hardware dealer in Buffalo, NY. A ¾" boxed bead has been reported with this imprint and a #105 incised on its heel. #105 is the style number for a ¾" boxed bead in the Greenfield Tool Company's (w.s.) 1854 price list. Also reported is a handled smooth plane incised #5, with a Sandusky iron and corresponding to Invoice #5 in the Sandusky Tool Co. (w.s.) 1877 illustrated list.

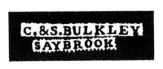

C. & S. BULKLEY
Saybrook, CT, planemakers ca.1850. Charles Bulkley was listed in the 1850 census for Saybrook as a toolmaker, age 55, and Samuel S. Bulkley as a toolmaker, age 33. The decorative cartouche that appears on the (C) imprint was also used on the planes of John Denison (w.s.). Several planes have been reported with both the C. & S. Bulkley and John Denison imprints, indicating a relationship between the two firms.   A & B: ★

A   B   C

C.F. BULKLEY & CO.
Possibly related to C. & S. Bulkley.

L. & C. H. BULL
Lorenzo and Charles H. Bull, Quincy, IL, hardware dealers 1845-61. ★★

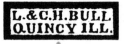

O.T. BULL & CO.
A Louisville, KY, hardware dealer 1851-66, consisting of Oliver T. and George W. Bull.

L. BUNDY
A combination match and plow plane (U.S. pat. 109,174, Nov. 15, 1870) was patented by Lewis Bundy. Imprint reads "L. Bundy's/comb'd/Match Plane/ & Plow/Pat'd. Nov. 15, 1870/Moores Forks/N.Y." ★★★★★

BUNTING & MIDDLETON

A probable hardware dealer whose imprint appears on a fore plane made by E. NUTTING (w.s.).

J. BURKE

James Burke, of Madison, IN, who in the 1850 census was listed as a planemaker, age 33, born in Maryland, and employing five people. ★★

JOHN BURLEY

Several examples have been reported. One plane is a coffin-shaped smoother with a double iron by Greaves & Son. Plane's appearance is mid-19c.

T. E. BURLEY

Thomas Burley (1723-1805), a joiner in Epping, NH, whose imprint has been found on various planes and molding tools. His molding planes are generally 10" long. The a wedge is from an example with flat chamfers; the b wedge is from a beech plane with rounded chamfers. The imprints are identical on all examples. ★★★

a   b

GEO. BURNHAM, JR.

George Burnham, an Amherst, MA, planemaker (b. 1817 in Connecticut) worked under this imprint 1844-53. He was listed in the 1840 and 1850 censuses as a planemaker and as an axe handle manufacturer in the 1860 census. In the Products of Industry census of 1850 he was listed as a tool manufacturer with a capital of $7000, using 20,000 feet of beech worth $800, 4 tons of boxwood worth $120, plane irons worth $2000, employing 14 male hands who were paid $364 total per month to make tools worth $12,000 annually. Burnham arrived in Amherst in 1841 after apprenticing in New Hartford, CT, probably with H. Chapin (w.s.). He became a journeyman for Luther Fox (w.s.) then in the bench plane business; and in about a year Burnham, together with Benoni Thayer, Hiram Fox, and Aaron Ferry bought Luther Fox out and formed Burnham, Fox & Co. (w.s.). In 1844 Burnham bought out his partners, trading as George Burnham Jr.   FF

BURNHAM & BROTHERS
An East Hartford, CT, planemaker ca.1850.   ★★

BURNHAM, FOX & CO.
A partnership of George Burnham, Benoni Thayer (who was listed as a mechanic in the 1850 census, age 41, in Amherst, MA), Hiram Fox and Aaron Ferry, who made planes 1842-44 in Amherst, MA. and were bought out by Geo. Burnham, Jr. (w.s.).   ★

THOMAS BURNS
Listed as a planemaker in the 1836-37 Newark, NJ, directory, but no example of his imprint has been reported.

E.T. BURROWES CO.
Edward T. Burrowes of Portland, ME, patented a sliding wire screen in 1878. The firm remained in business until 1928. The plane bearing the firm name was part of the installation package. A 12" level marked E.T. BURROWES has also been reported.

J. BURT
Molding planes made of beech, ranging from 9¼" to 9½", have been reported from five different sources. Appearance is early 19c.

S.M. BURT

Spencer M. Burt, a turner and wheelwright, who may also have been a planemaker. Burt died intestate in 1835 in Berkley, MA, which is close to Taunton and Norton.

BUSH

A number of planes have been reported with this imprint, several being found in eastern Pennsylvania. They are all made of beech with wide, flat chamfers. Appearance is ca.1800. An A B. DEAN (w.s.) imprint has appeared on a Bush plane, as has an owner imprint J. SHAUB, this on one of the planes found in eastern Pa. A John Bush of London, England, who worked —1794-99— is reported in *British Planemakers*, 3rd edition, using the same imprint. This suggests that the planes found in the U.S. were imported or perhaps came over with emigrants, or perhaps Bush emigrated. It seems that more examples have been reported in the U.S. than in England. ★★

a   b

CHARLES V. BUSH

This imprint was reported on a closed-handled match grooving plane. Penn Yan is most likely PennYan, NY.

H. BUSH

Henry Bush, Rochester, NY, was a planemaker and tool dealer during the period 1831-33, and later in partnership with William W. Bryan. (see Bush & Bryan) ★★

BUSH & BRYAN

A Rochester, NY, hardware partnership of William W. Bryan and Henry Bush. They operated during 1834-36 and again in 1849-53. (see H. Bush and also W.W. Bryan)

BUSHNELL

Believed to be a Philadelphia hardware dealer.

N.T. BUSHNELL & CO.

This imprint appears on the toe of a double iron nosing plane made by H. CHAPIN/UNION FACTORY (B imprint). Probably a hardware dealer.

BUTLER

Imprints B, C, C1, and D were used by both John Butler and George Butler. George Butler was a Philadelphia, PA, planemaker 1819-35. John Butler was one of the early Philadelphia, PA, planemakers. His first directory listing was in 1791 and he worked as late as 1830. He was listed in the 1790 census as a carpenter and in 1800 as a planemaker. A beading plane bearing his imprint (A) and also the owner's brand A. HAINS (Adam Hains, an important Philadelphia cabinetmaker, active —1790—) is owned by Winterthur, together with furniture made by Hains. The (E) imprint appears on a #12 hollow and combines BUTLER with the B1 imprint of M. LONG (w.s.).   A: ★★★★★   B, C & C1: ★   D: ★★★   E & F: ★★★★★   *(continued on next page)*

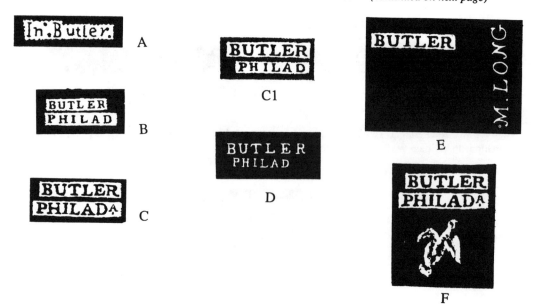

76

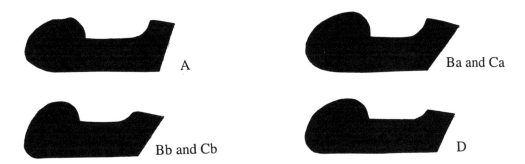

A

Ba and Ca

Bb and Cb

D

ANDREW BUTLER

Listed as a planemaker in the 1825 city directory at the same Philadelphia, PA, address as John Butler (see Butler) and in 1830 by himself. No example of his imprint has been reported.

FREDERICK BUTLER

Listed as a planemaker in the 1825 city directory at the same Philadelphia, PA, address as John Butler (see Butler). No example of his imprint has been reported.

BUTTLES & RUNYON

Joel Buttles and Clark Runyon, who operated in Columbus, Ohio, —1843-44—, and who may have been planemakers or tool dealers or both.   ★★★

W.H. BYRON

A Milwaukee, WI, hardware dealer in the late 1840's. A Z.J. M'Master/Auburn (w.s.) plane has been reported imprinted MADE FOR/W.H. BYRON/MILWAUKEE (designated C imprint).   A & B: ★★★

A

B

C. R. & W.

The meaning of these initials is not known. A hollow owned by the Farmers Museum at Cooperstown, NY, is also imprinted N.Y.C. The museum dates it 1878-83. There is an owner's imprint on the plane C.F. RAYMER. He may be the C.R. of C.R. & W.

C. S. C.

One example reported, a tongue plane with an eagle imprint. Probably a Chapin-Stephens & Co. imprint. (see Chapin-Stephens)

C.T. & CO.

Also stamped N.Y.C. Possibly an imprint for Charles Tollner. (see C. Tollner)

JAMES CAIN (or CAINE)

Listed as a plane manufacturer in the Cleveland, OH, directories of 1851-53. Earlier (1849-50) he was employed by J.J. Vinall (w.s.). In the 1863-67 directories he was listed as a toolmaker.

T.C. CAIN

Thomas Caine, a planemaker of Ravenna, Ohio, —1838-50—. ★★

E. CALDWELL

A Baltimore, MD, planemaker, —1840-56—. ★

B. CALLENDER & CO.

Benjamin Callender, a Boston, MA, hardware dealer who traded as Benjamin Callender 1851-61, and as Benjamin Callender & Co. 1862-87.   A: ★   B: ★★★

A

B

N. CAMPER

Napoleon Camper, a Baltimore planemaker, tool maker and tool store owner. He was listed in the 1850 census as age 26 and born in Maryland. His working dates were —1850-80.   A, B, C, D: ★

A

B

C

D

A and D

J.F. CARD

A probable hardware dealer in Toledo, OH, ca. 1850.

H. & W.T. CAREY

Planes have been reported, with a location imprint XENIA (probably Xenia, Ohio, a town close to Dayton). One example appeared on a screw stop dado with Ohio Tool Co. irons and stamped "48" on the toe, Ohio Tool Co.'s invoice number for screw stop dados, implying that Carey was a dealer.   ★★★

CARLIN & FULTON

James F. Carlin and David C. Fulton, hardware dealers and importers in Baltimore, MD, —1864-1900—.

E.W. CARPENTER

Emanuel Weidler Carpenter (1791-1856) was a fifth generation Pennsylvania German; the original family name was Zimmerman, German for carpenter. His ancestor, Heinrich Zimmerman (b.1673, d. ca.1749), migrated from Canton Bern in Switzerland to America about 1706. E.W. was a son of Samuel Carpenter (b.1765, d.1824), who moved, when Carpenter was 16, from his farm into Lancaster, PA, and later became mayor of Lancaster.

E.W. Carpenter, during his career, was a cabinetmaker, toolmaker, planemaker, and "practitioner of medicine" and was active in planemaking during most of his adult life. He left Lancaster around 1814, and in 1820 returned there; he was listed as a joiner 1821-25. At least part of the time away was spent in Maryland, where he married Sarah Stevens Sangston from Baltimore City in 1818 and where his oldest daughter was born in 1819. The Baltimore planes (Imprint C) were most likely made ca.1818-19.

The opening of E.W.'s shop apparently resulted from an inheritance from his father, enabling him to purchase, in 1826, a "large and commodious two-story BRICK TAVERN HOUSE" on the southwest corner of South Queen and German (now Farnum) Streets. In 1828, Joseph L. Hurst, a cabinetmaker, was apprenticed to E.W., probably only briefly. In a legal memorandum, E.W. agreed to "Learn-instruct and teach" Hurst in "the art, trade and Mystery of Plane Making" and to pay him "Customary Journeymans wages." Others who worked in E.W.'s shop included his sons Samuel Sangston Carpenter (see S. Carpenter), John Edwin Carpenter (b.1831; listed as a planemaker 1850-67, 1873-74, otherwise as a carpenter) and (Emanuel) Warner Carpenter (see W. Carpenter); also William Kieffer (w.s.), son-in-law of E.W.; Israel B. Carpenter (see I. Carpenter), nephew; John Kilheffer, a 16 year old planemaker living with E.W. in 1850; and probably J.F. Bauder (w.s.) and Samuel Auxer (w.s.) C.G. Siewers (w.s.), Carpenter's son-in-law and a Cincinnati planemaker, may have been trained by Carpenter in the 1830's. Carpenter retailed planes at his shop, sold them to New York and through hardware stores including Oglesby & Pool (see Kelker), John F. Steinman (w.s.), George Mayer (w.s.), John A. Duncan, Wilmington, DE, Yarnall & McClure (w.s.) and W.M. McClure (w.s.).

Carpenter is known among tool collectors for his Improved Arm planes, U.S. Patent 594, Feb.6, 1838 (D imprints). This involved cutting threads through the body of the plane and engineering arms "which regulate the fence with great ease and accuracy and give it an increased firmness." He also held two other patents: the first, issued Jan. 30, 1830 (National Archives restored patent 5807X), for an adjustable bit in tongue planes (E imprints), and the last, March 27, 1849 (no.6226), for a second wedge to adjust the throat opening on planes (Imprint B).

At a time when tools were becoming more standardized, Carpenter continued to produce a wide variety, made in a small shop, employing one or two journeymen with a few apprentices. He seemed willing to make any plane a customer might want: wedge, screw, or improved arm plow and match planes; screw and improved arm filletster and sash planes; regular or double wedge coffin, fore, miter, and panel raising planes; simple and complex molders in many sizes and cuts; sun planes and long jointers for coopers. He also produced marking, mortise, slitting and panel gauges in almost any length; yardsticks, board rules, clapboard gauges; sash templates; bitstocks with pad bits; double pistol routers; screw boxes, handscrews, violin clamps, screws for vises and large clamps; workbenches, etc. He usually used beech for his tools, but boxwood, rosewood, ebony, fruitwood, even hickory were also employed. Many of his patterns, including his distinctive wedge, are significantly larger or thicker than those of others. Some planes are massive.

Sarah Stevens Sangston Carpenter (ca.1796-1878), his wife, took over the shop when he died in 1856 and ran it, probably with help from William Kieffer. The property was sold by 1865, so E.W.'s shop lasted about 38 years. Newspaper ads shortly after E.W.'s death showed that Sarah continued the planemaking business, including the use of E.W.'s name and almost certainly his stamp: "E.W. CARPENTER'S PLANE MAKING BUSINESS WILL be continued in all respects as heretofore, and in his name, by the undersigned, his widow, who is confident she will be able to sustain the well known and long established reputation of his Planes. . .The business will be conducted by her under the name and style of E.W. CARPENTER, at the old stand. S.S. CARPENTER." The successors to the planemaking business were Kieffer & Auxer (w.s.), Auxer & Remley (w.s.), and Samuel Auxer (w.s.).

According to the 1850 Census of Manufacturing, E.W. Carpenter, Plane Maker, made 150 Bench Screws worth $140 and 1000 Planes worth $1500 from June 1849 to May 1850. He used 3000 feet of wood costing $100, employing five males. In the 1860 Census of Manufacturing, Sarah S. Carpenter, Plain Maker, produced 2000 "plains" worth $4000, employing three men.

Carpenter's planes are much sought after by collectors, particularly the rarer types such as the patented plow and the wide cornice plane. *(continued next page)*

A: FF A1: ★ A2: ★★ B: ★★★ C: ★★★★★ D: ★★★★ D1: ★★★★ D2: ★★★★
D3: ★★★★ E: ★★★ E1: ★★★ E2: ★★★★ *(continued next page)*

E.W. CARPENTER.
LANCASTER.

A

E.W. CARPENTER

A1

E.W. CARPENTER
LANCASTER·PA

A2

E.W. CARPENTER'S
PATENT
MARCH 27, 1849
LANCASTER

B

E.W. CARPENTER
BALTIMORE

C

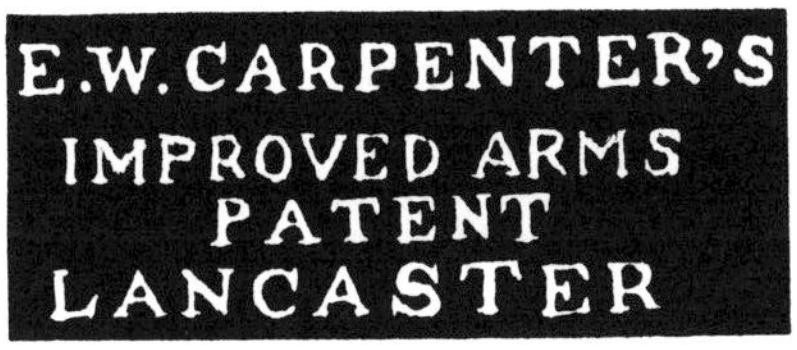

E.W. CARPENTER'S
IMPROVED ARMS
PATENT
LANCASTER

D

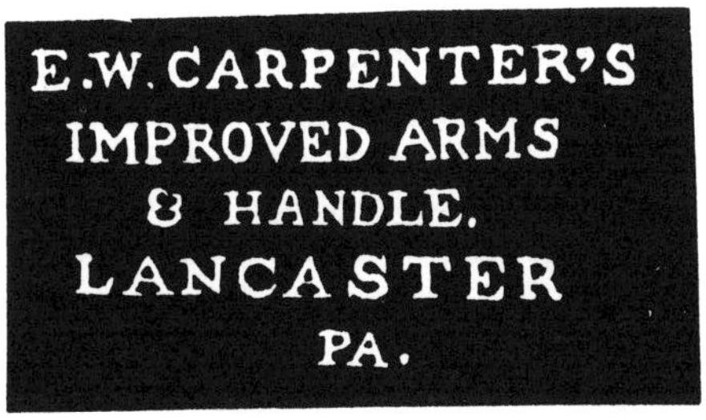

E.W. CARPENTER'S
IMPROVED ARMS
& HANDLE.
LANCASTER
PA.

D1

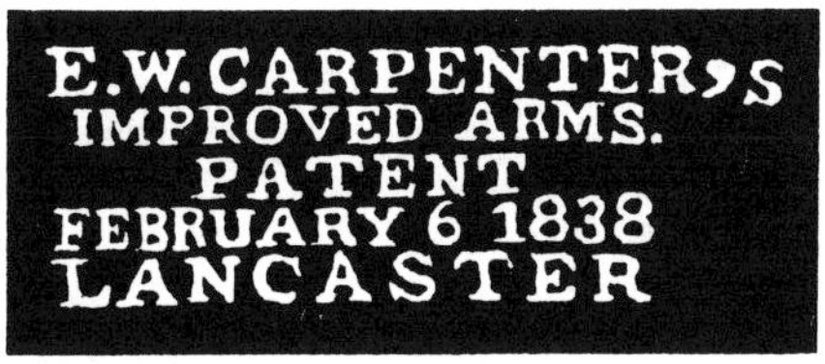

E.W. CARPENTER'S
IMPROVED ARMS.
PATENT
FEBRUARY 6 1838
LANCASTER

D2

E.W. CARPENTER'S
IMPROVD ARMS
PATENT
LANCASTER

D3

E.W. CARPENTER'S
PATENTBIT
LANCASTER

E

E.W. CARPENTER'S
PATENT
LANCASTER

E1

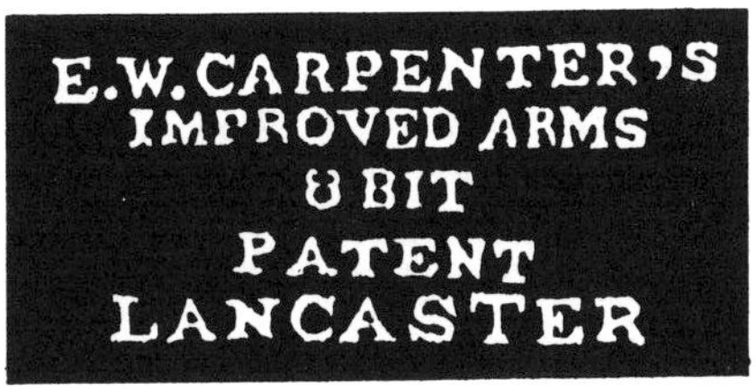

E.W. CARPENTER'S
IMPROVED ARMS
& BIT
PATENT
LANCASTER

E2

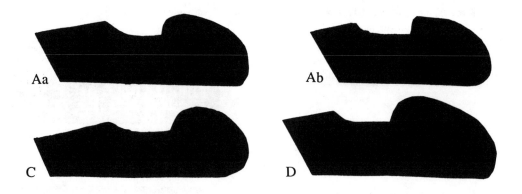

Aa

Ab

C

D

I. CARPENTER

Rev. Israel B. Carpenter (1824-1890), nephew of E.W. Carpenter (w.s.), son of his younger brother, Michael. Israel was listed as a planemaker in Lancaster, PA, 1847-48. He likely trained under Carpenter, then served him as a journeyman for these two years. In Reading in 1850, he was converted and became a minister of the United Brethren in Christ in 1852. He served ten churches, mostly in Lancaster, Dauphin, and Berks Counties, 1852-79. He had no church appointment during 11 of these years and, except when he was a private in Co. A, 12th Regiment, Militia of 1862, he probably had to help support himself with woodworking (he was listed as a carpenter in Reading in 1876). He lived in Reading from 1872-90, except for a one year appointment just outside Lancaster. He went blind about 1885 and ran a grocery from his home until his death in 1890.

On Aug. 25, 1868, F. Smith and I. Carpenter patented (no. 81425) a metal top for wooden bench planes (see *P-TAMPIA, Vol. I,* p.127 -Bibliography) intended to strengthen and lighten them and, with a double wedge like that of E.W., to adjust the mouth of the plane. Frederick Smith was a hatter married to Israel's sister. His shop address was given to write for further information on the patent. Presently known examples are patent smooth, jack, and fore planes, an all-wood fore plane, and all-wood astragal with E.W. style wedge, and a yardstick. Patented bench planes ★★★★ Regular wooden planes ★★★★

S. CARPENTER

Samuel Sangston Carpenter (1823-1889), eldest son of E.W. Carpenter (w.s.) When he turned 21, Samuel was listed as a planemaker in the 1844 Lancaster, PA, tax list (he probably helped made E.W.'s planes from about the age of 16). He also studied law, but seems not to have practiced it until he moved, in December 1844, to Cincinnati where his brother-in-law, C.G. Siewers (w.s.), was living. He was appointed a U.S. Commissioner, but declined to enforce the Fugitive Slave Law; this cost him most of his business as Commissioner. Late in her life, Sarah S. Carpenter paid annual visits to Samuel; she died in Cincinnati on her last visit. ★★★★★

W. CARPENTER

Possibly Emanuel Warner Carpenter (b.1834), referred to as Warner, son of E.W. Carpenter (w.s.). Warner was listed as a planemaker, age 17, living with this father, in the 1850 census. In 1856, when his father died, he was living in Hamilton County, Ohio, perhaps working for his brother-in-law, C.G. Siewers (w.s.), making tools while studying law with his older brother Samuel (see S. Carpenter). He became "a lawyer who removed South" and in 1864 he was in Capiah County, Mississippi. He may have received his own imprint stamp when he reached age 21 in 1855 and used it briefly before leaving E.W.'s shop.   ★★★★★

M.A. CARRINGTON

Miles A. Carrington was listed as a plane manufacturer in New Haven in the 1856-57 Connecticut directory. ★★★★

C. CARTER

Charles Carter made planes in Troy (1847-53 as R. & C. Carter and then E. & C. Carter, both w.s.), Utica (in 1855 working for others), Syracuse (1856-59), and Auburn, NY (1860-63 as a toolmaker at the Auburn Prison workshop). Born in England in 1826, he was the son of Richard Carter (see R. Carter), also a planemaker, with whom he formed a brief partnership. On October 6,1858, he received patent #82692 for a machine "for forming the throats of planes after the main part of the mortise has been roughed out." The machines were used by the Ohio Tool Co. and H. Chapin's Son (both w.s.). The Chapin assignment for the use of one machine was conveyed 10/22/1869, with Carter receiving $1000.   ★★★★

E. CARTER

This imprint has been reported from several sources. The planes are made of beech, with relieved wedges; length varies between 9½" and 10". Included are a single-iron sash plane, a coping plane, two beads and several other molding planes.

E. CARTER   see Edward Carter

EDWARD CARTER

1825-1903. Born in England, the son of Richard Carter (see R. Carter) and brother of Charles Carter (see C. Carter). He made planes in Troy, NY, under his own imprint 1854-57 and 1865-97. An advertisement in the 1866 Troy directory indicates the diversity of his firm. It had both a plane factory and a tool store (established in 1833 by his father, Richard Carter) and advertised manufacture of planes, mechanics' tools, wood moldings, and hand tenoning machines. Sawing, planing, turning, boring and mortising was done to order. Edward's son, Richard, took over management in 1898 and in 1903 planemaking was dropped. (also see E.& C. Carter and Carter's Tool Store)   A: ★   B & C: FF

E. & C. CARTER

A partnership of Edward Carter with his brother Charles, that made planes in Troy, NY, 1849-53; and later for a short period 1862-64 with his stepbrother Cyrus replacing Charles. Apparently the same imprint was used. (see C. Carter and also Edward Carter)   FF

I.M. CARTER

Carter, whose name and location HYDE PARK N.Y. appear on a bookbinder's plow plane, is reported in the *History of Dutchess County* (James Smith, 1882) as Israel M. Carter, an edge tool manufacturer, born in Hyde Park in June 1829, who began his business in 1847. His vita included being a tax collector, a constable, and trustee of the fire district for ten years.

L.R. CARTER

Lewis R. Carter, a Cincinnati, OH, planemaker in 1834 and also a partner in Carter, Donaldson & Fugate in 1831 and Carter, Donaldson & Co. —1832 (both w.s.).   ★★★

R. CARTER

Richard Carter (1802-1891), head of the Carter family, father of Charles and Edward Carter, and probably also of Leonard Carter, and stepfather of Cyrus Carter (b. Troy NY 1828). He came to the U.S. from England in 1831 and began making planes in Troy, NY, in 1833. He made under his own imprint 1833-41 and 1850-62. He was in partnership with Leonard 1842-46 (see R.& L. Carter) and with son Charles 1847-49. (see R.& C. Carter and also C. Carter and Edward Carter).   ★   *(see next page)*

R. & C. CARTER
A brief partnership (1847-49) between Richard Carter and his son Charles as planemakers in Troy, NY. (see C. Carter and also R. Carter)   ★

R. & L. CARTER
A partnership between Richard Carter and Leonard Carter (possibly his son or close relative) in Troy, NY, 1842- 46. Leonard earlier was a planemaker at the Carter factory 1836-41, boarding with Richard in 1836 and 1837. The imprint shown is incuse. (see R. Carter)   ★

R & L CARTER
TROY

CARTER, DONALDSON & CO.
Lewis R. Carter and James F. Donaldson, Cincinnati, OH, planemakers, 1832—. (see Carter, Donaldson & Fugate, and L.R. Carter)

CARTER, DONALDSON & FUGATE
Lewis R. Carter, James F. Donaldson and Thomas Fugate, Cincinnati, OH, planemakers, —1831. (see L.R. Carter, Carter, Donaldson, J. Donaldson, and T. Fugate)

CARTER'S TOOL STORE
Several molding planes have been reported. Probably the imprint for Edward Carter, alone or with one of both of his brothers (Charles and/or Cyrus), when he added a tool store to the family's various enterprises. (see Edward Carter)   ★★★

S. CARUTHERS
Samuel Caruthers is the earliest of the documented Philadelphia planemakers. He was the master to whom Benjamin Armitage (w.s.) was apprenticed. Caruthers advertised in the *Pennsylvania Chronicle* of March 6, 1767, that his wares included "double-ironed planes of a late construction far exceeding any tooth planes or uprights whatsoever for cross grained or curled stuff." Caruthers also sold tools. In 1768 he advertised "Samuel Caruthers. In Third Street, Continues to keep a general assortment of hard ware, particularly adapted to carpenters and joiners, also smiths, coopers, shoemakers, &c. A set of clockmaker's files to be sold together. . . seven and a half steel plate pit saws, very well finished and the utmost care is taken to keep the very best saws of all denominations, of various makers; also there is, and is intended to be continued, the making of all sorts of

carpenters and joiners planes, with the usual care and fidelity. . . N.B. Wanted beach [beech] wood in bolts, also in scantling; ash wood, ditto, both for plane making and wood saw frames." He was elected to the Carpenter's Company of the City and County of Philadelphia in 1771 and died in 1780.

Unlike those of the early New England planemakers, Caruthers' planes reflected the style of mid-18c English planes, quite understandable since Philadelphia was the colonies' largest city, and an important port, whose prosperous inhabitants followed the latest London fashions. ★★★

E.W. CASE

A Columbus, OH, planemaker and/or dealer whose dates are unknown. ★

L. CASE

Lorenzo Case (1821-1887) made planes in Watertown, NY, under his own imprint —1850—, after having earlier made planes as an employee of Benjamin F. Berry (see B.F. Berry) in the 1840s. The 1850 census lists him as employing six men and producing carpenters' tools worth $3500. It appears that his planemaking activities ceased in 1855. A: ★ B & C: ★★

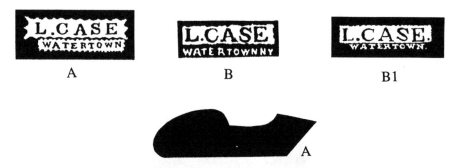

A   B   B1

A

CASEY & CO.

George Casey apparently made planes under this imprint in Auburn, NY, in 1857. He was otherwise in business with several sets of partners (see Casey, Kitchel & Co., Casey, Clark & Co., and the Auburn Tool Co.). These various enterprises all used prison labor. George Casey was actively involved in planemaking from 1847 into the 1880s. ★

CASEY, CLARK & CO.

George Casey bought out his partners in Casey, Kitchel & Co. and with new partners (J.N. Starin, Nelson and Adejiah Fitch, Noah P. Clark, and Alonzo Beardsley) manufactured under Casey, Clark & Co. in Auburn, NY, from 1858 to 1864 when the firm was reorganized into the Auburn Tool Co. (w.s.). The 1860 census showed 65 hands employed with $45,000 worth of planes and plane irons produced. The imprint shown below is incuse. (see Casey & Co. and Casey, Kitchel & Co.)   ★

CASEY CLARK&Co
AUBURN N.Y.

CASEY, KITCHEL & CO.

A partnership consisting of George Casey, Adam Miller, Joshua Douglass and Nelson Kitchel, which bought the Auburn prison labor contract from Z.J. McMaster & Co. (w.s.) in 1847 and made planes using prison labor 1847-58. The 1850 census indicated that the firm employed 40 convicts, used a steam planing mill and produced $22,000 worth of carpenters' and joiners' tools. (see Casey & Co. and Casey, Clark & Co.)   All imprints: ★

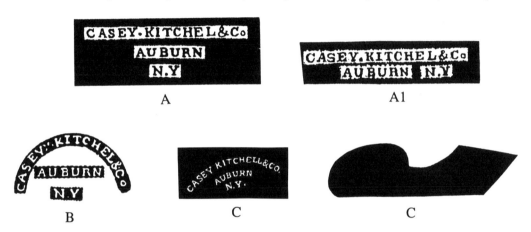

CASEY·KITCHEL&Co
AUBURN
N.Y

A

CASEY·KITCHEL&Co
AUBURN N.Y

A1

CASEY·KITCHEL&Co
AUBURN
N.Y

B

CASEY KITCHELL&CO.
AUBURN
N.Y.

C

C

H. CASSEBEER

This imprint has been reported on the heel of a quarter round with G.W. DENISON & CO. (w.s.) imprinted on the toe. Most probably a hardware dealer in Rochester, NY. (see Cassebeer Reed & Co.)

H.CASSEBEER
ROCHESTER N.Y.

CASSEBEER REED & CO.

A New York City hardware firm consisting of Herman Cassebeer, William A. Reed and Louis H. Auerbacher. It operated 1878-84 in the premises previously occupied by Nathusius, Kegler & Morrison (w.s.). (see H. Cassebeer and also Reed & Auerbacher)   ★★

CASSEBEER REED&Co
229 BOWERY
NEW YORK

H. CASSEL

Planes reported range between 9¾" and 10" long and are made of beech. Appearance is ca.1800-1820, probable location eastern Pennsylvania.

CATION

David W. Cation was a New York City planemaker who produced under this imprint 1835-44—, and earlier, in 1834, was a partner with J.W. Gibbs in Gibbs & Cation (w.s.). He was listed in the 1850 census as a merchant in NYC, age 48, and born in Connecticut. The imprint shown below is incuse. ★★★

A. CAUGHTER & CO.

An example with a location imprint LOUISVILLE, KY, has been reported.

CAVANACH & MILLER

A probable hardware dealer.

CAYUDUTTA FACTORY

Nothing factual is known about this imprint. Cayudutta Creek empties into the Mohawk River at Fonda, NY. The mark may be a trade name for one of the central NY state planemakers. One of Wm. H. Livingston & Co.'s (w.s.) imprints reads Wm H. LIVINGSTON & CO./CAYUDUTTA WORKS. ★★

CAYUGA, N.Y.

This stamp has been reported on various bench planes. Kenneth and Jane Roberts in *Planemakers of New York State* have postulated that this may be an imprint of the Auburn Tool Co. (w.s.), which was located in Cayuga County, NY. Confirming this a bench plane imprinted New York Tool Co., a brand name of Auburn Tool Co., also carries a CAYUGA N.Y. (A) imprint. "Cayuga" was also used as a brand name on first-line axes sold by Treman & Bros. (w.s.), a large hardware firm in Ithaca, NY. ★★★ *(see next page)*

 A

 B

R. CHAFFIN

Several coopers' planes, including a howel, croze, and topping plane, have been reported. Appearance is ca.1800. There are several Actons: in Massachusetts, Vermont, and Maine. Maine seems the most likely choice, since most examples have been reported from that state.

W.B. CHAMBERLIN

This imprint appears on an H.CHAPIN/UNION FACTORY dado plane (#38), with the additional location imprint WESTFIELD N.J. Probably a hardware dealer.

CHAPIN   see P. Chapin

H. CHAPIN

Hermon Chapin (1799-1866) apprenticed in 1822 with D. & M. Copeland (w.s.) and in 1826 became a partner with Daniel Copeland in the planemaking firm of Copeland & Chapin at Pine Meadow near New Haven, CT. In 1828 he purchased Copeland's interest and became the sole owner of the business, now called UNION FACTORY. No examples of a "Copeland & Chapin" imprint has been reported, and it is supposed that the D. Copeland (w.s.) imprint was used.

The Union Factory was one of the major manufacturers of planes in New England. The company employed 40 shop hands and produced $30,000 worth of product, according to the 1850 census. The 1860 census showed 36 employees and production worth $33,000. The firm was succeeded by H. Chapin & Sons (w.s.) in 1860. (see *Wooden Planes in 19c America*, Vol.II, in the Bibliography. This book contains an extensive history of the Chapin planemaking enterprises, as well as describing the large number of plane types produced, including the Rust-Chapin adjustable patent plow plane.)   A & B: FF

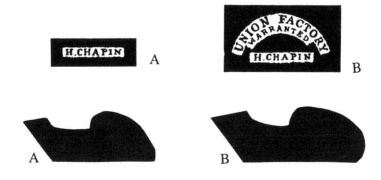

89

H. CHAPIN & SONS

Successor to H. Chapin/Union Factory. Formed in 1860 in New Hartford, CT, by Hermon Chapin and his sons, Edward M., George W. and Philip E. Chapin. No planes are known with this imprint. Edward and George assumed ownership under the name of H. Chapin's Sons in 1865 (w.s.; also see H. Chapin).

H. CHAPIN'S SON

Successor to H. Chapin's Sons (w.s.) upon the purchase in 1868 by Edward M. Chapin of his brother George's interest. Edward continued the firm until his death in 1897, when it was succeeded by H. Chapin's Son & Co. The 1870 census showed 28 employees producing 40,000 planes which sold for $45,000. Two water wheels produced 50 hp which ran three saws and other machinery. No planes are known with this imprint. (also see H. Chapin)

H. CHAPIN'S SON & CO.

Formed in 1897 upon the death of Edward M. Chapin by two of his sons, Hermon M. and Frank Chapin, and Rufus E. Holmes, as successor to H. Chapin's Son. No planes are known with this imprint. In 1901 it was merged into the Chapin-Stephens Co. (w.s.; also see H. Chapin)

H. CHAPIN'S SONS

Successor to H. Chapin & Sons in 1865. The firm continued in New Hartford, CT, until 1868 when George W. Chapin sold his interest to Edward M. Chapin, who continued the firm as H. Chapin's Son (w.s.). No planes are known with this imprint. (see also H. Chapin and H. Chapin & Sons)

N. CHAPIN & CO.

Nathaniel Chapin (d.1876) was an older brother of Hermon Chapin. In 1835 he was employed by H. Chapin (w.s.) as a supervisor under a five-year contract that paid him $450 the first year and $500 per year thereafter. Some time after 1838 he organized and made planes under the Eagle Factory name in New Hartford, CT. He moved his factory to Westfield, MA, in 1847 and was listed in the 1850 industrial census as a planemaker in Westfield, age 59, born in Massachusetts and owning real estate worth $3000. He employed six hands, used water power and produced 8000 bench and molding planes worth $7000. A plane has been reported with the Eagle Factory imprint only, omitting N. Chapin & Co.   A, B, & C: FF

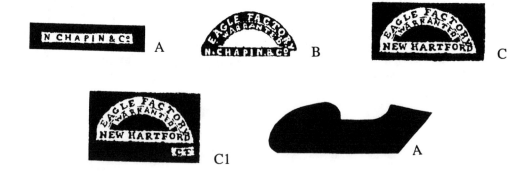

CHAPIN-STEPHENS

A merger in 1901 of H. Chapin's Son & Co. (w.s.) and L.C. Stephens & Co. at Pine Meadow, CT. The firm dissolved in 1929. Stanley acquired the line of rules but discontinued the line of wooden planes. (see H. Chapin)
FF   (see next page)

P. CHAPIN

Philip Chapin was among the most prolific of the Baltimore, MD, planemakers. He was a brother of Hermon Chapin (see H. Chapin) for whom he worked prior to 1830. He began planemaking in Baltimore around 1831, as Ward & Chapin, and made under his own imprint —1835-36 and —1842-55—. His advertisement in the 1853-54 city directory stated he operated a plane manufactory and tool store carrying "carpenters', carvers', cabinet, coach and pattern makers tools of American and English manufacture." He returned North around 1860 to Pine Meadow, CT, and apparently retired. Over his years in Baltimore he bought a large quantity of planes from H. Chapin. Whether these were sold under the H. Chapin/Union Factory imprint or were made to Philip Chapin's specifications for his imprint, we do not know. (see Chapin & Kendall, Atkinson & Chapin, Wm. C. Ross, E.L. Matthews, and A.B. Seidenstricker & Co.)   A: ★★   B: FF   B1: ★★   C: ★★

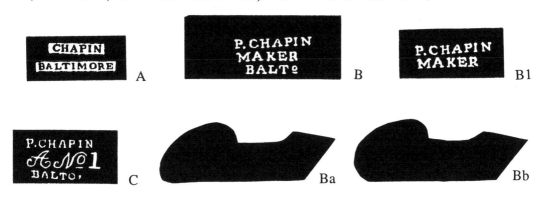

CHAPIN & KENDALL

A partnership of Philip Chapin and Thomas Kendall, that made planes in Baltimore, MD, —1833—. (see P. Chapin and also Kendall)   ★★

I. CHAPMAN

This name appears on a beech jointer also imprinted WILLISTON VT. (which is just east of Burlington). Isaac Chapman was listed as a carpenter, age 36, born in New Hampshire and living in Williston in the 1850 census.

J. CHAPPELL

James Chappell was listed in the 1839 Pittsburgh, PA, directory (and in no other) as a planemaker. Earlier he was a partner with A. Bright. (see A. Bright & J. Chappell)   A & B: ★★★★

 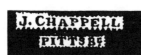 

A   B

C. CHASE

Several planes have been found in the Portland, ME, area, including a 9¹³⁄₁₆" molder and a 9¾" quarter round, both with wide rounded chamfers, and a double handled 14½" match plane with metal skate and runner.

G. CHASE

George Chase was a joiner and ship's carpenter —1841-46— in Portland, ME, who also, apparently, made planes. The imprint has appeared on a 13⅜" sash plane with two irons, an ovolo and a rabbet, all made of beech. (see G. Chase & Co.)

G. CHASE & CO.

This name has been reported on a 9¹³⁄₁₆" long beech rabbet and a 9⁷⁄₁₆" round. (see G. Chase)

J. CHASE

James Chase (1737-1812) of Gilmanton (later Gilford), NH, a joiner and cabinetmaker who made and sold planes along with other woodworking tools. Two examples have been reported, one a 9¾" complex molder with a Sleeper-type wedge. Both are made of beech.

S. CHASE

Several examples have been reported with the Sleeper-type wedge: a 9⅞" beech round, a 9⅞" beech tongue plane, and a yankee plow.

CHASE BROTHERS

This imprint has been reported on a slide-arm plow with thumbscrews and the additional location mark HAVERHILL.

CHASE, SARGENT & SHATTUCK

Horace B. Shattuck, Frederick W. Sargent, and John K. Chase traded as Chase, Sargent & Shattuck —1866-79, hardware dealer in Lowell, MA.

CE. CHELOR

Cesar Chelor is one of the most famous names in early New England planemaking. He was a black slave owned, perhaps as early as 1736, by Francis Nicholson (w.s.) who is the earliest documented American planemaker. Cesar Chelor quite possibly made many of the planes bearing the Francis Nicholson imprint. Chelor was admitted as a member to the Congregational Church in Wrentham Center in 1741 and probably was at least 21 years old at that time. In his will, recorded in 1753, Nicholson freed Chelor, giving him his bedstead, bed and bedding, a variety of tools, ten acres of land and grazing and timber rights. Chelor married Juda Russell in 1758, raised a family, and died intestate at Wrentham in 1784. His estate inventory was valued at 77 pounds 2 shillings, including sundry tools and old lumber. Jethro Jones (see I. Jones), another black planemaker, may have have had some association with Chelor during Jones's stay in Wrentham ca.1764-65.

The Chelor imprint has two major variations. The (A) imprint consists of three separate die stamps, one for each line. The LIVING IN is often omitted due to lack of room on the toe of the plane (imprint B). The (C) imprint is very rare; only four examples have been reported.   A, A1, & A2: ★★   B: ★★★★★

(continued on next page)

 A

 A1

 B

A2

Aa   Ab

B

E.V.A. CHICHESTER
Listed as a planemaker in Norwalk, CT. —1856-65. No example of this imprint has been reported.

GEORGE CHICK
Planes reported with this imprint also have a location stamp PORTLAND, and, in one example, BATH, MAINE. Examples are made of rosewood, ebony, or lignum and are ship builder types. Appearance is ca.1850.
★★★

J.E. CHILD
A Providence, RI, planemaker, —1850-75, who also supplied plane bodies to, and did contract work for, the Greenfield Tool Co. He was listed in the 1850 census as a planemaker, age 22, born in Rhode Island, living in his father's house along with Isaac Battey (see I.S. Battey), also a planemaker, who was married to Child's sister. (see J. Edwin Child)   A: ★   B: ★★

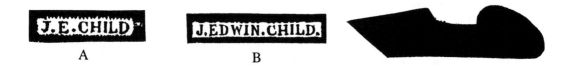

A   B

J. EDWIN CHILD   see J.E. Child

CHILD, FARR & CO.
Alonzo Child and Asa Farr ran a hardware business in St. Louis, MO, 1847-51, which was succeeded by Child, Pratt & Co. (w.s.).   ★

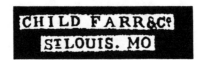

CHILD, PRATT & CO.

St. Louis, MO, successor to Child, Farr & Co. (w.s.) in 1852 that continued in the hardware business until 1859, when it was succeeded by Child, Pratt & Fox (w.s.).   ★

CHILD, PRATT & FOX

Successor to Child, Pratt & Co. (w.s.), St. Louis, MO, hardware dealers, in 1860 continuing to 1863 when it was succeeded by Pratt & Fox (w.s.). No example of this imprint has been reported.

CHIPAWAY

Trademark of the E.C. Simmons Hardware Co. of St. Louis, MO, and used on their second quality planes. The mark was applied to the side of the plane.

A. CHURCH

The imprint A. CHURCH/GRANBY appears on a 28" long jointer. Alonzo Church worked for Kennedy & Co. (w.s.) as a planemaker in 1837. He appears in Truman Nutting's journal (see T. Nutting) in 1842 and 1843 for plane transactions.

HORACE CHURCH

An Amherst, MA, planemaker who worked —1833—. He was listed as a joiner in the 1850 census, age 46, and born in Massachusetts. No example of his imprint has been reported.

J. CHURCH

Believed to be Jonathan Church, who appeared in the 1810-50 censuses as living in Granby, CT. In the 1850 census he was shown as a farmer, age 67, born in Connecticut, owning real estate valued at $4000. Several examples have been reported, including two $9\frac{1}{2}$" birch molders and a $9\frac{1}{2}$" beech sash plane with $\frac{3}{16}$" flat chamfers. Appearance is early 1800s.

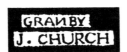

W.H.H. CLAFLIN

William H.H. Claflin (1815-1895) was listed as a carpenter in Northfield, VT, 1872-80. Most of the planes reported came from one lot, possibly a part of Claflin's own tool kit since none had any owner's marks on them. Two other planes in the group, one by M. Read and the other by A. Fish (both w.s.), have the "B" imprint. All the planes have a professional appearance.   *(see next page)*

A

B

C

A

J. CLAP
Several examples bearing this imprint have been reported. Two are made of birch, one has a relieved wedge. Appearance is late 18c or very early 19c.

U. CLAP
Several planes have been reported, a beech jack, a birch fore plane, a smoother, a plow, and a 9¾" hollow. All appear ca.1800. Possibly Uriah Clap (1769-1852), who was a cabinetmaker in Gardner, MA, —1817-1838—.

A   B

D. CLARK
Several planes have been reported, 9½" to 9⅝" long, beech, appearance early 19c.

DAVID CLARK
An 18c planemaker in Cumberland, RI, which is adjacent to Wrentham, MA, the home of Francis Nicholson, John Nicholson, and Cesar Chelor (all w.s.). Clark later changed his location imprint to IN CUMBERLAND when the Wrentham town lines were changed.   ★★★★★

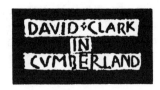

E. CLARK/HARTFORD

Probably Ebenezer Clark (1765-1801), who advertised in the Connecticut *Courant* (Hartford, CT) of February 2, 1796 "made, making, and will shortly be ready for market an (sic) universal assortment of joiners tools made in the neatest manner from English Patterns." Ebenezer Clark appeared in the 1790 and 1800 censuses for Hartford. The imprint and wedge outline shown came from a ½" beech round, 9⅜" long, with ¼" flat chamfers that was found with a group of Kennedy (w.s.) planes. The wedge bears a striking resemblance to early Leonard Kennedy examples. Leonard Kennedy was a listed creditor in Clark's petition to be declared insolvent in 1798. Clark's main vocation seems to have been as a builder, often on speculation, his business conducted both in New York City and Hartford.

E. CLARK/MIDDLEBORO

An 18c planemaker in Middleboro, MA, but as yet unidentified. Clark's planes bearing the "A" imprint are similar in appearance to those of H. Wetherel (w.s.) who made planes in nearby Norton before 1790, and to those of Levi Tinkham (w.s.). They also have the fluting characteristics of the mid-period Joseph Fuller (w.s.). Some of his plane irons bear the imprint N. BENNETT, having been made by Nebediah Bennett, a local blacksmith. The planes bearing the "B" imprint have a later appearance and may have been made by a next-generation E. Clark. The imprint is the same as "A" but without "Middleboro", and the wedge finial is rounded. Length is 9½", the wood beech, and the chamfers rounded. A: ★★★ B: ★★★★

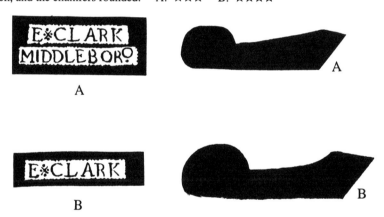

A

B

E. CLARK/MILWAUKEE

Edwin Clark, a Milwaukee, WI, planemaker who appeared in city directories in the late 1840s and 1850s variously as a planemaker, tool maker and plane manufacturer. (see E. & H. Clark) ★★

E. & H. CLARK

Edwin and Henry Clark, listed as toolmakers and planemakers in the 1854-55 Milwaukee, WI, city directory. (see E. Clark)

H. CLARK

This imprint has been reported on a large hollow that carries a W. Butcher iron. A Henry Clark was listed as a planemaker and joiner in the 1847-54 Milwaukee city directories, and Henry Clark was listed as a partner with Edwin Clark in E. & H. CLARK (w.s.) in the 1854-55 Milwaukee city directory. Utica may represent an earlier location for him.

H.H. CLARK

Henry H. Clark of Mercer, PA, appeared in the 1850 census, age 39, occupation wood turner.

I. CLARK

A number of examples have been reported, all beech with rounded chamfers. Appearance is early 19c.

JOSEPH CLARK

Three planes have been reported. All are rounds, 10" long, and made of birch. They look very early.

T. CLARK

Thomas Clark was a Pittsburgh, PA, planemaker who worked as a journeyman for Swetman & Hughes (w.s.), and in 1826 was listed a planemaker, Swetman & Hughes no longer being listed. His shop was located on the same block as that of William Evans (see W. Evans). His last listing was in the 1847 directory. Clark is believed to be the Thomas Clark, "an apprentice boy about twenty years of age" that Leonard Kennedy (w.s.) advertised for in the Hartford, CT, papers (Jan. 24, 1818), as having run away. Clark's last name was spelled with and without an "E" at the end.   ★★   *(see next page)*

CLARK & WISWALL

A New Haven, CT, planemaker —1856—. No example of this imprint has been reported.

D. CLAY

This imprint appears on a handled 14⅝" long birch hollow, 2" wide, with ⅜" wide flat chamfers. As for the location, there were Greenfields throughout New England, from Maine to Connecticut.

CLEAN CUT

Dunham, Carrigan & Hayden of San Francisco, CA, offered a line of wooden planes under this brand name in their 1914 catalog.

E. CLIFFORD

Ebenezer Clifford (1746-1821) of Kensington and Exeter, NH, a prominent joiner, cabinetmaker, master builder, architect and Justice of the Peace. Jeremiah Fellows, a Kensington blacksmith, clockmaker, and tavernkeeper noted in his day book the sale of quantities of plane irons and plow plane skates to Clifford during the period 1772-94. Clifford in turn made cases for some of Fellows' clocks. ★★★

H. CLOCK

Over a dozen planes bearing this imprint were found in a group. All appeared professionally made, 10" long, beech, with ¼" flat chamfers. Included were some complex molders with spring marks. None bore any owner's names. Probably Henry Klock, who was born in 1749 in the Mohawk Valley, NY, and died in Herkimer, NY, in 1810. He owned two farms and directed the building of the Octagonal Church in Little Falls, NY.

N.H. CLOSSON

A Middletown, CT, planemaker, —1849-58—. No example of the imprint has been reported.

J.L. CLUFF
A fruitwood block plane with this imprint was found in the Skowhegan, ME, area. A 22" razeed ship fore plane has also been reported.

J. COATES
James Coates, Washington, PA, (b. 1817) who was listed in the 1850 census as a planemaker age 33 and born in Pennsylvania. An 1855 map of Washington County shows his "Plane Factory" on Wheeling St., Washington. Some of his planes carry imprinted dates. The earliest among those reported is 1846. He owned the plane factory until 1859 and appeared in the 1880 census as a carpenter.   A: ★★★   B: ★★★★   C: ★★★★

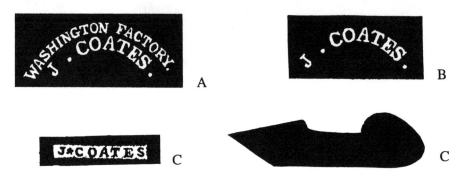

B. CODDINGTON
Benjamin Coddington (b.1814 in Ohio) was a Lafayette, IN, planemaker who appeared in the city directories from 1858 to 1886. He was listed in the 1850 census as having a plane "manufactory" producing 300 "plains."
★★★

COLLINS/HARTFORD
An imprint used by Robert J. Collins, Jr. (see R.J. Collins) as a planemaker in Hartford, CT, —1806-07—. (see Kennedy)   ★★★

COLLINS/RAVENNA

Fitch K. Collins and probably Robert Collins III, sons of R.J. Collins (w.s.), who together with their father made planes in Utica, NY (see Collins/Utica) —1831-34— and then moved to Ravenna, OH, where they were listed in the 1840 and 1850 federal censuses. A broadside catalog sheet dated July 5, 1838, lists a full range of joiner's planes "Manufactured and sold wholesale and retail by F.K. Collins" at Ravenna. Fitch K. Collins was born in New York state ca.1809 and Robert Collins III in Connecticut in 1807.   A: ★★   B: ★★★

 A    B

COLLINS/UTICA

An imprint used by Robert J. Collins, Jr. (see R.J. Collins) and his sons Fitch K. Collins and Robert Collins III —1831-34—. (also see Collins/Hartford and Collins/Ravenna)   ★★

COLLINS & ROBBINS

A planemaking partnership that probably comprised Enos Robbins (see E. Robbins) and Robert J. Collins, Jr. (see R.J. Collins) that operated in Utica, NY, —1829-30—.   ★★

DAVID COLLINS

An advertisement appeared in the April 12, 1809, *Connecticut Courant* (Hartford, CT) stating "David Collins has on hand a good assortment of Moulding tools, bench planes & etc.. . . .where he continues to manufacture all kinds of joiner tools."

R.J. COLLINS

Robert Johnson Collins, Jr., an important planemaker, father of several planemaking sons, and an associate of the Kennedys. Collins was born ca.1780 and married Leonard Kennedy's (w.s.) younger sister Eunice in 1802. He may very well have learned planemaking from Kennedy with whom he began a partnership in 1803 "to carry on the house carpenter and joiners business and manufacture joiners' tools." Imprints used were Kennedy & Collins and K & C (both w.s.). The partnership continued until around 1805, after which Collins apparently made planes under his own name (see Collins/Hartford). Sometime between 1807 and 1809 Collins moved to New York State. Between 1828-29 he worked at Leonard Kennedy Jr.'s (w.s.) factory in Utica, and ca.1830 probably was in a partnership Collins & Robbins (w.s.). Between —1831-34— he made planes under the imprint Collins/Utica (w.s.) and in 1834 was noted as an agent for Kennedy.

Sometime during this period and probably before moving on to Ohio, he also produced planes in Rochester. Collins died in Ravenna, OH, Nov. 1835, age 55. It is unlikely because of the short time period and the scarcity of the imprints that there was much planemaking during his Ohio residency. (see also Collins/Ravenna)

A: ★★★   B: ★★★★   *(see next page)*

101

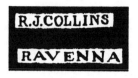

A

B

A.J. COLTON

Alfred J. Colton (b. ca.1839) was a Philadelphia, PA, dealer and planemaker, 1861-90, and the son of D. Colton (w.s.), with whom he worked 1861-80. He exhibited stair handrail planes, double routers and carpenters' molding planes (for which he received an award) in the 1876 Centennial Exposition. No planes with his imprint have been reported and it is believed that he used his father's stamps both during his father's lifetime and until he ceased planemaking ca.1890.

D. COLTON

David Colton (1815-1880), born in Massachusetts, father of A.J. Colton and brother of John Colton (both w.s.), was a prolific Philadelphia, PA, planemaker—1837-80. He worked with his brother intermittently during the early years and then with his son. The Colton plane imprints, which consist of several separate dies provide the collector with a number of varieties, many of which have their origin in the Israel White stamps (w.s.). The H imprint sugggests that the Coltons took over some of Henry G. White's (w.s.) stock in 1858. (see also D. Colton & J. Colton, D. Colton & B. Sheneman, and J. Colton)   A — E: ★   F: FF   G: ★

(continued on next page)

102

F

G

H

D. COLTON & J. COLTON

D. Colton and J. Colton imprints have appeared on the same plane. David and John Colton, who were brothers, worked together at "379 Market St., Phila" ca.1837-41, and at the "Corner of Callowhill and Fourth St. Phila" ca.1858-60. They took over Henry G. White's (w.s.) shop and used parts of the old Israel White (w.s.) stamps. Since the imprint consisted of several separate die stamps, there are variations in the position of the elements. (see D. Colton and also J. Colton)   A — C: ★★

A

C

B

103

D. COLTON & B. SHENEMAN

David Colton and Benjamin Sheneman, who were Philadelphia, PA, makers and dealers, 1846-52. (see D. Colton and also B. Sheneman)   A & B: ★★

A

B

J. COLTON

John Colton, a Philadelphia, PA, planemaker, brother of David Colton, with whom he sometimes worked in the early years. Between —1842-57 and 1861-89, he probably worked under his own name. He was born in Massachusetts ca.1807 and died in 1890. He was listed as having realty worth $16,000 in the 1850 census. (see D. Colton and J. Colton)   A, B & B1: ★   C — F: ★★

A   B   B1

C   D

E   F

COLUMBIA TOOL CO.

Planes are made of "Russian white beech" and, in the case of the A imprint, are ink-imprinted on their sides. They were imported from Germany ca.1925, and were distributed by the United Hardware & Tool Corp. of New York City. The company's 1925 catalog, which has been reprinted by the Mid-West Tool Collectors Association, lists six pages of various plane styles, including horn smoothing planes, jacks, jointers, T-rabbets, weather-stripping and various molding planes. Planes carrying the "B" and "C" imprints appear to be American-made and of earlier origin.   A: ★★   B & C: ★★★

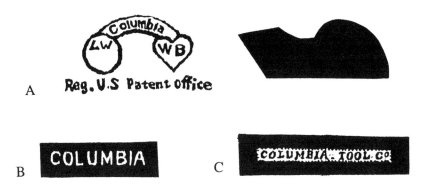

A

B

C

COLWELL & CO.

A wholesale and retail hardware dealer in Cleveland, OH, that operated under this name from 1860-68.

I. COMINS

Believed to be Issachar Comins, who was born in Charlton, MA, in 1782 and who died there in 1861. His estate included five molding planes and had a total value of $10,000. Early records list him as "a carpenter and finished workman" who had served earlier as an apprentice. He was the brother of Barnabas Comins (1771-1829) who was a woodworker and whose probate inventory included 12 planes. Comins' planes are made of birch. The molding planes have a relieved wedge. Appearance is ca.1800. ★★★

J. CONANT

Probably John Conant (b. ca.1773) who was trained as a carpenter and joiner and who came to Brandon VT in 1796, where he was also a builder. He was a partner in an ore furnace, produced the Conant Cook Stove and, with his sons, also had a store. Molding planes bearing this imprint range in length from $9\frac{5}{8}$" to $9\frac{7}{8}$", some of birch, others beech. An auger has been reported with the imprint "J. Conant c. steel."

L.G. CONKLIN

Luther G. Conklin, a St. Louis, MO, planemaker, —1840-54. He may have been the Luther G. Conklin who was listed as a planemaker in New York City in the 1831 American Advertising Directory. ★★★

JOHN CONOVER

Listed as a planemaker in the Cincinnati, OH, 1829 directory. He was believed to have moved to Louisville, KY, after 1831. No example of his imprint has been reported. (see T. Fugate and J. Conover)

CONWAY TOOL CO.

Founded by Alonzo Parker in 1850 at Conway, MA, and by 1851 employed 80 men. The factory was destroyed by fire July 1851. Parker and his associates reorganized, moved a few miles north to Greenfield, MA, and started the Greenfield Tool Co. (w.s.), one of the largest New England producers of planes during this period. A, B, C: ★★

A

C

B

J. P. COOK

John P. Cook, a Detroit, MI, planemaker, 1850-61. ★★

S. COOK

Solomon Cook (b. NY 1809), a rather peripatetic planemaker, who first worked in Cincinnati, OH. In 1829 he was reported boarding with John Conover (w.s.) and was probably a bench-hand for him. A plane has been reported with the imprint S. COOK & CO/NEW ALBANY, IND. A Solomon Cook appears in the 1830 federal census for Marion County, IN, and in the 1840 census for Clinton County, IN. During 1835 and 1836 advertisements in the Indianapolis *Journal* listed S. Cook as planemaker, sharing a shop with F.T. Luse, a cabinetmaker. He was listed as a planemaker in Clark County, IN, in the 1850 census. Examples exist with a location stamp JEFFERSONVILLE IA., which is next to New Albany and just across the river from Louisville. The Louisville City directory listed Solomon Cook as a planemaker at Wm. W. Richards (see W. Richards & Co.) in 1843-44, at Benchards in 1844-45, at Woodruff's (Alexander S, Woodruff, w.s.) in the 1845-46 directory, and at Woodruff & McBride in 1848 (w.s.). He was listed as a planemaker in Memphis, TN, 1859-60.
A:, B, C, & D: ★★★ *(continued next page)*

A

C

A

B

C

D

S. COOK & J. GILMER

This imprint, which suggests a partnership between Joseph Gilmer and Solomon Cook, incorporates the J. Gilmer/New Albany stamp that Gilmer used earlier when in business for himself in New Albany, Indiana. The firm probably operated for a short period in the 1850's. (see J. Gilmer)

S.C. COOK

Samuel C. Cook, a prolific New Brunswick, NJ, planemaker. Born ca.1800, he was listed as a manufacturer in the 1840 census. We believe he made planes —1825-45, and was probably succeeded by E. Danberry (w.s.). Imprint (A) is thought to be the earlier one and is very rare.   A: ★★★   B: ★

A

B

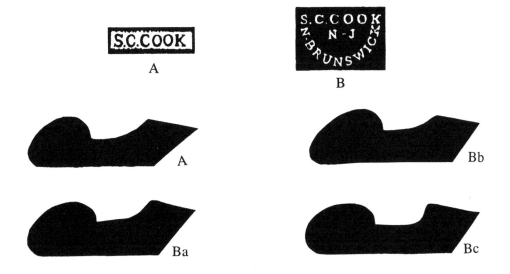

A

Bb

Ba

Bc

J. COOK & CO.
James Cook, who was born in 1798 in Morristown, NJ, moved to Terre Haute, IN, where he opened a hardware store in 1847. In 1858, his son, Louis M. Cook, became a partner and the name became J. COOK & SON, under which it continued until 1872. ★★★

S. COOK & CO. see S. Cook

W. COOLEY
William Cooley was a Boston, MA, planemaker who began as an edge tool maker in 1832 and produced planes under this imprint 1834-48, except for 1844 when the business was Cooley & Montgomery (w.s.). A, B, & C: ★

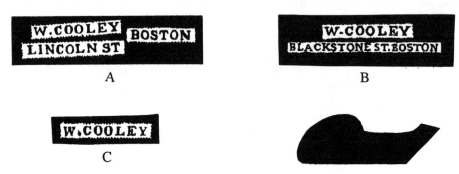

A   B

C

COOLEY & MONTGOMERY
A Boston, MA, planemaking partnership consisting of William Cooley and J.A. Montgomery. They operated in 1844 only. (see W. Cooley; also see Montgomery) ★★

COOPER
A number of planes have been reported. Molding planes are 9½" long, made of beech, and look ca.1830-40.

E.L. COOPER
Ebenezer L. Cooper was a New York City hardware merchant 1863-73, who also dealt in coopers' tools. No example has yet been reported.

G. COOPER

Also imprinted IN ROBSON. A group of five planes was found bearing this imprint; 9¼" long, with flat chamfers and oval wedge finials. Another plane, imprinted G. COOPER only, is 9⅜" long, beech, with ¼" flat chamfers.

A. COPELAND

A Columbus, OH, planemaker, whose working period is not known. However, if A. Copeland is Alfred Copeland, the dates would be sometime between the demise of M. & A. Copeland (w.s.) in 1831 and Alfred's death in 1858. Alfred Copeland's listing in the 1850 census was as a manufacturer in Chester, MA, age 48, and born in Connecticut. (see George Copeland)   ★★

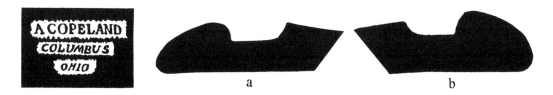

a   b

CHARLES COPELAND

Listed as a planemaker, age 33, born in Massachusetts, in the 1850 Amherst, MA, census. No example of his imprint has been reported.

D. COPELAND

Daniel Copeland (1794-1853) was born in Sturbridge, MA, the brother of Melvin & Alfred Copeland. He probably apprenticed with Leonard Kennedy Sr. and was a partner in D. & M. Copeland—1820-25 in Hartford, CT. In 1826 he joined Hermon Chapin in Copeland & Chapin, establishing what was to become the Union Factory. Chapin bought him out in 1828, after which Copeland made planes under this imprint. (see Kennedy, D. & M. Copeland, M. Copeland, and H. Chapin)   A & B: FF

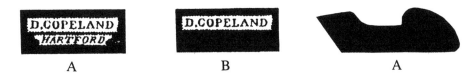

A   B   A

D. & M. COPELAND

A planemaking partnership in Hartford, CT, between brothers Daniel and Melvin Copeland, c1822-25. (also see D. Copeland and M. Copeland)   A & B: FF

A   B   A

GEORGE COPELAND

Listed in the 1850 census for Columbus, OH, occupation plane factory, age 55. Also listed was George Copeland Jr., age 27, same occupation. Both were listed as born in Vermont. No example of this imprint has been reported. (see A. Copeland)

M. COPELAND

Melvin Copeland (1797-1866) born in Sturbridge, MA, brother of Daniel and Alfred Copeland. He probably apprenticed with Leonard Kennedy Sr. in Hartford, CT, and then was a partner with his brother Daniel in D. & M. Copeland (w.s.) —1820-25. Between 1826-30 he made planes with his brother Alfred in Hartford (see M. & A. Copeland). He made planes under the M. COPELAND imprint in Hartford —1831-1842. In 1842 he moved his firm to Huntington, MA, where he was joined by brothers Daniel and Alfred. He was listed in the 1850 census as a manufacturer in Huntington, owning real estate worth $3000. In the 1850 industrial census he was reported employing 15 hands and producing planes worth $12,000. By about 1855 the firm was called Copeland & Co. (w.s.).   A, B, B1: ★★★   C, D, E: FF

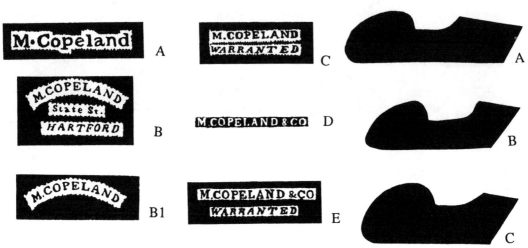

M. COPELAND & CO. see M. Copeland

M. & A. COPELAND

The brothers Melvin and Alfred Copeland, who made planes in Hartford, CT, under this imprint, 1826-30, after dissolving the D. & M. Copeland (w.s.) partnership in 1826. (see A. Copeland and M. Copeland. Also see H. Chapin for their relationship to the Union Factory).   A: FF   B: ★   B1: ★★★   C: ★★★

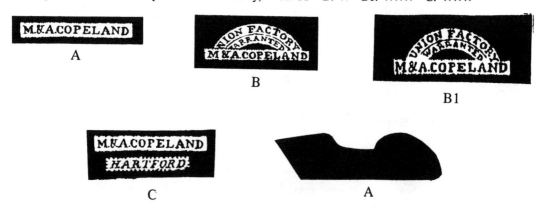

COPELAND & CO.

A Huntington, MA, planemaking firm, 1855-1866—, successor to M. Copeland (w.s.). The 1855 Massachusetts census indicated 15 hands producing $12,000 worth of product, and the 1860 census listed 16 hands who produced $22,000 in bench planes.   ★   *(see next page)*

COPELAND & CHAPIN
A partnership between Daniel Copeland and Hermon Chapin in Hartford (Pine Meadow), CT, 1826-28. No example of this imprint has been reported. (see D. Copeland and H. Chapin)

COREY, BROOKS & CO.
A Boston, MA, hardware dealer —1875—. ★★

S. COUDEN
Probably the S. Couden who worked for J. Burke and S. Sloop (both w.s.) and whose name appears alongside their respective imprints.

J. COUGHTRY
Joseph Coughtry (1824-97) made planes in New York City 1849-50, and then in Albany, NY.
A, A1, B: ★★★

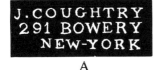

A   A1   B

D.O. CRANE
David Orville Crane (1804-1858) was a cousin of S.G. Crane (w.s.). He learned planemaking from Leonard Kennedy (see Kennedy) in Hartford, CT, and after his marriage in 1828 went to New Hartford, south of Utica, NY. He was recorded in the 1830 census as heading a household that included two other men between 20 and 30 years old. He next appeared in the 1850 census in nearby Seneca, having become a dentist. While Crane may have initially worked for Leonard Kennedy, Jr. in Utica, it is likely that he soon began operating independently. An advertisement by Rowe & Woodruff in the Utica *Intelligencer* of Jan.27, 1829, offered a "selected assortment of Bench Planes, also moulding tools of almost every description by L. Kennedy & Co. and D.O. Crane. Persons wishing to purchase can have the privilege of selecting from either of the above named manufacturer's make."   A: ★   B: ★★★

A   B   A

H. CRANE
Harvey Crane was listed in the 1840 census as living in East Hartford, CT, next door to Peter Brooks (see P. Brooks & Co.). By 1846 he was working in Springfield, MA, and was listed in the 1850 census as a planemaker, age 45, born in Connecticut. In 1860 he was listed as a mechanic in a railroad shop.   A: ★★   B: ★★★★

 A

 B

S.G. CRANE
Samuel Gustin Crane was born June 1809 in Connecticut and was a first cousin of D.O. Crane (w.s.). In 1849 he was working for D.R. Barton (w.s.). The Rochester, NY, city directories list him as a wood tool maker 1849-50, a cooper's tool maker 1851-52, a planemaker 1853-58, a mechanic in 1859, and a tool maker in 1861 at D.R. Barton. He was a partner with James Scott in Crane & Scott (w.s.), 1866-67, and in 1879 he was a foreman at D.R. Barton. It is not clear when he made planes under his own imprint, but judging by their scarcity, his output was limited.

STEPHEN H. CRANE
Appeared in the 1842-43 and the 1847-48 New York City directories as a planemaker, and in the 1850 census as a planemaker in Middletown, CT, age 40, born in Scotland and working for the Arrowmammett Works (w.s.). No example of his work has been reported.

CRANE & SCOTT
Samuel G. Crane and James Scott made planes in Rochester, NY, 1866-67. (see S.G. Crane)

CRANE & WAY
This name has been reported on a 22" beech jointer with a centered closed handle and the additional location imprint HARTFORD, presumably Connecticut where some of the Way family were hardware dealers (see William Way). Harvey Crane (see H. Crane) was a planemaker in East Hartford, CT, ca.1850. The jointer reported appears to have been made during that period.

M. CRANNELL
Matthew Crannell, Jr., (d. 1892) made planes under this imprint in Albany, NY, 1862-92. Earlier he was a partner in Bensen & Crannell (w.s.). From 1851 on, he operated a mechanics' tool store in addition to his planemaking business. He was listed in the 1850 census as an Albany planemaker, age 33, born in NY. J. Coughtry (w.s.) was probably at one time an employee. Both the A and B imprints are incuse.   A & B: FF

A

M. CRANNELL & CO
ALBANY

B

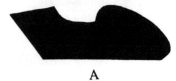

A

M. CRANNELL & CO. see M. Crannell

CREAGH See J. Creagh

J. CREAGH
John Creagh was an English-born Cincinnati, OH, planemaker, who made planes under his own imprint 1834-40 and also handled hardware 1839-40. He was succeeded by Lyon & McKinnell & Co. (w.s.) (Also see J. Creagh/J.W. Lyon, J. Creagh/E.F. Seybold, Creagh & Rickard, and Creagh & Williams)   A, B, C: ★★

A

B

C

C

J. CREAGH/J.W. LYON
Both marks have appeared on the same plane and probably represent left-over stock of J. Creagh purchased by J.W. Lyon (w.s.). Lyon, McKinnell (w.s.) listed itself as successor to J. Creagh in 1842. (see J. Creagh/E.F. Seybold)

J. CREAGH, J.W. LYON/McKINNEL
Probably J.W. Lyon & McKinnel using the old stock of J. Creagh. (see J. Creagh and Lyon, McKinnel & Co.)

J. CREAGH/E.F. SEYBOLD
Both these marks have been reported on the same plane (see E.F. Seybold D imprint). It is thought that Seybold may have purchased some of Creagh's "selling out" stock between 1840-42. (see J. Creagh)

CREAGH & RICKARD
John Creagh and Thomas J. Rickard were plane and brush makers in Cincinnati, OH, —1829—, who also sold edge tools made by others. (see J. Creagh and T.J. Rickard)   A & B: ★★

 A

 B

113

CREAGH & WILLIAMS

John Creagh and David W. Williams were hardware dealers in Cincinnati, OH, in 1831. (see J. Creagh)
A & B: ★★

 A

 B

J. CREAGH/W. WINTKLE

Still one more of the J. CREAGH combinations, this time with W. Wintkle of whom we know nothing.

B. CREHORE

This mark has been reported on a 10" birch ogee. A Benjamin Crehore (1765-1832) had a cabinet shop in Milton, MA, in 1791. By 1797 he was a pianoforte maker, the first in America. (see J. Crehore)

J. CREHORE

A Boston, MA, housewright whose name has appeared on several planes of 18c appearance. (see B. Crehore)

W. CRESY

This name has been reported on two sash planes (9¼" and 10") and on a round and molding plane, both 9¼". All are made of beech. Appearance is ca.1800. A 9¾" beech round of very early appearance has been reported imprinted W. CRESSY.

H.H. CRIE & CO.

A hardware dealer established in 1860 in Rockland, ME, by H.H. Crie and R. Anson Crie. Their last appearance in the business directories was in 1914. Their imprint H.H. CRIE & CO. has been reported stamped on the edge and side of a croze made by D.B. Titus (w.s.).

WM. CROOK & SON

A Baltimore hardware dealer 1874-94.

 A

 B

CROOK HARDWARE CO.   see Wm. Crook & Son

CROSS BROS/WARRANTED

This mark has been reported on a plow plane and a filletster. Appearance is mid-19c.

A

B

CRUM & SCHULTZ

This name has been reported on a plane with the additional location imprint WINCHESTER, VA. A John F. Crum, age 22, was listed as a merchant in the 1850 census for Winchester, VA.

W. CUDDY

William Cuddy made planes in New York City 1841-54. He also had a tool store 1850-54.   ★★

S. CULVER

A Samuel Culver was listed in the 1830 census of Barnard, VT. This imprint appears on a 9$\frac{1}{16}$" long beech groove plane.

A. CUMINGS

Allen Cumings was a Boston, MA, planemaker, appearing in the city directories in 1844-46 and 1848-54—. He lived in East Boston during the 1840's but moved to nearby Chelsea ca.1850. Note that the name also appeared in directories as CUMMINGS. He was listed in the 1850 census as a planemaker, age 38, born in NY. His next door neighbor was George A. Benton. The Greenfield Tool Co. (w.s.) ledger of 1854 showed the purchase of jointer, fore, and jack plane stocks from A. Cummings, Boston. (see G.A. Benton; also see Read & Cumings). Since Allen Cumings came from NY state, the imprints C, D and D1 probably represent his earlier work. Examples reported include a complete set of bench planes.   A, A1, B: ★   C, D, D1: ★★★★

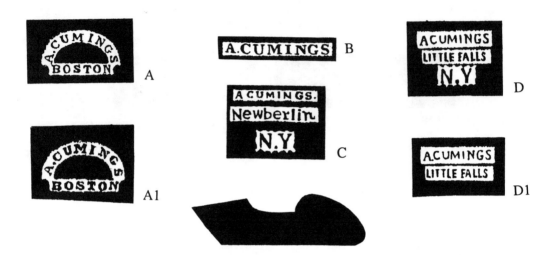

S. CUMINGS

Samuel R. Cumings was a planemaker in Providence, RI, —1828- 38. A 14⅞" open tote skewed rabbet has been reported with an ATTLEBORO location stamp. Whether there was a relationship between Samuel R. Cumings and Samuel R. Cummings (see S. & R. Cummings) is not known. (also see Cumings & Gale)
A: ★   B: ★★★★

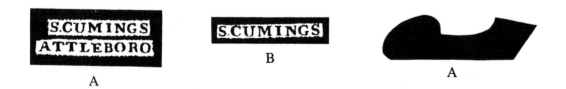

CUMINGS & GALE

Samuel R Cumings and Jonas R. Gale, a Providence, RI, planemaking partnership —1830-33. In 1833 Cumings sold his half interest to Gale. (see S. Cumings and also J.R. Gale)   ★★

JOHN CUMMINGS

The Art and Mystery of Tennessee Furniture by D.C. Williams and N. Harsh quotes an 1832 advertisement in the *Religious and Literary Intelligencer* placed by cabinetmaker John Cummings of Maryville (Blount County,

TN) in which he advertised his services as a cabinetmaker and wagonmaker and said he would make coffins as well as bench and moulding planes.

S. & R. CUMMINGS

Listed in the 1872 Business Directory under "Planes," located a few doors from P.A. Gladwin (w.s.). The 1864 directory listed Samuel R. Cummings, a carpenter in nearby Chelsea.

CUNNINGHAM & CO.

A Cincinnati, OH, planemaker, 1854—. No example of this imprint has been reported.

F. CURTIS

Frederick Curtis made planes in Boston, MA, ca.1820.   A & B: ★

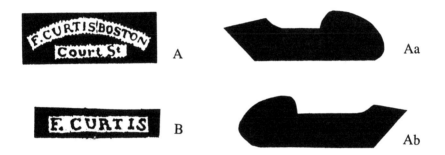

N. CURTIS

Nathaniel Curtis was a planemaker in Boston, MA, 1816-22.   A & B: ★★

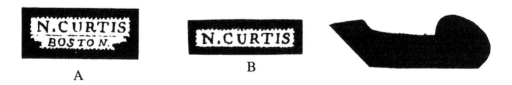

CUTLER & CO.

This name has been reported on a wedge-arm plow plane of mid-19c appearance, with the additional location imprint CLEVELAND OHIO.

DAGGETT & WALKER

This imprint appears on a 9⅜" long #11 round.

F. DALLICKER

This imprint was probably used by both Frederic Dallicker Sr. (b.1779-d.ca.1860) and his son Frederic Dallicker Jr. (b.1799-d.ca.1870), of Douglas, Montgomery County, PA, who made planes —1810-1860-. The wedge shapes and chamfer styles vary, reflecting the long period over which the planes were produced.   ★

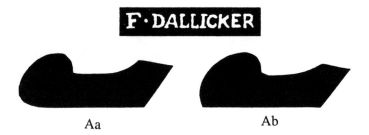

Aa   Ab

IOHN DALMAN

Examples reported range from 9½" to 9⅝" long. Appearance is ca.1830. Location may be central New York state. The wedge is similar to that of the Oothoudts (w.s.).

E. DANBERRY

Ellsworth Danberry (b.1818), a New Brunswick, NJ, planemaker who was probably associated at one time with S.C. Cook and succeeded him, substituting his name for Cook's on Cook's imprint, the location stamp being a separate die. (see S.C. Cook). A plane has been reported with its S.C. COOK mark overprinted by the E. DANBERRY name. Danberry was listed in the 1850 census as a planemaker. By 1855 he was listed as an express agent.   ★★   *(see next page)*

118

J.B. DANNER
Listed as a planemaker in the 1854 and 1859 Milwaukee, WI, city directories.

DANT & RYAN
This imprint appears on a 9½" hollow with the additional location imprint ALTON, ILL.

G. DARLING & CO.
Probably Gilbert Darling, a hardware dealer who was succeeded by his son, Charles H. Darling in 1877, who traded as C. Darling & Co.

M. DAUB
Reports have included several 9" long molding planes, a crown molder, and a panel raiser. An M. Daub appears in the 1850 census for the village of Bethel, Lebanon Twp., PA, as Martin Daub, age 50, a carpenter, born in PA.

H. DAVIDSON
The imprint has been reported on Sandusky and Ohio Tool Co. planes. Probably a hardware dealer.

J.T. & R.G. DAVIDSON
A McLean, NY, planemaking partnership, thought to be Robert G. Davidson (1827-1917), who was listed as a foundryman in the 1850 census, and perhaps a brother (John C. Davidson was his father's name).   ★★★

119

MOSES H. DAVIS

A New York City planemaker 1842-44. No example of his imprint has been reported. (see Davis & King)

Wm. B. DAVIS

A number of examples have been reported. Appearance is ca.1850. ★★★

DAVIS & KING

Possibly a partnership between Moses H. Davis and Josiah King (both w.s.) in New York City. Dates are not known but are probably before 1850. ★★

DAVIS, LAMB & CO.

A hardware dealer in Petersburg, VA. Appearance is ca.1850. ★★

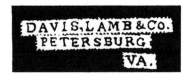

DAVIS & LESTER

Probably Wm. S. Davis (b.ca.1816) and John H. Lester (b.ca.1826), who were listed as planemakers in the Southampton, MA, 1850 census. In 1853 John Lester was producing small bench planes as a piece worker for the Greenfield Tool Co.; in 1860 he was listed as a planemaker in Chelsea, MA. A William S. Davis worked for H. Chapin (w.s.) as a journeyman planemaker 1837-40. ★★

I. DAY

At first believed to be John Day, apprenticed to Phillipson in London, 1756, and so recorded in W.L. Goodman's *British Planemakers,* 2nd ed. It was noted, however, that the five sightings reported were all in the United States and that two of the planes reported (a jack and a jointer), were made of birch and were therefore probably American in origin. Subsequently several planes were discovered double-stamped W. Raymond/I. Day. Only one would probably have been the maker, in this case W. Raymond (w.s.) and the other a merchant.

The search for a merchant named I. Day revealed only one, James Day of Gloucester, MA, who was in business before 1762 and died June 14, 1805 "between 73 and 80 years of age." The I. Day stamp appears also on a typical English keyed plow of the 1770-1780 period.

The marks below show the large W. Raymond stamp (the earlier imprint) used with the large I. Day stamp and the smaller W. Raymond stamp (the later imprint) used with the smaller I. Day stamp. The I. Day mark also appears alone. Data observed indicates an earlier starting date of ca.1785 for the large Day stamp and a starting date of ca.1795 for the smaller mark.   A, A1, B, B1: ★★★★

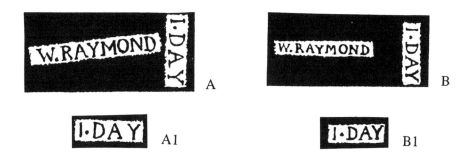

B. DEAN

Probably Benaiah Dean, born 1754 in the Taunton, MA, area. He served in the Revolutionary War and was noted as a joiner in Raynham, MA, in 1778 and in 1787. In 1804, 1810, and 1814 he was listed as a carpenter in Raynham and was referred to as a noted house builder. He died in Taunton ca.1831. His early wedge, A1, (unrelieved) usually appears on molding planes 9⅞" long with flat chamfers. His later wedge, A2, is relieved and appears on molding planes of 9¾" length with rounded chamfers and fluting.   ★★★

C.P. DEAN

Two planes with this imprint were found in a lot containing a number of Wm. Woodward planes in Taunton, MA. Planes are of beech. (see B.Dean and Wm. Woodward)

S. DEAN

A number of planes have been reported, in at least two cases with the additional imprint DEDHAM, (presumably Dedham, MA, home of I. Pike and S. Doggett). The appearance of the planes vary from 18c (imprints A & B) to early 19c (imprint C), suggesting perhaps two generations or two separate makers. A Samuel Dean (1700-75) was a joiner and lived in Dedham, MA, between 1737 and 1747. Before and after that he lived in Norton, MA. A lineal descendant, Samuel H. Dean (1767-1825) lived in South Dedham. His estate included a modest number of carpenter's tools.   A: ★★★★   B: ★★★   *(see next page)*

 A  B  C  A

WARREN DEARBORN

A cabinetmaker in Sandwich, NH, (1802-1863) whose working years were 1828-62 and who also made planes and other woodworking tools. (see Dearborn & Skinner)

DEARBORN & SKINNER

A partnership of Warren Dearborn (w.s.) and Elijah Skinner (1786-1871), which, from 1828 to 1831, did cabinetmaking and made planes in Sandwich, NH. No examples have been reported.

M. DEETER   see Deter

L. DeFOREST

Linson DeForest (b.1822 in CT) made planes in Birmingham (Derby), CT, —1850-1857, and in New York City 1857-58. The 1850 census listed him in Birmingham, age 28, employing six men and producing 8000 planes selling for $6000. The 1860 census showed him as a planemaker in Derby, CT.   A: ★   B: FF

 A  B  B

L. & C.H. DeFOREST

A Birmingham (Derby), CT, planemaking firm consisting of Linson DeForest (see L. DeForest) and Charles H. DeForest that operated ca.1860. Charles H. DeForest appeared in the 1860 census as a planemaker, born in CT and 38 years of age, the same age and birth location as Linson, possibly making them twins. The firm's 1860 price list offered what must be the most extravagant plow plane ever commercially proposed: "No. 494, handled ivory plow plane with solid gold nuts and washers, 22 carats fine, golden tips on arms and golden mounted, $1000." No example has been reported.

SIMEON DeFOREST

A planemaker in Birmingham (Derby), CT, 1849-56—. No example has been reported.

H.V. DEMING

H.V. Deming (1831-1903) had a varied career. He was at various times engaged in the lumber business, operated a woolen mill in Ontario, Canada, and worked for the customers' service at Windsor port, next to Detroit. To date there is no written evidence of planemaking, though perhaps he had some such dealings along with the lumber business.

W.J. DEMOTT

A compass plane has been reported with the additional imprint "No.7[?] Houston St. N.Y." (see Demott & Devoys)

DEMOTT & DEVOYS

This imprint has been reported on several Andruss (w.s.) planes. Probably a New York City hardware dealer. (see W.J. Demott)

G.W. DENISON & CO.

A planemaking partnership in Winthrop, CT, 1868-84, that comprised Gilbert Wright Denison (who was the son of Elihu Wright but assumed the Denison name after his marriage to Sarah Denison, niece of Lester E. Denison, w.s., in 1865), Gideon K. Hull, and Jedediah Harris. Each invested $750. In 1870 the firm grossed $8200 and employed between five and seven men, in addition to the partners. The three partners took a profit of $300 each that year, plus their wages of 27½ cents per hour.

J. DENISON

John Denison (1799-1876), who was in business himself ca.1840-76 in Saybrook, CT, and earlier with J.& L. Denison (w.s.) He was listed in the 1850 census as a toolmaker, age 51, with five employees, producing 1750 planes a year worth $3300, and owning real estate worth $3000. In the 1860 census the company claimed eight employees producing 12,000 planes worth $6000 during the year.   A & B: ★★   B1: ★★★   C: FF

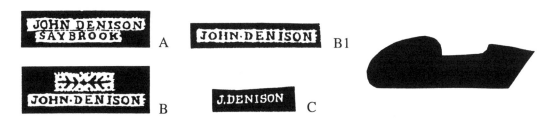

JOHN DENISON   see J. Denison

J.L. DENISON

This J.L. Denison imprint is very similar to the J. Denison stamp. There was a J. & L. Denison (w.s.) and John was also in business for himself, using three different imprints showing his name alone, with no record of his having a middle initial. The J.L. Denison imprint may therefore represent another variety of the John Denison stamp or possibly another member of the family. It may even be a typographical error that was soon after corrected to J. & L. Denison, thereby explaining its rarity.

J. & L. DENISON

A Saybrook, CT, planemaking partnership of the brothers John and Lester Denison (w.s.), that began in 1832 and in 1836 added a new partner, Jeremiah Gladding (see J. Gladding Jr.). The partnership was disbanded sometime during the 1840's. John Denison went into the planemaking business on his own and Lester opened a woodturning shop, which he continued until his death.   With cartouche - illustrated: ★★★   Without cartouche: FF

L. DENISON

Lester E. Denison (1801-66), planemaker and partner in J. & L. Denison (w.s.). There has been no example reported of this imprint.

C. DENNET

Two Yankee plow planes and a beech molding plane with lignum boxing have been reported bearing this imprint. Their appearance is ca.1800.

DENNING & CAMPBELL

A Chilicothe, Ohio, hardware dealer —1843-56. ★★★

C.H. DENNISON

Charles H. Dennison of Freeport, ME, (b.1835), was listed as a joiner in the 1860 census and as a carpenter in the 1895 and 1901 Maine register. Various planes have been reported, including a 9¼" beech spar plane. ★★★   *(see next page)*

DERRICKSON & FULLER

This imprint has appeared on a #116 Ohio Tool Co. skewed rabbet, on a pair of side rabbets (#123 Ohio Tool) and on several reverse ogees (#62 Ohio Tool). Probably a hardware dealer.

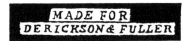

S. DESCHAUER

Stephen Deschauer was a Chicago, IL, hardware dealer, 1865-97. ★★

E. DETER

Several examples have been reported. Appearance is 18c; probable location Eastern Pennsylvania.

M. DETER (Also spelled DEETER)

Melchior Deter, one of the early Philadelphia, PA, planemakers who appeared in the city directories of 1797-1800 as a planemaker, but who may have worked both earlier and later than those dates.   ★★★

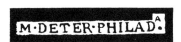

DeVALCOURT

Charles DeValcourt, who made planes in New York City, 1827-36, and subsequently became a grocer. A, B, B1, C, & D: ★★   *(continued next page)*

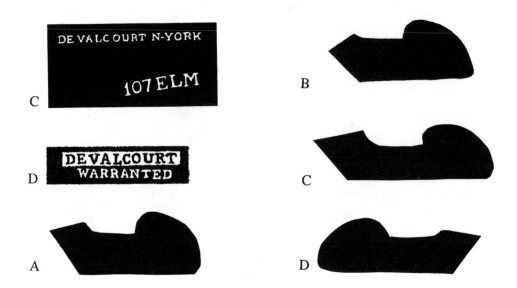

C · DE VALCOURT N-YORK · 107 ELM

D · DEVALCOURT WARRANTED

A

B

C

D

DEWEY & BROWN

There is a record of Brown & Dewey in Bellows Falls, VT, as manufacturers of "bench tools, piano and seraphine legs" in *Atwater's Vermont Directory & Commercial Almanac* of 1856. Henry S. Dewey of Bethel, VT, received Patent No. 16954 on March 3, 1851, on a machine that shaped the throat of a plane. Planes made by Dewey & Brown are stylistically similar to those of H.S. Dewey/L.W. Newton (w.s.) indicating a relationship. ★★★★

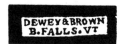

DEWEY & BROWN
B. FALLS · VT

H.S. DEWEY/L.W. NEWTON

Henry S. Dewey and Levi W. Newton, in Bethel, VT, who were listed as planemakers in *Atwater's Vermont Directory & Commercial Almanac* of 1857. On March 31, 1857, U.S. Patent No. 16954 was issued to Henry S. Dewey of Bethel VT, Assigned to H.S. Dewey and L.W. Newton. The patent was for a machine for cutting the throats of carpenters' plane stocks and was apparently used in the several examples of their bench planes reported to date. (see "The Dewey & Newton Bench Plane" *Plane Talk*, Fall 1990, pp. 274-5.) These planes are stylistically similar to those made by Dewey & Brown (w.s.) indicating a relationship between the two companies.

E.P. DICKINSON

Edward P. Dickinson was an Amherst, MA, planemaker 1869-85, who took over his father's hammer, fork, and edge tool manufacturing shop and smithy in 1879. ★★★ *(see next page)*

SAMUEL DICKSON

A March 16, 1796, newspaper advertisement refers to Samuel Dickson as a cabinetmaker and planemaker residing in Frederick Town, MD, (formerly of Wilmington, DE). His working period was ca.1772-96 and his name was probably also spelled "Dixon." No example of this imprint has been reported.

DILLWORTH BRANSON & CO.

Probably a Philadelphia hardware dealer. Appearance of the planes is mid-19c. Two examples have been reported of Conway Tool Co. planes (w.s.) overprinted DILLWORTH BRANSON & CO. ★★

I. DOGGETT

Probably Isaac Doggett (1758-1807), brother of Samuel Doggett Jr. and son of Samuel Doggett (see S. Doggett). Two examples have been reported, both with the additional location imprint DEDHAM. One is a $9\frac{7}{8}$" tongue, made of beech, with rounded chamfers and a wedge very similar to that of S. Doggett. ★★★★★

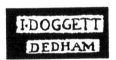 

S. DOGGETT / Dedham

Believed to be Samuel Doggett (1727-94) and perhaps his son, Samuel (1751-1831), of Dedham, MA. Samuel Sr. was a housewright and toolmaker in Dedham as early as 1751 and his estate inventory included, among many tools and supplies, a "Box of unfinished Tools and 37 pieces of Tool stuff." Samuel Jr. was both a millwright and a housewright. S. Doggett molding planes range in length from $9\frac{1}{2}$" to over 10", indicating production over a long time period, much as with Aaron Smith and Joseph Fuller. Samuel Sr. was almost certainly a planemaker and Samuel Jr. probably was. Planes were probably made as early as 1747 and into the early 19c. The A imprint has been reported on various planes including a $9\frac{7}{8}$" molding plane with $\frac{1}{4}$" flat chamfers and on a 10" birch molding plane with $\frac{5}{16}$" flat chamfers and is probably the earliest, preceding Doggett's move to Dedham. The B imprint is probably the later, usually appearing on planes with rounded chamfers. A: ★★★★ B: ★★

A   B

S. DOGGETT / Middleboro

Simeon Doggett, born in Marshfield, MA, in 1738, moved as a child to Middleboro, where he spent his working years. He served at Crown Point in 1759 during the French & Indian Wars and was a constable and tax collector for Middleboro —1771-73— and was listed as a joiner. He was apparently a loyalist during the American Revolution and spent the war years in Nova Scotia. He was back in Middleboro by 1783 and in 1796 he was on a committee to build the Town Hall. He died in 1823 at age 85. There is a record of his having had five apprentices: John Cobb (shop joiner) in 1762, Joseph Churchill 1765, Moses Samson 1769, Jeremiah Samson (w.s.) 1772, and Nathaniel Morton 1783. ★★★★★

E. DOLE

Several examples have been reported, all molding planes, 10¼" long, made of beech, with ⅜" wide flat chamfers and a Sleeper-style wedge. An Ebenezer Dole was listed as a cabinetmaker in Newburyport, MA, ca.1809, and an Enoch Dole who died in Newbury, MA, ca.1826.

W.F. DOMINICK   see W.F. Dominick & Co.

W.F. DOMINICK & CO.

A number of planes have been reported. Appearance is ca.1850.

 A
 B
 B

DOMINY

Planes were made by several generations of the Dominy family of East Hampton, NY, mostly in the period 1750-1815 and primarily for their own use. A number are in the Winterthur Museum as part of the restored Dominy workshop and are described by Charles F. Hummel in his excellent study of this family, *With Hammer in Hand.* (see Bibliography). There is however an entry in the account book of Nathaniel Dominy IV listing "two plane stocks, finishing, May 1, 1786, 5 shilling 6 pence" for Nathan Conkling Jr.

J. DONALDSON

James Donaldson, who made planes in Cincinnati, OH, —1834—, and later in Troy, OH. From ca.1842 to 1854 he was in partnership with J. Hall in St. Louis, MO, as a planemaker and then a hardware dealer. J. Donaldson seems to have been a restless sort, judging from his numerous changes in location and partners. The E imprint combining the D imprint with an S.E. Farrand (w.s.) imprint appears on a 9½" long very complex molder. (see Carter, Donaldson & Fugate, J. Donaldson/L.R. Carter, J. Donaldson/J.Hall, and J. Donaldson/J. Creagh/J.H. Hall)   A & D: ★   B & C: ★★★   *(see next page)*

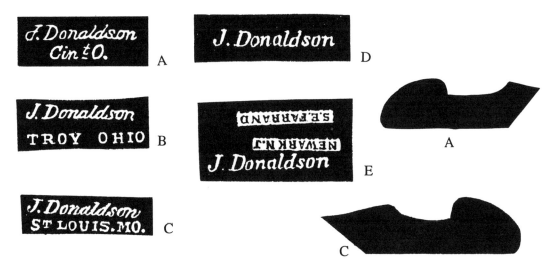

A   D

B   E   A

C   C

J. DONALDSON/L.R. CARTER

Examples reported with this imprint are possibly variants of the Cincinnati, OH, planemaking partnerships that sometimes appear as CARTER, DONALDSON & CO. (w.s.). (Also see CARTER, DONALDSON & FUGATE)

J. DONALDSON/J. CREAGH/J.H. HALL

Examples have been reported with this imprint and a CINN. OHIO location stamp. It is believed that J. Donaldson and J.H. Hall were planemaking partners between 1834 and 1836 and J. Creagh purchased their stock before Donaldson went to Troy, Ohio. (see J. Donaldson/J. Hall)

J. DONALDSON & T. FUGATE

Cincinnati, OH, planemakers ca.1840. (see J. Donaldson and also T. Fugate)   ★★★

J. DONALDSON/J. H. HALL

A St. Louis, MO, planemaking firm and hardware dealer that apparently also operated in Cincinnati and Troy, Ohio. It was composed of James F. Donaldson and John H. Hall, 1842-54, though planemaking may have ceased in 1847. (see Hall & Lynn; J. Donaldson; and J. Donaldson/J. Creagh/J.H. Hall)   A: ★★   B: ★★★
C: ★★   D: ★★   *(see next page)*

A   B   C

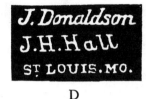

D   C

C. DONAT

Charles Donat, a Poughkeepsie, NY, planemaker, who was born there ca.1809 and died in 1842. ★★

T. DONOHO

Thomas Donoho was noted as a planemaker in the 1844 and 1845 Philadelphia directories. He was apparently working for Charlotte White, Israel White's widow (both w.s.), where he specialized in side beads. His initials T.D. appear on a number of the White imprints. Starting in 1846 he probably began working for himself, although judging from the rarity of his imprint, he did not pursue planemaking for long. ★★

J. DOREMUS

This imprint has been reported on a 9⅜" beech tongue with the additional location stamp NEWARK. Appearance is ca.1830.

MARTEN DOSCHER

Marten Doscher, b. 1852 in NY was a New York City hardware and tool dealer, 1879-94—. A Marten Doscher advertisement appeared in an 1887 issue of *Iron Age* listing himself as a commission hardware dealer at 88 Chambers St., New York, and offering "G.W. Bradley's Edge Tools, Axes, Coopers' Tools, Cleavers, Bush Hooks, Draw Knives, Ship-Carpenters' Tools, &c. Also a full stock of Planes, Brooks' Bright Wire Goods, Washita Stone and Taunton Tack Co.'s Rivets, &c." (see Doscher Plane & Tool Co.)   FF   *(see next page)*

DOSCHER PLANE & TOOL CO.

A planemaker in Saugatuck (now Westport), CT, —1886-1902. The company manufactured for Marten Doscher (w.s.) as well as for others. FF

DOUGLASS

Jeremiah and John Douglass, planemakers in New York City. They are listed in the 1796 directory only, but possibly produced earlier. Their imprint is probably the rarest of those of the early NYC makers. ★★★★

J. DOW

Thought to be James Dow (1792-1876) a joiner and builder (1812-76) in Littleton, NH, two of whose sons-in-law, D.P. Sanborn and F.J. Gouch (both w.s.), were planemakers. A: ★★★★

 A  B

C.C. DRESSER

Caleb C. Dresser was a Goshen, MA, planemaker, 1854-56—. He was one of the founders of the Union Tool Co. ★

SAM'L DRUCE

This name has been reported separately on several molding planes, 10" long, made of fruitwood or birch, with relieved wedges. There was a Samuel Druce (1767-1845), a Wrentham, MA, housewright, who appeared in the 1810 census. *(see next page)*

DUCHARME FLETCHER & CO.

A Detroit, MI, hardware firm, ca.1855. (see also Buhl, Ducharme & Co.)

CHRISTOPHER DUFFEY

Born 1810 in Ireland and listed in the 1850 federal census as a planemaker in New Albany, IN. No examples of his work have been reported.

T. DUKE

Tristam Duke was listed as a toolmaker in the 1833-35 Philadelphia, PA, city directories.   ★★★★

DUNHAM, CARRIGAN & HAYDEN   see Clean Cut

DUNHAM & M'MASTER

Samuel C. Dunham, in partnership with Truman J. McMaster (w.s.), made planes 1821-25, using convict labor at Auburn State Prison, NY.   A: ★★   B: ★★★   B1: ★★★

 A  A

 B

 B1  B1

S.C. DUNHAM/T.J. M'MASTER   see Dunham & M'Master

JOHN DUNLAP

John Dunlap (1746-1792) was a famous joiner/cabinetmaker of Goffstown and Bedford, NH, much of whose surviving work is in museum collections. There is no evidence that John Dunlap made planes, except for a fore plane stock noted as made and sold in his account book of 1782. An indenture agreement between William Huiston, apprentice, and Major [John] Dunlap, dated March 9, 1775, said in part "and at the end and expiration of the aforesaid time the aforesaid John Dunlap is to dismiss the said William from his service and help him to make the wooden part of a set of tools fit for the trade."

SAMUEL DUNLAP

1752-1830. Joiner/cabinetmaker of Goffstown, Bedford, Henniker, and Salisbury, NH, member of the renowned Dunlap family of furniture makers. His account book lists plane stocks made and sold 1800-15.

DUNN & SPENCER

Listed as a hardware store in Petersburg, VA, in an 1852 directory.   ★★★

CHARLES DUPEE

Charles Dupee Sr., 1734-1802, was born in Boston, MA. In 1750, at the age of 16, he became the ward of Joshua Clap (see J. Clap) of Walpole and subsequently became a housewright and most probably a planemaker (1755-65) in Walpole and then Wrentham (1765-1782-), where he died in 1802. Charles Sr. ran a tavern in Wrentham where, it is related, Captain Nathan Hale and his Company had breakfast on their way to relieve the siege of Boston in 1775. James Dupee, Charles' oldest son, was awarded power of attorney for Charles Sr. ca.1782. The earlier imprint A appears on a jointer that has an iron imprinted by Dalloway (Birmingham England —1770—). The later imprint B may have been used by Charles Dupee Jr., his son (1759-1803), who was a Lieutenant during the Revolutionary War, or by Charles Sr. during the later part of his working period. A & B: ★★★★★

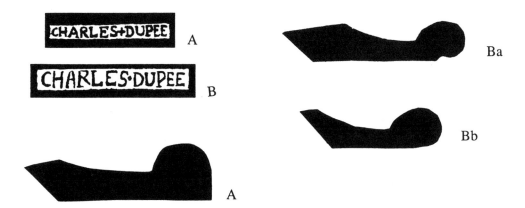

D. DURGIN

Daniel Durgin (1792-1847), who came from Durham, NH, and worked as a house carpenter and occasional planemaker in Dover, NH, from 1824 until his death. ★★★★

H. DURRIE

A Fort Wayne, IN, hardware dealer who advertised in 1855. ★★★

J.C. DURYEA

John C. Duryea operated a hardware store in Brooklyn, NY, 1836-49. The imprint shown below is incuse. The Duryea imprint has been reported on the toe of a J.J. Bowles (w.s.) side rabbet. ★★★

P. DURYEE

Peter Duryee ran a hardware store in New York City 1841-67. It became Peter Duryee & Co. in 1867, with Jacob A. Duryee and William H. Cowl as partners. ★★★

DUSTIN

Several examples have been reported, one a 10⅛" molding plane with heavy chamfers. A possible 18c maker.

WM. L. DUSTIN
William L. Dustin (d.1886), Lawrence, MA; listed in the directories as a planemaker 1866-75, and 1876-83 as a sashmaker. ★★

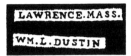 

EAGLE

This name, with the additional location imprint NEW YORK, has been reported on a 7¾" smoothing plane with an Auburn Tool Co. double iron.

EAGLE FACTORY   see N. Chapin & Co.

EAGLE MNG CO.

The B imprint gives a location for EAGLE as well as a possible clue to its origin. The location stamp is identical to that used in the H.L. James B imprint and the A wedge of each seems to be the same. James had a sizeable manufacturing operation and Eagle may have been a trade name.   A & B: ★★★

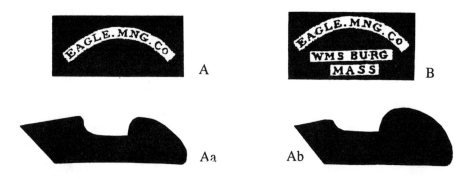

EAGLE TOOL CO.

This imprint has been reported on two jack planes, one of which carries the Auburn Tool Co. (w.s.) inventory style number for a jack.

A. EARL see A.R. Earl

A.R. EARL

Abel R. Earl was a St. Louis, MO, hardware dealer who sold tools and manufactured planes —1850-69—.
A & B: ★★   C & D: ★★★

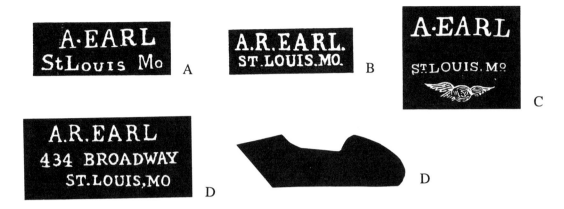

EASTBURN

Robert Eastburn (1774-1854) made planes in New Brunswick, NJ, —1802-26— (possibly as early as 1795), and was probably New Jersey's earliest planemaker. In 1802 he advertised that "he carries on the planemaking business and has on hand an assortment of fashionable molding planes and others of different kinds." During this period he also operated a hardware and grocery store. An example has been reported on which the Eastburn imprint has overprinted and all but obliterated that of Stothert (Bath, England, 1785-1841), the actual maker, whose planes were being imported into the New York City area during that period. The 1820 census listed Eastburn as a planemaker employing two journeymen, Collins Test and Robert Pumpton.

Eastburn may also have had a business relationship with the Grant family. Thomas Grant (w.s.) lived in New Brunswick —1787-1802 and the "Grant" crowned initials appear occasionally on Eastburn planes. The D imprint shows an owner's initial imprint "ILV". The same ILV imprint plus a crowned ILV appears on a Thomas Grant plane, again suggesting a relationship, and suggesting also that the crowned initials were used by both men to provide customers with identification of ownership and were applied probably at the time of sale.

Eastburn was one of the few early American makers to use friction-fit arms on plow planes and plank arm tongue and grooving planes. Others included T. Napier and T. Grant (both w.s.). All three lived and worked in the same region and probably knew or knew of each other. Some of the earlier Eastburn planes have flat chamfers and the later ones rounded.

Although the R. EASTBURN imprint is the later one, it is less frequently found than the earlier EASTBURN.
A: ★   B: ★★★   C: ★★

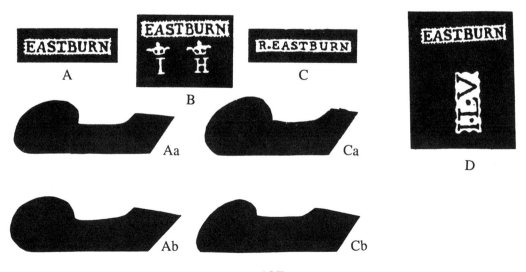

137

JOSEPH EASTBURN

Joseph Eastburn (1812-1891) was the son of Robert Eastburn and appeared in the 1850 census and in the New Brunswick, NJ, city directories of 1868-71 as a planemaker. No example of his imprint has been reported. He probably worked for his father and then for others. (see Eastburn)

R. EASTBURN   see Eastburn

EASTERLY & CO.

John Easterly (b. 1822) had a convict labor contract at Auburn Prison, New York State, and made planes there 1866—Dec. 1867. Augustus Howland, trading as A. Howland & Co. (w.s.), succeeded him. The Easterly imprint was also used on plane irons. The Easterly imprint has been reported on a single-boxed bead marked No. 105, the style number given single-boxed beads in the 1859 Auburn Tool Company price list. This suggests that the Easterly name continued to be used by Auburn Tool after Easterly's demise, or else Easterly shipped Auburn planes under its own name.   A & B: ★★

 A   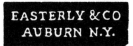 B

F.P. EASTMAN

This name has appeared on various planes including an 11⅞" long narrow shipbuilder-type coffin smoother, a lignum vitae razeed fore plane, two handled smoothers, one made of lignum, and an ebony-bodied handled plow plane. Appearance would indicate a New England seacoast maker ca.1860-70.

EAYRS & CO.

A partnership in Nashua, NH, ca.1850, of John and James Eayrs who made planes, but whose main business was the production of fine emery and the sawing of lumber.   ★★

ECLIPSE TOOL CO.

Made tools in New York City, 1901-02.

138

JAMES A. EDDY

The 1841 Providence, RI, city directory listed James A. Eddy as working in hardware at 5 Broad Street, which was the address of Battey & Eddy (w.s.), hardware and plane dealers. Earlier, in 1838, he was listed as working at Joseph Belcher's hardware establishment (see Belcher Bros.) presumably as a clerk. The imprint shown would suggest that at some time he was in business under his own name. The planes reported bear a very close resemblance to those of Isaac S. Battey (see I.S. Battey) and may have actually been made by him.   ★★

EDGERTON

Orrin (or Oren) Edgerton, a Buffalo, NY, planemaker 1836-47. Imprint A1 is a smaller version of A. (see Edgerton, Reed & Co.)   ★

A

A1

B

EDGERTON, REED & CO.

This name has been reported on a sash plane of mid-19c appearance, with the additional location imprint BUFFALO. (see Edgerton)

HOSEA EDSON

1753-1829. Edson was a member of the Shaker community at Harvard, MA, 1791-1802 and again —1829, during which time his planes were probably made. Earlier he had been a housewright. In 1774 he took the oath as a Minuteman and on April 19, 1775, responded to the Lexington Alarm. He was living in Pembroke, MA, in 1820. One example, a birch molding plane, is 10½" long.   ★★★★★

B.A. EDWARDS

Benjamin Alvord Edwards, (baptized 1757; will probated 1822), was a chairmaker and joiner in Northampton, MA. His planes have a relieved wedge, are made of birch, and were probably made in the last quarter of the 18c.   ★★★★

H.S. EDWARDS & BRO.

This imprint has been reported on a beech hollow, 9½" long with round chamfers. Probably a hardware dealer.

ELDER & SON

Henry L. Elder was listed as a merchant in the 1842-53 city directories. A combination tongue & groove plane has been reported with an A. Howland & Co. (w.s.) imprint along with the Elder & Son imprint.

JAMES A. ELDRIDGE

Listed in the 1860 census as a planemaker in Pittsfield, MA, employing three hands, using water and 20 hp of steam power to produce 6000 bench planes worth $2400, and other tools worth $1300. In the 1870 census he was again listed as a planemaker, but in Adams, MA, and owning real estate worth only $200. (see Allen & Eldridge)

S. ELDRIDGE

Samuel Eldridge was listed as a planemaker, age 23, in the 1850 census for Conway, MA. (see Allen & Eldridge)   ★★★

G. & S. ELFREY

George Elfrey (b. 1809 in PA) was listed as a planemaker in Philadelphia, PA, in the 1839-41 city directories ★★★★

J.M. ELLIS & CO.

A partnership consisting of Joseph M. Ellis and Charles Threshie that was listed in the New Orleans, LA, city directories from 1850 until 1861 as a hardware dealer. A complex molder has been reported with both the Ellis and A. & E. Baldwin (w.s.) imprint.   ★★★

ELLSWORTH & DUDLEY

This name has appeared on a Sargent & Co. (w.s.) bead with the additional location imprint PO'KEEPSIE N.Y. and also on a Union Factory rabbet (see H. Chapin). A probable hardware dealer.

EMERY, WATERHOUSE & CO.

A hardware dealer in Portland, ME, that began business ca.1846 and is still in operation. From 1846 to 1870, the firm logo read EMERY + WATERHOUSE. In 1871 it changed to EMERY WATERHOUSE & CO. and in 1894 changed once again to EMERY & WATERHOUSE CO. A handled matched tongue and groove with this imprint also carries the imprint of the Taber Plane Co. (w.s.). ★★

EMPIRE TOOL CO.

Possibly one of the imprints used by the Auburn Tool Co. to conceal its use of prison labor in making tools. A & B: FF

A   B

WM. ENDERS

Also imprinted OAK LEAF and ST. LOUIS. Believed to have been used on second quality planes and irons of the Keen Kutter brand of E.C. Simmons Hardware Co (1921-30). William Enders was a clerk for A.F. Shapleigh & Co. in 1871 and became a salesman in 1875. He joined the Simmons Hardware Co. (Keen Kutter) as a saleman in 1887 and eventually became a vice president of the company. (see Keen Kutter and also Shapleigh & Co.)

ENFIELD TOOL CO.

No information has been found. The imprint appears on a match tongue plane with the number 343.

ENGLISH & MIX

A probable New Haven, CT, hardware dealer. This imprint was found on a boxed side bead made by I. Hammond (w.s.).

ENSENORE WORKS

A brand of the Owasco Tool Co. ca.1875. Owasco Tool Co. was, in turn, a brand name of the Auburn Tool Co. The 1875 Russell & Ervin hardware catalog advertised the Ensenore brand as an Owasco Tool Co. product. The imprint below is incuse. (see Owasco Tool Co. and Auburn Tool Co.) ★ *(see next page)*

141

ENSENORE WORKS
NEW.YORK

W.L. EPPERSON
William L. Epperson was listed as a planemaker in the Louisville, KY, directories of 1858-59, 1876, and 1890, although he may have worked earlier. Examples reported have all been premium quality plow planes, using exotic woods, brass or silver fittings, and inlay. In the intervening years he was variously listed as a carpenter, machinist, fishing rod manufacturer, violin manufacturer, and cabinetmaker. A true renaissance man. ★★★

LOUIS ERNST
A Rochester, NY, hardware dealer who advertised as early as 1869. "Compliments of Louis Ernst & Sons" has been found printed on a 1900 Morse Twist Drill & Machine Co. catalog. The Louis Ernst imprint has been found on planes made by G.W. Denison and by L. & I.J. White (both w.s.). ★★

ERNST & SEIFRIED
A partnership of Louis Ernst (w.s.) and Ferdinand Seifried that advertisted in the *Rochester Union & Advertister* in 1857. No example of an imprint has been reported.

E. EVANS
Evan Evans (1811-1885, b. NY), a Rochester, NY, planemaker 1834-50—, who was listed in the 1850 census as a planemaker and who, in 1829, was employed by John Reed. (see Reed; see also E. & J. Evans)

E. & J. EVANS
A Rochester, NY, planemaking partnership (1841-85) consisting of Evan Evans and James Evans, who was listed in the 1850 census as a planemaker, age 44, born in NY. (see E. Evans) A: ★   B: ★★

A

B

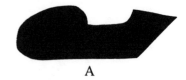

A

WILLIAM EVANS
Planes have been found bearing this name, with the additional imprint MARTINSBURG VA, but no record of Evans in Martinsburg, VA, (now WV) has yet been found.

W. EVENS

In Nov.1813, William Evens announced the opening of his planemaking business in Pittsburgh, PA, and was listed as a planemaker in the 1815 city directory. He was located on the west side of Market Street above Fifth, two blocks from the planemaking shops of W. Scott and Swetman & Hughes (both w.s.). He was again listed in the 1819 and 1826 directories at a new location on the same block as planemaker Thomas Clark (see T. Clark). In 1831 he moved from the central business district, across the Allegheny River to Allegheny Town, now part of Pittsburgh northside. He had a dual career as both a music teacher and planemaker and by the 1837 directory was listed as a "professor of music" only and continued so through the 1852 directory. He died in 1854. He was unusual among planemakers in that he advertised "mother planes." (see Wilson/Pittsburgh) ★★

EXCELSIOR WORKS

Possibly a trade name; appearance is ca.1850.

C. EYMAN(N)

A hardware dealer in Cincinnati, OH, 1856-81. The name only is shown imprinted on an H. & J.C. Taylor (w.s.) round (imprint A).   A & B: ★★

   A      B

H. EYRE

The 1875-76 NYC directory lists a Harry Eyre, smith, at 135 Lewis and an Elizabeth Eyre, tools, same address. Harry apparently minded the forge and Elizabeth minded the store. Elizabeth's listing begins in 1873 and extends to 1880 with "tools" her occupation 1873-77, "hardware" 1877-78, "saws" 1878-79, and back to "tools" 1879-80. ★★★

W.H. FAHNESTOCK

A hardware merchant who was first listed in the 1847 Pittsburgh, PA, directory. His last listing was 1860-61. During part of this period he was listed as FAHNSTOCK & BRO. His imprint has been reported on planes made by H. Chapin/Union Factory and Ohio Tool Co. (both w.s.), as well as alone.

ALEX FALL

Alexander Fall who was listed in the 1865 Nashville, TN, directory as a hardware dealer and earlier listed in various partnerships beginning in 1853 as Fall & Cunningham (w.s.) and 1861-65 as Alexander Fall & John M. Gray. ★★★

FALL & CUNNINGHAM

A Nashville, TN, hardware store partnership consisting of Alexander Fall and G.W. Cunningham that appeared in the city directories 1853-61. Its imprint has appeared on a number of Ohio Tool Co. (w.s.) planes, including a boxwood self-regulating center wheel plow. ★★★

B. FARLEY

Benjamin Farley of Hollis, NH, who made coopers' tools and was listed in the 1849 New England business directory. His imprint has been reported on a 4′ cooper's jointer.

FARLEY-CHRISTMAN & CO.

A Dubuque, IA, hardware dealer who operated in the early 1850's. ★★★

J.W. FARR [& CO.]

James W. Farr made planes in New York City 1832-36 and 1839-52 and in Brooklyn 1837-38. His indenture papers, dated Aug. 30, 1827 (he was 16½ years old), apprenticed him to Enos Baldwin of NYC (see E. Baldwin) for 4 years 5 months and 13 days "to learn the art, trade, and mystery of a planemaker." He promised not to "absent himself day nor night from his master's service without his leave; nor haunt ale houses, taverns, dance houses, or play houses." He was to be paid $2 per week for the first 2 years 5 months and 13 days and then $2.50 per week for the remaining 2 years.   A: ★   B: ★★★   C: ★   D & D1: ★   E & F: ★★★

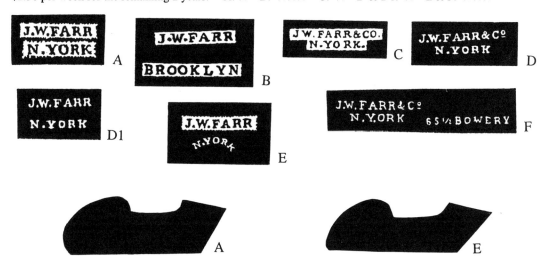

S.E. FARRAND

Samuel E. Farrand appeared in the 1835-36 Newark, NJ, directory as a planemaker, at the same address as Andruss (w.s.). In the 1840's he was listed as a machinist, in 1849 as a carriage dealer, and in the 1850 census he was listed as a farmer, age 60, living in Hanover, Morris County, NJ. His planes include a number of coachmaking types. (see J. Donaldson)   ★

FARRINGTON & BURDITT

Probably a Holyoke, MA, hardware dealer, mid- to late-19c. The imprint has been reported on an Auburn Tool Co. (w.s.) plane.

L.J. FARWELL & CO.

Leonard J. Farwell (b. 1819 in NY state) was a hardware dealer in Milwaukie (old spelling), W.T. (Wisconsin Territory), 1840-51. In 1841 he was a partner in Cady & Farwell and in 1843 in Clark, Shepardson, and then as L.J. Farwell & Co., becoming the largest wholesale and retail hardware company in the city. Earlier, before relocating to "Milwaukie" he operated a tinsmith shop and hardware company in Lockport, IL, and subsequently became the second governor of the state of Wisconsin in 1851.

JOEL FENN & CO.

Joel Fenn was a Wallingford, CT, planemaker —1849—. He was also agent for Sawheag Works —1850— (w.s.). He was listed in the Wallingford 1850 census as a planemaker, age 32, born in Connecticut, and owning real estate worth $4500. (see Gladwin & Fenn)   ★

Aa   Ab

ISAAC FIELD

A Providence, RI, planemaker —1824-57. He was listed as a toolmaker in an 1808 land transfer from Joseph Fuller (w.s.). There is also an Isaac Field listed in the 1850 census as a planemaker in Providence, age 29, born in RI. Isaac Field and his brother, William Field, also a planemaker, rented part of Jo. Fuller's shop in the years following Fuller's death. The following advertisement appeared in *The Providence [RI] Directory* 1836:

ISAAC FIELD

TOOLMAKER

GRATEFUL to his friends and the public for past patronage, respectfully gives notice that he continues to make all kinds of Carpenters' Tools; he also repairs Tools and whets Saws. Those in want of any thing in his line, are invited to call at No. 138 Westminster street [Joseph Fuller's old address] where the prices will always be found such as to give satisfaction.

In the 1840's Isaac Field and Joseph Fuller Jr. (Jo. Fuller's adopted son whose original name was Joseph Field) were listed at the same address. Since some Isaac Field planes have much earlier characteristics than others, there is the strong possibility of two generations of planemakers using this imprint. (see Jo. Fuller and also Fuller & Field)   A & A1: ★

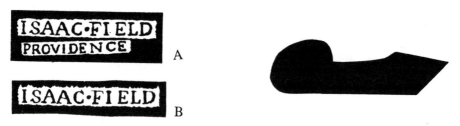

A

B

JOSEPH B. FIELD

Joseph Field, b. 1812, was noted in a property transfer in Fall River, MA, in 1835 and lost $300 of personal property in the great Fall River fire of 1843. He was listed as being in commerce in Fall River in the 1840 Massachusetts census and as a trader in the 1850 census and as a grocer in the 1855 and 1857 Fall River directories. A 9½" beech bead with round chamfers and a 5" wide cornice plane have been reported, with his imprint and the additional location imprint FALL RIVER

RICH'D M. FIELD

Richard M. Field was the partner of Joseph Fuller Jr. (see Fuller & Field). Several examples of planes bearing this imprint have been reported. They are 10" long and have relieved wedges. A 1799 deed referred to him as a toolmaker, while in an 1817 deed transfer, he was noted as a merchant.   ★★★★

FIELD & HARDIE

Believed to be a Philadelphia, PA, hardware dealer. There are reports of Sandusky Tool Co. planes overstamped FIELD & HARDIE/PHILA, and one by H. Chapin also overstamped. The planes are of mid-19c appearance.   A: ★★   B: ★★★

A

B

FIELDING & BARTLETT

A Lowell, MA, hardware dealer, listed in the city directories in 1866 and 1868.   ★★

E. E. FILLMORE

A hardware dealer in Zanesville, OH, (1842-63). Earlier he was a partner in Patterson & Fillmore (1835-42). Planes made by Ohio Tool Co. have been reported bearing this imprint.   ★★

L. FILLMORE

Two separate groups of planes (four found in Rhode Island; two in Vermont) have been reported, all 9½" long, beech, with 5/16" flat chamfers.

A. FISH

Ansel Fish, Lowell, MA, who was listed in the city directories as a planemaker in most years between 1836 and 1855, and in the 1850 census as a planemaker, age 44.   ★

Aa

Ab

J. FISH

Appearance is second quarter 19c.   A & B: ★★★

 A  B

J. & A. FISH

James and Alexander Fish were planemakers in Chicago, IL, 1853-55.   ★★★

FISHER

Several planes have been reported. Two are 10" long birch molders with flat chamfers. Appearance is 18c. (see C. Fisher, J. Fisher, and N. Fisher)

C. FISHER

Several examples have been reported, one a 10" birch round. Appearance is late 18c, and probable location is southern Vermont. (Planes were found in Woodstock and Newfane). (see Fisher, J. Fisher and also N. Fisher)

J. FISHER

Six molding planes have been reported, all made of birch, 9⅞" - 10" long, with relieved wedges. Probable location is southern Vermont (planes were found in Woodstock and Newfane); appearance is late 18c. (see Fisher, C. Fisher and also N. Fisher)

N. FISHER

Several examples of this mark have been reported; including three cornice planes with offset totes, and a 10½" long molding plane. Probable 18c maker. (see Fisher, J. Fisher and also C. Fisher)

FISHER & AGNEW

This firm, comprising E.H. Fisher and John Agnew, appeared in the 1859 Columbia, SC, directory (the earliest available) as dealers in hardware and cutlery, and again in the 1860 directory. John Agnew & Son was listed in 1875-76 (the first directory printed after the Civil War, as a dealer in hardware and groceries. In the 1879-80 directory John Agnew was shown as a dealer in hardware, agricultural implements, carriages, and buggies. ★★★

FISHER & CO.

This mark has been reported on a hollow, a smoothing plane, a jointer, and a handled beech screw arm plow. Appearance is ca.1850.

ABM:FISK

Abraham Fisk. Various examples of this imprint have been reported, including a Yankee style plow plane, a 10" rabbet, a 9⅜" birch ogee, and several 9⅞" beech molders with flat chamfers. (see Abraham Fisk) ★★★★

ABRAHAM FISK

Various molding planes have been reported, 9⅞" long, made of yellow birch, with flat chamfers and flutes; also a birch Yankee plow. Appearance is late 18c. (see ABM:FISK) ★★★★

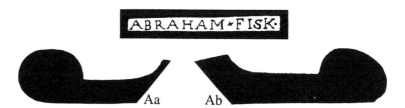

Aa   Ab

S. FISK

This mark has been reported on two panel raisers, a 30" jointer, a Yankee plow plane, and a 9⅞" astragal, all of yellow birch and 18c in appearance.

I. FITCH

Isaac Fitch (1734-1791) of Lebanon, CT, was a prominent cabinetmaker, architect and builder. His estate inventory included 44 planes. It is probable that he at least made planes for his own use and that of his employees. (see Bibliography)   *(see next page)*

H. FLAGLER & CO.
Henry Flagler was listed in the 1850 census as a 48 year old merchant, born in NY state and living in Lockport, NY.   ★★★

FLETCHER
Charles Fletcher was a New York City planemaker and hardware merchant 1875-83.   A & B: ★★★

 A    B

S.F. FLETCHER
A Richmond, IN, hardware dealer 1857—. (also see Fletcher & Benton)

FLETCHER & BENTON
A Richmond, IN, hardware firm, ca.1845-57, comprising S.F. Fletcher and Thomas H. Benton (both w.s.). ★★★

EDWARD F. FOLGER   See E.F. Folger & Co.

E.F. FOLGER & CO.
Edward F. Folger (1824-75) was a hardware merchant in Buffalo, NY, 1849-57.   A & B: ★★

 A    B

S.N. FONDER
A tongue plane has been reported with the additional imprint TERRA HAUTE.

THO. FOSS

Thomas Foss, b.1728, believed to have been a carpenter/joiner in Portsmouth, NH.

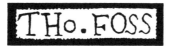

J. FOSTER

This imprint was reported on a jointer of mid-19c. appearance.

J.L. FOSTER

John L. Foster was listed as a ship's carpenter in the 1864 Boston directory. The imprint shown here appears on a 9⅜" beech sash coping plane with boxing. A razeed rosewood jack plane has also been reported.

FOSTER & PORTER

Probably a hardware dealer. The imprint has appeared on a Sandusky Tool Co. (w.s.) plane.

T. FOWLER

Thomas Fowler was a joiner in Salesbury, MA, ca.1800. A plow plane has been reported with early 19c characteristics.

FOWLER BROS.

An example has been reported additionally imprinted HARDWARE/187 FLATBUSH/BROOKLYN/L.I. on a moving filletster made by Shiverick (1865-67).

A. & E. FOX

Appearance is second quarter 19c.

B.F. FOX

Benjamin F. Fox (1826-1904) was a Springfield, IL, hardware dealer, 1855-70. ★★ *(see next page)*

G. FOX

An Amherst, MA, planemaker, whose working dates are not known. A George W. Fox was listed in the 1850 census as a planemaker in Middletown, CT, age 34, born in England and working for the Arrowmammett Works (w.s.).

HIRAM FOX

The son of Luther Fox (w.s.). He made planes in Amherst, MA, —1841. In 1841 he became a partner in Burnham, Fox & Co. (w.s.).

LUTHER FOX

An Amherst, MA, planemaker —1831-43. Between 1834 and 1836, he was a partner with Truman Nutting (see T. Nutting) in Nutting & Fox (w.s.). George Burnham worked for him as a journeyman and soon thereafter, in 1843, Fox sold out to Burnham, Fox & Co. (w.s.). (see L. Fox & Son and George Burnham)

L. FOX & SON

Luther Fox and son, of Amherst, MA, who probably operated in the 1830's. (see Luther Fox) ★★

FOX, NUTTING & WASHBURN

An Amherst, MA, planemaker; probably consisting of Luther Fox, Truman Nutting, and William Lyman Washburn, that operated ca.1835. (see W.L. Washburn, T. Nutting, and Luther Fox)

FOX & WASHBURN

Probably Luther Fox and William Lyman Washburn, who operated 1835-36—. (see W. L. Washburn) ★

JOHN FRACE

A rosewood plow plane and a grooving plane of mid-19c appearance have been reported with the additional imprint NEWTON, N.J. A John Frace appeared in the 1860 census as an 18-year old carpenter. There is no record of any Fraces in the 1870 census.   *(see next page)*

152

ELIAS FRANCIS
Possibly an earlier appearance of Elias Francis of Mockridge & Francis (w.s.) which operated 1835-68.

P.S. FRANCISCO
A planemaker whose working dates are unknown. Ohio City was incorporated in 1836 and became part of Cleveland in 1854. Francisco was listed in the 1850 census as a planemaker living in Brooklyn, OH (next to Cleveland), age 32 and born in NY.   A & B: ★★★

A   B   B

WILLIAM FRANKLIN
A planemaker in Cincinnati, OH, 1842-58. No example of his imprint is known.

G. FREBURGER JR.
George Freburger Jr., a Baltimore, MD, planemaker listed in the city directories 1849-51.   ★★★

C. FRESE & CO.
Charles Frese, an Indianapolis, IN, hardware dealer who appeared in the 1866 and 1876 city directories. (see Frese & Kropf)   ★★

FRESE & KROPF
Charles Frese and Gustav Kropf, Indianapolis, IN, hardware dealers 1863-65. (see C. Frese & Co.)

REUBEN FRETZ

Inventor of a patented Carriage Wheel Trimming Plane; for details refer to *Patented Transitional & Metallic Planes in America, Vol. II,* pp.68-70, Roger K. Smith,.

T. FUGATE

Thomas Fugate, a Cincinnati, OH, planemaker who worked under his own name 1829-31 and intermittently between 1839 and 1870. In 1831 he was a partner in Carter, Donaldson & Fugate (w.s.). Between 1832 and possibly as late as 1839 he was a partner in T. Fugate & J.D. Conover, Louisville, KY, planemakers (w.s.). In the 1850-51 directory he was listed as a foreman at G. Roseboom (w.s.). (see also B. King/T. Fugate) ★★

T. FUGATE & J.D. CONOVER

A Louisville, KY, planemaking partnership comprising John D. Conover (see John Conover) and Thomas Fugate (see T.Fugate). They were listed in the 1832 city directory and may have continued until 1839. ★★

WILLIAM W. FULGHUM

Listed as a planemaker in Richmond, IN, in the 1860 census. No example of his imprint has been reported.

C. FULLER

Charles Fuller was a Boston, MA, planemaker, 1836-87. He was listed in the 1850 census as age 32, born in NH. He started his own business in 1852; worked at Causeway Street 1852-66, at Pine Street 1867-72, and at Waltham Street 1873-87. The D imprint (Green Street/Boston) is very similar to the L Gardner imprint (w.s.) which Gardner used between 1843-55. Apparently Fuller used it sometime after 1855. The 1860 Massachusetts industrial census showed him employing two hands and producing 700 planes worth $1700.   A, B, & C: ★
D: ★★★

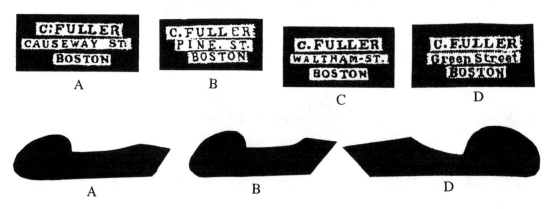

154

CHARLES H. FULLER

Charles H. Fuller worked as a planemaker for, and boarded with, C. Fuller (w.s.) 1866-69 and may have made under his own name 1870-75, all in Boston, MA.

D. FULLER

David Fuller (1795-1871 b. MA) was a joiner in 1819 and planemaker in West Gardiner, ME. His name appears in the 1820 census and he is listed as a planemaker and carpenter in the Maine register of 1855-56, although his personal papers also indicate planemaking activity during 1853-54, and as a carpenter in the 1850 census.   A: ★★   B & B1: ★★★★

G. FULLER/D. FULLER

This imprint appears on a 9½" beech side rabbet.

JAMES H. FULLER

This name has been reported twice, with the additional incised imprint CAMBRIDGEPORT MASS. Appearance is mid-19c.

JO. FULLER

Joseph Fuller (1746-1822, b. Lisbon, CT), worked in Providence, RI, and was one of the most important and prolific of the early planemakers.   An advertisement in the *Providence Gazette* of Dec. 26, 1772, annouced "Joiners' Tools made and sold by Joseph Fuller."   He was listed as a joiner (1773), and in 1808 as a toolmaker. He served as an officer during the American Revolution and, like Francis Nicholson (w.s.), was a deacon of his church.   He was a charter member of the Providence Association of Mechanics and Manufacturers in 1789.   He had no children of his own, but adopted Joseph Field, who then changed his name to Joseph Fuller Jr. (see Fuller & Field).   Joseph Jr. was left a quarter share in Joseph Fuller's estate.   Judging by the quality and quantity of his work, he probably was among the relatively few early makers who earned a significant part of their income from planemaking.   There is a notice in the *Providence Gazette* of April 28, 1798, announcing that the partnership of Joseph Fuller and son (i.e., Joseph Fuller Jr.) was "this day dissolved by mutual consent."   It is possible that the partnership began at or about 1794 when Joseph Jr. came of age.   There is some evidence to suggest that among possible Jo. Fuller employees were George and James Snow III, who were brothers.   Both were listed as toolmakers in land transactions with Jo. Fuller.

The evolution of planemaking from the 18th to the 19th century can be seen in the style changes Fuller made over his long planemaking career.   During his early period, his planes were 10" or longer, with flat chamfers and decorative fluting on toe and heel.   In later years, when he adopted the standard 9½" length, his chamfers became rounded and the fluting disappeared.   The wood he used evolved from yellow birch to beech, and his wedge shape became relieved after his early period and then rounded.   Also changing over this timespan was his maker's imprint.   These are shown in probable chronological order A through E.   A: ★★   B: ★★★★★   C: ★★★ D, D1, D2: ★   E: ★★   *(see next page)*

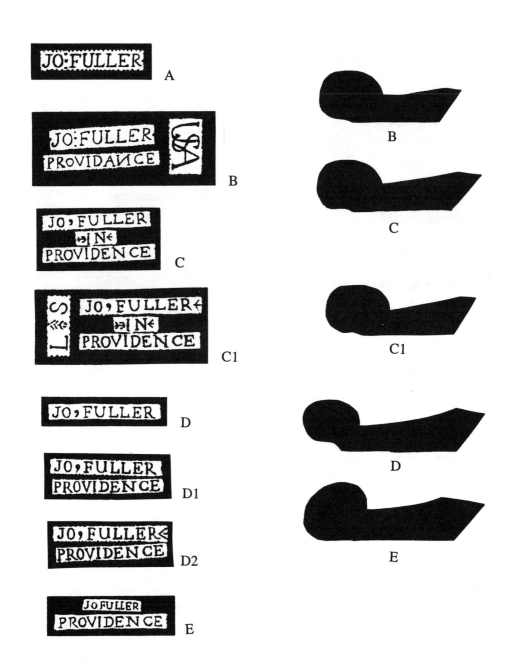

A

B

C

C1

D

D1

D2

E

B

C

C1

D

E

FULLER & FIELD

Possibly a partnership between Joseph Fuller Jr. (1773-1845; born Joseph Field, and the adopted son of Joseph Fuller) and Richard Montgomery Field (w.s.), who were listed as toolmakers in 1799. In 1817 Joseph Fuller Jr. was a blockmaker and Richard M. Field a merchant. However, because of the early appearance of these planes, their 10" length, use of yellow birch, flat chamfers, and fluting, it is also quite possible that the partnership consisted of Jo. Fuller (w.s.) and one of the many other Fields then living in Providence. ★★★

S.J. GAGE

Sylvester J. Gage of Vergennes, Vermont, appeared as a carpenter and joiner in the 1849 New England directory, and as a manufacturer of sash and window blinds in the 1850 "Products of Industry for Vermont." A smooth plane has been reported with the imprint S.J. GAGE/VERGENNES.

CHARLES C. GAINES see C.C. Gaines & Co.

C.C. GAINES & CO.

Charles C. Gaines began business in New Orleans as a crockery and glassware merchant, becoming a hardware dealer in 1849. His partners included William Heyl, Feret Jerdy, and L.A. Stone. The store experienced a fire in 1862 that apparently terminated the business.   A & B: ★★★

 A

 B

JAMES GALBREATH

Appeared in the Cincinnati, OH, 1850 directory as a planemaker, but no example of his imprint has been reported.

J.R. GALE

James R. Gale was a Providence, RI, planemaker who was a partner in Cumings & Gale (w.s.) 1830-33, and who worked under his own name 1833-36—. An advertisement of his "Plane Manufactory" in which he claimed "to make Planes and Tools of every description" appeared in the 1836 Providence directory.
A & B: ★   C: ★★

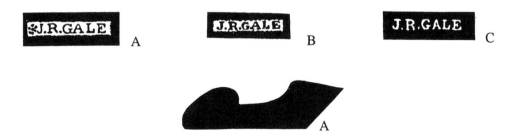

CHARLES GARDNER

A planemaker in Cornwall, CT, —1857-58—.

L. GARDNER

Leavitt Gardner made planes in Boston, MA, from 1825 to 1855; and under this imprint 1843-55. He was listed in the 1850 census as a planemaker, age 50, born in MA, and owning realty worth $7000. He employed three hands and made planes worth $3500. A boxed bead has been reported with an additional imprint "Patent April 9, 1851," probably referring to its adjustable double iron. (see also Gardner & Murdock and Gardner & Brazer) ★

S. GARDNER & CO.
Thought to be a Boston, MA, hardware dealer; working dates unknown.

GARDNER & APPLETON
A Boston, MA, planemaking partnership whose working dates are not known.

GARDNER & BRAZER
A Boston, MA, planemaking partnership that operated in 1825 only. Its address was Green Street, the same as that of Gardner & Murdock (w.s.). The partners were Leavitt Gardner (see L. Gardner) and Benjamin Brazer (see Brazer), who appeared in the Lowell, MA, directories 1832-35. ★★

GARDNER & MURDOCK
Leavitt Gardner and Amasa Murdock, who were Boston, MA, planemakers 1825-41. (see L. Gardner and also A. Murdock) ★★

D.N. GARRISON
David N. Garrison, a Dayton, OH, planemaker and tool merchant —1850-54— who worked earlier as a planemaker for Samuel Sloop (w.s.) in Cincinnati, OH, 1839-40. He was listed in the 1850 census as a tool merchant in Dayton, age 32, who operated a tool factory using water power and employing four hands. Total value of tools produced was $3330. (see D. N. Garrison/T.A. Heim) ★★

D.N. GARRISON/T.A. HEIM
A probable partnership of David N. Garrison and T.A. Heim in Dayton, OH, ca.1849-50. (see Heim & Smith and D.N. Garrison) *(see next page)*

158

D.S. & S.P. GEER

David S. and Samuel P. Geer were Syracuse, NY, hardware dealers —1853-65—. Previously they operated as Geer Bros. (1851-52), the firm consisting of David S., John R., John R. Jr., and Samuel P. ★★

D. GEHRET

This name has been reported on a complex molder, a jointer with an offset handle, and two massive plow planes, 12" long and 2" wide. Appearance is ca.1800; probable location is eastern PA.

J. GEHRIG

Various examples of this imprint have been reported, including a 10" tongue, a 9½" beech round, a 9" torus bead; all with flat chamfers and a very distinctive wedge finial. Appearance is ca.1800, probable location is eastern PA.

GENESEE TOOL CO.

This may be one of the trade names used by the Auburn Tool Co. The Genesee River flows through Rochester, NY and Genesee County is nearby, both within 100 miles of Auburn Tool. A 16" jack has been reported, found together with a "Cayuga" jack and an "Ontario" fore plane (both w.s.). The A and B imprints are incuse. A & B: ★   C: ★★★

GENESEE TOOL Co
A

B

C

GERARD TOOL CO.

The appearance and quality of the planes suggest a "second" line product. Gerard Tool may have been a trade name used by the Auburn Tool Co., much like Owasco Tool Co. and Genesee Tool Co. (both w.s.). James Watson Gerard (1794 - 1874) was a New Yorker who was responsible for the incorporation of the Society for Reformation of Juvenile Delinquents and who was the first to sponsor the wearing of uniforms by police, suggesting a possible Auburn Prison connection.   *(see next page)*

159

C. GERE

This imprint very much resembles the A and A1 imprints of Ebenezer Gere (see E. Gere), who was born in New London, CT, in the late 18c, lived in Groton, CT, and in Ulster County, NY, in the early 1800's and made planes in Brooklyn Twp., PA, in the 1830's and 40's. Ebenezer had a brother Charles. Susquehanna County, PA, records show that Charles Gere was a carpenter, that he came to Brooklyn Twp. from Hartland, VT, ca.1804-07, and that he died in Hartland in 1842, aged 65.

C.M. GERE

Christopher M. Gere, planemaker, and son of E. Gere (w.s.). He was born in New London, CT, in 1814 and came with his parents to Brooklyn Twp., Susquehanna County, PA, in 1821. At age 16 he entered his father's planemaking shop and continued to work as a planemaker until he was elected sheriff in 1848 and moved to Montrose, PA.   A & B: ★★

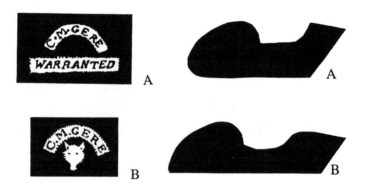

E. GERE

Ebenezer Gere, a planemaker, and father of C.M. Gere (w.s.). He came to Brooklyn Township, Susquehanna County, PA, from Preston, CT, and bought a farm for $600. He was subsequently listed as a planemaker and apparently operated a shop. He was listed in the 1830 and 1840 censuses as being in Brooklyn Twp., and in the 1800 census in Ulster County, NY. He was probably in Groton, CT, during part of the early 1800's. His earlier stamps, A and A1, appear on planes with late 18c-early 19c characteristics, most of which were found in southeastern New England.   A: ★★★   A1: ★★★★   B: ★★   C: ★★★

N. GERE

Several planes have been reported, including a 9⅜" beech ogee with ⅜" flat chamfers and single lignum boxing. Appearance is late 18c.

GERE, ABBOTT & CO.

This firm was listed as a hardware merchant in the Columbus, OH, city directories of 1848-56. The Gere was George Gere, who later became the first president of the Ohio Tool Co. Abbott was James S. Abbott, who was listed as a tool merchant as early as 1845-46 and continued in the hardware business by himself after the dissolution of Gere, Abbott, and later, in 1860-62, with his son H.J. Abbott as J.S. ABBOTT & SON. All were located in Columbus, Ohio. A & B: ★★

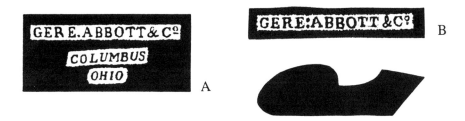

B

A

J.W. GIBBS

John W. Gibbs, a New York City planemaker 1829-33. (see also Gibbs & Cation) A, A1, B: ★

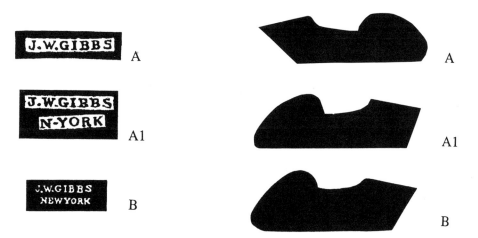

A

A

A1

A1

B

B

GIBBS & CATION

A partnership of John W. Gibbs and David W. Cation that made planes in New York City 1830 - 34. (see John W. Gibbs and also Cation) ★★★

J. GIBSON

John Gibson (1795-1868) was born in Ireland and made planes himself and in two partnerships in Albany, NY, 1823-52. He manufactured under his own name 1823-24, 1829-35, and 1839-52. John Gibson's advertisement in the 1842-43 Albany directory listed his establishment as a Plane Factory, Plane & Board planing and sawing, and a Plaster Mill. The B imprint shown below is incuse. (see Rowell & Gibson and J. & J. Gibson)
A & B: FF

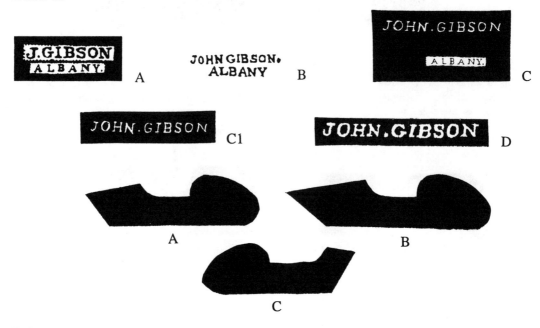

J. & J. GIBSON

An Albany, NY, planemaking partnership —1837-38 consisting of John Gibson and his brother Joseph. The imprint shown below is incuse. (see J. Gibson and also Joseph Gibson)   ★

JOHN GIBSON   see J. Gibson

JOSEPH GIBSON

A brother of John Gibson who made planes under his own imprint in Albany, NY, 1839-46. (see J. & J. Gibson)   ★

GIDDINGS & MEEK

A Hartford, CT, planemaker and/or hardware dealer. Appearance of the planes is mid-19c. ★★

A. GILBERT & SONS

A. Gilbert & Sons "Plane Manufactory" appeared on an early map of Derby, CT. The 1860 census listed an Ager Gilbert, age 42, as a joiner, born in CT. No example has been reported.

H. GILBERT

A Harrisburg, PA, hardware dealer whose imprint has been reported on both an ISRAEL WHITE and a BURNHAM & BROS. plane, and who appeared as late as 1890 in the Harrisburg city directory.

J. GILBERT

53 molding planes bearing this imprint were found in a tool chest that also included a C. Morehouse (w.s.) plane. Patten's 1840 New Haven, CT, directory listed a John Gilbert as a joiner with his own shop.

W. F. GILBERT

William F. Gilbert was listed in the 1850 census as a planemaker, age 16, and working for DeForest (see L. DeForest and also L. & C.H. DeForest) and in the 1860 censuses as age 26, a planemaker, born in CT. ★★★

GILBERT, SWEET & LYON

A New York City hardware dealer who sold planes 1887 - 89. The partners were John A. Gilbert, Edwin S. Sweet, and Henry M. Lyon. They were succeeded by Sickles, Sweet & Lyon (w.s.). The imprint shown below is incuse. ★★

GILBERT, SWEET & LYON
NEW. YORK

GILLESPIE

This name has been reported on a G.W. DENISON rabbet (A imprint). Probably a NYC hardware dealer.

A. GILLET

Six examples have been reported, including a 10" beech ogee, a round, and a 10" bead, all with a Sleeper-style wedge and $\frac{3}{16}$" flat chamfers.

S. GILLIS

Two examples of this imprint have been reported; one a $10\frac{3}{8}$" long bead, with interrupted lignum boxing, a style characteristic of eastern Pennsylvania, where it was acquired. A group of nine planes, found together and all stamped S. Gillis, has been reported. Three are imprinted E.W. Carpenter/Baltimore, four are imprinted E.W. Carpenter/Lancaster, one is imprinted Kneass, and one is imprinted S. Gillis only, raising the questions of whether Gillis was an owner as well as a maker, whether he retailed planes made by others, or whether he was a maker/user.

G.D. GILMAN

Several planes have been reported, including a crown molder and a mast plane. Appearance is ca.1825-50.

J. GILMER

Joseph Gilmer was listed as a planemaker in New Albany, IN, city directories of 1848, 1856, and 1859, and was noted in the 1850 census as age 41 and gone off to California to dig for gold (with apparently little success). ★★

J. GLADDING JR.

Jeremiah Gladding was a planemaker in Saybrook, CT, ca. 1830 - 40—. (see J. & L. Denison)   ★★★

P.A. GLADWIN & CO.

Porter A. Gladwin was a Boston, MA, planemaker —1857- 82—. He made planes under his own imprints 1857-73 and 1877-82. Earlier he was a partner with Joel Fenn in Gladwin & Fenn (w.s.) and between 1873-77 was a partner with Thomas L. Appleton in Gladwin & Appleton (w.s.). A pair of handled match planes have been reported with the "P.A. Gladwin" imprint struck over "J. Kellogg" (w.s.). Before moving to Boston, he made planes in Wallingford, CT, both under his own imprint and in partnership as Gladwin & Fenn (w.s.) and probably Gladwin & Platts (w.s.).

He was also an active inventor, having registered six patents, four of which concerned planes. The first, imprint C, (June 9, 1857, #17541) was for an improved match plane that permitted, through the use of fences, the cutting of a tongue or a groove without having to reverse the direction of the plane. The second (February 16, 1858, #19359) was for an eccentric lever that would adjust the position of the iron. The third, imprint E,

(December 19, 1926, #185442) provided adjustable fences for his first patent, the match plane. His last plane patent (April 9, 1878, #202105) was a combination tool handle and plane and is found made of wood or metal. A, A1: ★ B: ★★★ C: ★★ D: ★ E: ★★★★

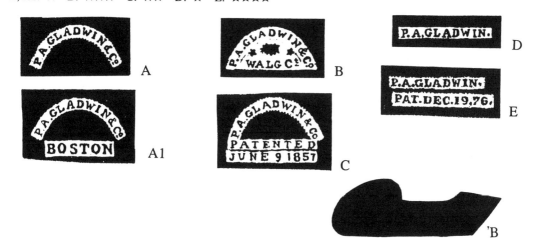

GLADWIN & APPLETON
A partnership, 1873-77, consisting of Porter A. Gladwin and Thomas L. Appleton that made planes in Chelsea, MA, but stamped them Boston, MA. (see P.A. Gladwin & Co. and also Thos. L. Appleton)   ★

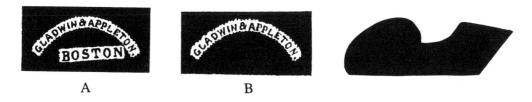

A   B

GLADWIN & FENN
Probably Porter A. Gladwin and Joel Fenn, a planemaking partnership in Wallingford, CT, ca.1850-55. (see P.A. Gladwin and also Joel Fenn & Co.)   ★★

GLADWIN & PLATTS
A Wallingford, CT, planemaker whose working dates are not known. The Gladwin is probably Porter A. Gladwin and the time period ca.1850-55. (see P.A. Gladwin and Gladwin & Fenn)   ★★

G.W. GLAESCHER
A Cincinnati, OH, hardware dealer 1859-79. (see Glaescher & Co.)

GLAESCHER & CO.
A Cincinnati, OH, hardware dealer 1879-89. (see G.W. Glaescher)

A.L. GLEASON
Albert L. Gleason worked in Watertown, NY, 1859-1909, in a variety of occupations. He was listed in the 1850 census as a toolmaker in Pamelia (a few miles north of Watertown), age 21 and born in NY. In 1860 he was shown as a partner in Gleason & Wood (w.s.) and in 1869 as a planemaker. The A.L. GLEASON in the A imprint is incuse and WATERTOWN is embossed.   A & B: ★★

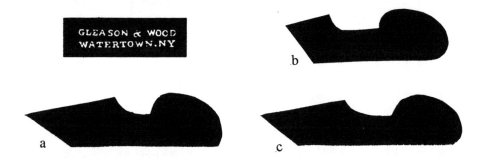

A    B

GLEASON & WOOD
Albert L. Gleason and William W. Wood were listed as manufacturers of joiners' tools in Watertown, NY, in 1860. The firm existed no longer than 1863. (see A.L. Gleason and also W.W. Wood)   ★★

a   c

I. GLEIM
Two 9¼" beech quarter rounds and a complex molding plane have been reported from two different sources. Appearance is ca.1800.

I·GLEIM

GLENN & DUKE
A tool and hardware dealer partnership listed in Philadelphia, PA., city directories 1837-40 and probably consisting of Wm. B. Glenn and Tristam Duke (see T. Duke).   ★★★★

166

GOTTFRIED GOEBBEL

A New York City planemaker 1855-57. No examples of his imprint have been reported.

GOEDEKING & NEWHOFF

This imprint appears on a boxed, 9½" beech ogee of mid-19c appearance, with the additional location imprint BELLEVILLE ILL.

GOLDSMITH - see William Goldsmith

ELI GOLDSMITH

Listed as a planemaker in the 1850 Philadelphia, PA, census, age 22, and born in PA. No examples of his work have been reported.

GEORGE GOLDSMITH

A Philadelphia, PA, planemaker, 1805-55. He was listed in the 1850 census as a planemaker, age 68, born in England. No examples of this imprint have been reported.

T. GOLDSMITH

Thomas Goldsmith was an early and prolific Philadelphia, PA, planemaker, 1801-37. In the 1850 census he was listed as a farmer, age 71, born in England, and owning realty worth $28,000. A T. Goldsmith plane has been reported overprinted R.A. PARRISH (w.s.).   A: ★★   A1: FF

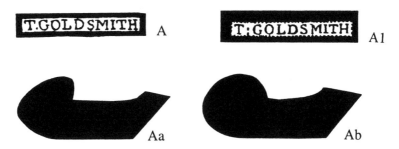

WM. GOLDSMITH

William Goldsmith was a Philadelphia, PA, planemaker, — 1837-68. The 1850 census listed him as a planemaker, age 45, owning realty worth $10,000. His son, Wm. Goldsmith Jr., age 18, was shown as a planemaker, living with his father. The 1857 city directory listing also had him making spirit levels. He was succeeded by John Veit (w.s.).   All imprints: ★   *(continued on next page)*

167

A

C

D

B

D1

J.W. GOODALE

John Willard Goodale (b. Amherst, MA, 1834 — d. 1905). His mother was Mary B. Hills, the daughter of Samuel Hills (see S. Hills). He was listed in the 1869 Amherst directory as a mechanic, in the 1873 directory as a planemaker, and in the 1879 directory as a toolmaker. The 1880 Federal census described his occupation as "Works at Plain Making (sic)." By 1889 he was listed as employed as a box maker. During several of his planemaking years he worked for William Kellogg (w.s.)   ★★★

GOODERICH, ANDREWS & CO.

The 1837 Detroit, MI, city directory listed Gooderich, Andrews & Co. as a planemaking company on Michigan Ave., making it probably the earliest of the Detroit planemakers. No examples have been reported.

E. GOOLD

Planes reported include five molding planes ranging from 9½" to 9⅞" long, all with Sleeper-type wedges; and a narrow panel raiser and a handled complex molder, both made of beech, with flat chamfers. Appearance is ca.1800 and professionally made.

Jn. GORDON

John Gordon appeared in the 1808 Philadelphia, PA, directory as a planemaker. Judging by the variety and quantity of the planes that have survived, he was apparently active over a longer period.   ★★

168

ISAAC GOSLIN

Listed as a planemaker in the 1844 St. Louis, MO, directory. No example of his imprint has been reported.

J.W. GOSNELL

A St. Louis, MO, planemaker listed in the 1847-48, 1850, and 1854 city directories. (see also J.W. Gosnell/W. Hall) ★★

J.W. GOSNELL/W. HALL

John W. Gosnell and William Hall were partners in St. Louis, MO, as planemakers, hardware and tool dealers, 1849-52—. (see J.W. Gosnell and also William Hall) ★★

F.J. GOUCH

Franklin J. Gouch was a planemaker in Worcester, MA, 1847-68. (see also J. Dow, Sanborn & Gouch, and Gouch & Demond) ★

GOUCH & DEMOND

The 1850 census listed a Daniel Demond, age 59, joiner, born in Massachusetts. The Gouch may have been Franklin J. Gouch (see F.J. Gouch), or it may possibly have been George Gouch, who in 1850 was a 28 year old carpenter in Springfield, MA. ★★★

I. GOULD

Three molding planes of early appearance have been reported: birch, 10" long, with an I. Walton (w.s) type of small rounded wedge finial. Also reported is a 12" birch jack.

L. GOVE

This name has been reported on a 9¾" beech molding plane with a Sleeper-type wedge, and on two birch, handled sash planes.

T.B. GOVE

Four examples have been reported; two are beech slide arm plows with thumbscrews. Appearance is early 19c. A Timothy Blake Gove was born in Hampton Falls, NH, in 1781 and died in 1831 in Lowell, MA, occupation unknown.

JO. GRAMLING

Johann Adam Gramling, born in Berks County, PA, in 1757, died in 1841, and fought in the American Revolutionary War.   A & B: ★★★★

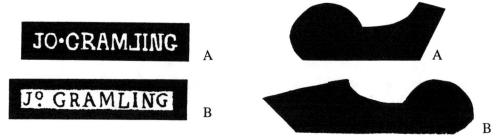

THO. GRANT

There were several Thomas Grants in 18c New York City who were variously planemakers and merchants. The imprint THO GRANT/NEW YORK is the earlier and rarer mark, and appears on planes that may have been made by Thomas Grant Jr., the joiner, and sold by his cousin Thomas Grant, the merchant and ironmonger (married 1755 - d. 1802). The varying styles of the Grant planes, plus anecdotal evidence, indicate they were the product of various makers and include examples that may have been imported from England. Thomas Jr. was probably the first New York planemaker and among the earliest American planemakers. Grant molding planes from this early period (probably —1750-60) range up to 10¼" in length, with flat chamfers up to 5/16" wide.

Thomas Grant, the ironmonger/merchant, advertised in 1770 a disposition sale of the remainder of his ironmongery and left New York City with the onset of the American Revolution, strongly suggesting that Grant planes were made prior to 1775. He lived the last part of his life in New Brunswick, NJ, a fellow church member and neighbor of Robert Eastburn (w.s.), New Jersey's first planemaker.

Also adding interest is the appearance of crowned initials on some of the Grant planes (both imprints) as well as on American-made planes of Eastburn, W. Raymond, and L. Little and on a few English planes by Cauldwell, Holbrook, I. Cogdell, and Phillipson. The B imprint illustrated below, showing the crowned initials ILV and an owner's imprint ILV tends to confirm the theory that the crowned initials were the owner/purchaser's and were applied to the planes by the ironmonger on request. In another instance supporting that theory, an I. NICHOLSON IN CUMBERLAND and two THO. GRANT planes were found together, each bearing the crowned initials "P P". In another group of seven planes that were bought together, six had crowned initials "B B" and one "I B". It's been recently discovered that two different types of crowened initials were used. The usual type appears on imprint B. The new type (so far reported only once) is shown as C. It has a distinctive "A" and reverse "P" that is different from the set used in B. A characteristic common to Grant, Eastburn, and J. Stiles (w.s.) was the use of friction fit (rather than wedge- or thumbscrew-secured) arms on some of their earlier plow planes and fenced plank match planes.

For additional information on the Grants and their period, see the monograph *Thomas Grant Ironmonger* by Daniel Semel, and the June 1982 Chronicle article on Robert Eastburn, Thomas Grant and the crowned initials. (see Bibliography) A: without crowned initials ★★ with crowned initials ★★★ B: without crowned initials ★ with crowned initials ★★ C: ★★★★★

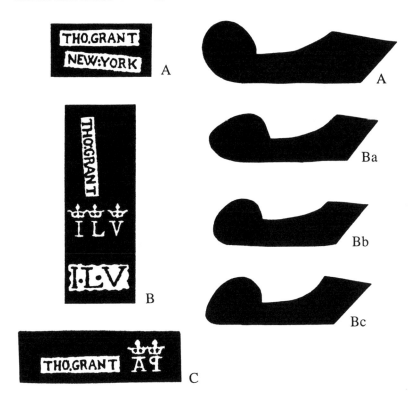

GRAY & KIRKMAN
A hardware dealer who was listed in the Nashville TN city directories from 1867-70. ★★

J. GREEN
Jacob Green made planes in New York City 1850-54. A & B: ★★

GREENFIELD TOOL CO.

Greenfield Tool was one of the major wooden plane manufacturers in 19c America. It was the successor to the Conway Tool Co. (w.s.), whose factory burned down in 1851 and whose stockholders decided to rebuild in Greenfield MA as the Greenfield Tool Co. Construction began in August 1851 and Alonzo Parker (see Parker, Hubbard & Co.) was appointed agent of the company.

In the 1850's power was supplied by a steam engine and distributed to the shop machinery by a system of overhead shafts and leather belts. The factory was two-story and comprised 10,000 sq.ft. employing 60 or 70 and producing 10,000-12,000 planes a month.

The 1860 Massachusetts Industrial census showed Greenfield Tool using 60 hp of steam, employing 30 hands with a monthly payroll of $1560 and producing $40,000 worth of carpenters' tools for the year.

In the 1870's, the company continued to decline, feeling the increased competition of metal planes, and on January 8, 1883, the company was declared insolvent with liabilities of $104,000. All imprints: FF

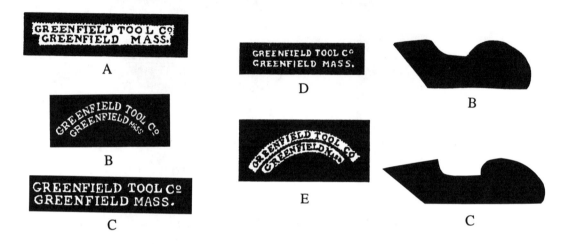

GREER & LAING

A hardware company whose name appears in the 1884, 1886, and 1887 Wheeling, WV, city directories and continued in business until 1965. (see Ott & Greer) ★★

I. GREGG

A dozen or so examples have been reported. The molding planes are 9½" long, made of beech with wide flat chamfers. Appearance is ca.1800. (see J. Gregg)

J. GREGG

This name has been reported on a 9½" beech hollow with round chamfers, single boxed. Of interest is the close stylistic resemblance of the imprint stamp to that of I. GREGG (w.s.). The J. Gregg stamp is slightly longer. Based on appearance, the J. Gregg plane would probably have been made a generation later.

J.H. GREGG

A John H. Gregg of New Boston, NH, was declared insane in 1883. An inventory taken at that time listed carpentry shop tools valued at $100, and a blacksmith shop, $50, both of which represented about one half of his estate.

M. GREGG

Mahlon Gregg, who appeared in the Rochester NY city directory from 1853-59 as a "millwright in wood and iron." An 1861 advertisement listed "cooper's, shipwright's, & carpenter's tools" produced at the race and sold at Searl's hardware store. The race was Brown's Race that served as a power source for most of the flour mills and was the second location of D.R. Barton (purchased in 1858). In the 1864-65 directory the address for the factory was the "flats," which is a lower area below the 90 ft. second falls and below D.R. Barton and the flour mills up along the race. Entries continued through at least 1870 as an edge tool maker with an interlude in 1866-67 in which "Gregg & Hamilton" was listed as a short lived partnership. An 1884 *History of Rochester* listed "Mahlon Gregg & Son [J.N. Gregg] Manufacturing cooper's tools on the flats. Foot of Falls." They employed 15-20 hands. ★★★

GREGG & HAMILTON   see M. Gregg

GREGORY   see G.W. Gregory

G.W. GREGORY

G.W. Gregory, a Binghamton, NY, hardware dealer 1850—. The A imprint is embossed.   All imprints: ★★

A

B

C

JOSEPH GRIBBLE

Listed as a planemaker in the 1850 census, living in Brownville, IN, four houses away from B. Lape (w.s.) for whom he may have worked. No example of his imprint has been reported.

GRIFFIN

A plane has been reported with the additional imprint 438 E. HOUSTON ST./N.Y.

173

GRIFFIN

Probably Orlando H. Griffin, who, in the 1850 census, was listed as a planemaker in Ravenna, OH, age 32, from NY state, and who was still listed as a planemaker in the 1860 census. At some time in his career in Ravenna he worked with Algernon S. Collins at carriage-making. In an advertisement dated Nov. 1842, O.H. Griffin announced "At the old stand of F.K. Collins & Co. [see Collins/Ravenna]. Will be kept constantly on hand or made to order every variety of planes. Good white beach (sic) timber taken in exchange for planes." The 1850 census of industry listed him as employing two men and producing 800 planes worth $800.   ★★

C.M. GRIFFITH

Listed in the 1850 census as age 35 and a merchant in Evansville, IN.

W. GRINEL

William Grinel (sometimes spelled Grinnel), was a Philadelphia, PA, planemaker 1814-19—. (see also White and Grinel)   A & B: ★★★

 A  B

GRISWOLD & DICKINSON

A Springfield, MA, planemaker, whose working dates are not known. Appearance is mid-19c.   ★★★

D.H.

More than 30 examples have been reported bearing this imprint, most from the Auburn to Skowhegan section of Maine. The initialed imprint is similar to that used by L. Sampson (w.s.). Appearance is ca.1800.

H.S. & CO.

An imprint used by Hammacher Schlemmer & Co. (w.s.).

J. HAAS

Johannes Haas of Upper Mahantongo Township, Schuylkill County, PA., who lived from 1814 till 1856. He was a well-known cabinetmaker of decorated Mahantongo furniture and also operated a smith shop and carpenter shop with his sons, David and Samuel. His account book, which has been passed down through the family, was kept in High German. It recorded that he made many things besides furniture: e.g., rakes, wheelbarrows, straw benches, cabbage cutters, complete wagon wheels, handles for chisels and shovels, planes, and harrows. A J. Haas plane described as a wedged arm plow was sold at auction in 1984. It was $10^{15}/_{16}$" long, made of applewood. It was most probably a plank match groove, since the arms were only $5\frac{1}{2}$" long overall. It had $^7/_{16}$" flat chamfers, a riveted skate and a snecked iron.

H. HAIGHT & CO.

The B imprint, which appears on a 22" fore plane, would seem to indicate that Haight was a hardware dealer.

 A

 B

HALB

Two examples have been reported, both with the owner imprint "L.L.K." Both are beech complex molders, with flat chamfers, and $9^7/_8$" long. Appearance indicates eastern PA, early 19c.

HUDSON HALE

Hale was listed in the 1850 New Haven directory as a planemaker. No example has been reported.

L.F.HALE

A 28⅜" jointer has been reported with the additional imprint E. CORINTH VT.

HALE &CO.

This name has been reported on a pair of match planes and on a screw arm plow.

A. HALL

A number of examples have been reported, including a cornice plane with an offset tote, a panel raiser, and several 9⅞"-10" molding planes with relieved wedges and flat chamfers; all beech; probably a southern New England planemaker, ca.1800.

J. HALL

Possibly John Hall, who made planes in Cincinnati, OH, ca.1840. The imprint J. Hall/St. Louis (incuse) appears on a skewed rabbet.

S.H. HALL

Two sash planes and a molder have been reported with this imprint. Appearance is early 19c.

W. HALL

William Hall was listed as a planemaker in Cincinnati, OH, 1842-44; then appeared in St. Louis, MO, directories as a planemaker in 1844, 1865 and 1866. He was also a partner in Gosnell/W. Hall and Hall & Hynson (w.s.). ★★

HALL, CASE & CO.

A Columbus, OH, planemaking firm that was started in 1847 and dissolved in 1852 after losing the contract for the use of convict labor at the Ohio Penitentiary to the newly-formed Ohio Tool Co. (w.s.), which then absorbed Hall, Case. The principals included John S. Hall (b. ca.1810 in CT), Harvey Case (b. ca.1798 in CT),

Joseph A. Montgomery (b. ca.1810 in MA - see Montgomery), and James F. Ward (b. ca.1802 in NJ). In the 1850 Products of Industry Census the company was listed as having 100 employees, using steam power, and producing 48,000 tools worth $75,000 for the year. (see Hall Stone & Co.)   All imprints: FF

HALL & HYNSON
William Hall and August Hynson were partners as hardware dealers and planemakers 1851-60 in St. Louis, MO. (see William Hall and Hynson & Coleman)   All imprints: ★

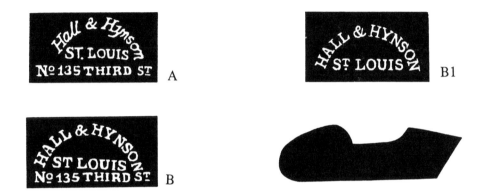

J.H. HALL/J.W. LYON
John H. Hall and Joseph W. Lyon were Cincinnati, OH, planemakers 1839-40. (see Joseph W. Lyon)

HALL STONE &CO.
This imprint may represent a partnership formed —1845 by John S. Hall and A.P. Stone, using convict labor at the Ohio Penitentiary to produce tools. (see Hall, Case & Co.)   ★★

HAMLIN

A combination tongue and groove plane has been reported, with the additional location imprint DETROIT.

A. HAMMACHER & CO.

Albert Hammacher was a hardware merchant and owned a tool store under this name in New York City 1864-84. Both imprints shown below are incuse. (see Hammacher, Schlemmer and also C. Tollner & A. Hammacher)   A: ★   B: ★★

A

B

HAMMACHER, SCHLEMMER & CO.

Albert Hammacher in partnership with William Schlemmer as hardware merchants in New York City 1885-1900. William Schlemmer worked for A. Hammacher & Co. from 1867-84 (except for 1871-72 when he had his own hardware store). In 1885 he became a partner. The successor firm still operates today in NYC. The imprints shown below are all incuse (see A. Hammacher & Co. and also H.S. & Co.)   A & B: ★   C: ★★★

A

HAMMACHER SCHLEMMER & C°
209 BOWERY, N.Y.
B

C

HAMMITT & BRO.

A probable hardware dealer.

I. HAMMOND

Isaac Hammond was a New Haven, CT, planemaker —1840- 45.   A & A1: ★

(continued next page)

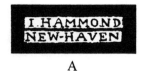
A

A1

178

 A

 A1

HANDERSON

This mark has been reported on several occasions on various planes: a dado, hollows and rounds, and a rabbet. All are 9½" long, beech, with round chamfers. Most have imprinted owners' initials that look to be made from the same set of die stamps; in the case of the rabbet E.W., the dado A.S.H., and the hollow and rounds E.B.T. in one case and J.Y.S. on another group of five (found in Lancaster County, PA). The rabbet carries a Newbould iron and one round an iron by Green. Although the planes are somewhat English in appearance, Handerson is not listed in *British Planemakers, 3rd ed.*, nor has he been reported by any English dealer or collector. The planes look to be early 19c. Two examples read I. HANDERSON, the others .HANDERSON, suggesting that the stamp was subsequently altered. The wedges remained the same.

 A

 B

G.C. HANES

This imprint was reported on a handled razeed smooth plane with a location imprint LOWELL/MASS. Appearance is mid-19c.

DAVID HANLEY

Listed as a planemaker in the 1837 and 1841 Philadelphia, PA, directories. He worked for the Whites (see Israel White), making two-arm plows, using the initials D.H.

HANEY & DEBOW

A Milwaukee, WI, hardware dealer ca.1850. An example has been reported imprinted on a plane also marked CASEY & CO/AUBURN/N.Y. (w.s.).

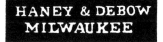

J. HANNAN

James H. Hannan manufactured planes in New York City 1849-57. During 1856-57 he also operated a tool store. He apparently made planes at one time in Middletown (probably NY state). The B imprint appears on a 3¼" long beech miniature smoother with a metal sole. Miniature planes made and imprinted by a planemaker are quite rare. A & B: ★★★ C: ★★★★

 A

J.HANNAN

B

J. HANNAN MIDDLETOWN

C

179

B. HANNIS

B. Hannis was listed in the 1803-08 Philadelphia, PA, city directories as a planemaker.   ★★★★

L.W. HAPGOOD

Lyman W. Hapgood was listed as a planemaker in the Lowell, MA, directories 1835-37.   ★★★

C. HARIMAN

Various examples of molding planes have been reported. They are 9⅞" to 10" long, beech, with flat chamfers, and a Sleeper-type wedge. Appearance is ca.1800.

A

B

H.J. HARPEL

Henry J. Harpel was listed in the 1840 and 1850 censuses, as living in Douglas, Montgomery County, PA. He was a neighbor of Frederick Dallicker Jr. (w.s.) Examples reported include two 9½" molding planes boxed with rosewood. Appearance is early 19c.

HARPER & HOUSMAN

A probable hardware dealer whose imprint has been reported on an Ohio Tool Co. match plane, among others.

HARPER & STEEL

A probable hardware dealer. (see Alex Steel)

C.E. HARRINGTON
This imprint has been reported on a G.W. Manning (w.s.) plane. A probable hardware dealer.

BENJAMIN HARRIS
Listed in the 1808 Philadelphia, PA, directory as a planemaker. No example has been reported.

N. HARRIS & CO.
A Cincinnati, Ohio, planemaker 1856-57. ★★★

S.A. HARRIS
This imprint appears on a 28" H.L. James (w.s.) jointer. Hyde Park is located in north central Vermont, about 40 miles east of Burlington. A probable mid-19c hardware dealer.

T.W. HARRIS
This imprint appears on an adjustable sash plane. Appearance is ca.1850.

W. HARRIS
We now have three separate sightings of this imprint. The two instances where we have fuller descriptions are a 9⅞" long quarter round, and a 9¹¹⁄₁₆" complex molder, both made of birch. The third example is a round and is described as early. The appearance of the first two is clearly 18c New England, possibly as early as the third quarter.

HARRIS & AMES

A New London, CT, planemaker that operated —1857-58. No example of the imprint has been reported.

HARRIS & SHEPHERD

Isaac Harris (b.1815) and Alexander Shepherd (b.1832) operated a hardware and cutlery business in Little Falls, NY, 1864-69. ★★★

J. HARRISON & CO.

John Harrison was a Zanesville, OH, planemaker who was listed in the 1856-57 city directory and again in 1860-61. In the 1850 census he was listed as 50 years old, employing one planemaker to whom he paid $40 per month, and producing $800 worth of planes. Born in New Jersey, he also appeared in the 1830 and 1840 Zanesville censuses. ★★

J.W. HARRON

John W. Harron made planes in New York City 1863-1917. (see R. Harron) The A imprint shown below is incuse; the B embossed. A: FF   B: ★★

J.W. HARRON
208 BLEECKER ST. N.Y.
A

B

A

R. HARRON

Robert Harron, who was probably the father of J.W. Harron (w.s.), made planes in New York City 1844-65. The 1850 census listed him as having three employees making 1200 planes worth $2100 annually. A & A1: FF

A

A1

N.F. HART & CO.

A Meriden, CT, planemaker —1857-58—. No example of the imprint has been reported.

J. HARTWELL

A number of examples have been reported. Probably New England, early 19c.

C. HARWOOD

Almost certainly a planemaker, his location probably southern New England, his working period ca.1800. His earlier planes have flat chamfers and a relieved wedge. The later planes have rounded chamfers and wedges with round finials. All the molding planes reported are 9⅛" long and are made of beech. ★★

.a   b

G. HASTINGS & CO.

Planes of mid-19c appearance have been reported. (see S. Hastings)

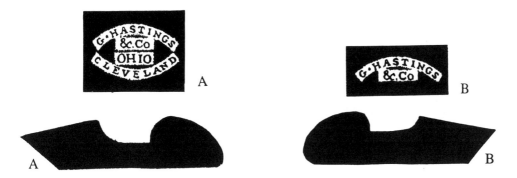

A   B

A   B

S. HASTINGS

A Samuel Hastings is listed in the 1850 Federal census as a 34 year old toolmaker in Amherst, MA. He was listed in 1840 as living in Amherst and "in manufacturing." There is also a listing of an S. HASTINGS of Mason, OH, as a plane manufacturer in the 1853-54 Ohio business directory. No example of the Ohio Hastings has been reported. (see G. Hastings & Co.) ★★

A. HATHAWAY

A number of examples by this maker are known. Planes are made of birch. The molding planes are 9" long and maple is used for the boxing. Appearance is ca.1800. There is some indication of a relationship with the planemaker Jn. Tower (b.1755) of Rutland, MA. ★★

P.C. HATHAWAY

A number of examples have been reported. Appearance is early 19c. Probably a planemaker. ★★

ALBERT S. HAVEN

A Boston, MA, hardware dealer who appeared in the city directories 1858-83. ★★

C. HAWES

A grooving plane has been reported with the additional imprint N.Y.

G. HAWES

The imprint illustrated below is on a molding plane, 9¾" long, made of birch, with round chamfers, fluting on the toe and heel, with a relieved wedge and chamfered wedge slot. Several other examples have been reported, also made of birch, between 9⅞" and 10" long, all with the Wrentham imprint. ★★★★★

HAYDEN

Joseph T. Hayden, a Syracuse, NY, planemaker —1850-51. (see Hayden & Nolton and E.T. Hayden; also see W.H. Blye) A: ★ B ★★★

A

B

E.T. HAYDEN

The location die stamp "Syracuse N.Y." seems to be the same as used by HAYDEN and also HAYDEN & NOLTON (both w.s.).

P. HAYDEN & CO.

Peter Hayden was a planemaker in Columbus, OH, who began to employ prison labor to produce carpenter, joiner and cabinet tools in 1842. The firm continued at least until 1851, when it became the Ohio Tool Co. (w.s.). Hayden was subsequently a director of the Ohio Tool Co. and instrumental in getting it the Ohio Penitentiary convict labor contract in 1851. (see Hall, Case & Co.) All imprints: ★★ *(see next page)*

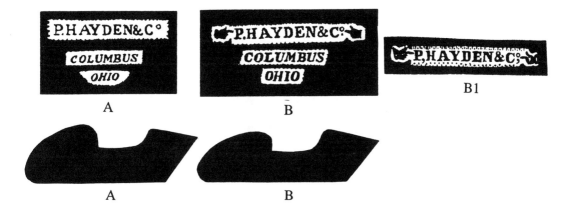

A   B   B1

A   B

HAYDEN & NOLTON

A Syracuse, NY, partnership of Joseph T. Hayden (see Hayden) and Lyman Nolton (w.s.) that operated as a tool and hardware store ca.1850 and probably sold planes made by the two partners.   ★★★

HAINES & SMITH

Haines & Smith/Portland was reported on a handled 9½" long beech smoothing plane.

A. HAYWARD

A number of examples have been reported. The molding planes are 9⅜" - 9½" long, most beech, with both round and flat chamfers. Appearance is ca.1800. Probable location, New England.

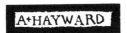   

HAYWOOD, CARTLEDGE & HONORE

This imprint has been reported on bench planes. Appearance is mid-19c.

R. HAZARD

This imprint has been reported on a 9⁷⁄₁₆" long beech hollow with round chamfers.

HAZLET

Hugh Hazlet, a Philadelphia, PA, planemaker who appeared in the 1817 city directory, and who worked at the same address that Tho. Napier (w.s.) had used. ★★★

  a  b

ADDISON HEALD

A prominent NH planemaker, cabinetmaker, and a Congregationalist minister (1817-1895). Starting around 1856, he made planes in Nashua, NH, and then as Warren & Heald (w.s.). In 1868 he moved to Milford, NH, where he set up a plane shop under his own name in the steam-powered furniture factory of his brother, David. In 1873 he was joined in a partnership by his son Daniel Milton Heald (1852-1929, see A. Heald & Son), specializing in bench planes and coopers' tools and a variety of other woodworking items. Planemaking continued after Addison Heald's death until 1906. Some of the bench planes incorporate the plane iron cap patented by Daniel Heald (No. 209969, Nov. 19, 1878). Earlier, some wedges utilized an unpatented screwing device at the top of the wedge that caused the toe of the wedge to press the plane iron against the plane bed and secure it. This device is unique to Heald planes and is thought to be a precursor of the patented iron cap.
A & A1: ★★   B: ★

 A  A1  B

A. HEALD & SON

A planemaking partnership of Addison Heald and his son Daniel Milton Heald in Milford, NH, 1873-1906, which continued under the same name after the death of Addison Heald in 1895. Daniel Milton Heald received a patent (No. 209969, Nov. 19, 1878) for a device that held the plane iron and permitted it to be adjusted for proper depth of cut by turning a screw. (see Addison Heald, and Warren & Heald)   ★★

H. HEALY

Five planes have been reported, including two grooving planes and two hollows. All are 10" to 10⅜" long, birch, with a relieved wedge and some fluting. Appearance is late 18c, southern New England. Possibly Harmon Healy (d.1800), a cabinetmaker in Beverly, MA.

HEATHER & WELLMAN

A Cincinnati, OH, hardware dealer 1871-78. ★★

HEGNY & BOLLERMANN
Probably a New York City hardware dealer ca.1870, whose imprint has appeared on G.W. Denison & Co. and Shiverick (both w.s.) planes.   ★★

HEIM & SMITH
Thomas Heim and Charles J. Smith, who were Cincinnati, OH, hardware and edge tool dealers 1849-50. (see C.J. Smith & Co. and J.&C. Smith; and D.N. Garrison/ T.A. Heim)

CH HEINIKE
CH HEINIKE planes have been found in eastern PA, both with and without English planemaker imprints, raising the question whether he was both a dealer and a maker. The English makers include Blizard (1800-28), I. Cox (1770-1843), and Wm. Moss (1775-1843). Planes with the CH Heinike imprint only are reported to be 9¾" long.

D. HEIS   see D. Heiss

D. HEISS
1745-1819. Dietrich Heiss (also spelled Heis) was a Lancaster, PA, joiner, carpenter and planemaker. His working years were spent mostly in Lancaster, except for the period ca.1782-85 when he worked in Philadelphia. He was the father of John and Jacob Heiss (both w.s.). A is the earlier imprint.   A: ★★★   B: ★★

 A    B
B

IACOB HEISS
Jacob Heiss (b. ca.1780; d. 1841), the son of D. Heiss and brother of Iohn Heiss (both w.s.), was listed as a planemaker 1807-40 in Lancaster, PA, but probably made planes earlier.   ★★

IOHN HEIS
1770-ca.1825. John Heiss, the son of Dietrich Heiss (see D. Heiss) and brother of Iacob Heiss (w.s.), worked as a joiner, carpenter, and painter in Lancaster, PA, 1792-1825.   ★★★★   *(see next page)*

J. HEISSER

Jacob Heisser ran a hardware store at 481 8th Ave., NYC, from 1851-70 and at 511 8th Ave. from 1870-77. Heisser died ca.1876 and was succeeded by his son, Wm. H. Heisser. It's interesting to note that Wm. Ward was operating at 513 8th Ave. during part of this period. (see W.J.C. Ward) ★★

R.W. HENDRICKSON

Richard W. Hendrickson made planes and ran a tool shop in New York City 1859-67 at 65½ Bowery, an address he shared with A.G. Moore (w.s.) during 1859-61. Hendrickson subsequently moved to Brooklyn and made planes there 1869-70. A: ★★ B: ★★★★

A

B

HENDRIK see Co. Hendrik

CO. HENDRIK

A number of examples have been reported, indicating a planemaker. Molding planes are between 9½" and 9⅝" long, are of beech, and appear to have been made ca.1800. A Cornelius Hendrik appeared in the 1790 census in Canajahorie, NY, located on the Mohawk River west of Albany, an appropriate place for someone with a Dutch name. The 1800 census listed a Cornelius Hendricks in NYC and the 1810 census listed two by that name in Ontario County, south of Rochester. A: ★★★ B: ★★★★

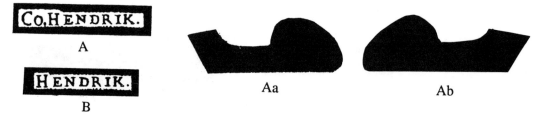

A

B

Aa   Ab

WM. HENRY JR.

Probably a hardware dealer. His imprint appears on a combination tongue and groove made by Hall Case & Co. of Columbus, OH (w.s.).

G. HERDER

Gustavus Herder was a Cincinnati, OH, hardware dealer 1839-66. ★★ *(see next page)*

HERMAN & MOHR

This imprint has been reported on a 9½" beech bead and on an open-tote 13¾" ogee. There is a Muncy in Lycoming County, PA, which was founded in 1827. Appearance is ca.1850. ★★★

J. HERRICK

John Herrick, of Burlington, VT, appeared in the 1842-44 city directory as a planemaker and was listed in the 1850 census as a house joiner, age 56, born in MA. He also used a smaller version of the imprint shown. ★★★

J.L. HERSEY

Joel Hersey appeared in the Portland city directories as a joiner 1834-49. Several molding planes have been reported, all 9½" long and beech.

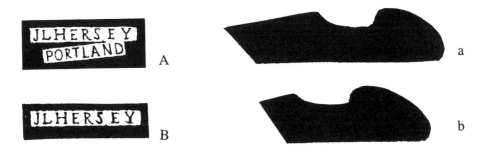

HIBBARD, SPENCER, BARTLETT & CO.

A major Chicago, IL, hardware company that private-branded planes made for them by Sandusky Tool Co. (w.s.) under the brand name A.C. BARTLETT'S OHIO PLANES (w.s.). The company began in 1883 as a successor to Hibbard, Spencer & Co. with William G. Hibbard, president, Franklin F. Spencer, vice president, and A.C. Bartlett, secretary, and continued operations into the 1920's. (see Tuttle, Hibbard & Co.)

W. O. HICKOK

This imprint was found on a bookbinder's plow. The W.O. HICKOK M'F'G. CO. is listed in the 1890 Harrisburg, PA, directory as a manufacturer of bookbinder's machinery, sash weights, cellar grates, and steam and gas fittings at its new factory, THE EAGLE WORKS, "with electricity as motive power and light."

(see next page)

A.G. HICKS

Andrew G. Hicks appeared as a plane manufacturer in the 1857, 1859-61, and 1864-65 Cleveland, OH, city directories. (see Higley & Hicks and also Asa Hicks)   All imprints: ★★

A

B

C

ASA HICKS

Listed in the 1850 census as a planemaker in Brooklyn, OH (on the outskirts of Cleveland), age 40, born in Michigan, but living in Ohio at least since 1838. (see A.G. Hicks)

A. HIDE

Examples have been reported, including a plow plane, a rabbet, a round, and several molding planes. All are made of birch. Two examples have been reported with the additional IN NORWICH imprint, one a 10" ovolo with astragal. A. Hide is possibly Asa Hide who was born in 1741 and died 1797. He lived in Norwich, CT, until 1780. The Hide family was one of the founders of Norwich and there are seven male Hides with first initial "A" in Asa Hide's generation. The appearance of the planes is mid- to late- 18c, making A. Hide possibly the earliest Connecticut planemaker.   A: ★★★★★   B: ★★★★★

A

B

M.E. HIGLEY

Believed to be Martin Higley (who was also a partner in Higley & Hicks, w.s.) of Ohio City, which was incorporated in 1836 became part of Cleveland in 1854, indicating a working period—1854—.   A & B: ★★★

A

B

HIGLEY & HICKS

Martin Higley and Andrew G. Hicks made planes ca.1850. Ohio City was incorporated in 1836 and became part of Cleveland, Ohio, in 1854. (see A.G. Hicks, Asa Hicks, and M.E. Higley)

A. HILL

Hill planes fall into two categories. Some dozen or so examples have the A. Hill imprint and appear on Jo. Fuller complex molders (D2 imprint). Another dozen or so examples have only a double or single A. HILL imprint. Most of these are dated "1828", are 10" long with ¼" flat chamfers. The majority are made of cherry, a few of birch.

I+HILL

John Hill was a Portsmouth, NH, joiner. A plane that is dated 1792 and bears the location PORTSMOUTH has been reported.

J. HILL   see John Hill's Tool Store

JOHN HILL'S TOOL STORE

John Hill opened his tool store in New York City in 1813. The "397 Broadway" imprint was used 1825-51 and the "390 Broadway" imprints 1852-61. John Hill imprints have been reported on planes made by Bensen & Crannell and Greenfield Tool Co. (both w.s.).   A: ★★   B, C & D: ★★★

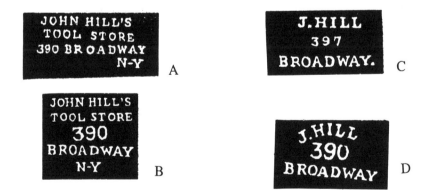

L. & C. HILL
An example with the additional imprint QUINCY ILL has been reported.

HILL, SWINSELLE
A Springfield, MA, planemaker, whose working dates are unknown.

H. HILLS

Hervey Hills was a manufacturer of joiners' planes "wholesale and retail" who worked in Springfield, MA, —1845-51—. (see S. & H. Hills and Hills & Wolcott)   FF

S. HILLS

Believed to be Samuel Hills of Springfield, MA, ca.1850. (see S. & H. Hills and H. Hills)   ★

S. & H. HILLS

Samuel and Hervey Hills were planemakers who succeeded Hills & Wolcott in Amherst, MA, in 1829 and continued until 1830. They also apparently operated in Springfield, as indicated by the imprints used. (see Hills & Wolcott, H. Hills, and S. Hills)   A & B: ★★   C: ★★★   D: ★★

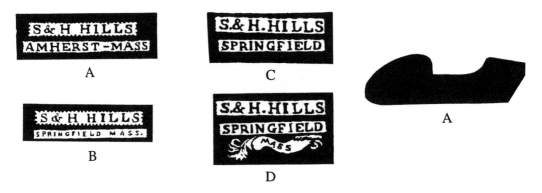

HILLS & RICHARDS

A Norwich, MA, planemaker whose working dates are not known.   ★

HILLS & WINSHIP

A Springfield, MA, planemaker —1832— that included William Winship who earlier (1826-32) had worked for H. Chapin (w.s.).   ★

192

HILLS & WOLCOTT

A partnership of Hervey Hills and perhaps Gideon Wolcott (a Connecticut planemaker who earlier, in 1828, had worked with Leonard Kennedy in Utica, NY). Hills & Wolcott made planes for one year, 1829, in Amherst, MA. (see S. & H. Hills, G. Wolcott, and Kennedy) ★

HENRY HISER

Listed as a planemaker in the 1859-60 Wooster, OH, directory. No example has been reported.

E. HOADLEY

A New Haven, CT, planemaker; possibly Erastus Hoadley (1781-1831) who came to New Haven ca.1809 and was a joiner. ★★★

R. HOE

R. Hoe was a major producer of printing presses. This imprint appears on what its owner describes as a "handled steel clad (on three sides) wood plane that could be a printer's block shoot plane."

R. HOEY

Robert Hoey made planes in New York City 1834-36. (see Hoey & Taber) ★

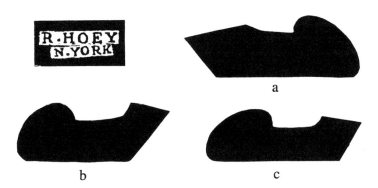

a

b   c

HOEY & TABER

A partnership of Robert Hoey and probably Wing H. Taber (w.s.), that made planes in New York City 1836-40. (see R. Hoey)   A & B: ★★   *(see next page)*

 A  B

W. HOFFMANN

William F. Hoffmann made planes in New York City 1856-87, his beginning year coinciding with Marley's (w.s.) last year (1820-56). Marley's last address was 360 Broome St., which is where Hoffman opened his business. The overprinted imprint B would seem to confirm that Hoffmann succeeded Marley.

A: ★   B: ★★★

 A  B

H. & J. HOGHENHULL

This name was reported on a 16" long gutter plane. Jacksonville is located about 30 miles west of Springfield.

HOLCOMB & SLENTZ

Planemaker in East Dayton, OH, whose working dates are not known.

C.W. HOLDEN

Charles W. Holden was a Norwich, CT, planemaker —1850-75—, who was listed in the 1850 census as age 33, born in CT, and owning real estate worth $2000.   ★

C.W. HOLDER & CO.

Charles W. Holder was a Bloomington, IL, hardware dealer —1855-56—.   ★★★

THOMAS HOLLIDAY & CO.

A Cincinnati, Ohio, hardware dealer ca.1860.   ★★

HOLLIDAY & SMITH

A Cincinnati, Ohio, hardware dealer ca.1870.

I.P. HOLMES

A Berwick, ME, planemaker whose working dates are unknown. Appearance is ca.1850.   ★★★

J. HOLMES

Examples reported are made of yellow birch or cherry, all 9⅜" to 9½" long, with wide flat chamfers. Several have irons with a blacksmith touch mark SS. Appearance is ca.1800.

HOLYOAKE-LOWNES & CO.

A Memphis, TN, hardware company 1851-54. It was one of the predecessors of what was to become ORGILL BROS & CO. in 1857. From 1854-57 the firm name was LOWNES, BEEKMAN & CO.

HOMER, BISHOP & CO.

A Boston, MA, hardware dealer that was succeeded in 1873 by Macomber, Bigelow & Dowse (w.s.). One example reported shows this imprint on a plane made by the Taber Plane Co. (w.s.).   ★

W.C. HOPPER'S PATENT

A patent received by William C. Hopper, Pittsburgh, PA, on January 16, 1855 (No. 12,234), that provided an iron mouth piece in the sole which could be adjusted closer to the mouth (in bench planes) as the stock was worn. One imprint used was crescent-shaped and read "Wm. C. Hopper's patent/Jan. 16 1855"; the other was a three line imprint "Wm. C. Hopper's/ Patent/1855". Hopper was listed in the 1850 census and in Pittsburgh business directories of the 1850's and 60's as a cabinetmaker and in 1874 as a lumber merchant.

195

BENJ. F. HORN
Several examples, including a coopers' sun plane and a croze, have been reported. There is an additional location imprint E. ST. LOUIS, ILL, and in one instance EST. 1861.

HORNOR & SON
A Philadelphia hardware dealer whose imprint appears on planes made by H. CHAPIN/EAGLE FACTORY, H. CHAPIN/UNION FACTORY, HILLS & WINSHIP, and FOX & WASHBURN (all w.s.). Joseph P. Horner, at 47 Market Street, Philadelphia (the same address as Hornor & Son), was listed as a customer of H. Chapin (w.s.) in 1836. ★★

J.W. HORTON & CO.
A Nashville, TN, hardware dealer who was listed in the 1859 city directory. The imprint has been reported on an Ohio Tool Co. (w.s.) rabbet.

HORTON & CRANE
A Buffalo, NY, hardware dealer. ★★

B.S. HOWE
Probably a hardware dealer. This imprint appears on a boxed bead made by J.A. McCELLUS (w.s.) who we believe was located in north central NY state. The Otsego location would tend to support that supposition.

W. HOWE
Four examples of this imprint have been reported, including a 9½" long hollow and round made of birch. Appearance is ca.1800.

ALFRED HOWES
This name has been reported on a jack plane and a jointer with the location imprint WATERTOWN/MASS. Appearance is ca.1850.

I. HOWES
This imprint has been reported on four molding planes of 18c appearance, and has also appeared on a Cesar Chelor (w.s.) complex molder as an apparent owner.

A. HOWLAND

Abraham Howland (1810-1892) lived in Kellogsville and nearby Moravia (Cayuga County, NY). He was listed in the 1850 census as a cabinetmaker, in 1855 as a toolmaker, and in 1865 as an undertaker. He may have had some business relationship with J. Sawyer (w.s.), as their planes resemble each other's, and the Moravia, NY, stamp that each used seems to be identical.   A & B: ★★★

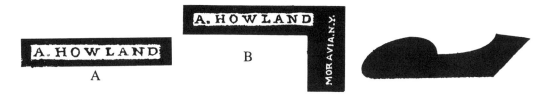

A. HOWLAND & CO.

Augustus Howland (b.1811) a bank president, along with Nelson and C.P. Fitch, Edward Myderse, and C.N. Tuttle, held a contract for convict labor used in making planes at Auburn State Prison 1869-74, having taken the contract away from Auburn Tool Co. (w.s.). Testimony of A. Howland & Co. before the NY State Commission on Prison Labor in 1870 revealed that it employed 100 prisoners @$73\frac{1}{8}$ cents per day; that the hardware trade did not consider prison work quality equal to that on the outside; that most of its production was sold to wholesalers in the west, some to the southern states, Texas, and California; that the total commercial value of the year's production was about $80,000; and that each prisoner made a part of a plane, none the whole.
A, A1, & A2: FF   B: ★★★   B1: ★★

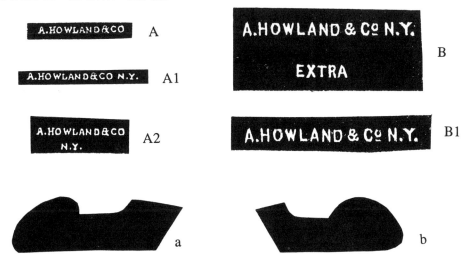

W.S. HOWLAND

Warren S. Howland was an Amherst, MA, planemaker —1852- 60, who was listed in the 1850 Amherst census as a joiner, age 50, and born in MA.   ★

D. HUBBARD

Daniel Hubbard (1778-1866) of Royalston, MA, was a housewright and carpenter. The majority of the 20 or so examples reported are bench planes, one of which was signed on the back of the wedge in pencil "Made by D. Hubbard Royalston Mass. 1834 for C. Bacon." ★★★

HUBBELL & LUNNAGAN

Benjamin Hubbell and John Lunnagan were listed as planemakers at 292 Division Street in the 1842-43 NYC directory. (see John Lunnagan) ★★★

A. HUBER

Several examples of this imprint have been reported, one a 10" molder with flat chamfers, another a handled cove with ⅜" wide flat chamfers. Probably ca.1800, eastern PA.

G. HUBER

This name has been reported on a 10" side bead with four lignum boxing inserts.

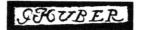

J.H. HUEPEL & CO.

A Cincinnati, OH, hardware dealer. The imprint has appeared on an Ohio Tool Co. hollow.

B. HUFF

Benjamin Huff was a Baltimore, MD, planemaker (and sign painter) —1849-51—. ★★

J. HUGHES

John Hughes was listed as a carpenter in the 1850 census, age 65, living in Wayne Twp., Wayne City, IN. This example of his imprint was reported on a beech smoother with a RICHMOND/IA location stamp.

J. HUGHES/H.M. PARK

Both of these Richmond, IN, planemakers' names appear on a 12¼" long handled plow plane. At this time we don't know whether this was a partnership , whether J. Hughes succeeded H.M. Park, or whether Hughes bought out some or all of Park's stock. (see H.M. Park)

WILLIAM P. HUGHES

William P. Hughes was a partner in the planemaking firm of Swetman & Hughes (w.s.) —1819— and never appeared in any listing as an independent planemaker.

HULINGS

Americus Hulings was a Cincinnati, OH, planemaker and tool store operator 1843-60—, who was listed in the 1848 Louisville city directory as a planemaker at Woodruff & McBrides (w.s.), and in the 1850 census as a planemaker, age 29, born in Ohio, and again in the 1860 census as a planemaker. (see Hulings & Kemper)   ★★

HULINGS & KEMPER

Americus Hulings and Samuel Kemper, who were plane manufacturers in Cincinnati, OH, in 1842. (see Hulings and also Samuel Kemper)

W. HULL

William Hull was a Boston, MA, planemaker who made under this imprint 1847-48. (see also Hull & Montgomery)   ★★

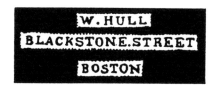

199

HULL & MONTGOMERY
William Hull and Joseph A. Montgomery, who made planes in Boston, MA, 1845-46. (see W. Hull and also Montgomery) ★★★

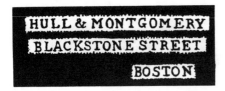 

D. HUNT
Several examples have been reported, including a jack, two panel raisers, and a 9¹³⁄₁₆" long round. Appearance is ca.1800, possible location Pennsylvania.

E. HUNT
Two planes have been reported. Appearance is ca.1850.

HOSEA HUNT
The 1860 census lists Hosea Hunt as a Huntington, MA, planemaker, age 31, and born in MA.

LEWIS HUNT
Several planes have been reported, including a plow with the imprint HUNT/CHARLESTOWN. A bead has been reported with a Spear & Wood (w.s.) imprint and an additional location stamp CHELSEA. Below is is the LEWIS HUNT/CHARLESTOWN/MASS. imprint. Both Charlestown and Chelsea are part of the Boston environs.

S.C. HUNT
Sheridan C. Hunt was listed in the 1864-65, 1868, and 1869 St. Louis, MO, directories as a plane manufacturer. Hunt was also a hardware dealer 1863-71. No example of his imprint has been reported. (see also Hunt & Wiseman)

W.J. HUNT
This imprint has been reported on a rabbet. The location stamp RACINE is probably Racine, Wisconsin.

HUNT & WISEMAN

Sheridan C. Hunt and James R. Wiseman were manufacturers of planes and wholesale and retail dealers in hardware and tools in St. Louis, MO, 1850-60. (see S.C. Hunt)   FF

HUNTINGTON

Possibly Sylvanus Huntington, who was listed as a 50 year old carpenter in Oswego, NY, in the 1850 census.

   A      A1

J. HUSSEY

John Hussey (b.1844 in Ireland; d.1877), a planemaker in Cummington, MA, ca.1870. (also see J.M. Taber)
★★

HUSSEY, BODMAN & CO.

Made planes in Norton, MA; working dates unknown.

HYNSON

Augustus R. Hynson was a St. Louis, MO, hardware dealer 1861-63. (see Hall & Hynson and Hynson & Coleman)

HYNSON & COLEMAN (or Colmann)

Augustus R. Hynson and ? Coleman were hardware dealers and plane manufacturers in St. Louis, Mo, 1864-73. No example of the imprint has been reported. (see Hynson)

HYNSON & GORMLY

A rosewood plow plane with a boxwood fence and arms has been reported with this imprint, incuse and stamped upside down on the toe of the plane. (see Hynson)

HYNSON TOOL & SUPPLY CO.

A St. Louis, MO, hardware dealer 1899-1920 that handled coopers' tools. This imprint was reported on a Sandusky Tool Co. (w.s.) applewood sun plane. (see Hynson)

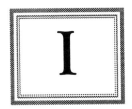

INGLIS   see A. Inglis

A. INGLIS
   Archibald Inglis (also spelled INGLISS and ENGLIS) made planes in Delhi, NY, 1850-76. He was listed in the 1850 census as a planemaker, age 40, born in England. The C imprint shown below is incuse.
A: ★★★★   B: ★★   C: ★★★★   D: ★★★★

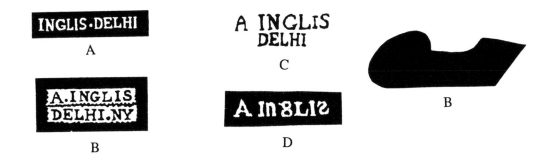

I. IONES   Listed under the J's.

R. IONSON   Listed under the J's

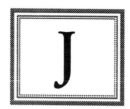

J

G. JAMAIN

The example reported was a 10¼" complex molder with an applewood body and birch wedge, and wide flat chamfers. A Gerrit Jamain was born in NYC in 1728.

C.B. JAMES & CO.

A probable hardware dealer; appearance ca.1850- 60. The B imprint appears on an Auburn Tool Co. (w.s.) hollow.   A & B: ★★

A

B

H.L. JAMES/EAST ORANGE

This imprint has been reported on both the toe and heel of a DeFOREST/BIRMINGHAM 9½" tongue plane. There was also an owner imprint, I.W. Smith.

H.L. JAMES/WILLIAMSBURGH

Henry L. James was a plane manufacturer in Williamsburg, MA, —1855-1870—. His shop was burned out some time before 1879. He was listed in the 1850 census as a merchant, age 31, with real estate worth $15,000. The 1860 Massachusetts Industrial Census listed him as a tool manufacturer, employing 11 hands, utilizing water power and producing 5000 planes. In the 1870 census he was shown as a manufacturer with real estate worth $50,000; in the 1880 census he was a woolen manufacturer. The WMSBURG/MASS location stamp on the B imprint also appears on an EAGLE MNG. CO. (w.s.) panel raiser, suggesting a relationship between the two. A & B: FF

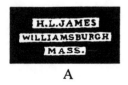
A

B

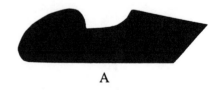
A

HENRY A. JAMES

Made planes in New York City in 1851 only. No example of his imprint has been reported.

JAMES MFG. CO.

Made planes in Williamsburg, MA; the working dates are not known but probably were ca. 1850.   ★

C.E. JENNINGS & CO.

This imprint has been reported on a smooth plane. The iron is also imprinted C.E. Jennings & Co. C.E. Jennings manufactured a variety of tools, including bits, augers, draw knives, chisels, and saws under its name, with an arrowhead trademark. Its 175-page 1913 catalog was reprinted in 1985 by the Mid-West Tool Collectors Assn. Interestingly, it did not include any planes. The firm traced its beginnings back to 1818.

C. JENSEN

Conrad Jensen of Boston, MA, received patent no. 126707 dated May 14, 1872, in which Jensen claimed that his plane combined in a single tool a tenon-cutter, a dado, a filletster, and two rabbets of different widths, using only two irons that didn't need to be changed in performing the various operations. Examples are known with both beech and rosewood bodies. J.H. Lamb (w.s.) was the probable manufacturer of the Jensen patent.

J:JEWET

A Yankee plow plane with a Sleeper-type wedge has been reported. It is made of beech, the skate is riveted, and the arms are mortised into the fence. I. Sleeper (w.s.) made planes in the Newburyport area during this period. A "James Jewet" was a prominent Newburyport, MA, merchant, whose estate was inventoried at 13,000 pounds sterling. (It included 50,000 nails!) He died in 1792.

J.C. JEWETT

A number of planes have been reported, including a jack, a bead, a hollow, a sash plane and a side rabbet. The planes show an additional location imprint WATERVILLE. A "John C. Jewett" is listed in the 1830 census for Waterville, ME.

G. JOHN

Several molding planes have been reported with this imprint. They are 10" long, made of beech, have $5/16$" flat chamfers and blacksmith-made irons. Possibly Pennsylvania.

D.D. JOHNSON

Probably a hardware dealer in Vincennes, IN, ca.1850.

J. JOHNSON

Several examples have been reported. Appearance is second quarter 19c.

 A    B

W. E. JOHNSON   see W.E. Johnson & Co.

W.E. JOHNSON & CO.

A planemaker in Goshen, MA, ca.1855, at which time he was reported employing six hands. A William Johnson was listed in the 1850 census as a 20 year old planemaker living with Wm. Webb (see W. Webb); and in the 1860 census as a master planemaker in Pittsfield, MA.

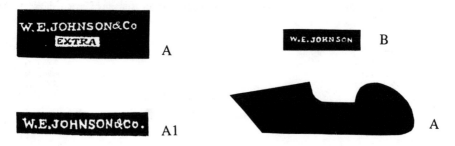

E:IONES

E. Jones has been reported a number of times. The molding planes have been $9\frac{3}{8}$" and $9\frac{1}{2}$" long, made of beech with flat chamfers. Probable location, New England ca.1800.

I. JONES/ALBANY

Isaac Jones (d.1921) was an Albany, NY, planemaker who was self-employed 1891-95, and earlier 1857-91 probably worked for others.   A & B: ★★★

 A   B

I. IONES/MEDWAY and HOLLISTON

Jethro Jones (1733-1828), like his contemporary Cesar Chelor (w.s.) with whom he may have been associated, was an early black planemaker —1764-67—. He appeared in Holliston, MA, records in 1771, and from 1777-83 served in the Continental Army (he had also served during the French and Indian Wars). He moved in 1790 to Blanford, MA, where he spent the remainder of his life. It's not known whether the Medway (A) imprint preceded or succeeded the Holliston (B) imprint. In any event, both imprints are extremely rare, indicating that Jones's output, at least under his own name, was much less than that of Cesar Chelor.   A & B: ★★★★

 A    B

J.F. JONES

John F. Jones was a Philadelphia, PA, planemaker 1825-35. No example of his imprint has been reported.

J.T. JONES

John T. Jones was a Philadelphia, PA, planemaker, 1831-46.   A, B, B1 & B2: ★   C, D, & E: ★★
E1, F, & G: ★★★   *(continued next page)*

A

B1

B

B2

C

J.T.JONES
St JOHN S^{t}
PHILADA

D

207

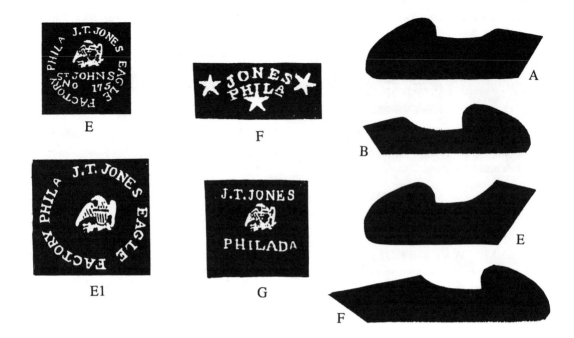

R.L. JONES

A raising plane has been reported, with a location imprint, WILLIAMSBURG, MASS.

S.E. JONES

Samuel E. Jones placed this advertisement in *The Northern Sentinel and Lansingburgh Advertiser* on July 2, 1787 (Lansingburgh is now part of Troy, NY): "Samuel E. Jones, Joiner & Tool-Maker, Takes this method to inform the public, that he carries on his business at the corner of Queen-St. opposite Mr. Thomson's tavern, where gentlemen may surply (sic) themselves with Joiners Tools of all sorts, of the best kinds, as cheap as those imported from Europe. Cash or Country Produce will be received."

The S.E. Jones wedge style and imprint resembles that of C. Allen of Lansingburgh (w.s.) who may have apprenticed or worked for Jones. One of Jones' planes is in the Farmers Museum at Cooperstown. ★★★

T. JONES

A number of examples have been reported. including one group of 14 found in New Hampshire (A imprint), eight of which were single sash coping planes of different varieties. All were 9½" long, beech, nearly all had round chamfers. An owner's name appears on 10 of the planes. Several other examples, also 9½" long, are made of birch, also with round chamfers and a relieved wedge (B imprint).

A   B

WALTER F. JONES & CO.

This imprint has been reported on a side bead.

R. IONSON

R. Jonson was most probably a late 18c and early 19c planemaker. A number of examples have been reported: the molding planes are beech, ranging in length from 9¼" to 10". An ovolo is boxed with lignum, a rounding plane is made of rosewood, another molding plane is made of an exotic wood, and a plow plane is reported with ebony inserts dovetailed in the arms to prevent wear from the thumb screws. He double-stamped his name when there was room. Most examples have been found in the lower VT-NH section of the Connecticut Valley, although the use of tropical wood also suggests the southern New England seacoast. A: ★★ B: ★★★ C: ★★

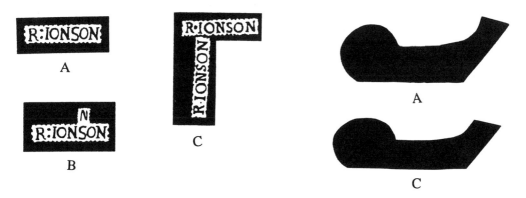

J.T. JORDAN

This name has been reported on a rosewood razeed fore plane and on a jack, with the additional imprint "MAKER". Both examples were reported from California.

JORDAN HARDWARE CORP.

This name appears incised on a Joh. Weiss & Sohn (Austria) horned smoothing plane with a Chapin-Stephens iron. The imprint appears on the top of the plane, between the mouth and the horn, and reads JOH. WEISS & SOHN WIEN (with eagle and bitstock emblem)/SOLE AGENT/JORDAN HARDWARE CORP/NEW YORK U.S.A. - AUSTRIA.

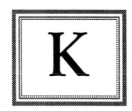

K

K. & C.   see Kennedy & Collins

C. KALTENBACH
Reported on a 28" jointer with a D.R. Barton iron. Probably a hardware dealer.

H.A. KAMMERER
An imprint H.A. KAMMERER INC/MT. VERNON N.Y. appears incised on the nose of a 9½" long, narrow round, possibly modified from a rabbet. Also incised on the side is NO. 10 PEERLESS/JORDAN/H.A. KAMMERER INC/MT. VERNON N.Y. Jordan Hardware (w.s.) of New York was the American agent for Joh. Weiss & Sohn of Vienna, Austria.

I. KAMP
Several examples of this stamp have been reported. Probable location is eastern Pennsylvania; working period ca.1800.

KANE MFG CO.
This imprint appears on the nose of a Sandusky Tool Co. (w.s.) weather strip plane.

A. KASSON
This imprint was reported on a 4" wide, 16¼" long, cornice plane.

JULIUS KATZ

Julius Katz was a cabinetmaker in Cincinnati, OH —1868-72—, who patented "An Improvement in Plane-Stock" (Pat. No. 102,406, April 26, 1870). His improved facing device for the sole of a plane consisted of "strips of bone, ivory, or similar hard organic substance glued together in two pieces or slabs."

JOHN C. KEEN

Listed in the 1799 and 1800 Philadelphia, PA, directories as a planemaker.

R. KEEN

Reuben (or Rubin) Keen who was listed in the 1814 Philadelphia, PA, directory as a planemaker. Some of his planes bear a FRANKFORD location stamp. Frankford, formerly just outside of Philadelphia, is now part of the city. Both imprints: ★★★★

A   B

KEEN KUTTER

A trademark of The Simmons Hardware Co., a major St. Louis, MO, hardware merchant. The trademark first came into use around 1870 and appeared on various hardware products well into the 20th c. (also see Shapleigh & Co.)

A   B

I. KEIM

There have been three different reports on this late 18th or early 19th century-looking, Pennsylvania Dutch-sounding, possible planemaker: a $9\frac{9}{32}$" long washboard plane with $\frac{1}{4}$" wide flat chamfers and a Newbould iron, a $9\frac{3}{8}$" long beech side bead with $\frac{5}{16}$" wide flat chamfers, and a $9\frac{3}{8}$" long molding plane.

W. & J.H. KEIM

An E.W. Carpenter combination tongue and groove plane carries an ink imprint "From/W. & J.H. Keim's Hardware/North 3rd Street/Reading PA."

KELKER

A hardware dealer in Harrisburg, PA. It was apparently the successor to OGLESBY & POOL and in the 1840's was known as Kelker & Co. and by the 1850's Kelker & Bro. An 1890 Harrisburg directory lists Luther R. Kelker as a dealer in hardware including "mechanics tools." Three imprints are known: a small incuse KELKER, a MADE FOR KELKER & BROTHER, and KELKER & SON.

KELLER   see I. Keller

I. KELLER

John Keller made planes —1796-1808— in Baltimore and was probably the earliest of that city's planemakers. The earlier imprint A appears on a 10⅛" hollow with ⅜" flat chamfers.   A: ★★★★   B & C: ★★★

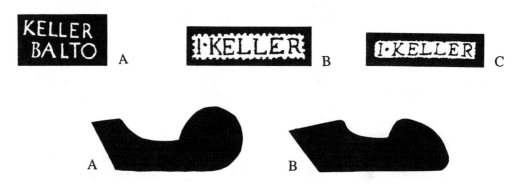

VICTOR KELLER

Victor Keller was a hardware dealer from Alleghany, the name for the old North Side of Pittsburgh before it was incorporated into the city. He was listed as a hardware dealer in directories from 1856 to 1861. His imprint appears on planes made by the Greenfield Tool Co. (w.s.).

GEO. W. KELLEY

Listed as a tool maker and planemaker in the 1854-57 Milwaukee, WI, directories. No example has been reported.

C.F. KELLNER

An incuse imprint C.F. KELLNER/PHILADELPHIA has been reported on an H. Chapin (w.s.) side bead. A probable hardware dealer.

H.S. KELLOGG

Henry S. Kellogg, was in the hardware business in Cincinnati, OH, 1839-46: as Kellogg, Wells & Ogden 1839; Kellogg & Ogden 1842-44; H.S. Kellogg 1846. He then became H.S. Kellogg in Cambridge City, IN, 1846-47, and Indianapolis, IN, 1847-55. In 1855 the firm became H.S. Kellogg & Son (Charles H. was the son) and continued until 1858. A J. Burke (w.s.) plane has been reported with the H.S. Kellogg imprint.   ★★

H.S. KELLOGG & SON   see H.S. Kellogg

J. KELLOGG/CLEVELAND OHIO

Several examples have been reported. Appearance is mid 19c.

J. KELLOGG/AMHERST MS

James Kellogg of Amherst, MA, made planes —1835— and 1840-67. During this period he also operated a mercantile store. The 1850 industrial census noted that he employed 14 hands, used water power and produced $12,000 worth of tools. He was listed in the 1860 general census as a merchant, age 68, and born in MA, but in the 1860 industrial census he was shown as a manufacturer using 15,000 feet of beech, water power, and eight hands to produce $8000 worth of tools. (scc also William Kellogg, J. Kellogg and Son, J. Kellogg & Co., Kellogg Fox & Washburn, and Kellogg & Fox)   A: ★★   B: FF

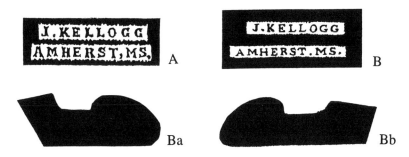

J.D. KELLOGG

A Northampton, MA, planemaker —1848—. The same eagle imprint shown below was used by H. Wells, Arnold & Crouch, and Peck & Crouch, all of Northampton (all w.s.).   ★★

J. KELLOGG & CO.

Amherst, MA. Working dates are not known. It may be a successor company to J. Kellogg & Son (w.s.) after the retirement of James Kellogg in 1867. (also see J. Kellogg)   ★★

213

J. KELLOGG & SON

James Kellogg and his son William manufactured planes and ran a mercantile store in Amherst, MA, —1865—. (see J. Kellogg and also William Kellogg)

WILLIAM KELLOGG

The son of James Kellogg. He joined his father in both the planemaking business and the store and in 1867 bought both from his father, who then retired. William continued to operate until 1886 when a flood damaged the plane factory and it was closed. No examples of this imprint have been reported. He presumably continued to use the J. KELLOGG/AMHERST MS. imprint (B). (see also J. Kellogg, J. Kellogg & Son, and J. Kellogg & Co.)

KELLOGG & CO.

The firm name of Charles A. Kellogg, listed in the New Orleans, LA, city directories in 1853 and 1854 as a hardware dealer. ★★★

KELLOGG & FOX

An Amherst, MA, planemaking partnership consisting of James Kellogg and Hiram Fox, that succeeded Kellogg, Fox & Washburn in 1839 and was dissolved in 1840. No example of an imprint has been reported. (see J. Kellogg, Kellogg Fox & Washburn and Hiram Fox)

KELLOGG, FOX & WASHBURN

A planemaking partnership probably consisting of James Kellogg, Hiram Fox and W.L. Washburn that operated in Amherst, MA, —1839. It was succeeded by Kellogg & Fox in 1839 (w.s.). No example of an imprint has been reported.

KELLOGG & HASTINGS

A Cleveland, Ohio, planemaker —1846-48—. No example of an imprint has been reported.

S. KELLUM

Various examples have been reported; the planes seem professionally made. Appearance is mid-19c.

A. KELLY

Possibly an earlier stamp of Abner Kelly of A. Kelly & Co. (w.s.). Several examples of mid-19c appearance have been reported.

A. KELLY & CO.

Probably Abner Kelly, a planemaker who was listed in the 1856 Ashfield, MA, directory, but probably worked for some time before then. The 1854 ledgers of the Greenfield Tool Co. (w.s.) show purchases of "best plough plates, plough and fillester stops" from A. Kelly. He was listed in the 1840 Ashfield census as age 37. In the 1860 industrial census A. Kelly & Co. was shown as employing two hands, using water power, and producing 3600 planes worth $1200. (see A. Kelly)   ★

SAMUEL KEMPER

A Cincinnati, OH, planemaker, 1843-44. No example has been reported. (also see Hulings & Kemper)

KENDALL

Thomas Kendall was a Baltimore, MD, planemaker —1831-33 and 1835-42. (see also Kendall & M'Cubbin) ★★

a   b

H.L. KENDALL

Henry Lee Kendall was a Baltimore, MD, planemaker and hardware merchant (among other vocations). He made planes —1849-59—. On June 8, 1858, he received patent number 20483 for an adjustable wedge that compensated for the wear on a plane's mouth opening. The patent imprint "H.L. Kendall/Patd. June 8, 1858/Balto" has been reported on fore planes and is extremely rare. Two planes bearing the H.L. Kendall imprint with the location stamp WASHINGTON have been reported. (see also Kendall & Schroeder and H.L. Kendall & Co.)   A, B, & B1: ★★   C: ★★★★★

A   B   B1

   C

H.L. KENDALL & CO.

Appeared in the 1860 Baltimore, MD, directory, but no example of this imprint has been reported. (see H.L. Kendall)

J. KENDALL

Examples exist with the additional location imprint N. LEBANON N.Y. No listing for this planemaker has been found, though a John Kendall was a thermometer maker in New Lebanon in 1835, succeeding his father,

Thomas Kendall, and was reported as a thermometer maker again in New Lebanon in the 1850 census, age 40, and born in MA.

THOMAS KENDALL   see Kendall

KENDALL & M'CUBBIN

Thomas K. Kendall and Robert W. McCubbin were Baltimore, MD, planemakers 1837-39—. No example of this imprint has been reported. (see R.W. McCubbin)

KENDALL & SCHROEDER

Henry Lee Kendall and Richard F. Schroeder made planes in Baltimore, MD, —1858—-. No examples of this imprint have been reported. (see H.L. Kendall)

KENEWA TOOL CO.

A brand name of Sargent & Co., New Haven, CT. (w.s.).

KENEWA TOOL CO.

KENNEDY

Leonard Kennedy Sr. was born in Hartford, CT, in 1767 (died 1842). He advertised himself as making all kinds of "joiner's moulding tools" as early as 1797 and may have supplied some of the planes that Ebenezer Clark (see E. Clark/Hartford) advertised in January 1796. In 1800 he advertised for journeymen, joiners, and apprentices, and was also selling lumber. By 1802 he was advertising all types of planes and also wooden screws and a few sets of "Scotch braces and Bitts," suggesting the sale of imported tools. From 1803 to 1805 he was a partner with Robert J. Collins Jr. in Kennedy & Collins (w.s.). The Pocket Register for the City of Hartford [CT] dated 1825 listed L. Kennedy & Co., probably comprised of Leonard Kennedy and Leonard Kennedy Jr., as a manufacturer of joiner's tools.

Leonard Kennedy Sr. had two sons who became planemakers, Samuel Lewis Kennedy (1792-1840) and Leonard Kennedy Jr. (1800-1879). Leonard Jr. worked in Hartford, CT, sometime before 1825; in Utica, NY, 1825-32; in Rochester, NY, 1838; in Hartford again 1838-46; in Milwaukee, WI, 1847-50 (where he was shown as an insurance agent in the 1850 census); after which he returned to Hartford and other pursuits. An advertisement in the Utica Directory of 1828 stated that L. Kennedy & Co. "manufacture all kinds of moulding Tools and bench planes" and that "all tools manufactured by L. Kennedy & Co. Hartford, Conn., Kennedy & White New-York or L. Kennedy & Co. Utica not proving good will be repaired gratis," indicating a business relationship among these firms, with Leonard Jr. making planes in Utica, brother Samuel in New York and perhaps father Leonard Sr. still making planes in Hartford.

Samuel Lewis Kennedy, the older brother, probably worked at Kennedy & Co., Hartford, —1813-17—; under the Kennedy name in New York City 1817-22; as a partner in Kennedy & White (w.s.), NYC, 1822-40; and Kennedy, Barry & Way, NYC (w.s.), 1840. In addition to his two sons, other planemakers who probably learned the trade from Leonard Kennedy were Daniel and Melvin Copeland, D.O. Crane, and Robert Collins Jr. (all w.s.).

The L. KENNEDY and L. KENNEDY/HARTFORD imprints were probably used by Leonard Sr. The KENNEDY & CO/HARTFORD may have been a partnership of Leonard Sr. and Samuel Lewis Kennedy during the early 1820's. At least one example of an L. KENNEDY/MILWAUKEE imprint is known. (see K & C, Kennedy & Bragaw, Kennedy & Way, Benton Evans & Co., Kennedy & Collins, and R.J. Collins)

A & B: ★   C: ★★★★   D & E: ★★   F & G: ★★★★   *(see next page)*

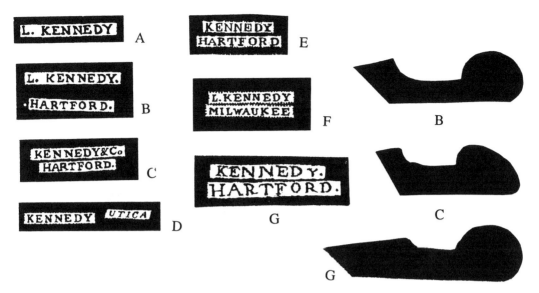

KENNEDY-N.YORK

Samuel Lewis Kennedy (1792-1840), a brother of Leonard Kennedy Jr., made planes in New York City 1817-22. He may have succeeded Consider Alford (see Alford, Kennedy, Barry & Way, Kennedy & White, and Kennedy) ★★

L. KENNEDY   see Kennedy

KENNEDY, BARRY & WAY

Samuel L. Kennedy and Samuel S. Barry, both planemakers, and William Way, a hardware merchant, were partners in this NYC hardware store in 1840. The firm became Barry & Way (w.s.) upon Kennedy's death in 1840. The imprint below is embossed. (see Kennedy, Samuel S. Barry, and William Way) ★★★

KENNEDY & BRAGAW

This firm made planes in Hartford, CT, 1844-46. Since Leonard Kennedy Jr. was back working in Hartford 1838-46, he may have been the Kennedy. No example of this imprint has been reported. (see Kennedy)

KENNEDY & COLLINS

A partnership of Leonard Kennedy and Robert J. Collins Jr. formed in Hartford, CT, in 1803 to "carry on the house carpenter and joiners business and manufacture joiners tools." It was dissolved in early 1805. (see also Kennedy, R.J. Collins, and Collins/Hartford)   A & B: ★★★

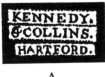

A

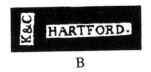

B

217

KENNEDY & WAY

Made planes in Hartford CT, 1838-43. Since Leonard Kennedy Jr. was back working in Hartford 1838-46, he may have been the Kennedy. No example of this imprint has been reported. (see Kennedy and also Kennedy, Barry & Way)

KENNEDY & WHITE

A New York City planemaking partnership 1822-40 consisting of Samuel L. Kennedy and Dyer White (1788-1852; born in CT). Samuel L. Kennedy (1792-1840) was the older brother of Leonard Kennedy Jr. and like his brother, he learned planemaking from his father, Leonard Kennedy Sr. Samuel had made planes earlier in New York City from 1817 to 1822. (see Kennedy, Kennedy/N. York, and Charles White)   ★

L. KENNEY

Leonard Kenney (also spelled Kenny) was listed as a planemaker in Albany, NY, 1818-19, and from 1820 to 1824 was a partner in Rowell & Kenney (w.s.)   A: ★★   B: ★★★

 A  B

I. KENT   see J. Kent

J. KENT

Justice Kent (1771-1858) who was born in Massachusetts and came to Windsor, NY (Broome County) in 1795, where he lived until 1811 when he settled in Brooklyn Twp., Susquehanna County, PA. There he farmed, built and operated a gristmill and was a carpenter, meanwhile managing to raise 11 children. A number of examples of his imprint have been reported. One, a 10½" birch plow plane has wooden thumbscrews, a relieved wedge, a riveted skate and arms mortised into the fence. A hollow is in the collection of the Farmers Museum at Cooperstown, N.Y. His early planes may have been made in MA. Most are ca.1800 in appearance.
A & B: ★★★

 A   B

KIEFFER & AUXER

Lancaster, PA, planemakers Samuel Auxer, who was listed as a planemaker in Lancaster PA in the 1860 census, age 26, and William Kieffer, a son-in-law of E.W. Carpenter (w.s.), who was also listed as a planemaker, age 37, in Lancaster in the 1860 census (and also in the 1857-59 and 1866-67 directories), The firm of Kieffer & Auxer was listed in the 1869-70 Lancaster city directory as a planemaker. Its planes are similar in style to those of E.W. Carpenter, particularly the wedge. (also see Auxer & Remly)   ★★   *(see next page)*

KILBOURNE KUHNS & CO.

A hardware firm consisting of L. Kilbourne, W.J. Kuhns, and John Joyce that was listed in the 1856-57 Columbus city directory.   ★★★

J. KILLAM

James Killam was a Glastonbury, CT, planemaker 1822-60. He was listed in the 1850 census as a planemaker, age 52, born in CT. Living with him was James L. Killam, a planemaker, age 26, born in CT, and presumably his son and fellow worker. Production for 1850 was estimated at $1200.   A: ★   B & B1: ★★★
B2: ★   C: ★★★

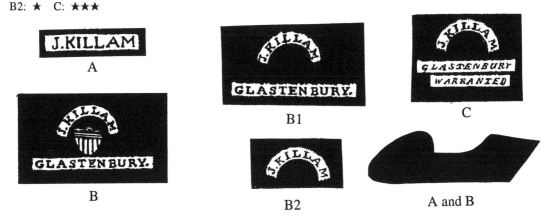

LYMAN KILLAM

Made planes in Glastonbury, CT —1857-58—. No example of an imprint has been reported.

S. KILLUM

Several examples have been reported. All are 9½" long. Appearance is second quarter 19c.

W.A. KIMBALL & CO.

An example is reported with this imprint on the heel of a Gladwin & Appleton (w.s.) round, suggesting that Kimball was a hardware dealer ca.1870.

KIMBERLY & ROWE

A 1¾" x 1¹⁄₁₆" tan printed label reading "Manufactured for/Kimberly & Rowe/Dealers in/Carriage and General Hardware/Joiners and Mechanics Tools/276 Chapel St. New Haven Conn" (just up the street from J.E. Bassett & Co., w.s.) was reported on a W.H. Pond (w.s.) bead. Kimberly & Clark operated from 1869 through 1874. They were preceded by Smith & Kimberly and succeeded by James Rowe & Co. In 1879 James B. Rowe was listed as a salesman for the Bassetts.

B. KING

Benjamin King was a Cincinnati, OH, planemaker —1825-44—. Earlier, in 1819, he worked for Swetman, Hughes & Co. (w.s.) in Pittsburgh, PA, per the city directory. Since he appeared in no other city records it is likely that he went down river to Cincinnati. (see B. King & T. Fugate, B. King/J. Walker, and King & Cunningham) ★★

B. KING & T. FUGATE

Two examples have been reported which suggest a partnership between these two Cincinnati, OH, planemakers, ca.1830.

B. KING/J. WALKER

A wedge-armed plank tongue plane has been reported stamped with the names of both these contemporaneous Cincinnati, OH, planemakers.

H. & J.W. KING

This imprint has been reported on an 8" block plane with a thistle brand Auburn Tool Co. iron and the number 48 (which is Arrowmammett Works style number for a smoothing plane), indicating a hardware dealer.

I. KING

Various examples of this imprint have been reported, including a beech hollow, a 9⅞" beech skewed rabbet with a relieved wedge, and an ogee crown molder made of yellow birch, with a rounded wedge and the imprint struck twice.   Appearance is ca.1800.

I. KING/NEWARK N.J.

Listed as a planemaker in the Newark directories of 1835-37 at 29 Plane St..   A handled three-arm self-regulating plow, very similar in style to several examples manufactured by Mockridge & Francis (w.s.), has been reported.

J. KING   see Josiah King

J.A. KING

John A. King was listed as a "colored" (black) planemaker in the Newark, NJ, directories of 1835-37 at 20 Academy St. His planes are similar in appearance to those by Andruss and by Searing (both w.s.). A J. Searing complex molder with the J. SEARING overprinted by the J.A. KING imprint was sold at auction in 1989.
★★★★

JOSIAH KING

A prolific NYC planemaker who, together with his two sons, made planes under various entities from 1835 to 1887. After being located on Houston St., then Grand and 4th Ave. (in 1849), he moved to 383 Bowery in 1851, and in 1858 to 373 Bowery. In 1870 the business became Josiah King & Son (with Josiah N. King as his partner). The E imprint (Josiah N. King) was presumably used during the 1870-85 period, when it was listed in the city directories. The firm was listed as Josiah Kings.Sons during the final two years, 1886-87. The 1850 census reported the firm employing two men who produced 1880 planes worth $1800. (also see Davis & King)
A & B: ★★   C: ★   D: FF   E: ★   F: ★★★   *(continued next page)*

A

B

C

D

E

F

221

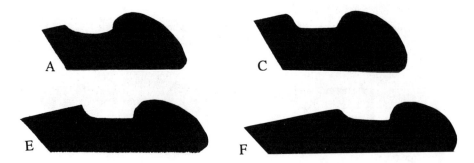

JOSIAH N. KING, JOSIAH KING & SON, and JOSIAH KINGS SONS   see Josiah King

S. KING
A number of examples have been reported indicating a planemaker. Both beech and yellow birch, flat and round chamfers, and molding plane lengths from 9¼" to 9⅞" are found, indicating a transitional maker, ca.1800, from southeastern New England. Not to be confused with S. King of Hull, England.

THOS. KING
Several examples have been reported, birch with flat chamfers and an owner imprint. Appearance is ca.1800.

WM. KING
William King, a New York City cooper's tool maker, 1841-45. His imprint has appeared on a howel.

KING & CUNNINGHAM
Reported on a bead and a pair of match planes. Possibly a partnership of B. King and Cunningham & Co. (both w.s.).

JOHN KINTZEL
Several examples have been reported. One is a 10" skewed rabbet made of beech and date-stamped 1830; another a handled 13" molding plane dated 1831. The B imprint appears on a 9½" long beech dado. Possibly a woodworker. *(see next page)*

A

B

A. KIRKMAN & CO.
An example reported was imprinted on a M'Master complex molder. Probably a hardware dealer.

OTTO KLEIST
Appeared in various Milwaukee, WI, city directories between 1870 and 1890 as a tool maker and in 1884 as a planemaker. No example of his imprint has been reported.

H.H. KNAPP
A Henry H. Knapp was listed in the 1850 census as a planemaker in Rochester NY, age 36, born in MA. "Detroit" sometimes appears inverted, and the shield device appears in different positions. ★★

KNEASS
There were two Kneass's who were Philadelphia planemakers, Frederick F., who worked —1819—, and who, in 1819, had a "Plane Manufactory & Tool Store" at 10 South Eighth St.; and Michael, who worked 1818-30. This imprint may have been used by either one or by both. Michael Kneass (b.1784 in Lancaster PA) was the son of Christopher Kneass (b.1756 in Philadelphia PA - d.1793). The NYC 1835 directory lists a Michael Kneass as a manufacturer at 9 King St. Michael was listed in the 1850 census as a pauper and a resident of the Philadelphia Alms House. (see Kneass & Co.) ★

KNEASS & CO.
A Philadelphia, PA, plane manufacturer which was listed in the 1818 Philadelphia directory at 8 South Eighth St., the same address as Michael Kneass. (see Kneass) ★★

KNOWLTON & STONE
A Keene, NH, hardware dealer who was active into this century.

E.F. KRAFT   see E.F. Kraft & Co.

E.F. KRAFT & CO.
Emilius F. Kraft & Co. was a St. Louis, MO, planemaker and dealer 1853-60.   A & B: ★★

A

B

B

E.R. KRUM
Emil R. Krum was a New York City hardware and cutlery dealer 1869-96. The imprint appears on a Greenfield Tool Co. (w.s.) rabbet.

L. KRUSE
Lewis Kruse was a Cincinnati, OH, hardware dealer 1850- 59, and was succeeded by Kruse & Bahlman. The B imprint is on a double boxed skew rabbet made by H. Taylor (w.s.).

A

B

L. KRUSE & CO.   see L. Kruse

KUHLMAN HDWE CO.
A Cincinnati, Ohio, hardware dealer 1889-1900.

D. KUNS
Several examples have been reported. Probably another of that early group of ca.1800 eastern Pennsylvania country woodworkers/planemakers.

L

L.G. & CO.

Four different examples of this imprint have been reported: a smoothing plane and a fore plane, each with an Empire Tool Co. iron, a 26" razeed jointer with an Ohio Tool Co. iron, and a 9½" long beech center bead.

 A  B

LAIRD

Planes reported are all between 9⅜" and 9⁷⁄₁₆" long and have flat chamfers ranging between ¼" and ⁷⁄₁₆". All are made of beech and most have one or more owners' stamps. The workmanship seems very crisp and professional. One example has the LAIRD imprint overstriking the EASTBURN on an Eastburn plane (w.s.). Planes have been reported with Green and Newbould irons that appear to be original to the plane. Appearance is ca.1800 and likely location the New York - New Jersey area.

G. LAKE

Several examples of this imprint have been reported: 9⅜" long, beech, with flat chamfers. Appearance is ca.1800.

CHARLES H. LAMB

Listed as a planemaker in the New Bedford, MA, directories, 1869-72. No example has been reported.

J.H. LAMB

James H. Lamb was a brother of William G. Lamb and an active New Bedford, MA, planemaker —1869-74. (see Charles H. Lamb, W.G. Lamb, J. & W. Lamb, Taber Plane Co., and also New Bedford Tool Co.) ★

R.T. LAMB & CO.
A Memphis, TN, hardware dealer 1847-49, who was succeeded by Lownes & Co. (w.s.).

W.G. LAMB
William G. Lamb, brother of James H. Lamb, was a New Bedford, MA, planemaker —1869-72. (see J.H. Lamb, J. & W. Lamb, Taber Plane Co., and also New Bedford Tool Co.)   ★

J. & W. LAMB
Presumably the brothers James H. and William G. Lamb, New Bedford, MA, planemakers. The firm was listed in the 1869 city directory. The various Lamb enterprises frequently used rosewood and boxwood in their manufacture of plow planes, producing some very lovely examples of the planemaker's art. (see J.H. Lamb and also W.G. Lamb)   ★★★

LAMB & BROWNELL
A New Bedford, MA, planemaker; listed in the 1871 city directory.   ★★

T. LAMSON
Examples have been reported, all between 9³⁄₁₆" and 9⁵⁄₁₆" long, with flat chamfers. Appearance ca.1800.

P.A. LANAUZE
Pierre Alexandre Lanauze operated a hardware store in New Orleans, LA, from ca.1845 to 1871, the year of his death.   ★★★

R.A. LANCEY
Roswell A. Lancey, who worked in Townsend, MA, ca.1900. Several examples of cooper's planes have been reported with his label, "Made by R.A. Lancey".

M. LANG
Probably Michael Lang, who was listed as a joiner in 1853 and between 1853 and 1876 as a toolmaker, hardware dealer, grocer, and planemaker. (see Lang & Co.   ★★

R. LANG
Robert Lang, Jr. was a Cincinnati, OH, planemaker and hardware store proprietor 1842-51.

LANG & CO.
A Buffalo, NY, hardware dealer 1858-71. Michael Lang was the proprietor. (see M. Lang)   ★★

H.A. LANGHORST
A Cincinnati, OH, hardware dealer 1866-80. His imprint has been reported on planes made by both Sandusky Tool Co. and J.C. Taylor (both w.s.).   ★★

B. LAPE
Benjamin Lape (b.1820 in Ohio) was a Cincinnati, Ohio, planemaker 1842-46—, who later moved to Madison, IN, and was a partner in the planemaking firm of J.S. & B. Lape (w.s.). He was listed in the 1850 census as a planemaker in Brownsville, IN. Both Madison and Brownsville are within a 50-mile radius of Cincinnati.

JACOB S. LAPE
Listed as a planemaker in the 1843-44 Cincinnati, OH directory, as a sash maker in 1846, and as a partner in the planemaking firm of J.S. & B. Lape (w.s.) in Madison, IN, ca.1850.

J.S. & B. LAPE
Jacob S. and Benjamin Lape made planes in Madison, IN, ca.1850. (see B. Lape and Jacob S. Lape)   ★★★

P.H. LAUFMAN

Philip Laufman operated a hardware firm in Pittsburgh, PA, from 1852 until 1859. His imprint P.H. LAUFMAN/NO. 78 WOOD ST/PITTSBURG has been reported on a screw arm sash plane made by Casey, Clark & Co. After 1859, the firm became P.H. Laufman & Bro., continuing until 1876.

J. LAUTNER

Joseph Lautner first appeared as a hardware dealer in the 1859-60 Pittsburgh, PA, city directory, with the listing continuing through 1913. The Allegheny City 1896 directory (Allegheny City was incorporated into Pittsburgh in the early 1900's) listed a Lautner Hardware Co., whose proprietors were Joseph and H.E. Lautner. A famous instance of the Lautner imprint appears on an ebony, ivory-tipped, center wheel plow plane, one of the classic rarities.   A & B: ★★

A   B   C

J. LAUTNER & CO. and LAUTNER HARDWARE CO.   see J. Lautner

J. LAWTON and J. LAWTON & CO.

Cincinnati, Ohio, hardware dealers, 1849-52.   A & B: ★★★

A   B

J. LEAVITT

Several molding planes, all made of yellow birch and between $9\frac{7}{8}$" and 10" long, with $\frac{7}{16}$" wide flat chamfers, have been reported. A Jacob Leavitt, a joiner of Fairfield, CT, died in 1759, leaving an extensive inventory of tools; as did John Leavitt (1724-98) of Suffield, CT. Appearance is certainly 18c, and a New England location.

a   b

F. LENDER

Fredric Lender, a Cincinnati, OH, planemaker who worked for S. Sloop (w.s.) in 1839-40 and was listed as an independent planemaker in the 1849-50 city directory. The C imprint consists of the B imprint overstamping the E.F. SEYBOLD A imprint (w.s.), suggesting that Lender possibly succeeded the Seybold planemaking business or at least acquired some of its stock. There is also a report of an F. LENDER imprint overstruck twice on a Schaeffer & Cobb (w.s.) B imprint.   A & B: ★★

A

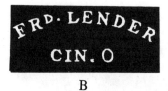

B

C

E. LEONARD
Examples of molding planes reported range between 9" and 9¼" long, have round chamfers, and a ca.1800 appearance.

FROM G.W. LEONARD & SON
Probably a hardware dealer. The imprint appears on the heel of a 9½" boxed molding plane made by F. UNDERWOOD/C.B. SCHAEFFER (w.s.).

JOHN H. LESTER   see Davis & Lester

E.S. LEROY
The example reported appears on a Varvill & Son/York (England 1829-40) plane, suggesting that Leroy was a hardware dealer.

DB. LEWIS
This imprint has been reported on a 9⁷⁄₁₆" birch skew rabbet with heavy rounded chamfers and the additional location stamp GROTON MS.

LEWIS-WILKES & CO.
Charles H. Lewis and William Wilkes were hardware dealers in Louisville, KY, —1855-56—.   ★★★

H. LIBHART
Four examples have been reported; one a 9½" long molding plane made of beech with an early 19c appearance, another a slide arm plow plane.

A. LINCOLN

Amos Lincoln was listed as a planemaker in the 1841 Boston, MA, directory. The imprint has been reported twice, on a jack and a molder.

LINDENBERGER

Appears on a $9\frac{3}{8}$" long beech round of early 19c appearance. Possibly the work of one or more of I. Lindenberger's (w.s.) sons, before or after their move to Ohio in 1817. Ebenezer (b.1793) was listed in the 1820 Kingston Twp, Ohio, census as a head of a household, and engaged in manufacture; John (b.1796) was also listed as a head of household and engaged in manufacture; and Christopher (b.1798), who was not listed. This imprint is slightly different from the Lindenberger portion of the C. Lindenberger (w.s.) embossed imprint A. However, the wedges are identical. (see I. Lindenberger and also C. Lindenberger)

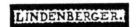

C. LINDENBERGER

Probably Christopher Lindenberger, the son of I. Lindenberger (w.s), who most likely learned planemaking from his father and probably followed his brothers John Jr. and Ebenezer when they moved to Ohio in 1817, after the death of their father. He is listed in the 1850 Ohio census as a planemaker, age 52 in Porter Twp., owning real estate valued at $3000. In the household are John Lindenberger, age 28, and Christopher Lindenberger, age 23, both planemakers, both born in Ohio, and both sons. In the 1860 Ohio census Christopher, age 62, is listed as a farmer. (see Lindenberger) A & B: ★★

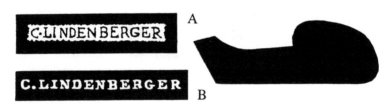

I. LINDENBERGER

John Lindenberger, who was born in Baltimore, MD, in 1754. He was trained as a cabinetmaker and served in the American Revolutionary War, at the battles of Brandywine and Germantown, Trenton, and Princeton. He resigned from the army in 1778, probably arriving in Rhode Island some time before 1785 and settling in Providence in 1786. By 1787 he was advertising that he was carrying on the planemaking business, which he continued until he died insolvent in 1817. His estate inventory included 962 molding plane irons, 1500 feet of beech and birch stuff, 14 float files, and 391 molding planes, 59 bench planes, 2 moving filletsters, and 3 plow planes. Besides making planes Lindenberger was also a blacksmith/toolmaker, taught architecture, and traded various goods.

Like the other transitional planemakers, his earlier planes were made primarily of yellow birch and had flat chamfers. Later examples were made of beech and sometimes cherry, and tended to have narrower, flat or rounded chamfers. There were probably hands other than Lindenberger's at work that added slight variations. Several planes similar in style to his have been reported with the PROVIDENCE imprint only. (see also Lindenberger and C. Lindenberger) A: ★★ A1: ★   *(continued next page)*

A

A1

JOHN LINDENBERGER (JR.)

The son of Christopher Lindenberger (see C. Lindenberger), the grandson of I. Lindenberger (w.s.) and the third generation of Lindenberger planemakers. He was listed in the 1850 Ohio census for Porter Twp. (some 20 miles north of Columbus) as a planemaker, age 28, born in Ohio and living with Christopher Lindenberger (almost certainly his father). He again appeared in an 1859 directory as operating a plane factory in Kingston Center, Ohio. There is a Kingston, Ohio, at the present time (but no Kingston Center). Kingston is located about 40 miles south of Columbus. There has been no report of a John Lindenberger imprint.

LINDNER & CO.

Reported on a bead. It appears to be American.

J.F. & G.M. LINDSEY

James F. and George M. Lindsey were brothers and planemakers in Huntington, MA. —1856-79—. They were listed in the 1850 census as mechanics in Chester, MA, ages 21 and 24 respectively, both born in MA. They were listed in the 1870 census as planemakers in Huntington, MA, and in the 1880 census, James was again listed as a planemaker but George was a deputy sheriff.   A & B: FF

 A  B  A

D. LINES

A number of examples have been reported, all made of beech, between 9⅛" and 10¾" long, and all with wide flat chamfers. Appearance is ca.1800.

LITHGOW

Walter Lithgow was among the earliest of the Pittsburgh, PA, planemakers. His name appeared in the 1810 census, and in Cramer's Pittsburgh Almanac of 1813, the year in which he died, as a planemaker.
A & B: ★★★★   *(see next page)*

 A  B

THOMAS LITTELL   see T. Littell/T. Atkinson

T. LITTELL/T. ATKINSON
Thomas Littell and T. Atkinson (both w.s.) were partners in a plane factory 1838-39 in Louisville, KY.
★★★

C.S. LITTLE & CO.
Charles S. Little was a hardware dealer, —1846-72, and planemaker, 1857, in New York City. (see Osborne & Little)   A: ★★   B: ★★★   C: ★★

 A  B  C

L. LITTLE
Levi Little, 1770-1802, was a Boston, MA, housewright, tool dealer and planemaker. Born in Newbury, MA, in 1770, son of John Little and Hannah Noyes and brother of Noah Little (see N. Little), he married Mary Lovering in 1794, and died in 1802.

Little made planes of both beech and birch; they range from 9½" to 10" long, and have ¼" flat chamfers. They are occasionally found with irons by Sheffield makers. It is usually impossible to distinguish between planes he made himself and those he imported for sale, though if made of birch or of beech boxed with rosewood, it is probably of his own manufacture. Several examples have been reported of I. COX (John Cox, planemaker of Birmingham, England, 1770-1808) imprinted planes also bearing the L. Little imprint and presumably imported by Little for resale.

He was first listed in the Boston Directory in 1796 as a carpenter at S. Bennet Street; then as a carpenter's tool maker in 1798 and 1800 on Orange Street. The house he occupied in 1798, which included his workshop, was described as two-storied, 936 sq. ft., 11 windows, and was valued at $900.

At his death his shop inventory was sufficiently detailed to be very helpful. Random entries reveal that he made planes as well as importing them: "2715 feet beech ----," "491 feet beech plank," "949 plain stocks," "518 plain stock jointures," "iron wood," "crese plains" and "tools made." There is an entry of 6 doz. planes 24.00 ($4/doz. at wholesale). Retailing at $6 per dozen or 50c each, makes them priced at 3/2 (3 shillings, 2 pence) "old money." In 1796 in England, hollows and rounds in the Seaton chest sold at 3/0. In the 1790's LAZARUS SAMPSON, MIDDLEBORO, MASS. (see L. Sampson) sold small planes priced from 3/2 to 3/6. This seems to be a common price range for that time. Some of his planes were wholesaled to the New York market, where at least one (shown below) was stamped with the buyer's "crowned" initials. (see Tho. Grant)

The A imprint appears on a plane bearing a Sleeper-style wedge and may in fact have been made by his brother Noah, who had adopted this style wedge on his planes. A: ★★★   B: ★   C: ★★★★   C1: ★   D: ★★★★
(see next page)

232

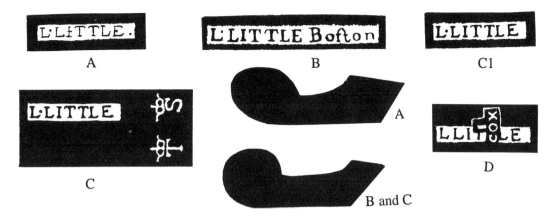

A   B   C1

A

C   B and C   D

N. LITTLE

Noah Little, 1772-1852, was a brother of Levi Little (w.s.) and was born in Newbury, MA. He was listed as a housewright in 1800 and as a yeoman when his estate was probated in 1852. His molding planes have Sleeper-style wedges leading to conjecture as to whether he learned planemaking from I. Sleeper (w.s.) or possibly bought his planes from Sleeper for resale. The appearance of his planes is ca.1800.   ★

WM. H. LIVINGSTON & CO.

An importer and dealer in hardware and cutlery in New York City 1840-66.   A & A1: ★   B: ★★

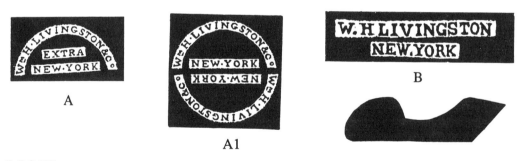

A   A1   B

J. LOCK

The Lock family were woodworkers who lived in Bennington, NH (near Concord).

LOCKPORT EDGE TOOL CO.

Lockport Edge Tool Co. operated between 1860 and 1870. Boyd's 1865 Central N.Y. Business Directory carried an ad by Phineas Smith as sole agent for the Lockport Edge Tool Co. "Manufacturers of superior axes, hatchets, hammers, picks, and every description of Cooper's Tools." Smith also offered planes in the body of the ad. This imprint has been reported on a 12" long jack with an EXCELSIOR WORKS, AUBURN N.Y. double iron, and on an Auburn Tool Co. dado.

LOGAN & GREGG

A Pittsburgh, PA, hardware company that in 1857 succeeded Logan, Wilson & Co. (w.s.) and continued in business until 1962. It sold many lines of both wooden planes and wood-bottomed transitional planes under its own name and under the trade name "Sterling."

LOGAN & KENNEDY

A Pittsburgh, PA, hardware dealer, founded in 1831 by John T. Logan and his cousin, Robert T. Kennedy, and continuing until at least 1847. It was succeeded in 1848 by Logan, Wilson & Co. (w.s.).

 A    B

LOGAN, WILSON & CO.

A Pittsburgh, PA, hardware dealer partnership of John T. Logan and Philip Wilson, successor to Logan & Kennedy (w.s.) in 1848. It was succeeded in 1857 by Logan, Gregg & Co. (w.s.). The imprint has appeared on an H. Chapin grooving plane.

J.H. LOHR

A Cincinnati, OH, hardware dealer 1858-71. The imprint has appeared on an H. & J.C. Taylor (w.s.) dado plane.

D. LONG

A number of planes have been reported with this imprint, several from eastern PA, including a sash plane with lignum boxing (which again suggests an eastern PA location). Appearance is early 19c. In the 1820 census for Wheatfield, Indiana County, PA, a David Long and a Mathias Long lived next door to each other, and there is a resemblance between the D. Long A imprint and the A imprint of M. Long, as well as the use of a triple imprint. (see M. Long)   A: ★★   *(see next page)*

 A  A1

G. LONG

Various examples have been reported, all made of beech. One, a molding plane, is 10" long with flat chamfers. Appearance is ca.1800.

I. LONG

Probably Isaac Long (1764-1840), a Hopkinton, NH, joiner whose probate inventory included four sets of bench planes, 70 molding planes, 9 cornice molding planes, and 6 smoothing planes, among other tools. He was related to Joshua Morse (see J. Morse Jr.) through the marriage of their children. A hollow and round imprinted by I. Long has been reported overprinted J. MORSE, suggesting that Morse may have succeeded Long, acquiring his stock. Long is not to be confused with the English planemaker, I. LONG (Jeremiah Long —1770—). ★★

M. LONG

Mathias Long was listed as a planemaker, age 59, in the 1850 census for Reading, PA. He was born in PA and appeared in the 1830 and 1840 censuses as living in Reading. In the 1820 census, a Mathias Long and a David Long were living next to each other in Wheatfield, Indiana County, PA. The B3 imprint appears on a plane by Butler (w.s.) (also see D. Long) A, B, & B1: ★★

 A

 B

 B2

 B3

 B1

J.T. LOOMIS

A Hartford, CT, planemaker 1847-63. ★★

A. LORD

This imprint has been reported twice. An Abraham Lord (1805-1889) was a documented Ipswich, MA, cabinetmaker.

C.D. & O.H. LORD

A Norton, MA, planemaker —1875—. No example has been reported.

D. LORD

Two 9¾" long molding planes made of yellow birch have been reported. They have ⁵⁄₁₆" flat chamfers and are late 18c in appearance.

J. LORD

Judah Lord, a Watertown, NY, planemaker who was listed in the 1850 census as a 48 year old machinist.

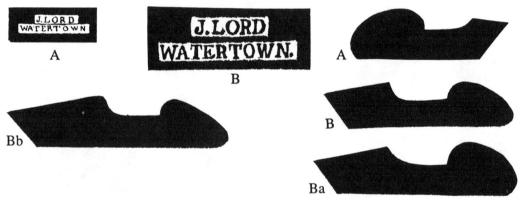

A

B

A

Bb

B

Ba

LORD & RANSOM

Listed in the 1850 census as a planemaker in Watertown, NY, with three employees, making tools and patterns worth $2000. The principals were probably Judah Lord and John F. Ransom. No example has been reported. (see J. Lord and J.F. Ransom)

D. LORING

Various examples have been reported. Some molding planes 9¾" to 10" long, made of yellow birch, bear the A imprint and look 18c. Others run about 9½" and seem to be second generation (B imprint). Location is probably eastern New England.

A   B

C. LOUD

This name has been reported on a 9¼" beech molding plane with round chamfers.

C. LOUD JR.

This name has been reported on a 9³⁄₁₆" long beech ogee, professionally made. Appearance is second quarter 19c.

F. LOUD

Nine examples have been reported, including a side rabbet, a coping plane, a round and a bead. The planes are 9½" long with round chamfers and are made of beech. Appearance is early 19c and location may be in the Northampton, MA, area.

D. LOVEJOY

Daniel Lovejoy was a Lowell, MA, planemaker —1870-71— who was listed earlier in the 1850 census as a Lowell blacksmith, age 23. The imprint shown is, however, probably from an earlier generation and appears on a 15¾" long, 5¾" wide cornice plane with flat chamfers. A birch jointer of early 19c appearance has also been reported.

H. LOVEJOY

Hubbard Lovejoy (b.1807), who is believed to have worked as a builder 1830-68 in Wayne and then Auburn, ME. Between 1848 and 1850, together with Wm. Burgess, he manufactured doors, sash, and blinds. A 28" jointer has been reported, as well as a screw arm plow.

J. LOVELL

Jacob Lovell (b.1829), of Cummington, MA, was listed as a wood turner in Goshen, MA, in the 1850 census, as a merchant in Cummington, MA, in the 1860 census and as a planemaker in Cummington in the 1870 and 1880 censuses. He was married to the sister of Hiram Barrus (see H. Barrus & Co.). He first worked for the

Union Tool Co. and then for himself. He died February 14, 1882, from injuries sustained when he fell down a flight of stairs at his factory and the box of planes he was carrying fell on top of him.   ★

LOVELL & CO.
A Boston, MA, 19c hardware dealer, whose working dates are unknown.

W. LOVLAND
Several examples have been reported, a hollow, two complex molders made of beech, and a bead with lignum boxing. Appearance is ca.1800.

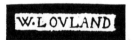 

A. LOW
Asa Low, a planemaker who was born in Maine, ca.1791, and died in Warren, Ohio, in 1831, age 40, a victim of smallpox. The 1820 census for Warren listed him as a manufacturer of bench and molding planes of every description, employing two men with total annual wages of $200, and the annual value of goods manufactured $1000.   ★★

LOWNES & CO.
Henry Lownes operated a Memphis, TN, hardware company. He was successor to R.T. Lamb & Co. (w.s.) in 1849 and was succeeded upon his death in 1857 by Orgill Bros. & Co. (w.s.).   ★★★

JOHN S. LUNNAGAN
Appeared in the 1843-45 New York City directories as a planemaker at 23 Catherine St, and again in the 1847-48 directory (this time spelled Lununagen) at 48 Hamilton St. In 1854-55 he once again appeared as a planemaker (this time spelled Lunnigan) at 346 Third Street. No example of his imprint alone has been reported. (see Hubbell & Lunnagan)

238

H. LUTTGEN

Several examples have been reported with the imprint FROM/H. LUTTGEN/JERSEY CITY: one on a skew rabbet by G.W. DENNISON & CO. (w.s.), another on a sash plane by SHIVERICK (w.s.). A probable hardware dealer.   ★★★

F.M. LYNCH

There have been several reports of complex molding planes bearing this imprint. Appearance is ca.1840-50.

J.P. LYNE & SON

Probably a hardware dealer, location unknown. The imprint has been reported on a Greenfield Tool Co. rosewood plow plane with ivory tips and nuts; and on a complex molder with an Auburn Plane Co.-style wedge and "141" imprinted on the heel, coinciding with the profile of style no. 141 in the Auburn 1869 catalog. A & B: ★★★

A

B

J.W. LYON

Joseph W. Lyon, was listed as a Cincinnati, OH, planemaker in the 1834 Cincinnati directory. (see Hall & Lyon; Lyon, McKinnell; and Lyon & Smith)

LYON & KELLOGG

This imprint has been reported on the heel of a boxed skewed rabbet made by Phoenix Factory/W. Warner (w.s.). Probably a hardware dealer.

J.W. LYON/McKINNEL

Most probably Joseph W. Lyon and Henry and William McKinnel; possibly a variant of the imprint of Lyon/McKinnell (w.s.). The example shown is an overprint on a J. Creagh (w.s.) plane.

239

LYON, McKINNELL & CO.

Joseph W. Lyon and Wm. McKinnell, plane and edge tool manufacturers in Cincinnati, OH, 1842-46. They were listed as successors to John Creagh in 1842. (see Lyon & Smith, Joseph W. Lyon, Hall & Lyon, J.W. Lyon/McKinnel) ★★

LYON & SMITH

Joseph W. Lyon and John H. Smith of Cincinnati, OH, who made and sold planes, edge tools and hardware 1849-53. In the 1850 census they reported manufacturing 14,000 planes worth $12,000 and edge tools worth $14,000, employing 20 workers who were paid $6000. (see Joseph W. Lyon; Lyon, McKinnell & Co.; Hall & Lyon) ★★

D. McARTHUR

This imprint was reported on a matched pair of handled, wedge arm tongue and groove planes, 13" long. Appearance is early 19c. Location may be Ohio since that is where they were found and where Dayton existed then, as well as now.

A. McBRIDE

Alexander McBride of Louisville, KY, who was listed variously between 1843 and 1846 in the city directories as an architect, a carpenter, and a hardware merchant. In the 1844-45 directory he advertised himself as a manufacturer of planes and dealer in hardware and cutlery. He was a partner in Woodruff & McBride (w.s.) in 1848-49, and was a sole proprietor in the hardware business 1851-66.

THOMAS J. McCALL

(d.1851) Listed in the 1834 and 1835 Albany, NY, directories as a planemaker, but no example of his imprint has been reported. He was a partner in Bensen & McCall (w.s.), Albany, in 1842.

J.A. McCELLUS

This name has been reported several times. Probable location is north central NY state; appearance is mid-19c.

Wm. M. McCLURE

William M. McClure of Philadelphia, PA, most probably a hardware dealer who entered six planes made by E.W. Carpenter (w.s.) in the Franklin Institute 1848-49 exhibits. A patented (No. 6226) smoother and a plow plane, made by Carpenter, bear the McClure imprint. (see Yarnell & McClure) ★★★

P. McCUEN

A 19c maker of cooper's tools in Brooklyn, NY.

J. M'CULLY

Possibly John M. McCully, who was listed in the 1815 Pittsburgh, PA, directory as a carpenter. The examples reported include an all boxwood screw arm plow that might be from a generation later.   A & A1: ★★★

 A    A1

J.M. McCUNE & CO.

A Columbus, OH, planemaker. A hollow and round have been reported stamped "1887".

WILLIAM McDANIELS

Listed as a planemaker in the 1837, 1839-42, 1845-50, and intermittently through the 1850's in the Philadelphia city directories. He worked for the Whites (see Israel White ??? imprint) making panel raisers that carry the initials W.M.D. No example of his imprint has been reported.

McDONALD-FOSTER & PORTER

The A imprint has been reported on a D.R. Barton (w.s.) complex molder and the A1 on an Ohio Tool Co. (w.s.) round. Most probably a mid-19c hardware dealer.   *(see next page)*

242

A

A1

JAMES McGENNIS
Listed as a planemaker in the Cincinnati, OH, 1819 directory. No example of his imprint has been reported.

A.O. McGREW
A.O. McGrew was listed as a hardware dealer in the 1850 Pittsburgh, PA, city directory. The imprint has been reported on a Hall, Case & Co. (w.s.) crown molder.

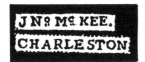

JA. McKEE
The C.H. in the location part of the imprint may be "Court House."

JNO. McKEE
Reported on a beech plow plane of mid-19c appearance.

McKINNELL & CO.
William and Henry McKinnell of Cincinnati, OH, who were plane and edge tool manufacturers in 1848-50. The McKinnell & Co. imprint has been reported overstamping the G. Roseboom A imprint on a panel raiser. (see J.W. Lyon/McKinnel and McKinnel & R.A. Ward)   ★★★

McKINNEL & R.A. WARD
Reported on a 9⅜" long 1/4 tongue plane.

McKINNEY & ALLING

John McKinney and Charles Alling, hardware dealers in Madison, IN, 1857-65. The predecessor firm was Wells (Wm. W.) & Alling (John), 1852-57, and the successor firm was Alling & Lodge 1865—. Its imprint has been reported on an Ohio Tool Co. plane.

T.J. M'MASTER & CO.

Truman J. McMaster (1797-1880) made planes at both Auburn and Sing Sing prisons, using convict labor under the contract system. In 1839 he defaulted on his contract and it was taken up by Young & McMaster (Alonzo D.). His working dates were Auburn 1825-39 and Sing Sing 1829-38. Earlier he was a partner in Dunham & M'Master (w.s.). McMaster's 1833 contract for planemaking at Sing Sing called for 30 men (convicts) at $37\frac{1}{2}$¢ per day. (see Z.J. M'Master and Young & McMaster) A & A1: FF B & B1: ★ C & C1: ★★ D & D1: ★ E: ★★ F: ★★★ G: ★★ G1: FF *(continued next page)*

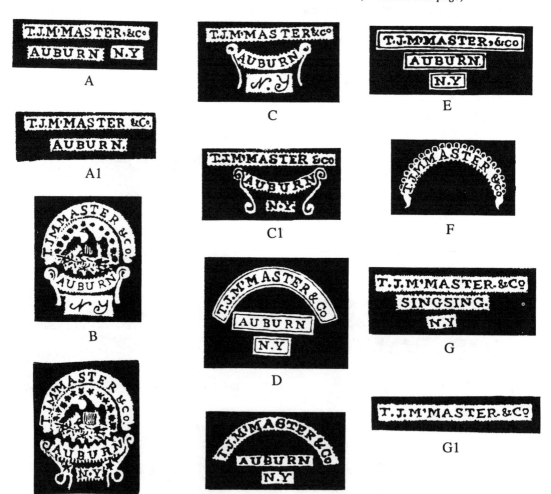

244

Z.J. M'MASTER & CO.

Zalmon J. McMaster (1808-60) was a brother of Alonzo D. and Truman J. McMaster. He made planes with convict labor at Sing Sing 1839-43 and Auburn 1846-47, when the tool contract was sold to Casey, Kitchell & Co. (w.s.). In 1847 Z.J. McMaster's contract at the Auburn Prison included 21 convicts at 32¢ per day, four at 16¢ and one at 24¢. (see T.J. McMaster)   A, B, & C: ★★   D: FF   E: ★   F: ★★   G: ★   H & J: ★★★

(continued next page)

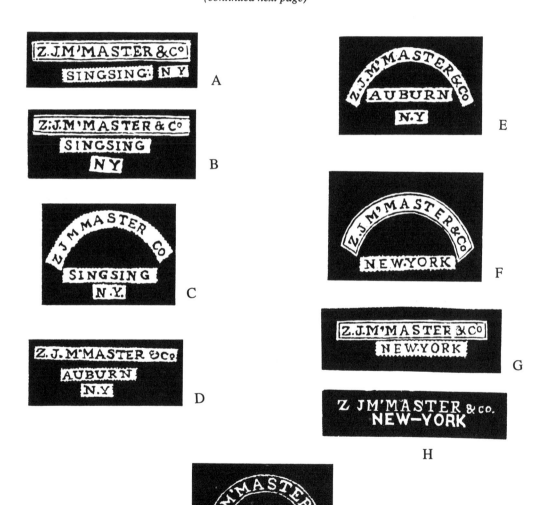

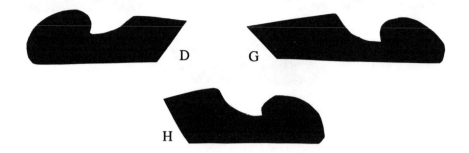

D   G

H

McQUAID & CO.

James A. McQuaid (b.1818, Clearfield, PA) operated a hardware store in Canton, IL, from 1855-63. His imprint has been reported on an Ohio Tool Co. (w.s.) panel raiser.

R.W. MACCUBBIN

Robert W. Maccubbin was a Baltimore, MD, planemaker listed in the city directories in 1840, 1845-58, and 1865-77. (see Kendall & M'Cubbin)   A & B: ★

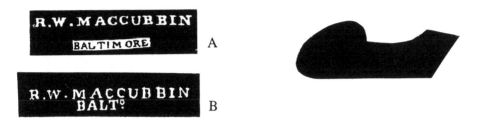

MACEY & HAMILTON

Hardware dealer in Nashville, TN, 1855-57.

A.W. MACK

Alford W. Mack, brother of J.B. Mack (w.s.) was a planemaker in Brooklyn Twp., Susquehanna County, PA, ca.1840.   ★★

J.B. MACK

John B. Mack was a planemaker who appeared on the 1836 tax records of Brooklyn Twp., Susquehanna County, PA. (see A.W. Mack)   A & B: ★★

A   B

247

MACK & CO.

Wm. R. and Royal L. Mack joined D.R. Barton and Co. (w.s.) in 1865, providing needed capital. In 1874 David R. Barton and his sons, Charles and Edward, left to organize a new firm, D.R. Barton Tool Co.(w.s.). The Macks then changed the firm name to Mack & Co. but retained "D.R. Barton & Co." as their trade name. The D.R. Barton Tool Co. failed in 1879 and the Macks took it over. Mack & Co. was in business until 1924, continuing to use the D.R. Barton trademark. No planes have been reported with a Mack & Co. imprint.

J.F. MacNEIL

A John F. MacNeil was listed in the 1880 census for Poughkeepsie, NY, as a toolmaker. Examples reported include a quarter round dated 1881, a cooper's chiv dated 1878, a molding plane dated 1879, and a miter plane dated 1880..

MACOMBER, BIGELOW & DOWSE

A Boston, MA, hardware dealer who was listed in the 1874-83 city directories. It was the successor to Homer Bishop & Co. (w.s.) and in 1884 became Bigelow & Dowse.

J.G. MADDIN

This name has been reported on a left-handed beech sun plane, with the additional imprint 204 ST. JOHN STREET.

GEO. G. MAHAN

George G. Mahan (1825-1875) was listed as a hardware merchant in the 1856 Muscatine, Iowa, directory.

FREDERICK MALCOLM   see Shiverick & Malcolm

P.H. MANCHESTER

Pardon H. Manchester, a Providence, RI, planemaker 1843-59 who was listed in the 1850 census as a planemaker, age 32, and born in Massachusetts.   ★

MANDER & DILLIN

James Mander and Maurice R. Dillin were Philadelphia, PA, planemakers —1865—, who also patented (No. 314338, March 24, 1885), and subsequently produced, an improved chamfer plane. This English style chamfer plane may have originated from Mander, who was a British citizen. The A1 imprint appears on a regular Mander & Dillin chamfer plane, apparently made before the patent was granted, the "applied for" putting potential imitators on notice.   A: ★★

A   A1

MANNEBACH

The Mannebach brothers, Charles J. and Julius, were New York City planemakers 1858-1898. In 1891 the firm was called Mannebach Brothers and advertised miter planes as a specialty. There have been three different imprints reported: MANNEBACH, MANNEBACH BROS., and MANNEBACH BROS/112 STANTON ST. N.Y. The 112 Stanton St. address was occupied from 1880-98 by one or more of the entities.

MANNEBACH BROS.   see Mannebach

J. MANNEBACH

Probably Julius Mannebach, brother of Charles J., who together operated as Mannebach Bros., (see Mannebach). The 112 Stanton St. address was occupied by one or more of the entities between 1880-98. A & B: ★

G.W. MANNING

George W. Manning (1853-1948) was a maker of cooper's tools in Hollis, NH, from 1880 to 1886. A 4 ft. cooper's long jointer, made of cherry, double-ironed and reversible for head and stave in one stock, has been reported. Also reported is a cherry cooper's topping plane with brass adjustment screws. Both are marked MADE BY/G.W.MANNING. A 9" mahogany coffin-shaped smoothing plane with a C.E. HARRINGTON/LOWELL MASS. (w.s.) imprint has the G.W. MANNING stamp on its heel.   ★★★

F.B. MARBLE

Francis B. Marble was a manufacturer and dealer in joiner's and cooper's tools in Cleveland, OH, 1846-56. He was associated with J.J. Vinall (w.s.) 1850-51 and with Marble & Smith (w.s.) in 1856. A patent #46372 was granted to an F.B. Marble residing in Columbus, OH, on February 14, 1865, on a machine for dressing throats in plane stocks.   A & B: ★★

MARBLE & SMITH
A Cleveland, OH, planemaker listed in the city directory in 1856 and comprising Francis B. Marble and ? Smith. (see F.B. Marble)   ★★★

MARKET HARDWARE CO.
Market Hardware Co./293 Market St/Newark has been reported as a purple ink stamp on the side of what appears to be a French rabbet.

MARLEY
Luke Marley was a New York City planemaker 1820-56. He worked at the Elm St. address 1822-28. William F. Hoffmann opened his planemaking shop in 1856 at 360 Broome St., which is where Marley last operated, until 1856. (See /W. Hoffmann and his B imprint) Imprint C is incuse.   A, A1, B, & C: ★★

L. MARLEY   see Marley

A. & W. MARSH
Archibald Marsh and W. Marsh, Cleveland, OH, planemakers, who appeared in the 1837-38 city directory though they probably were active for a longer period of time. An Archibald Marsh worked for H. Chapin (w.s.) as a planemaker 1831-35.   ★★

M. MARSH

Four planes have been reported, all 9" long and made of beech. All are owner imprinted J.E. COLEGROVE and I. CRAIG. These same two owner imprints appear on a R. HOEY/N.Y. plane (see R. Hoey). Appearance is mid-19c. A 9⁷⁄₁₆" boxed molding plane has been reported with an inverted, "& SON" added, the "&" next to MARSH and the "SON" above.

MARSHALL & BROWN

A Westfield, MA, planemaker whose working dates are not known. Appearance is second quarter of the 19c. ★★★

M. MARTIEN

What are believed to be variations on this name appear in the early Philadelphia, PA, directories as HIBSAM MARTIN (1799 and 1800), HIBSAM MARTIEN (1803), MIBSAM MARTIEN (1801 and 1807). Both the HIBSAM and MIBSAM variations occupy the same address as William Martin (see W. Martin) and all may be the same man. ★★★★

MARTIN

A number of planes have been reported, mostly from the Philadelphia, PA, area. One example is side-slipped, a characteristic of Philadelphia and Baltimore planemakers. Appearance is ca.1800. The planes are very similar in style to those of W. Martin (w.s.) and this may, in fact, be another version of his imprint. ★★★

I. MARTIN

Two large groups, totalling 17 planes, were reported found in the Woodstock, VT, area. A sash plane with narrow flat chamfers has also been reported, as has a 9½" birch round, also with flat chamfers, and a 30" jointer.

251

J. MARTIN

Three examples have been reported, a 9⅜" molder, a complex molder boxed with lignum, and a 9½" beech round with round chamfers. Appearance is early 19c.

W. MARTIN

William Martin was one of the early Philadelphia, PA, planemakers who worked —1773-1801—. In 1773 Martin took as an apprentice one Hugh Fegan. It was William Martin who bore the standard of the planemakers in the Fourth of July Grand Procession of 1788 in Philadelphia (an important annual ceremony in the early days of the Republic). His banner included four planes, spring dividers, a square and a gauge. (see also M. Martien and Martin)   A & B: ★   C: ★★

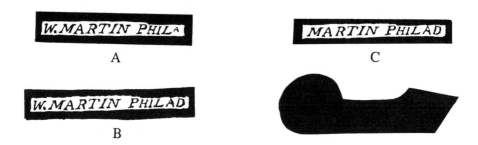

MARTIN & COREY

Howard R. Martin and William E. Corey were hardware store operators in New York City 1857-65. Martin left in 1865 and Corey continued, first alone and then with William H. Neve. The imprint has been reported on a J. Denison (w.s.) boxed bead (C imprint).   ★★

C.R. MASON & CO.

Charles R. Mason & Co., a Lawrence, MA, hardware dealer who was listed in the 1875 city directory.
A: ★   B: ★★

JAMES W. MASON

Made planes in New York City 1874-78. No imprints have been reported from New York City. In 1869-70, a Connecticut directory listed him as a planemaker in Saybrook. Saybrook imprints are known. The 1850 census listed a James W. Mason, age 28, blacksmith, living in Sterling, CT, and born in Rehoboth, MA.

J. W. MASSEY
James W. Massey, a Philadelphia, PA, planemaker 1808-31. (see Stall & Massey)　★★

SAMUEL MASSEY
Listed as a plane manufacturer in Paxton's 1818 Philadelphia, PA, directory, and as operating a hardware store 1821-32. No examples of his imprint have been reported.

MATTESON & SULLY
This imprint has been reported on a 14½" long pair of open handled tongue and groove planes with #48 imprinted on the toe.

MATTHEWMAN & CO.
Probably a hardware dealer in New Haven, CT. Two examples have been reported with Sandusky Tool Co. imprints and one with an Auburn Tool Co. style number.

E.L. MATTHEWS
Emerson L. Matthews was a Baltimore, MD, planemaker ca.1856-59. A 9½" long complex molder has been reported with both a P. Chapin (w.s.) B imprint and the E.L. Matthews imprint, suggesting a relationship.
A & A1: ★★★

 A　　E.L.MATTHEWS BALTᵒ A1

J. MATTISON
Joseph Mattison was a Chicago, IL, hardware dealer, 1845-51.

G. MAYER

A hardware dealer in Lancaster, PA. A match plane made by J. Stamm, as well as planes made by John Bell & H. Chapin/Union Factory (all w.s.) have been reported with the G. Mayer imprint. ★★

J. MAYER

Johannes Mayer (1794-1883), a documented furniture and tool maker of the Mahantango Valley in Pennsylvania, whose work is described and illustrated in *Decorated Furniture of the Mahantango Valley*, by Henry Reed. A painted chest by Mayer sold at a January 1989 auction for $203,500. Over a dozen examples of his planes have been reported, including four that bear owners' stamps: a $13\frac{3}{8}$" sash plane, a 14" panel raiser with offset tote, a $10\frac{7}{16}$" rabbet, and a $9\frac{1}{2}$" bead. All are made of beech. Appearance is early 19c.

W. MAYHEW

Various examples have been reported. All are made of beech, the molding planes are $9\frac{1}{2}$" long with flat chamfers; a tongue and a narrow panel raiser have offset handles and flat chamfers. Appearance is early 1800's.

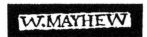 

MEAD SELDEN & CO.

Consisting of A.J. Mead and Samuel Selden, this was a wholesale hardware and cutlery company in Cincinnati, OH, in 1853. Its predecessors were A.J. Mead & Co. (1850-52) and Mead & Winston (1849-50).

 A

 B

MECHANICS TOOL CO.

Reported twice, one a 16" beech jack and the other a 22" beech fore plane, both with an Ohio Tool Co. iron and a late 19c manufactured appearance.

A. MEIER & CO.

Adolphus Meier was a successful businessman who ran, among other enterprises, a hardware business in St. Louis, MO, from 1838-72. Note that the C imprint spells the name MEIR. A & B: ★ B1: ★★ C & D: ★

A

B1

C

B

D

ADOLPHUS MEIER & CO.   see A. Meier & Co.

HERMAN H. MEIER

A St. Louis, MO, hardware dealer in 1853-64. Dr. Murphy, in his study of St. Louis hardware dealers, mentions an imprint but none has been reported to the authors.

MEIGS PATENT

Restored Patent 673OX, Feb.9, 1831, was granted to P. Meigs of Madison, WI, for an adjustable cap iron on a bench plane. The cap iron is stamped Meigs Patent in an enclosed double circle.

A. MEIR & CO.   see A. Meier & Co.

MERRICK   see G.G. Merrick

G.G. MERRICK

George G. Merrick (b.1814) worked as a ship's joiner in Thomaston, ME, ca.1840-60; then moved to Libertyville, IL.   A, B, & B1: ★★★

A

B

B1

I. MERRILL

Jacob Merrill (1763-1841) a Plymouth, NH, cabinetmaker and carpenter whose account books (1784-1812) show that he made smoothing planes, rabbets, and fore planes, as well as other joiners' tools. The imprint has been reported on a 10¼" rabbet and on a beech jack plane.   *(see next page)*

MERITT & CO.   see Merritt & Co.

J. MERRITT
James Merritt, a Hanover, MA, planemaker who appeared in the 1878 Massachusetts business directory.
★★

MERRITT & CO.
Jacob T. Merritt was a New York hardware dealer, chandler, and agent (in the 1840's) for Z.J. McMASTER (w.s.). The firm operated as Jacob T. Merritt & Co. in 1841 and Merritt & Co. 1842-60. It was listed in the 1848 and 1850 city directories as a planemaker.   A & B: ★★

A

B

MEYER & SCHULZE
August Meyer and Charles E. Schulze were St. Louis, MO, hardware merchants 1857-59. Schulze continued as a hardware dealer after Meyer's death in 1859.   ★★

MILLER
Probably a Providence, RI, hardware dealer ca.1870. A jack and a smooth plane have been reported with Auburn Tool Co. (w.s.) style numbers and the Miller imprint.   (see I. Miller)

A. MILLER/NEW YORK
One of the examples reported is a 16" panel raising plane, with the additional imprint of CHAS ASHLEY/OGDENSBURG, a hardware dealer (w.s.). Appearance is mid-19c; location possibly upstate New York.

A. MILLER/PHILADELPHIA

Adam Miller was a planemaker in Philadelphia, PA, 1839-50, and was a journeyman for Israel White (w.s.). His initials A.M. appear on some White imprints (see Charlotte White and Henry G. White). No imprint bearing his name has been reported.

A.R. & G.H. MILLER

Albion R. Miller and George H. Miller were listed in the Chicago, IL, 1865-66 directory as importers and jobbers of hardware and cutlery

E.W. & L.R. MILLER

This imprint was reported on an Arrowmammett (w.s.) plow plane. Probably a hardware dealer.

F. MILLER

Frederick Miller, born 1816 in PA, was a planemaker in Philadelphia, PA, 1837-52. During part of this period he was a journeyman for the White family (see Israel White, Charlotte White, and Henry G. White). His initials F.M. appear on some White imprints. No plane bearing his imprint has been reported. (see Pennell & Miller)

G. MILLER

Various examples have been reported. All are made of beech; the molding planes have wide flat chamfers; a 13" long cornice plane has an early offset handle. Appearance is ca.1800; location probably Pennsylvania.

H. MILLER

Henry Miller was a St. Louis, MO, hardware merchant 1850-54 and 1860-65 who had previously clerked for M. & N.H. Stout (w.s.). From 1857 to 1860 Miller was agent for W.W. Miller (w.s.) and during 1863 Henry Miller operated at W.W. Miller's address.

A

A1

H.B. MILLER

Henry B. Miller of Lebanon, OH, was listed as a cabinetmaker between 1828-31, and was a partner of Peter Probasco in Miller & Probasco (w.s.) in Cincinnati, OH, —1834—.

I. MILLER

This name has been reported on a small smoother with the location mark PROVIDENCE. (see Miller)

J. MILLER

This name has been reported on a round plane with the location imprint N. YORK.

J. MILLER & BRO.

This name has been reported on two hollows of mid-19c appearance.

J.D. MILLER

Appears with the additional imprint BRIDGEPORT; working dates are not known.

JOHN P. MILLER

Listed as a planemaker in Cincinnati, OH, in 1842. No example of his imprint has been reported.

M. MILLER

Reported on an Ohio Tool Co. (w.s.) round and on a Weiss & Sohn (Austria) rabbet. Most probably a NYC hardware dealer.

W.W. MILLER

William W. Miller was a St. Louis, MO, hardware merchant 1857-60. (see H. Miller) ★★

MILLER & PROBASCO

Henry B. Miller and Peter Probasco made planes in Cincinnati, OH, —1834—. (see P. Probasco) ★★★

MILLIGAN

An Auburn Tool Co. (w.s.) razeed jack plane has an additional imprint on his toe "Sold by/Milligan/229 Federal St/Boston".

E.D. MILLIKEN

This imprint has been reported on several hollows and rounds. Appearance is mid-19c.

J. MILTON

Joseph Milton (1789-1864) the father of M.H. Milton (w.s.), was a cabinetmaker and planemaker in Canaan, NH, 1818—. A & B: ★★

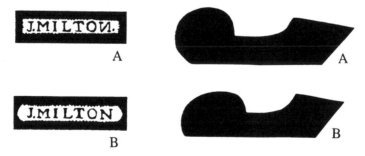

M.H. MILTON

Matthew Harvey Milton (1819-1905), the oldest son of J. Milton (w.s.). A cabinetmaker, he made planes in Canaan, NH, ca.1850, but became a merchant in 1854. Examples exist bearing the imprints of both father and son. ★★

J. MINOT

A number of examples have been reported. Appearance is early 19c; the location is unknown.

MISSOURI PREMIUM/H.C. & T.

This imprint has been reported on a screw-arm plow of mid-19c appearance. (see G.H. Nichols)

ISAAC D. MITCHELL

Listed in the Dayton, OH, city directories as a planemaker from 1871 to 1890 and again 1898-1900. During this period he also made cooper's tools, was a saw filer, and dealt in various craftsman tools. No example of his imprint has been reported.

R. MITCHELL

Reported on a coping plane and a nosing plane.

JOHN T. MIX & CO.

This name appears on a jack plane imprinted W.H. POND/NEW HAVEN (w.s.). There is an incomplete location imprint NEW ___. Very probably a New Haven, CT, hardware dealer.

A. MOCKRIDGE

Abraham (or Abram) Mockridge (d.1873) was a partner of David Bensen in Benson & Mockridge, Albany, NY, 1830-31 (w.s.). Mockridge left Albany for Newark, NJ, in 1833. He appeared in the Newark directories 1835-36 and 1840-41 as a plane and coach tool maker under his own name, and 1835-68 as a partner in Mockridge & Francis (w.s.) at the same address. He was listed in the 1850 census as a plane manufacturer, age 47, born in NJ and owning real estate worth $7500. ★

MOCKRIDGE & FRANCIS

A Newark, NJ, partnership of Abraham (or Abram) Mockridge and Elias Francis (b. in NJ ca.1813) that made planes and dealt in hardware 1835-68. Their planes are the most plentiful of any New Jersey maker. A three arm adjustable plow plane, with a metal center adjusting mechanism, both handled and without handle, was apparently developed and sold by the firm. The firm was succeeded by Mockridge & Son. (w.s.; see also A. Mockridge and Elias Francis)   A. B, B1: FF   Three arm adjustable plow plane ★★★★   *(see next page)*

x

260

 A  B  B1

MOCKRIDGE & SON

The successor to Mockridge & Francis (w.s.) in 1868. It was headed by Oscar B. Mockridge, son of Abraham. The firm made planes and dealt in hardware and tools in Newark, NJ, 1868-98. ★

MONTGOMERY

Joseph A. Montgomery was a Massachusetts-born planemaker, who worked under these imprints in Boston in 1848 only. In 1850, at age 40, he was a principal in Hall, Case & Co., Columbus, OH (w.s.) and owned real estate worth $2000. He later became the Superintendent of the Sandusky Tool Co. (w.s.). (see also Cooley & Montgomery, Hull & Montgomery, and Montgomery & Woodbridge)   A & B: ★★

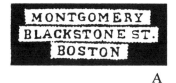 

A   B

MONTGOMERY & WOODBRIDGE

A Boston, MA, planemaking firm comprising Joseph A. Montgomery and Edwin C. Woodbridge in 1847. (see E. Woodbridge; also see Montgomery)   A & B: ★★

 A  B  A

MOON & LABY

A Cincinnati, OH, planemaker and coach tool manufacturer 1849-50.

MOORE

William Moore was listed as a hardware dealer in NYC 1844-47. (see William H. Moore)   A & B: ★★

A

B

A.G. MOORE

Albert G. Moore was a New York City planemaker who worked 1853-61 at 65½ Bowery, the same address that R.W. Hendrickson (w.s.) worked at between 1859 and 1861; and J.W. Farr (w.s.) —1852.
A, A1, & B: ★

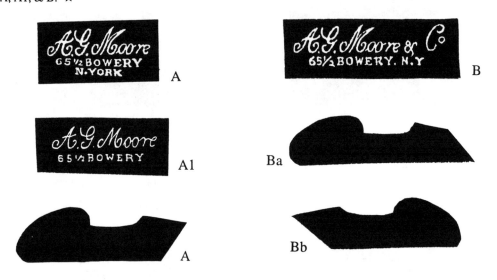

A

B

A1

Ba

A

Bb

A.G. MOORE & CO.   see A.G. Moore

JAMES MOORE & SONS

A Concord, NH, hardware dealer 1872-83, whose partners were James, Byron, and Ira B. Moore. An imprint has been reported but was not legible enough to reproduce.

T. MOORE

This imprint was reported on a 9⅜" long beech skewed rabbet with wide rounded chamfers. Appearance is second quarter 19c. A Thomas Moore appeared in the 1850 census for Richmond, VA, as age 28, a cabinetmaker, born in VA.

THEOPHILUS MOORE

A Baltimore, MD, planemaker 1819—. No example of his imprint has been reported. A Theophilus Moore is also listed as making planes in Liverpool, England, 1823-67—, with the imprint MOORE/LIVERPOOL. (see Thomas Moore)

THOMAS MOORE

Thomas Moore was listed as a planemaker in Baltimore, MD, —1814-16—, 1823, and —1829-36. No examples have been reported. A Thomas Moore made planes in Liverpool, England and was listed as planemaker in 1794 and 1807. Because of the similarity of the working dates, and the possible Liverpool origin of each of them, it is felt that Thomas Moore and Theophilus Moore (see entry above) may be the same, or closely related persons.

WILLIAM H. MOORE

Appeared in the Baltimore, MD, city directories as a planemaker —1835-36 and a hardware dealer 1847-51. A William Moore (see Moore) was a hardware dealer in New York City, 1844-47, and it is possible, considering the working dates, that they were the same person.

A.C. MORE

Abner C. More (or Moore) was a planemaker in Goshen, MA, 1848-51. He sold his millsite and machinery to the newly formed Union Tool Co. in 1851. ★★

C. MOREHOUSE

A New Haven, CT, planemaker —1840-46 and a joiner 1850-57. ★★

Z. MORGAN JR.

This name has been reported a number of times. The molding planes are 9½" long, beech, some boxed, all look professionally made. Appearance is ca.1840.

M. MORIARTY

Matthew Moriarty (d.1911). He arrived in Bangor, ME, in the 1860's and operated a cooperage for 40 years, retiring in 1906. He was listed as a toolmaker in the 1873 Maine directory, making cisterns and cooper's tools to order. On July 16, 1872, he was issued Patent No. 129419 for an adustable howel.

JULIUS MORISSE

(d.1891) A St. Louis, MO, hardware dealer, 1848-91. Julius Morisse was formerly a clerk at T.J. Meyer Hardware Co. in 1847.   A, A1, & B: ★

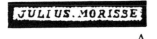
A

A1

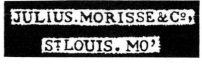
B

JULIUS MORISSE & CO.   see Julius Morisse

A. MORRILL

This name appears on a rosewood 11⅛" miter plane.

B. MORRILL

Benjamin Morrill (1789-1862) was a joiner and tool maker in Bangor, ME, 1832-51. He also served in the state legislature and was a captain in the state militia. His father was a carriage maker. The minutes of the Bangor Mechanics' Association for Dec. 4, 1832, gave his occupation as planemaker.   A, A1, & B: ★★

A

A1

A

B

B

I. MORRISON

This imprint was reported on a complex molding plane found in a Pennsylvania flea market. Earlier a pair of handled match planes were reported as coming from the Erie, PA, area. Also reported was a 9⅜" beech round and a 9⅜" side bead, both with interrupted lignum stripes in their soles, and rounded chamfers. An owner's brand, JNo. COGGINS, was burned into the side of the round. The side bead was found in eastern PA.

J. MORRISON

Three planes have been reported, a 9½" ogee, a 9½" cove and bead, and 9⁷/₁₆" hollow, all beech with flat chamfers and a Sleeper-type wedge.

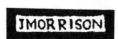

J. MORRISON [OHIO]

John Morrison advertised as a planemaker in the Chillicothe, Ohio, *Supporter and Scioto Gazette* during May and June 1826.

J. MORSE JR.

Joshua Morse, Jr. (1774-1826) was a carpenter, joiner and toolmaker of Hopkinton, NH, who advertised in 1816 and in 1819 that he made tools for joiners, cabinetmakers and coopers "with stocks and irons for bench tools and moulding tools of all descriptions, of the best quality in the newest fashions and warranted good. He will take most kinds of Country Produce, Cash, or approved notes in payment. Orders by Post-Riders will be particularly attended to the same as if purchasers themselves were present." (see I. Long) ★★

A.S. MORSS

Anthony S. Morss, a Boston, MA, hardware and chandlery dealer 1847-1900—, who offered carpenter's and cooper's tools.

A

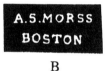

B

C.W. MORSS

Charles W. Morss, a Boston, MA, hardware dealer 1868-76.

A. MORTON & CO.

This imprint, with the additional location imprint CLEVELAND has been reported on several planes. Appearance is mid-19c. Likely location is Cleveland, OH.

Q. & W.L. MORTON

Quinn and W.L. Morton were listed in the 1852 Virginia directory as Petersburg, VA, hardware merchants.

(see next page)

265

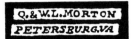

J. MOSELEY

James Moseley was listed as a planemaker in the 1850 census, living in Richmond, IN, age 39. He advertised his planemaking in the Richmond *Jeffersonian* at intervals between 1846 and 1851, moving his shop several times during that period. He was born in England where Moseley was an important name in English planemaking.

MOSES   see E. Moses

E. MOSES

Edward Moses (b.1815 in CT) made planes in Deposit, Hastings, and Ashford, NY, ca.1850. A rabbet has also been reported with an E. HARTFORD location imprint.   A, B, B1, & B2: ★★   C, C1 & D: ★★★ E: ★★★★

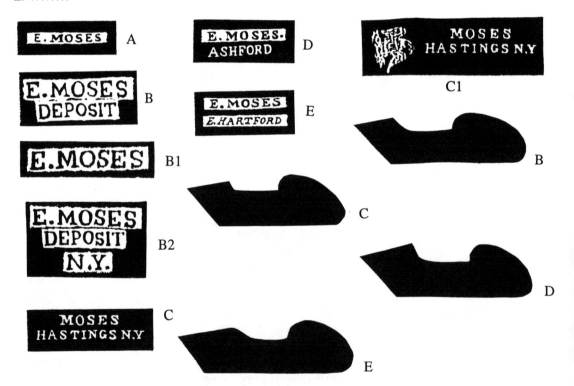

WILLIAM MOSEY

Listed as a planemaker in Cincinnati, Ohio, 1849-50. No example of an imprint has been reported.

A.H. & W.V. MOSS

This imprint appears on a ¾" bead with #18 stamped on the heel. The plane came from the Cleveland area, so the Sandusky may well be Sandusky, OH. In the 1850 census for Portland, OH, Augustus H. Moss, age 39, and William V. Moss, age 29, were both listed as merchants and both born in NY.

MOUND CITY PLANE CO.

This name has been reported on a plane whose appearance is ca.1850. There is a Mound City in Illinois, in Kansas, and in Missouri, and it is also the nickname of St. Louis, MO.

WM. MUIR & CO.

Made planes in Windsor Locks, CT. Working dates are not known, and no imprint has been reported.

MULTI-FORM MOULDING PLANE CO.

Founded by Thomas D. Worrall in 1856 and operating 1856-58 in Boston, MA (Charlestown being part of Boston). The company manufactured planes with interchangeable soles, based on a patent granted on Aug. 29, 1854 (No. 11,635). The company made a wide range of types and sizes, including complex molders and plow planes, tongue and groove combinations, beads, etc. Several examples have been reported with the C imprint, indicating that Multi-Form supplied planes to the Ohio Tool Co. (w.s.). For a much more complete description of the company and its products, see *Patented and Transitional Planes in America, Vol. I* pp.25-36, listed in the Bibliography.

A	B	C

G. MUNDORFF

This name has been reported on a beading plane with the location imprint BERLIN and on a jack plane with the location imprint BERLIN PA. Berlin, PA, is south of Johnstown near the Maryland border. Appearance of the planes is early 19c.

A. MURDOCK

Amasa Murdock, made planes in Boston, MA, 1825-41 and, in 1828, became a member of the Massachusetts Charitable Mechanics Assn. as a planemaker. Three planes reported are a $10\frac{1}{16}$" beech center bead, and two 10" rounds. All three have $\frac{1}{4}$" flat chamfers, suggesting an earlier starting date, or the existence of two generations of planemakers.

W.D. MURRAY

This imprint was reported on a $9\frac{1}{2}$" long moving filletster and a rosewood plow with boxwood arms and nuts made by J. Kellogg/Amherst Mass (w.s.). A probable hardware dealer.

J. MYERS II

Jeremiah Myers, a South Boston, MA, planemaker 1858—. No example of the imprint has been reported.

T. NAPIER   see Thos. Napier

THOs. NAPIER

Thomas Napier was born in 1747 near Glasgow, Scotland, where he was apprenticed, became a journeyman toolmaker, and finally opened his own business in 1773. Shortly thereafter, in 1774, he joined the Scottish migration to the American colonies, presumably to escape the political unrest and depressed economic conditions plaguing Scotland during that period.

He landed in Philadelphia during November 1774 and set up a planemaking shop. Among his first orders was one from James Stiles (see J.Stiles), the New York City planemaker, in the amount of one pound one shilling "for makin Sudry plans." In 1785 Napier was again recorded as having a shop in Philadelphia and in 1786 advertised that he carried "all manner of carpenters, joiners, cabinet makers, chair makers, coach makers and coopers tools made in the best and neatest manner." Again in the *Pennsylvania Mercury* for April 28, 1786, he advertised 57 different types of planes "by Thomas Napier, a planemaker from Edinburgh" adding that he could make "any kind of planes - to drawing or pattern, to the greatest exactness, the charge according to the work in them."

In 1794 Napier moved to nearby Wilmington, Delaware, where he apparently was engaged in coopering, returning to Philadelphia and planemaking in 1796. By 1797 he was also manufacturing and selling "Fishers Pills" and then "Napiers Pills." He died in 1812, leaving an estate of approximately $500. William Grinel (see W. Grinel) was an appraiser of the estate, and Hugh Hazlet (see Hazlet) was the administrator of Napier's wife's estate in 1820, while George White (see G. White) was an appraiser.

Napier was the only planemaker we know who imprinted his name on planes made both in Great Britain and the United States. Only one example is known of his Scottish planes. It is a molding plane, 9¾" long, with flat chamfers and the "THO" lacking the upper case "S". Only one example of the B stamp with the location imprint PHILAD. has been reported (designated as B1). The T. NAPIER B imprint probably is the later of the two American imprints. Like so many planemakers of the period, making a living was difficult for Napier and financial success elusive. Also, despite a planemaking career of over 40 years, relatively little of his work survives, leading us to question how successful he was in making and marketing his product. [Acknowledgement is made to Alan G. Bates, author of "Thomas Napier - The Scottish Connection" (see Bibliography) from which most of the foregoing information was obtained.]   A: ★★   B: ★★★   B with "Philad." (B1): ★★★★★

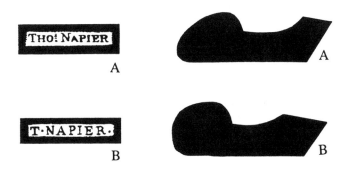

H.L. NARRAMORE

Henry Lyman Narramore (1836-1898), born in Massachusetts, made planes in Goshen, MA, 1865-72. He was also listed as a planemaker in Cummington, MA, in 1859.   A: ★★   B: ★

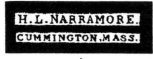
A

B

A

NATHUSIUS, KUGLER & MORRISON

A hardware dealer in New York City 1859-76. The partners were Oscar A. Nathusius, Charles E.A. Kugler, and Robert Morrison. An example has been reported imprinted on a J.H. LAMB/NEW BEDFORD (w.s.) toothing plane. (see Cassebeer Reed & Co.)   A: ★★   B: ★★★

A

B

JOHN M. NAYLOR & CO.

Probably a hardware dealer in Tiffin City, Ohio. John Naylor, 37 years old, was listed in the 1850 census as a merchant living in the village of Clinton, a suburb of Tiffin City. He owned $10,000 in realty and $2000 in personal property. The appearance of the planes is mid-19c. The stamp shown below is overstruck on a plane imprinted by Casey & Co/Auburn N.Y. (w.s.). Examples also exist overprinted on Sandusky Tool Co. and Auburn Tool Co. planes.

HENRY J. NAZRO

Henry J. Nazro (d.1905) operated as a hardware dealer in Milwaukee, WI, —1847. (see H. Nazro & Co., J. Nazro & Co., and Nazro & King)   ★★

H.J. NAZRO & CO. (HENRY J. NAZRO & CO.)

Henry J. Nazro & Co., a Milwaukee, WI, hardware dealer, 1848-59, consisting of Henry J. and John Nazro Jr. (1826-88). (see Henry J. Nazro, J. Nazro & Co., and Nazro & King).   A: ★   B: ★★

A   B

270

J. NAZRO & CO.

A Milwaukee, WI, hardware dealer. John G. Nazro, a cousin of Henry J. Nazro, was the owner and was in business 1860-80. It succeeded H.J. Nazro & Co. (w.s.).

JOHN NAZRO & CO.   see J. Nazro & Co.

NAZRO & KING

Henry J. Nazro, from Massachusetts, and Henry U. King, from Troy NY, were hardware dealers in Milwaukee, WI, 1844-47. (see Henry J. Nazro)   ★★

B.B. NEALS

Reported on a 22" long fore plane with an Auburn Tool Co. Thistle brand iron.

S. NEEL

Samuel Neel was a hardware dealer in Wheeling, VA. (now WV) -1837-51.   ★★

PETER NEFF & SONS

A Cincinnati, OH, wholesale hardware dealer, 1849-65.   ★★

THOS. NEGUS & SONS

A probable hardware dealer. The name has been reported on a bead with #123 marked on its heel. This is H. Chapin's (w.s.) style number for single boxed beads.

NELSON & HAYNER

Arba Nelson and John E. Hayner were hardware dealers in Alton, IL, 1853-73.

 A   A1

NEW BEDFORD TOOL

Listed in New Bedford, MA, directories 1873-79 as a manufacturer of bench and molding planes, as well as a hardware and tool dealer. The company employed W. G. Lamb and his brother J. H. Lamb (w.s.) and is believed to be the successor to the Taber Plane Co. (w.s.).

NEW HAVEN PLANE CO.

This imprint has been reported on a 16" beech jack plane of mid-19c appearance with an additional location imprint "N. H. Ct", presumably New Haven, CT.

NEWARK PLANE RULE & LEVEL CO.

This company was listed in the Newark, NJ, directories from 1878-86. In an advertisement in the 1879 city directory E. Francis, late of Mockridge & Francis (w.s.), was listed as Superintendent and "full sets of planes and all kinds of tools for carpenters, coopers, carriage and cabinetmakers furnished to order or made to draft. Level glasses reset, repairing and cutters made to order." ★★★★

A.H. NEWBOULD

Alexander H. Newbould, a hardware dealer in Detroit, MI, 1837-55; succeeded by Buhl & Ducharme (w.s.). Charles Ducharme was a clerk with Newbould in 1845 and 1846. ★★

J.A. & F.W. NEWBOULD

This name has been reported on a plow plane and a round plane with mid-19c appearances.

A. NEWELL

Various examples of this imprint have been reported: an ovolo with double fillet and narrow flat chamfers, a hollow and round, and a 9⅞" long cherry ovolo. Appearance is late 18c. A rabbet of early 19c appearance, was found near Lanesboro, MA, home of E. Newell (w.s.). The B imprint appears on a plane that seems to have been made a generation later than that of the A.

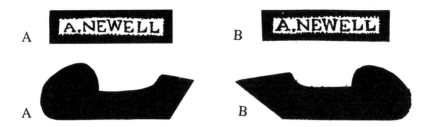

A. NEWELL/NEW YORK CITY

Andrew Newell made planes in New York City 1886-92 and then was a tool dealer 1898-1905.

E. NEWELL

Capt. Ebenezer Newell of Lanesboro, MA (1747-1808), served in the revolutionary army. His estate inventory, dated October 5, 1810, included $25.50 of sundry joiner's tools, as well as 20 "chisells", 20 files, 8 gouges, 5 handsaws and a lathe. His earlier planes are made of birch and the molders are generally 9¾" to 10" long. They have flat chamfers and a Nicholson-style wedge. One example has fluting on the toe and heel similar to the early Jo. Fuller style, as well as wider chamfering than usual. Later examples are 9½" long, made of beech, with flat chamfers. The wedge outlines are the same as those for the earlier birch planes.   A & A1: ★★

A	A1

NEWHALL & STEBBINS

This imprint appears on an M. Copeland & Co. (w.s.) molding plane. A probable hardware dealer.

NEW YORK TOOL CO.

A brand name of the Auburn Tool Co. (w.s.). It was used 1864-93. The imprints shown below are incuse. A, A1, & A2: FF

A

A1

A2

273

NEW YORK WORKS

Reported on a manufactured 8" smoothing plane.

G.H. NICHOLS

This imprint appears on a 9½" round. Appearance is ca.1850. (see Missouri Premium/H.C. & T.)

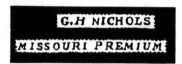

F. NICHOLSON

Francis Nicholson of Wrentham, MA (1683-1753), is generally believed to be the first American planemaker who imprinted his name. He was the father of John Nicholson (see I. Nicholson) and the owner of the slave Cesar Chelor (see Ce. Chelor). He was listed as a joiner in 1716 in Rehoboth, MA, and moved to Wrentham in 1728. He was married four times, was a deacon of the church, and died in Wrentham in 1753. In his will, in which he referred to himself as a toolmaker, he left most of his tools to his son John, and some to his slave, Cesar Chelor, also giving Chelor his freedom.

At least two examples of the B imprint exists with a dot after the "F" rather than a star. By the nature of the die-making process this would have to be the first state of the stamp, assuming the same die stamp continued to be used. The presence or absence of the location stamp LIVING IN/WRENTHAM or just the LIVING IN stamp seemed to depend on the space available on the toe of the plane. There were three separate dies (one for each line) making up the complete imprint, allowing this flexibility. The three wedge variations shown apparently have no chronological significance, nor do the variations from 9¾" to 10⅛" in the length of the molding planes. A: (large Wrentham, A and M joined): ★★★★★ (unique) B, B1, B2: ★★ C (with dot instead of star): ★★★★★

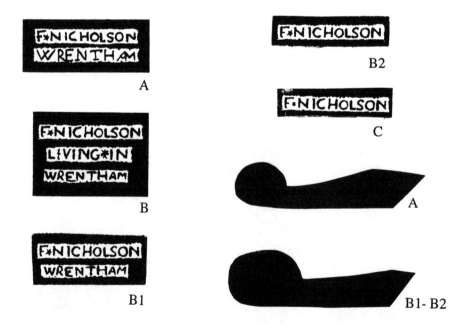

I. NICHOLSON

John Nicholson (1712-1807) was the son of Francis Nicholson (w.s.). In 1739, he was noted as a joiner in Wrentham, MA. He later was noted as living in Cumberland, RI, which resulted from a change in town boundary lines. In 1751 he was referred to as a yeoman and joiner and afterwards (1763) as a gentleman, having presumably acquired sufficient property. He died, aged 96, in Union, ME. His planes are rarer than those of his father and of Ce. Chelor.

John Nicholson's plane imprint appears in a number of variations. [1] A (and perhaps A1 and A2): LIVING IN/WRENTHAM (a separate die for each line) were possibly used between 1733 when he attained age 21 and was probably working with his father until 1739/40 when he acquired land and moved his wife and family some six or seven miles away. [2] B and B1: IN/WRENTHAM. Having moved away he a acquired a new "IN" stamp, and possibly a very close copy, or else a duplicate, of the WRENTHAM stamp (1739/40-1747). [3] C: IN/CUMBERLAND. In 1747 the Wrentham town lines were changed and Nicholson found himself living in Cumberland, RI. He remained there until 1763.

He returned to Wrentham in 1763 and may have used the Wrentham stamp once again, though now he was referred to as a gentleman (a gentleman didn't make planes, or he wouldn't have been considered a gentleman). Further complicating matters was Nicholson's tendency to simply imprint his name only, even though there was room for his location stamp. The reasons are subject to all sorts of conjecture.

A, A1, A2, B, B1, C: ★★★

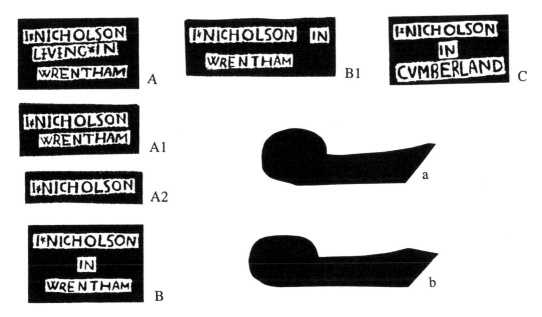

H. NILES

Possibly Hezekiah Niles, brother of S. Niles (w.s.) or more likely, a relation from an earlier generation. The name has been reported on various planes, including a 12⅛" handled molding plane. All have heavy flat chamfers and are made of beech. The molding planes usually range from 9⅞" to 10⅛" in length.   ★★★★

S. NILES

Samuel Niles of Wilmington, DE, advertised in the *Delaware Gazette* in 1791 that he carried on the planemaking business. He was also a carpenter and cabinetmaker and was killed in 1796 when a sign blew down on him. His younger brother Hezekiah offered the business for sale, stating in an advertisement "Carpenters, Joiners &c are respectfully informed that he has on hand a variety of plains which he will sell low for cash." (see H. Niles)   ★★★★   *(see next page)*

275

J.R. NOBLE

This name has appeared on a 9½" long bead. Appearance is mid-19c.

TIMOTHY B. NOE

Listed in the Newark, NJ, 1837 directory as a planemaker. No example of his imprint has been reported.

LYMAN NOLTON

A Salina, NY, planemaker —1850—. No example of his imprint has been reported. (see Hayden & Nolton)

W. NORCROSS

Probably a hardware dealer. The imprint appears on a Collins/Utica (w.s.) molding plane.

B. NORMAN

Benjamin Norman was born in New Jersey, probably in North Brunswick, in 1812. It is likely he was one of the four apprentices to Samuel C. Cook (w.s.) enumerated in the 1830 U.S. census. In the 1840 census Norman was "employed in manufacturing and trades" in North Brunswick, and one of his planes is known bearing an 1840 date. The 1850 census found him in Trenton, NJ, occupation planemaker. He was listed in the first general Trenton city directory (1854-55) as a planemaker but apparently left the city and planemaking in 1856, as he was not listed in the 1857 or subsequent directories. By the 1860 Federal census he was living in Pennington, NJ, occupation "store and livery." Because his planes are so rare, it is possible that most of his North Brunswick work was for S.C. Cook and bears Cook's mark. A: ★★★ B: ★★★★

NORRIS & BROTHER

Richard N. Jr., George W., and George S. Norris were hardware dealers in Baltimore, MD, 1840-58. ★★

N. NORTON

Nathan F. Norton was a planemaker in Philadelphia, PA. He first appeared in the city directory of 1837. He was later listed in the Camden, NJ, section of the Philadelphia directories of 1850-56. Earlier he worked as a journeyman for the Whites. His initials N.N. appear on some of the White imprints. (see Israel White, Charlotte White, and Henry G. White) ★★

B.B. & W.R. NOYES

Benjamin B. and William R. Noyes were hardware dealers in Detroit, MI, 1846-59.

D. NOYES

Planes reported with this imprint are similar to those of S. Noyes (w.s.), made of beech and a very early 19c appearance.

E.O. NOYES

This imprint appears on a 7/8 beech screw stop dado made by GLADWIN & APPLETON, which also has a SOUTHWORTH & NOYES imprint. Southworth & Noyes (w.s.) were hardware dealers. E.O. Noyes could have been a predecessor or successor. Brockton and Bridgewater are close to each other.

S. NOYES

A Samuel S. Noyes (1785-1832) was a successful East Sudbury, MA, cabinetmaker. This imprint appears on the heel of a 10" molding plane having an E. Clifford (w.s.) imprint on its toe. A number of other examples have been reported, made of beech, heavily chamfered and of very early 19c appearance, including a $9^{15}/_{16}$" hollow with $^3/_8$" flat chamfers and a Sleeper-style wedge.

I. NUTTER

Various examples have been reported, made of both birch and beech, with molding planes ranging between 9½" and 9¾" in length and with flat to heavily rounded chamfers. A James Nutter (b.1775) was an architect and master joiner in Portsmouth, NH —1804-09—. The appearance of the planes would fit into this time frame.

E. NUTTING

Ebenezer Nutting (1803-86), a planemaker in South Amherst, MA, —1830-57. He was the elder brother of Truman Nutting (w.s.) and operated a small plane factory just downstream from him. He was listed in the 1830 and 1840 censuses for Leverett, MA, as a toolmaker and in the 1850 census for Amherst, MA, as age 50, engaged in tool manufacturing and owning real estate worth $1000. Living with him was his son E.P. Nutting (w.s.) and three other planemakers. In 1837 $8000 worth of planes were manufactured with 10 employees. In 1845 the value of tools manufactured was $14,975 utilizing 22 employees. The 1850 industrial census showed him employing 11 male hands and two females. During his nearly 30-year career, Nutting sold large amounts of lumber, lathe, and shingle, some wooden planes, primarily bench types, and very large quantities of plane handles for other plane manufacturers or as a subcontractor. His account books listed 32 different recognized planemakers as customers. Planes with his mark are quite rare. (see T. Nutting)   A & B: ★★★

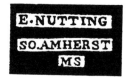 A    B

E.P. NUTTING

Edward Porter Nutting (b.1828), the oldest son of Ebenezer Nutting (see E. Nutting), made planes in So. Amherst, MA, —1852-56—, part of which time he was in partnership with his father. In 1855 $18,000 worth of tools were manufactured. He was listed in the 1850 census as age 22, a planemaker living with his father. ★★★

J.H. NUTTING

John Hastings Nutting, son of Truman Nutting's half-brother George, boarded with Truman Nutting in 1834 when he was 16, and presumably learned planemaking. Entries in Truman Nutting's journal, 1840-41, indicated that John bought planes from, and sold planes to, Truman Nutting. In April 1847 the journal reported that John H. sold Truman 669 smoothers. (see T. Nutting)   ★★★

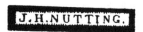   

N. NUTTING

Nathan Nutting (1804-1867) became a journeyman carpenter in 1833 and was listed as such in the 1855 and 1867 Maine business directories, and as a mechanic in the 1850 census. His imprint has also been reported on

a large hollow with the additional location stamp OTISFIELD. (see N. Nutting & H.C. Smith)
A, B & C: ★★★

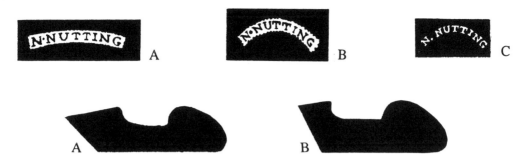

N. NUTTING & C.H. SMITH
An example has been reported with the location imprint NORTHAMPTON. (see N. Nutting)

T. NUTTING
Truman Nutting (1807-91), a planemaker in Amherst, MA, 1829-52, was the brother of Ebenezer Nutting (see E. Nutting) and operated a sawmill and shop just upstream from him. He also made plane parts, such as handles and stocks, for other plane manufacturers. He was listed in the 1850 census as a tool manufacturer, age 42, born in MA, and having real estate valued at $8000. Wyman Hoyt, age 21, and Henry H. Nutting, age 20, both planemakers, were listed as living with him, as were Alonzo Nutting, age 18, and Frank Nutting, age 16, who were described as toolmakers (and sons). In the 1850 Industrial census he was listed as having 18 male and two female employees, utilizing water and steam power to produce 500,000 shingles worth $1000, 300,000 lath worth $1500, 200,000 feet of lumber worth $200, and 90,000 plane handles worth $6600. In 1852 Nutting left Amherst for Olean, NY, where he did carpentry and then moved on to Minnesota, where he ran a hotel, farmed, and manufactured brooms. ★★★

NUTTING & FOX
A planemaking partnership consisting of Truman Nutting and Luther Fox (w.s.) 1834-36, in Amherst, MA. No examples have been reported.

JOSEPH NUZUM
This imprint has been reported on a molding plane with a location imprint FAIRMONT VA. (now WV). A Joseph Nuzum was listed in the 1850 census as a cabinetmaker, age 28, born in VA and residing in Marion County, VA (in which Fairmont is located).

B.W. OAKLEY & SON

Benjamin W. Oakley (b.1805) was a Fort Wayne, IN, hardware dealer —1858-72. (see Oakley & French)

OAKLEY & FRENCH

Benjamin W. Oakley was in partnership with ? French as a Fort Wayne, IN, hardware dealer —1858—. (see B.W. Oakley & Son)

CHARLES ODELL

Charles Odell was a Salem, MA; hardware dealer 1869-76.

ELI ODELL

Eli Odell (1806-1878) was a tool maker and planemaker in Winterset, IA. He was granted Patent No. 41317 on January 19, 1864, for a device that closed the throat of a bench plane, adjusting for wear.

OGONTZ TOOL CO.

A brand name of the Sandusky Tool Co. (w.s.), used on tools distributed by Hibbard, Spencer & Bartlett (see A.C. Bartlett) and possibly others, and most often found on bench planes. Ogontz was a chief of the Ottawas who lived in Sandusky, Ohio, during the early 19c.   A: FF   B: ★★

A

B

OHIO KING

Possibly a trademark of the Sandusky Tool Co. or the Ohio Tool Co. (both w.s. - also see O.K./OHIO)

(see next page)

OHIO KING

OHIO PLANE CO. see A.C. Bartlett

OHIO TOOL CO.

A major plane manufacturing company in the 19th and early 20th centuries. It was incorporated in Columbus, OH, in 1851 by Peter Hayden (see P. Hayden & Co.) and others, and had a tradition of periodically utilizing prison labor. The first president was George Gere, a hardware dealer (see Gere, Abbott & Co.). In 1851 the company was reported employing 200 hands, with carpenter's planes as the main line. By the 1870's and 1880's, the ready acceptance of metal and transitional planes, and other competition, was increasingly felt. In 1887 the company employed only 70 hands (the use of prison labor having ceased in 1880) and in 1893 Ohio Tool merged with Auburn Tool Co. (w.s.), with Ohio Tool the survivor. In 1913 the Ohio factory was destroyed by a flood and in 1914 manufacturing was re-established in a new plant in Charlestown, WV. Operations ceased in 1920. The 1910 price list still offered an extensive line of wooden planes. A style number usually appears on imprint H in the space under "Ohio Tool Co." A through E: FF   F: ★   G & H: ★★

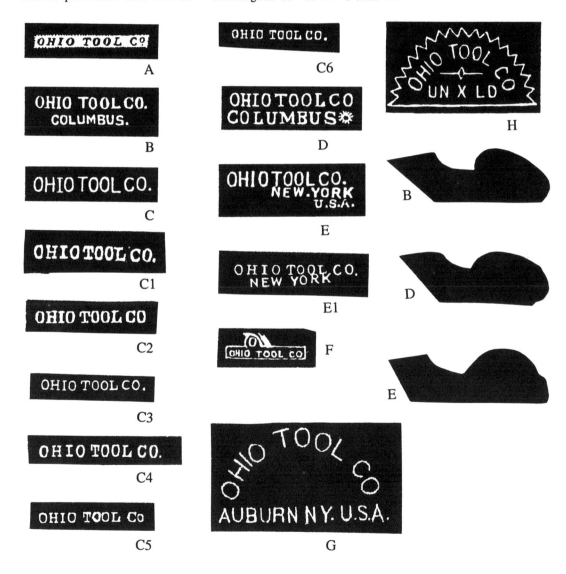

281

O.K./OHIO

Possibly another variation of the OHIO KING (w.s.) trademark.

OLNEY

A planemaker in Providence, RI, who worked ca.1800. The molding planes reported are made of birch, have a relieved wedge, and range from 9⅝" to 10" in length. ★★★

ONTARIO 2

This mark has been reported on a D.R. Barton & Co. (w.s.) jack, as well as on an unmarked wide round and several other jack planes. There was a ferry called Ontario II , built in 1915, that ran between Coburg, Ontario, and Rochester, NY. Service was discontinued in 1951. The planes bearing the imprint all appear to be late 19c, early 20c and factory made.

J. OOTHOUDT

A number of planes have been reported. Appearance is ca.1830-40; location probably the Hudson Valley of NY. The two Oothoudt imprints, "J" and "W", are similar in appearance. Their molding planes range in length from 9¼" to 9½" and are made of beech. Their wedge styles are quite distinctive, having an extended narrow finial. Chamfers are narrow and rounded. Several examples have W. Butcher irons. The planes have a crisp professional look. Several are boxed. A pair of hollow and rounds, 9½" long (J. Oothoudt), have "1833" imprinted on their toes. (see W. Oothoudt) ★★

W. OOTHOUDT

A number of planes have been reported. Location is thought to be the Hudson Valley of New York, based on where the planes have been found and the Dutch name. Appearance ca.1830-40. (see J. Oothoudt) ★★

ORGILL BROS. & CO.
A Memphis, TN, hardware company that succeeded Lownes & Co. (w.s.) in 1857 and continues today as one of the largest wholesale hardware companies in the U.S.

ORMSBY-BLAIR & CO.
A Louisville, KY, hardware merchant 1851-56, comprising Robert J. Ormsby and Henry S. Blair.

ORMSBY & OWEN
Reported on a screw arm plow of ca.1850 appearance. (see Ormsby-Blair & Co.)

OSBORN & LITTLE
A New York City planemaker —1846 consisting of Charles Osborn and Charles S. Little. After 1846 it was continued by Little as a hardware dealer under Little's name. (see C.S. Little & Co.)

OTT
Reported on a 9½" long beech bead.

OTT & GREER
A hardware company that only appeared in the 1851 Wheeling directory. The partners were Jacob R. Greer and either, or both, Samuel L. Ott and Morgan L. Ott. By the next Wheeling directory in 1856, Greer had become a partner in Greer & Laing (w.s.).

OWASCO TOOL CO.

A trade name owned and used by the Auburn Tool Co. (w.s.) —1875—. All imprints shown below, including A, are incuse.   A, B, & B1: FF   B2: ★★

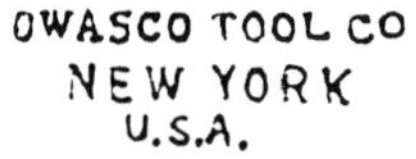

OWASCO TOOL CO
NEW YORK   A
U.S.A.

OWASCO TOOL CO
NEW.YORK   B

A and B

OWASCO TOOL CO   B1

B

OHIO TOOL CO.
NEW.YORK
U.S.A.   B2
OWASCO TOOL CO

WARREN PACKARD

Six planes have been reported, all carrying Ohio Tool Co. style numbers, as well as this imprint. Warren Packard (1828-97) was a hardware dealer in Warren, OH, (1865-72) and was the father of the two brothers who founded the Packard Motor Car Company.

I.W. PAINE

Various examples have been reported, all beech molding planes, 9⅜" to 9½" long. Six are from one group. One of these is also imprinted D.O. CRANE and another COLLINS/UTICA (both w.s.).

T. PALMER

This imprint has been reported on a pair of cherry handrail planes and on a beech dado. Appearance is mid-19c.

EDWIN C. PARK

Edwin C. Park was born in 1821 in Pennsylvania and was listed in the 1850 general census as a planemaker in Richmond, IN. During the period 1857-71 he was variously described as a plow maker, a carpenter, and a woodworker. At least one example has been reported. (see H.M. Park)

H.M. PARK

A Harvey Park was listed as a planemaker (probably as a journeyman) in the 1836-37 Cincinnati, OH, directory, but apparently went on to become a planemaker under his own name. (see Edwin C. Park, J. Hughes/H.M. Park)

BENJAMIN PARKER

Made planes in Hingham, MA, —1849—. He was listed in the 1850 census as a carpenter in Hingham, age 71, owning real estate worth $7,500. There has been no report of an imprint.

J. PARKER

Joseph Parker was listed in the 1850 Federal census as a planemaker in Newark, NJ.

PARKER, HUBBARD & CO.

Alonzo Parker (1807-1892) and Horace Hubbard made planes in Conway, MA, 1842-49—, and shortly thereafter founded the Conway Tool Co. (w.s.). In the 1850 Industrial census the company was reported employing 64 hands, using steam power, and producing 130,000 molding tools worth $50,000 and 60,000 bench planes worth $25,000. Alonzo Parker was listed in the 1850 census as a tool manufacturer in Conway, MA, born in MA; and Horace Hubbard was listed the same, age 42, born in CT. Hubbard was shown living in East Hartford, CT, in the 1830 and 1840 censuses. Both A and B imprints are embossed.   A: FF   B: ★★

 A  B  A

C. PARKHURST

Charles Parkhurst (b. ca.1793 in NJ) appeared in the 1835-36 Newark, NJ, directory as a planemaker and in the 1850 census as a turner. (see Parkhurst & Coe and J. Parkhurst)   ★★★

J. PARKHURST

A John D. Parkhurst was listed in the 1850 Federal census as a 57-year old carpenter, born in NJ and living in Springfield, NJ. (see C. Parkhurst)

L. PARKHURST

A plane has been reported with this imprint and the location imprint HARTFORD.

PARKHURST & COE

Charles Parkhurst and Joseph D. Coe were listed in the 1835-36 Newark, NJ, directory as toolmakers and planemakers. Joseph D. Coe was listed in the 1850 census as a turner, age 50, born in NJ and owning real estate worth $20,000. No example of an imprint has been reported. (see C. Parkhurst)

GEO. PARR

George Parr & Co. was listed as a maker of awls, saw sets, and other carpenter's tools in Buffalo in 1866. Earlier, in 1861, George Parr was listed as a Buffalo edge tool maker and may have been the Parr in Parr & Parmelle, who made edge tools in Buffalo in 1865.

JOHN PARR

A 3¾" long smoothing plane has been reported with JOHN PARR/47 8TH AV. N.Y. incised across its nose and containing an iron stamped in a circle JOHN PARR ● NEW YORK with "cast steel" across the middle of the circle. A John Parr Jr. was listed as a hardware dealer at 546 8th Ave. in the 1856 NYC directory.

PARRISH

Robert Parrish advertised planemaking in 1775 and continued in the trade until after 1800. A record of early Philadelphia apprenticeships lists the apprenticing of one William George Dorrington to Robert Parrish, Philadelphia, on January 20, 1773, for 8 years 9 months 7 days. Parrish was described as a "Wheat fan maker and Plain maker." In 1776 Robert Parrish and a John Nicholson advertised in the *Pennsylvania Ledger* of February 10, 1776, for the return of two runaway indentured servants, one a gunstocker, the other a "plainmaker."
★★★★★

R.A. PARRISH

Robert A. Parrish was a Philadelphia, PA, planemaker —1807-45. A marking gauge marked PARRISH and with his 1819 directory address (238 N. 3rd St.) has been reported, and a T. Goldsmith (w.s.) plane has been reported overprinted R.A. Parrish. (also see Parrish, Parrish & Barry, and Parrish & Massey)   A & A1: ★
B & C: ★★★

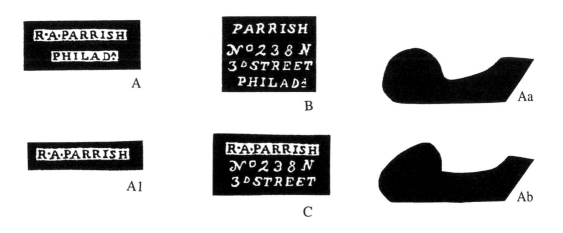

PARRISH & BARRY

A planemaking partnership in Philadelphia ca.1820, probably comprising Samuel Barry and Robert A. Parrish. (see Barry & Co. and R.A. Parrish)   ★★★   *(see next page)*

PARRISH & MASSEY

Listed in the Philadelphia, PA, directory of 1817 and 1820-22 as a hardware dealer at 238 No. 3rd. (see Parrish & Barry, R.A. Parrish, and J.W. Massey)

PARRY

John S. Parry made planes in New York City in 1832; in Albany, NY, 1833-37 and 1840-41; and in Brooklyn, NY, 1842-54. He also was a partner in Bensen & Parry (1838-39; w.s.). A & B: ★★

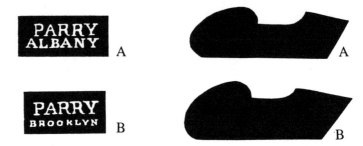

A.C. PARSONS

Amasa Chester Parsons (1826-1913) was born in Massachusetts, made planes in Cummington, MA, —1874-80— and was listed in the 1870 census as a plane handle manufacturer, and in the 1880 census as a planemaker. No example of an imprint has been reported.

E. PARSONS/J.M. BABBIT

These names have been reported on a molding plane. An Elisha Parsons was listed as a planemaker in the 1834 Cincinnati, OH, directory and J.M. Babbit (w.s.) was noted as a planemaker in Mason, OH, —1850-56.

S. PARTRIDGE

The A imprint appears on a birch Yankee plow plane, 9⅞" long, with wood screws, square inset arms, wood depth stop, and a riveted skate. A Stephen Partridge married Jemima Taft in Mendon, MA, in 1776. (see E. Taft) A & B: ★★★★★

E. PASQUARELLI
Both a match and a plow plane has been reported with this imprint. Appearance is mid-19c.

JOHN PASSCUL
Listed in the early Philadelphia directories as a planemaker, probably as John Paschal in 1797 and 1799, and as John Pascue in 1796. All located in Cable Lane.   ★★★★★

MATTHEW PATTEN
Matthew Patten (1719-1795) was a woodworker and toolmaker in Bedford, NH (1754-73) who made smoothing planes, fore planes, rabbets, ogees, plows and cooper's jointers. No example of his imprint has been reported.

W. PAWLETT & CO.
This imprint has been reported on various planes. Appearance is mid-19c.

J.A. PEALE & CO.
Probably a hardware dealer in Vicksburg, MS, whose imprint has been reported on Ohio Tool Co. planes.

J. PEARCE
This imprint has been reported on bench planes and is thought to represent the second line (non-warranted) of planes sold by the Union Factory/H. Chapin (w.s.) to New York tool stores and wholesalers (C imprint)..
A: ★   B, B1, C1: FF

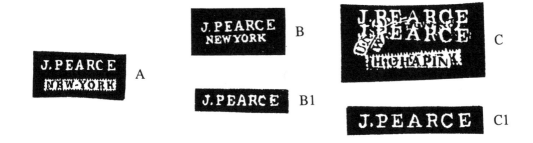

J.W. PEARCE

Jonathan W. Pearce (b.1815) was a planemaker who worked in Fall River, MA, —1840-52 and Providence, RI, 1853-79. "J.W. Pirce" is believed to be an earlier variant spelling of his name. The name stamp has appeared without the location stamp even where there is adequate room for both on the toe of the plane. The C imprint was reported on a beech plow with birdseye maple arms, fence and nuts of ebony, and wedge of rosewood; possibly a presentation piece.   A: ★   B: ★★★   D, D1: ★★

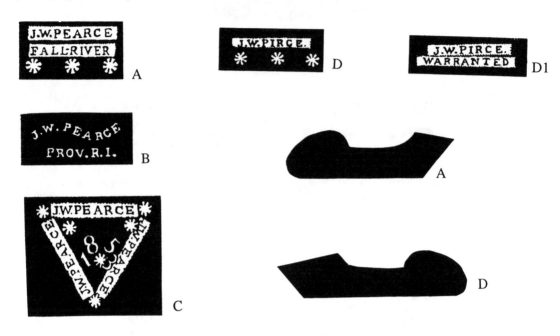

E. PEARSON

This name has been reported on various 10" long beech molding planes of mid-18c appearance. Probable location is Pennsylvania.

E.B. PEASE & BRO.

This name has been reported on a side bead.

PECK & CROUCH

A Northampton, MA, planemaker ca.1850 whose name imprint often included the same eagle motif as appeared with H. Wells, Arnold & Crouch, and J.D. Kellogg, all of Northampton, MA. A Francis Peck and a Charles Crouch worked for the Greenfield Tool Co. (w.s.) 1853-54. (see Arnold & Crouch)   ★★   *(see next page)*

290

P.M. PECKHAM

Perry Mumford Peckham (1789-1880) was a planemaker in Fall River, MA, —1850-60—. At various times he was also a cabinetmaker, a maker of deck plugs, wedges and steering wheels (for ships), and a saw filer. He was born in RI and appeared in the 1820 census in Bristol RI, 1830 in Troy RI, and in 1840 and 1850 in Fall River. In 1850 he was listed as a planemaker. Found with a group of 13 P.M. Peckham planes, all owned by the same user, was a plane imprinted PMP, 10¼" long, with a relieved wedge (see below). It probably represents the early work of Perry Mumford Peckham or else a like-named ancestor from a previous generation.
B: ★★ B1: ★

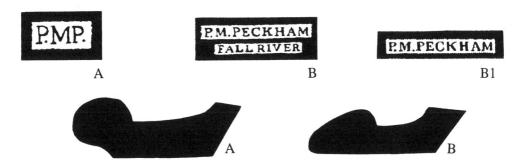

A. PEELER

Various examples of this imprint have been reported, including an 8¾" long round made of beech, a 10⅛" long birch hollow, and a jack made of yellow birch. Appearance is ca.1800. A 9¾" birch plow plane with oak thumb screws and wedge, a maple depth stop, and arms mortised into the fence, imprinted PEELER, has also been reported, as has a 14½" x 2¼" birch panel raiser. The PEELER and A PEELER stamps are identical, and since the first initial "A" is a separate die, they probably represent the same maker. The improbable looking wedge is authentic.

H.W. PELL

This imprint was reported on an Ohio Tool Co. (w.s.) B imprint jack plane, suggesting that H.W. Pell was a hardware dealer and very possibly related to Pell & Wright (w.s.).

PELL & WRIGHT

This imprint has appeared on a plow plane and a tongue. Appearance is ca.1850. (see H.W. Pell)

(see next page)

291

E.W. PENNELL

Edward W. Pennell (b. ca.1814) was a Philadelphia, PA, planemaker —1839-59. He was listed in the 1850 census as a planemaker, age 36, born in PA. George Gorbutt, also a planemaker, was listed as living with him. The B1 imprint is shown as a variant, made possible by the separate die stamps (see Pennell & Miller)

A & B: ★★

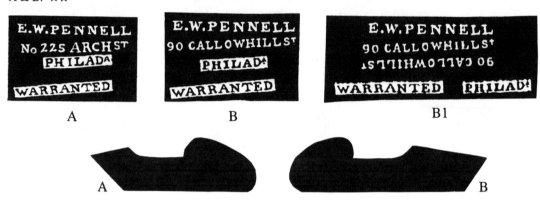

A   B   B1

A   B

PENNELL & MILLER

A Philadelphia, PA, planemaking partnership comprising Frederick Miller and Edward W. Pennell that was listed in the Philadelphia city directories of 1848, 1850-52, and 1854. (see E.W. Pennell and also F. Miller)

A & B: ★★★

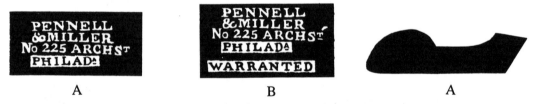

A   B   A

A.W. PERKINS

A number of planes with this imprint have been reported, including a plow plane with wood screws and depth stop, a 9⅝" boxed complex molder, a 9½" long beech rabbet, and a 14" beech panel raiser with centered tote; all with round chamfers. Appearance is early 19c.

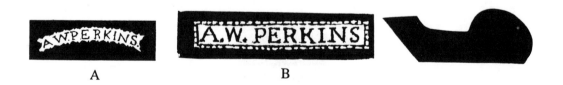

A   B

H. PERKINS

Hiram Perkins (1822-72), who advertised in the *Cabot Advertiser* (VT) Jan. 1869: "Tools! All Kinds of Carpenters and Joiners Tools made to order. Also cash paid for Second Growth White Beech Butts." In the 1870 census he was listed as a farmer and toolmaker in Cabot, VT.   A & B: ★★★★

H. PERKINS & CO.

This imprint has been reported on an H. Chapin plow, suggesting that Perkins was a hardware dealer.

J. PERRY

There may be more than one generation of J. Perrys involved in planemaking (who may or may not be related). The A imprint has appeared on an 18c-style crown molder, a Yankee plow, and three 9⅞" long molding planes with 5/16" flat chamfers. The B imprint appears on planes that have an early 19c appearance.   A: ★★★★ B: ★★★

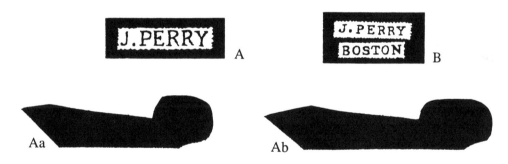

J.B. PERRY & CO.

This name has been reported on a 9¼" beech molding plane. Appearance is second quarter 19c.

293

J.H. PERRY
John H. Perry was a New York City planemaker 1850-63. ★★★

W. & E. PERRY
William Perry and ? Perry, planemakers in West Haven, CT, whose working dates are unknown, but based on the appearance of their planes could be ca.1820-30. ★★★

PETERS & TRIMBLE
Norris Peters and Joseph M. Trimble were hardware merchants listed in the 1857 Richmond, IN, city directory.

JOHN PETTINGELL
A Lowell, MA, planemaker —1875—, who was listed in the directories as a carpenter 1844-78 and who supplied wood for plane stocks. No example of an imprint has been reported.

J. PHELPS
Several examples of this imprint have been reported. The planes are made of beech. The maker stamp looks early, the chamfers are flat on the toe and heel and rounded on the top of the stock. Appearance is ca.1800.

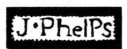 

PHILADA. WORKS
Probably an abbreviation for "Philadelphia Works." Nothing is presently known about this company. Two planes have been reported, a side bead and a toted beech plow plane. Appearance is ca.1850.

T. PHILLIP

Several examples have been reported. The planes are thought to be from Pennsylvania and made in the early 19c.

B. PHILLIPS

Benjamin Phillips, a Cincinnati, OH, planemaker, —1836-52.

N. PHILLIPS

Nathaniel Phillips was a Boston, MA, planemaker 1807-23.   ★★

S. PHILLIPS WORKS

This imprint has been reported on a beech fore plane and on a gutter plane. Appearance is mid-19c. A Silas Phillips was listed in the 1850 census as a 33-year old coachmaker living in Greenfield, MA.

PHOENIX COMPANY

A planemaking company that was housed in Lambert Hitchcock's former chair factory at Hitchcockville, CT, and was founded by Arba (1807-81) and Alfred Alford. The firm started in 1853 as a reorganization of A. & A. Alford & Co. (1849-53; w.s.). The plan was to make carpenter and furniture tools as well as chairs and furniture. In 1864 the company was sold to Delos Stephens, who continued tool manufacturing on the site until 1901, when the firm moved to Pine Meadows and became Chapin Stephens Co. (w.s.). (also see Warner & Driggs and W. Warner)   FF

PHOENIX FACTORY   see W. Warner and Warner & Driggs

J. PICKERING
Several planes have been reported, all made of beech, with Sleeper-type wedges and narrow flat chamfers. Probably made in southeastern New England during the early 19c.

JOHN PICKERING
John Pickering was listed in the 1813-14 Philadelphia, PA, directory as a planemaker. No example of his imprint has been reported.

T. & A. PICKERING
A Cincinnati, OH, hardware dealer 1866-1965. (also see J.W. Wayne & Co.)

E. PIERCE
Various examples have been reported, made of yellow birch (except one of cherry). The molding planes are all between 9" and 9¼" long, with ¼" flat chamfers. Appearance is 18c. A $9^{15}/_{16}$" round made of yellow birch, with $^{7}/_{16}$" flat chamfers and fluting, and a tongue plane, bear an even earlier-looking E. Pierce imprint that appears to be mid-18c and may be the work of a preceding generation. A is the earlier imprint; B the later.   B: ★★★★

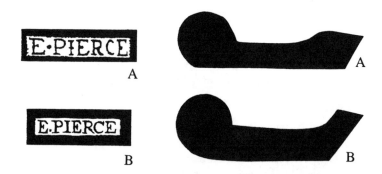

A

A

B

B

E.G. PIERCE JR.
Elisha G. Pierce Jr. (b.1822) was listed as a carriage manufacturer in 1861 and 1864 and in *Walton's Vermont Register* as a "manufacturer of Carriages and Sleighs" from 1881 to 1899. Earlier he was listed in the 1850 census as a carpenter. Among the various planes reported is an 18" long shipbuilder's dado and a twin match plane on a single stock, similar to the P.A. Gladwin & Co. (w.s.) 6/9/1857 patent.   ★★★

J.W. PIERCE   see J.W. Pearce

I. PIKE
Probably Jarvis Pike Jr., who appeared in the Dedham, MA, records from 1738-42 and/or his father, Jarvis Pike, who appeared in 1726 and 1733. One of the earliest of the New England planemakers.   ★★★★★

J. PIKE
Various examples have been reported. The molding planes range between $9\frac{5}{8}$" and $9\frac{3}{4}$" in length, are made of beech, and have wide flat chamfers. Appearance seems to indicate ca.1800.

A.M. PIPER
Several examples have been reported. Appearance is early 19c.

B. PIPER
A planemaker in Newton, MA, 1881—. No example of an imprint has been reported.

R. PIPER
Rufus Piper (1791-1874), a carpenter and planemaker in Dublin, NH.   A & B: ★★★★

 A    B

T.P. PIPER
This imprint appears on a $9\frac{1}{4}$" long beech grooving plane with two sets of owners' initials.

297

T.W. PIPER

This name appears in the maker's slot on a 10" beech hollow and a 10" molding plane with rounded chamfers. S.A. Piper is incised twice on the toe and once on the heel of the hollow and A.M. Piper (w.s.) once on the heel.

J.W. PIRCE   see J.W. Pearce

J.T. PLATT

John T. Platt was listed as a planemaker in Bridgeport, in 1868 and again in the 1870 census, age 45, and born in CT. Earlier he was listed in the 1850 New Haven, CT, directory, also as a planemaker.   ★★★

J.T. PLIMLEY & CO.

This imprint appears on a 9¼" beech single-boxed complex molding plane, whose appearance is ca.1850.

S. PLUMER

Several examples have been reported, one a 9¹¹⁄₁₆" long molding plane with wide flat chamfers and a Sleeper-style wedge. There were a number of Samuel Plumers in Massachusetts during the 18c. One Samuel Plumer, born in Newbury, MA, on June 16, 1737, was a carpenter and lived in in the Newbury area until his death in 1817.

S. PLUMMER

Silas Plummer (b.1822) was listed as a carpenter in Lisbon Falls, ME, in the 1850 census. In the 1870 Products of Industry census, he was shown as making $700 worth of plane stocks and tool chests.   ★★★★

L. POLLARD

A number of planes have been reported with this imprint, including a group owned by the Fruitlands Museum, Harvard, MA. The planes are generally 9½" long and made of beech, though several examples are almost 10" long with flat chamfers. Appearance is ca.1800. Possibly Luke Pollard, who was born in Harvard, MA, in 1774 and died some time after 1830.   A & B: ★★★

A   B   A

S. POMEROY

Believed to be Simeon Pomeroy of Northampton, MA. These planes range from 10" long, made of birch, to 9½" long, made of beech; indicating a long period of planemaking, —1800—.   ★★

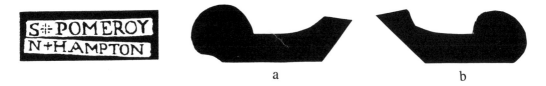

a   b

DAVID POND

A New Haven, CT, planemaker 1853-68. In 1868 he worked at the address of Pond & Briggs (w.s.). No example of his imprint has been reported.

W.H. POND

Wadsworth H. Pond made planes in New Haven, CT, 1844-80—. The William H. Pond listing which appeared in the New Haven 1847-48 directories is believed to be a misprint for Wadsworth H. Pond. The 1860 Industrial census listed six employees who had produced 18,780 planes worth $15,000 during the year. The Pond imprint is most often found without the decorative stag imprint. (see Pond & Briggs; Pond, Malcolm & Welles; and Pond & Welles)   A, A1, B1: ★

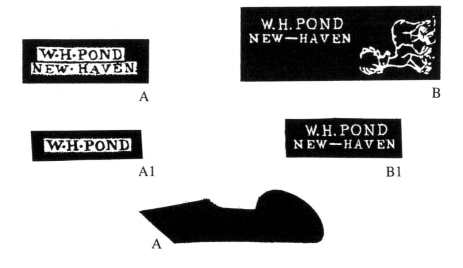

A   B

A1   B1

A

POND & BRIGGS

Wadsworth H. Pond and William A. Briggs made planes in New Haven, CT, 1868-69. (see W.H. Pond)

POND, MALCOLM & WELLES

Wadsworth H. Pond, Frederick S. Malcolm, and ? Welles made planes in New Haven, CT, ca.1860. (see Pond & Welles, W.H. Pond, and Shiverick & Malcolm)   A & A1: ★★

 A

A1

POND & WELLES

Various examples have been reported. Appearance is ca.1850. (see Pond, Malcolm & Welles and W.H. Pond) ★★

L.T. POPE

Lemuel Thomas Pope was listed in the 1837-41 Boston, MA, directories as a planemaker. He also received a U.S. patent dated March 17, 1838, covering a machine for punching and shearing iron. ★★

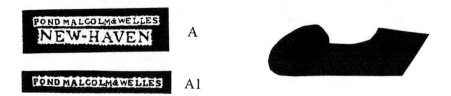

PORTER & SPERRY

Listed as planemakers in the New Haven, CT, directory of 1860. No example of an imprint has been reported.

C.D. POTTER & CO.

This name has appeared on a pair of 14" handled tongue and groove plank planes with threaded fence arms. Delaware is just north of Columbus, OH.

N. POTTER

Possibly Nathaniel Potter (1693-1768) who was a carpenter in Lynn, MA, and whose estate inventory listed "3 fore planes," "three long plaines," "three smoothing plaines," a plow plane, plus 69 other planes and "9 new plaines" and plane irons. Several planes have been reported, made of birch: a $10\frac{7}{16}$" rabbet, a $9\frac{7}{8}$" bead, a $10\frac{3}{8}$" halving plane, and a 10" long Yankee plow.   *(see next page)*

S.H. POTTER

A Terre Haute, IN, hardware dealer, 1844-63. Known as S.H. Potter & Co. in 1844 (a partnership of Samuel H. Potter and Lucius Ryce); listed as S.H. Potter 1858-63.

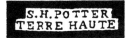

POTTER & RICHEY

Wm. W. Richey (w.s.) and ? Potter, planemakers 1844-45, in Louisville, KY. Their imprint reads POTTER & RICHEY/LOUISVILLE KY.

POTWINS

A.C. & W.S. Potwin, who were hardware dealers in Terre Haute, IN, 1863-64—. They were successors to Potwin & Bush (ca.1858) and their predecessor was Potwin & Burnham (ca.1852).

T. POULTNEY & SONS

Thomas Poultney was listed as an ironmonger in Philadelphia, PA, in the 1790 Federal census. The imprint was found on a plane made by Mutter, London, England (1766-99).

W. POWEL

The records of the mayor of Philadelphia, PA, for the years 1770-74 include the record of one Benjamin Thomton, apprenticed to William Powell of Philadelphia on October 8,1771, for 4 years, 6 months, and 12 days for the sum of £21/9 shillings to be taught planemaking and given 5 quarters of school. Powell's molding planes are beech, just under 10" long and have ¼" flat chamfers.   ★★★★★

H. PRATT

This name has been reported on a beech Yankee plow plane with the location imprint WRENTHAM, and also on a cherry molding plane. A Henry Pratt was born in Wrentham, MA, May 14, 1771, and appeared in the 1800 census in nearby Sherburn.

PRATT & CO.

A large Buffalo, NY, hardware firm that operated 1836-60. The 1850 census listed Samuel F. Pratt as the proprietor, aged 43. (see S.F. Pratt & Co.)   A, B, B1, & C: ★

A   B   B1   C

S.F. PRATT & CO.

Samuel F. Pratt (b.1807 in Vermont) was a partner in Pratt & Co., Buffalo, NY (w.s.).

A

B

PRATT & FOX

A St. Louis, MO, hardware dealer 1863—. It was the successor to Child, Pratt & Co. (w.s.). No example of an imprint has been reported.

D. PRESBREY

Probably Daniel Presbrey (1785-1856) of Taunton, MA, son of S. Presbrey (w.s.). Both imprints appear on molding planes that vary in length from 9¼" to 9½" and have rounded chamfers and boxing.   A & B: ★★

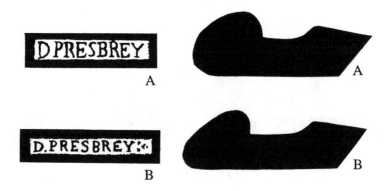

A   A

B   B

S. PRESBREY

Thought to be Simeon Presbrey (1758-1840), a carpenter who lived in Norton, MA —1781-1810—. One of his sons, Simeon Jr. (1792-1858), may also have made planes using these stamps. (see also D. Presbrey)
A & B: ★★★   C: ★★★★

C. PRESCOTT

Charles Prescott was a Lowell, MA, planemaker who appeared in the Lowell city directories 1832-55 and 1861-78. He was listed in the 1850 census as a carpenter, age 45, born in MA; and in the 1850 Industrial census as employing one male hand and producing planes worth $600.   ★★

GEORGE E. PRICE

A George Price, age 26, was listed as a merchant in the 1850 census for Staunton, Augusta County, VA. This imprint appears on a Greenfield Tool Co. (w.s.) hand rail plane.

PRIESTLEY & BEIN

A New Orleans, LA, hardware firm founded ca.1841 by John D. Bein and William Priestley (who died shortly thereafter). Priestley was succeeded by his mother, Margaret Foulke Priestley, and Bein's brother-in-law, Henry D. Richardson. In 1860 the firm became J.D. Bein & Sons and after the Civil War was absorbed by Rice Brothers & Co.

303

PROBASCO   see P. Probasco

G. PROBASCO

This imprint has been reported on a professionally made 14" wedge-arm plank plane (tongue) with a James Cam iron. Appearance is second quarter 19c.

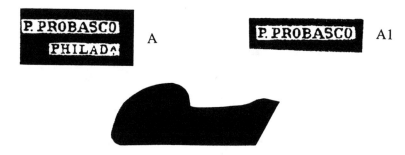

P. PROBASCO

Peter Probasco was a planemaker who appeared in the 1823-30 Philadelphia, PA, directories; then moved to Ohio, signing an apprentice agreement on February 10, 1829, in Lebanon, OH "to teach the art, trade, mystery, and occupation of plane making" to one Charles Webber, age 11, the agreement to expire on January 11, 1839. (This was an unusually early age to begin an apprenticeship). Probasco appeared in the 1830 census as living in Turtle Creek Twp., which was part of Lebanon. By 1831 Probasco was in Cincinnati, boarding with J.D. Conover (see John Conover). During —1834— he was a partner in Miller & Probasco (w.s.) and in 1839-40 he worked for E.F. Seybold (w.s.), all in Cincinnati. Finally a Peter Probasco appeared in the 1840 census in Hancock County, Indiana, near Indianapolis and some 75 miles northwest of Cincinnati.   A & A1: ★★

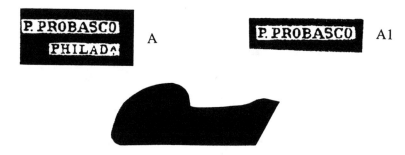

J.S. PRUDEN & SONS

A New York City hardware dealer. The imprint illustrated showing "751 and 753 8th Ave/New York" appears on a Shiverick (w.s.) hollow and a Shiverick dado, and represents a location that was not advertised by Pruden in the NYC directory.   ★★

E. PUFFER

Thought to be Elijah Puffer (1738-1816), who was born in Norton, MA, and later moved to Medway, two towns that are notable in early American planemaking history. His mother, Rebekah Ware, was the cousin of Mercy Ware, who married John Nicholson (see I. Nicholson), and both were nieces of Mary Ware, Francis Nicholson's third wife (see F. Nicholson). In 1764 he moved to Peterborough, NH. A plane has been reported imprinted E. PUFFER IN PE_____, which is presumed to be Peterborough.

Q.T. & CO.   see Quackenbush Townsend Co.

J.E. QUACKENBUSH & SON
John E. and Abram Quackenbush were listed as hardware dealers at 535 Eighth Ave. in the 1872-73 New York City directory. In 1874 "& Son" was added. Earlier John had a listing under "umbrellas" and Abram was a carpenter.   A & B: ★★

A

B

QUACKENBUSH TOWNSEND CO.
A New York City hardware firm that operated 1865-92. The partners were Charles E. Quackenbush and William H. Townsend. In later years, Robert Townsend joined the firm. The A imprint shown below is incuse.
A & B: ★★   C: ★★★★

A

B

C

QUEEN CITY TOOL CO.
A Cincinnati, Ohio, hardware dealer; dates not known.

Jno. B. QUEGLES

A Natchez, MS, planemaker; appearance is ca.1840.

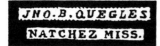 

P. QUIGLEY

Philip Quigley was born in Ireland, came to the U.S. in 1845 and first appeared in the Newark, NJ, directory of 1849-50 as a manufacturer of spirit levels and carpenter's tools. The 1850 general census listed him as a carpenter's tool maker, age 25. Quigley left New Jersey for California, arriving in San Francisco in 1852. His first listing in the San Francisco directory was in 1862 as a carpenter; and from 1867-70 he manufactured spirit levels and carpenter's tools on Market Street. He died in 1871. From the little information available, it's likely that he was a tool dealer as far as planes were concerned. After Philip Quigley left Newark, a John Quigley appeared in the 1852 Newark directory as a grocer and a carpenter's tool maker, continuing through the 1856-57 directory. No examples of his imprint have been reported.   A, B, C: ★★★

A   P. QUIGLEY   P.QUIGLEY. 822 MARKET ST.S.F

A   B   C

S. RANDALL

Samuel Randall made planes in Albany NY 1826-41 under various entities. Though he appeared in the city directory only in 1833-34, it is probable he also made under his own name as early as 1830. The A imprint shown below is incuse. (see Randall & Bensen, Randall & Co., Randall & Cook, and Randall & Shepard.)
A & B: ★   C: ★★

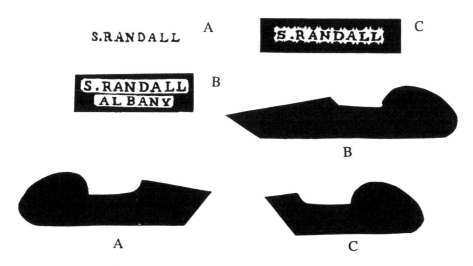

RANDALL & BENSEN

A planemaking partnership of Samuel Randall and David Bensen in Albany, NY, 1827-29. (see S. Randall and also David Bensen)   ★★

RANDALL & CO.

An Albany, NY, planemaker 1840-41. Successor to Randall & Cook (w.s.) with the same partners. No example of an imprint has been reported. (see S. Randall)

RANDALL & COOK

A planemaking partnership of Samuel Randall and Moses Cook in Albany, NY, 1835-39. (see S. Randall)
A: ★★   B: ★   *(see next page)*

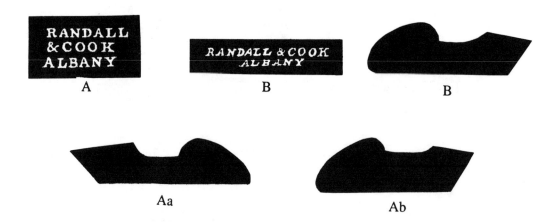

A   B   B

Aa   Ab

RANDALL & SHEPARD

Albany, NY, planemakers 1826. No example of an imprint has been reported. Principals were Samuel Randall and Daniel M. Shepard. (see D.M. Shepard and also S. Randall)

J.F. RANSOM

John Ransom was listed in the 1840 Watertown, NY, directory as a planemaker. The 1840 general population census had him living next door to Benjamin Berry (B.F. Berry, w.s.) another Watertown planemaker who had a shop on Bebee's Island in the Black River. The 1850 census listed John F. Ransom as a 30 year old, born in Vermont. Living with him was William Wood (W.W. Wood & Co. and Wood & Smith, w.s.), a 22 year old planemaker. A plow plane has been reported imprinted J.F. RANSOM/CINCINNATI. It is likely that Ransom spent some time between 1840 and 1850 in Ohio before moving back to Watertown in 1850. The 1850 industrial census listed Lord & Ransom (w.s.) as planemakers in Watertown. Their three employees made tools and patterns worth $2000. The 1855 Watertown business directory listed Ransom as a sash manufacturer. ★★

A.L. RAPLEE

This imprint appears on a ⅞" dado 9⅝" long. The plane iron is also imprinted A.L. Raplee. Appearance is mid-19c.

T.B. RAYL & CO.

A major Detroit, MI, hardware firm, founded by Thomas B. Rayl in 1880. One of its later (ca.1905) catalogs, listing a small selection of all-wooden planes, has been reprinted. (see Bibliography) *(see next page)*

 A

 B

B. RAYMOND

This name has been reported on a 9½" rabbet. Thought to be Benjamin Raymond (1793-1879) son of W. Raymond (w.s.), who was a toolmaker 1836-46 in Beverly, MA.   ★★★★

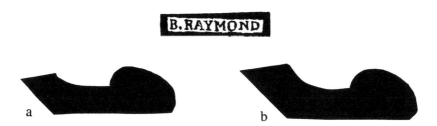

a

b

N.H. & C.H. RAYMOND

Nathan H. Raymond (b.1792 in Connecticut) and his son, Charles H. (b.1820 in New York City), were hardware dealers in Cambridge City, IN, 1845-55. When Edward, another son, became a partner in 1855, the name was changed to C.H. & E. Raymond, and then to E. Raymond & Co. In 1867 it became C.U. Raymond & Co.

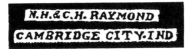

W. RAYMOND

William Raymond (1762-1836) was listed as a cabinetmaker (1791), toolmaker (1799), and gentleman (1810). He was also an active planemaker in Beverly, MA, probably from the late 18c into the first quarter of the 19c. The most dramatic example of his work is what must be the largest cornice plane in existence: 16¾" long, 9⅛" wide, with a 7¾" iron (in the collection of the North Andover, MA, Historical Society). His son, Benjamin Raymond (1793-1879) (see B. Raymond), was listed as a toolmaker, 1836-46, in Beverly. His stepson, Ebenezer Berry, also made planes. (see E. Berry)

The large Raymond stamp (A) is the earlier. The finial on the wedge A used with these planes is also significantly larger than the later B wedge. The earlier planes are usually between 9⅝" and 9⅞" long rather than the standard 9½" and have wide flat chamfers, though those bearing the later stamp occasionally are also up to 9⅞" long with wide flat chamfers. Either Mr. Raymond could not make up his mind regarding his style or else imprinted his planes as he sold them rather than when he made them.

The Thomas Grant-type crowned initials (see Tho. Grant) have been reported on at least one Raymond plane (C). The I.DAY imprint (D) which appears on some Raymond planes is believed to have been James Day (w.s.), a Gloucester, MA, merchant (1730-1805).   A: ★★★   B: ★   C: ★★★★★   D: ★★★★★

(see next page)

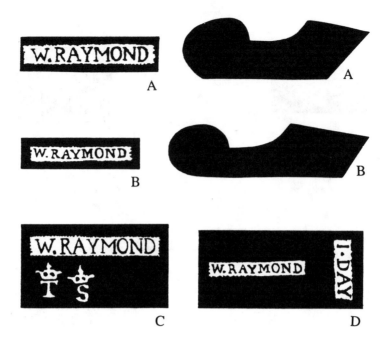

A

B

C D

H.N. RAZE

A planemaker in Williamstown, MA, ca.1860. No example of his imprint has been reported.

H.H. READ

H.H. Read, sometimes spelled REED; was listed as a planemaker in the Vermont directories of 1854-59.

M. READ

Marcus Read was a Boston, MA, planemaker 1842-44. (see also M. Read & Co. and Read & Cumings)
★★

M. READ & CO.

Marcus Read made planes in Boston, MA 1845-46. No example of an imprint has been reported. (see also M. Read, and also Read & Cumings)

READ & CUMINGS

A Boston, MA, planemaker 1846-47, consisting of Marcus Read and Allen Cumings. No example of an imprint has been reported. (see M. Read and also A. Cumings)

F. REAGER

Probably Frederick Reager (1808-88) who lived for part of his life and died in Aaronsburg, Centre County, PA, occupation carpenter. The estate inventory of his wife, Rebecca, who died in 1892, included over 20 "plain" entries, with prices ranging from $.10 to $1.10 and a box of "plain Pts." $.30.

C. RECHT

The imprint C. RECHT/183 Bowery N.Y. has been reported on a Sandusky Tool Co. (w.s.) side bead. Probably a NYC hardware dealer.

REED

John Reed came to Utica, NY, in 1820 from Wales (Great Britain), where he had been named as a planemaker, and shortly thereafter began making planes in this country. The 1850 census listed John Reed as a "plain maker" with $3000 in capital, using 5 men and horsepower to produce 7200 planes that sold for $4500. The 1855 NY state census showed that he employed 3 men and one boy to make 5000 planes that sold for $7000. The last listing for John Reed appeared in the 1867 Utica city directory. In 1868 his son, Edward, took over the business and continued until 1894, all under this imprint. Evan Evans (see E. Evans) worked for Reed in 1829.

A: FF   B & B1: ★★

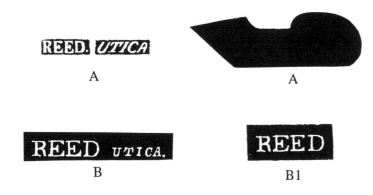

A   A

B   B1

REED & AUERBACHER

A New York City hardware firm —1884-1910. The partners were William A. Reed and Louis H. Auerbacher. The firm was the successor to Cassebeer, Reed & Co. (w.s.). This imprint has been reported on planes made by W. Hoffman and Marten Doscher (both w.s.) ★★

REILY

This name appears on a screw arm plow plane of mid-19c appearance. "Cape G" is probably CAPE GIRARDEAU, MO.

WM. RENFREW

At least seven examples of this imprint are known, all bench planes. One is a 10" razeed smoother with a closed tote. It has a double iron and an adjustable throat opening with an ebony insert. The planes bear the additional location imprint ST. JOHNSBURY VT. William Renfrew was listed in an 1887 directory as a manufacturer of sash, doors, and blinds for E.& T. Fairbanks Co., St. Johnsbury, VT.

REVONOC

This is the brand name used by HIBBARD, SPENCER, BARTLETT & CO., an important Chicago, IL, hardware dealer (1883-1960—) whose initials are H.S.B. & Co. Revonoc is Conover spelled backwards. Mr. Conover was a vice-president of the company in 1907. This imprint was reported on a transitional type jointer.

BENJAMIN F. RHOADES

Listed as a planemaker in the 1850 census for Worthington MS. No example of an imprint has been reported.

GIDEON W. RHOADES

Listed in the 1850 Massachusetts industrial census for Chesterfield, MA, as a manufacturer of plane handles, using steam power and six employees to produce 55,000 for the year. No example of an imprint has been reported.

C.W. RHOADS

Charles W. Rhoads (1810-1873) made planes in Amherst, NH. No example of an imprint has been reported.

RICHARDS

John Richards, a Philadelphia, PA, planemaker who appeared in the 1809 city directory.   A & A1: ★★★★

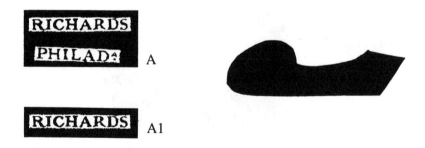

C.J. RICHARDS & CO.

This imprint was reported on a 9½" long hollow. The wedge shown closely resembles those used by T.J. McMaster (w.s.).

F. RICHARDS & CO.

Frederick Richards was a tool maker in Springfield, MA, who advertised in 1846 that he had on hand and manufactured all kinds of bench and molding planes. He appeared in the 1847 directory as a toolmaker and in 1848 as a hardware dealer. He was listed in the 1850 census as age 39, born in CT, and employed as a toolmaker by H. Chapin (w.s.). ★★★

H.B. RICHARDS

Henry B. Richards (1810-1901) was a hardware dealer in Lynchburgh, VA, 1834-41.

J.P. RICHARDS

Imprint A appears on a rosewood screw-arm plow plane. Appearance is mid 19c.

A

B

W. RICHARDS

This name appears on a dado plane.

313

RICHARDS & FLEURY

A New York City hardware dealer —1852—, comprising Charles J. Richards and James A. Fleury.
A & B: ★★★★

 A

 B

D. RICHARDSON

This imprint was reported on the side of a 9½" long beech round. The plane has very narrow flat chamfers.

W.W. RICHEY

William W. Richey was a plane manufacturer in Louisville, KY, 1838-39. (also see Potter & Richey) ★★★

J. RICHMOND

Jacob Richmond was a planemaker in Troy and Dayton, OH. Planes have been reported with various dates imprinted: 1839, 1843, and 1844. Richmond was listed in the 1850 census as a planemaker in Dayton, OH, age 40, born in MD. He came to Ohio ca.1836 and in the 1860 census was listed as a carpenter, still in Dayton.
A & B: ★★★

 A

 B

SAMUEL H. RICHMOND

Samuel H. Richmond was listed in the Pittsburgh, PA, 1819 directory as a planemaker at Swetman & Hughes (w.s.). He also appeared as a "plainmaker" on an 1818 Pittsburgh tax list. No example of an imprint has been reported.

RICKARD

Thomas J. Rickard was listed in the Cincinnati, OH, directories as a plane and edge tool maker, —1831-32—, and also worked in St. Louis, MO. The eagle emblem on the St. Louis imprint is the same as that used by H. Stout (w.s.). The B imprint reads "T. Rickards" (possibly the possessive form). All other sources read "Rickard". The T. RICKARDS imprint is shown with an overprint of C.J. Smith (w.s.), a hardware dealer whom he apparently supplied with planes. (see Creagh & Rickard)   A: ★★★   B: ★★★★   C: ★★★

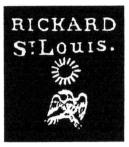

A

C

B

T. RICKARDS   see Rickard

P.B. RIDER

Perry B. Rider (b.1808) was a planemaker in Bangor, ME, 1834-48, after which he moved to Boston, MA. ★★

T.J. RIDER

This name has been reported on a beech molding plane. The plane's iron is incised BANGOR ME. Probably Thomas J. Rider, born in 1806, who was a joiner in Thomaston, ME, and also a guard at the state prison in Thomaston. Thomaston is some 65 miles south of Bangor. The imprint has also been reported struck four times in the form of a square on a 22" long beech fore plane.

RIES & SCHUBER

A partnership between Franz Joseph Ries and John Schuber that first appeared in the 1861 New Orleans city directory. The partnership ended in 1864 after the death of Ries. One example with the imprint RIES & SCHUBER/NEW ORLEANS was reported on a handled 13" long, 3½" wide complex molder.

J.H. RIGBY'S TOOL STORE

Apparently a New York City tool dealer, whose imprint appears on a J.Denison (w.s.) plow plane.

E.C. RING

Ethan C. Ring (b.1812) made planes in Worthington, MA, 1843-55. Ringville was a village in the town of Worthington. He was listed as a planemaker in the 1850 industrial census, employing five hands, using water power, and producing planes worth $4000. A & B: ★

A   B

ELKANAH RING JR.

(b.1810 in MA) Made planes in Worthington, MA 1840-47—. He was listed as a mechanic in the 1850 census and was a manufacturer in Huntington, MA, in the 1860 census, owning real estate worth $10,000. No example of an imprint has been reported. (see E. & T. Ring & Co.)

E. & T. RING & CO.

Probably Elkanah and Thomas Ring, who were mill owners and manufacturers at this time. Planes were made —1840-55—. In 1840 they were listed as having 17 people in their household working at manufacturing or a trade, and in 1855, 8 employees producing $4000 worth of product (probably including tools other than planes). Thomas Ring was shown as a mechanic, age 38, in the 1850 census. (see Elkanah Ring Jr.)   ★

E. ROBBINS

Enos Robbins (spelled with one or two b's) (b.1806 in CT) made planes in Utica, NY, as a partner in Collins & Robbins —1828-30 (w.s.). He boarded with L. Kennedy (see Kennedy) in Utica in 1829. Robbins moved to Newport, NY, in 1841 and was listed as a planemaker in the 1850 census, and a toolmaker in the 1855 state census. Perhaps he, early on, or an E. Robins of a previous generation, made planes under the imprint below, which appears on a complex molder "of early appearance with deep chamfers."

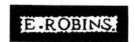

316

CHAS. ROGERS

Charles Rogers was a St. Louis, MO, hardware dealer 1853-57. In 1857 the firm was listed as Rogers, Anderson & Co. Rogers was a partner in the hardware firms of Rogers & Field in 1844, Rogers, Shapleigh & Co. 1843-47, and Rogers & Barney 1847-52. No imprint is known for any of these, only for CHAS. ROGERS.

D. ROGERS

These imprints have been reported on planes of mid-19c appearance.

 A

 B

G.W. ROGERS

G.W. Rogers was a co-patentee of Tidey's Double Beveling plane (Pat. # 11,235, July 4, 1854). One of his fellow patentees, M.B. Tidey (w.s.), also made planes in Dundee, NY. Rogers was listed in the 1850 census as age 30, a planemaker, living with Marcus Spaulding, 17, also a planemaker, in Starkey, Yates County, NY. This imprint was reported on a 22" fore plane.

JACOB ROGERS & CO.

Rogers was a hardware dealer in Lowell, MA, listed in the city directories from 1853 through 1870. His imprint has been reported on an Addison Heald/Milford, N.H. (w.s.) jointer, and on a Warren & Heald (w.s.) fore plane.   A: ★★   B: ★★★   C: ★★★

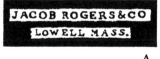 A

 B

 C

W. ROGERS

Various molding planes and a sash plane have been reported with this imprint. Appearance is ca.1800.

ROGERS & FOWLER

A planemaker in Dayton, Ohio, —1856-57—.

ROGERS, TAYLOR & CO.

This imprint appears on a razeed jack plane with a Baldwin Tool double iron.

H. ROHRKASSE & CO.

A hardware dealer in Cincinnati, Ohio, 1849-57.

ROOSEVELT. HYDE & CLARK

A hardware dealer partnership in Charleston, SC, that consisted of H.L. Roosevelt, Simeon Hyde, and Robert A. Clark. The firm first appeared in the 1849 city directory (there apparently were no directories between 1841 and 1849) and again in 1852. In 1855 Clark, Hyde & Co. (Robert A. Clark and Simeon Hyde) appeared under Wholesale Hardware & Cutlery, and in 1860 as Hyde, Gregg & Day (Simeon Hyde again). After 1860 the Civil War intervened. Earlier, in 1840-41, there was a firm of Harris, Roosevelt & Barker, the earliest mention of any of the three partners.

ROOT & PLATT

Augustine K. Root and Anson B. Platt were hardware dealers in Alton, IL, 1858-72.

G. ROSEBOOM

Garret Roseboom made planes in Cincinnati, OH, in 1839-40 for Seybold and during most of the period 1842-61 under his own name and as a member of various firms. (see G. & W.H. Roseboom, Roseboom & Magill, Roseboom & Roe, and McKinnell & Co.)   A & B: ★   *(see next page)*

 A  B

G. & W.H. ROSEBOOM

Garret and William H. Roseboom made planes in Cincinnati, OH, —1850-52. In the 1850 census Garret was listed as a Cincinnati hardware merchant, age 44, and William as a Cincinnati planemaker, age 25; both were from Indiana. In that year the firm produced $4950 worth of planes, employing six hands. William was also listed as a planemaker in the 1853 and 1859-60 Cincinnati directories. (see G. Roseboom)   ★★

ROSEBOOM & MAGILL

A partnership consisting of Garret R. Roseboom and Wesley M. Magill who made planes in Cincinnati, Ohio, 1855. (see C.J. Smith & Co.)   ★★★

ROSEBOOM & ROE

A partnership consisting of Garret Roseboom and Frank Roe, who made planes in Cincinnati, Ohio, 1853. No example of an imprint has been reported. (see G. Roseboom)

I. ROSS

Various examples have been reported including a 10" cherry sash ovolo and a 10" birch corner bead, both with flat chamfers. Appearance is 18c.

WM. C. ROSS

William C. Ross was a Baltimore maker of edge tools and planes —1849-68—. He was listed at the same address, 44 Light St., 1862-66, that P. Chapin (w.s.) occupied 1845-55. An example of a Ross A1 imprint on a P. Chapin plane bearing the B imprint has been reported. (see P. Chapin, Wm. C. Ross/A.B. Seidenstricker & Co., and Wiseman & Ross)   A, A1, B, C: ★★   D: ★★★   *(see next page)*

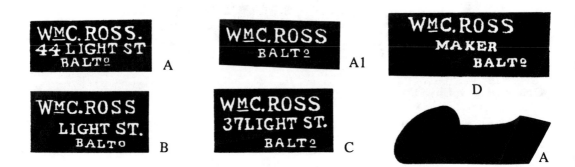

Wm. C. ROSS/A.B. SEIDENSTRICKER & CO.

William C. Ross made planes at 37 Light St., Baltimore, MD, 1867-69. Albert B. Seidenstricker made planes at this address 1871-72 and at 27 Light St. in 1870 and therefore may have been a successor to Ross and overstamped his remaining stock. (see Wm. C. Ross and also A.B. Seidenstricker & Co.) ★★★

C.S. ROWELL

Charles S. Rowell made planes under this imprint in Troy, NY, in 1832 only, having taken over his father's (Simeon Rowell's) business. After 1832 he was no longer listed as being in the city. (see S. Rowell) ★★★

S. ROWELL

Simeon Rowell, father of C.S. Rowell (w.s.) made planes in Troy, NY, under his imprint (1828-32) and in Albany prior to that time. (An example has been reported with the S. Rowell/Troy imprint overstamped on a Rowell & Gibson/Albany imprint, confirming the chronological sequence of these two firms.) He was also a partner in Rowell & Kenney and Rowell & Gibson (both w.s.). In 1832 he turned his business over to his son. The B imprint is embossed. A, A2, & B: ★ A1: ★★★ C & D: ★★ *(continued on next page)*

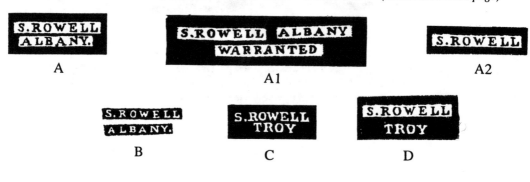

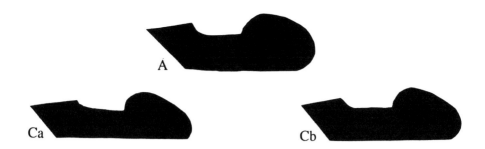

ROWELL & GIBSON
Simeon Rowell and John Gibson made planes in Albany, NY, 1824-28. The imprint shown below is embossed. (see S. Rowell and also J. Gibson) ★★

ROWELL & KENNEY
Simeon Rowell and Leonard Kenney made planes in Albany, NY, 1821-24. No example of this imprint has been reported. (see S. Rowell and also L. Kenney)

GEO. A. RUBELMANN HDWE. CO.
A wholesale and retail hardware firm in St. Louis, MO, 1883-1974.

A   B

E. RUGG
Thought to be Elias Rugg Jr. (1803-1882) carpenter and pattern maker of Keene, NH, whose imprint has been reported on several planes.

JAMES RUMRELL
Made carpenter's planes and various measuring tools in Boston, MA, 1852-61—. In an advertisement appearing in Adams' 1856 Boston Directory, he stated that he manufactured carpenter's planes, rules, tailor's squares, plumbs and levels, scales, bevels, T-squares &c with "particular attention paid to repairing." No example of his imprint has been reported.

RUNYON & KING

A hardware store in Springfield, Ohio, —1852—.

G.E. RUSSELL

This imprint was reported on a J.F. & G. Lindsay (w.s.) round. A probable hardware dealer. (see J. Russell & Co.)

H. RUSSELL

Various examples have been reported, including three crown molders and a threaded-arm plow plane. Appearance is early to middle 19c.   A, B, & C: ★★★

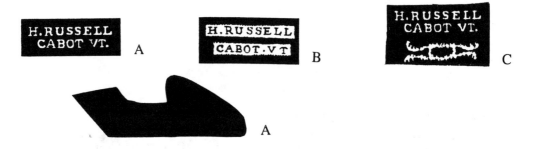

J. RUSSELL & CO.

This imprint has been reported on a J.F. & G.M. Lindsay (w.s.) quarter round. A probable hardware dealer. (see G.E. Russell)

W. RUSSELL

Various examples have been reported. The planes have $5/16$" flat chamfers. One is birch; the others beech. The length of the molding planes is $9\frac{3}{8}$", two have boxing, and a grooving plane has a riveted skate. Appearance is ca.1800.

RYAN & BRO.

Daniel Ryan (1819-1897) was a hardware dealer in Alton, IL, —1858—.

E. SAFFORD

Elias Safford appeared in the Albany, NY, directories —1813-21 as a toolmaker and planemaker. It is likely however that he was active for some time before that.   A: ★★   B & B1: ★

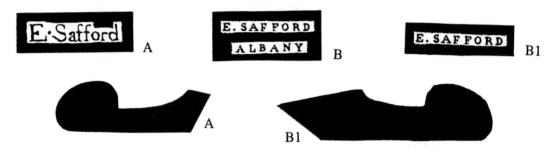

A. SAMPSON

Abel Sampson (b. 1790 in Turner, ME - d. 1883) was a joiner, tool maker, and planemaker in Portland, ME, —1823-37. A very colorful account of his life will be found in the article "Abel Sampson, Maine Privateer Turned Planemaker." (see the Bibliography)   A & A1: ★★

L. SAMPSON

Lazarus Sampson, a cooper by trade as well as a planemaker, lived in Middleboro and Fair Haven, MA, where he died in 1816. He was probably a cousin of Jeremiah Samson (see Jer. Samson) and of Deborah Sampson who, in 1782, enlisted as a soldier in the American Revolution under the name of Robert Shurtleffe and was discovered to be a woman after being wounded in battle. He appears in land records for Middleboro, MA, in 1791 and in 1805. Planemakers John and Nicholas Taber (see J. Taber and N. Taber) inventoried his estate (total value $85.50). His name stamp has the same "arrowhead" touch marks as those found on Jo. Fuller and Jo. Wilbur stamps (both w.s.) and may have been made by the same engraver.

Sampson price-marked his planes right behind the wedge slot, in shillings and pence (presumably before 1792 when Congress instituted a national currency), and in cents sometime after 1792, when the new dollars and cents decimal system gradually came into use. Various examples are shown below. The use of the initial imprint

324

"L.S." appears on planes with both types of currency. This stamp may have derived from its use in stamping the chine of the bung stave, when, as a cooper, Sampson identified his work with his mark. A 9½" Jo. Fuller plane has been reported with the L.S. imprint.

Sampson's planes are 10" long, made of birch, and have a relieved wedge.   A: ★★★   B: ★★★

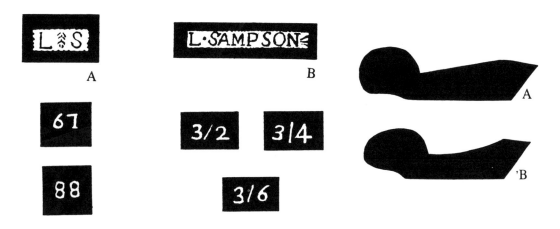

JER. SAMSON

Probably Jeremiah Samson (1755-1830) who spent most of his life working as a housewright in Kingston, MA. He was probably a cousin of L. Sampson (w.s.). Samson was apprenticed to Simeon Doggett of Middleboro in 1772 (see S. Doggett/Middleboro). Several of the molding planes reported are 9½" long, made of beech, boxed, have flat chamfers and a rounded finial on the wedge (see Wedge A). Other examples appear to be earlier. These include a 10¹⁄₁₆" long cherry reeding plane with a relieved wedge (see Wedge B).

A: ★★★★   B: ★★★★★

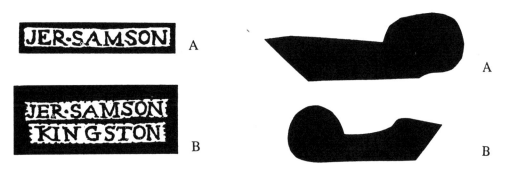

D.P. SANBORN

David Page Sanborn (1810-1871) was a planemaker in Littleton, NH, before 1840 and was shown in the 1840 census as living in Lowell, MA, with three in his household in manufacturing or a trade. He was a partner in Sanborn & Gouch, Worcester, MA (w.s.) 1845-48, and, based on imprint D, probably also made planes there under his own name. He returned ca.1850 to Littleton where he continued planemaking until 1871, by the middle 1860's with his son, Francis Davidson Sanborn (1834-1880), and by 1869 with his son-in-law Minot Weeks (1841-1873) in Sanborn & Weeks (w.s.). He was one of the few American planemakers who made crown molders with two separate single irons. In a letter dated September 5, 1866, he quoted prices on "beanch, four, and other planes" (sic). He was married to a daughter of James Dow (see J. Dow) and was a brother-in-law of F.J. Gouch (w.s.). (also see Sanborn & Co.)   A: ★★   A1: ★   B & B1: ★★   C & D: ★★★

(see next page)

325

 A  A1

B  B1

C D

SANBORN & CO.
A planemaker in Worcester, MA, whose working dates are not known. Very possibly D.P. Sanborn (w.s.) was involved.

SANBORN & GOUCH
A partnership of David P. Sanborn and Franklin J. Gouch, brothers-in-law, who made planes in Worcester, MA, 1845-48. (see D.P. Sanborn and also F.J. Gouch) A: ★★ B: ★★★

 A B

 B

SANBORN & WEEKS
D.P. Sanborn (w.s.), Francis Davidson Sanborn, his son, and Minot Weeks, his son-in-law, who made planes, log calipers, and board rules together in Littleton, NH, 1864-73. No example of an imprint has been reported.

H.M. SANDERS & CO.
A Boston, MA, hardware dealer 1892-1973.

H.M. SANDERS & CO
BOSTON. MASS.

J. SANDERSON & J. SANDERSON & CO.
John Sanderson (b.1815 in MA) was listed in the 1850 census as a toolmaker in Amherst MA. He moved to Concord, NY (Erie County) in 1852 and made planes there 1852-73. In 1860 he reported his annual production at $800. In 1874 he became a partner in Sanderson & Warren (w.s.). The 1855 census listed him employing two men to produce "350 sets" of planes worth $2000 each year. (see J. Sanderson/S. Shepard)   A & A1: ★★★   B: ★★★★

 A  A1  B

J. SANDERSON/ S. SHEPARD   see S. Shepard

J.E. SANDERSON
According to local records, Sanderson was a "pedlar" for tools owned by J.E. Sanderson's mills of South Worthington, MA 1848—.

SANDERSON & WARREN
John Sanderson and ? Warren formed a partnership in 1874 to manufacture planes. Their location was probably in the Buffalo, NY, area. No example of an imprint has been reported. (see J. Sanderson)

J.G. SANDKUHL
(b.Germany 1827) John G. Sandkuhl dealt in hardware and made planes in Poughkeepsie, NY, 1850-84. The 1860 census listed one employee (possibly himself) producing $675 worth of planes. In 1881 he advertised in the Poughkeepsie directory as a Mechanician "Coopers tools, saws, files, molding irons, pattern making, models made for patents" and noted that he was established in 1850   A & B: ★★★

 A  B  A

SANDOE & EDELEN
Manufactured planes in Philadelphia, PA, including Shelabarger's Patent Beech Smooth Plane (pat. no. 5486 -March 28, 1848), which provided a cap iron made to close the plane's throat as the stock was worn. Examples were exhibited in the Franklin Institute Fairs of 1849 and 1850. There is a B1 imprint that is the same as B with an additional address line that reads "7 N, 9th ST PHILA"   A & B: ★★

 A  B

SANDUSKY TOOL CO.

This company, located in Sandusky, Ohio, was organized in 1869 and continued making planes into the 1920's under its label and private brands. It was one of the largest planemakers in the country, also producing plane irons for itself and others. The company issued printed catalogs and distributed its products throughout the country. While most of the imprints that were used are commonly found, certain types of Sandusky planes, such as the self-regulating center wheel plow, are extremely rare.

After a series of unprofitable years and a destructive tornado, the company was essentially shut down in 1925, at the end employing 100 superannuated workers and struggling unsuccessfully to market wooden planes, plane irons, wooden clamps, and hand hoes, all of which had been largely supplanted by newer, cheaper, or improved products. Imprint C1 appears on a weatherstripping plane. (see Bibliography for catalog reprints)

A, B, C, E, F, G, H: FF   C1: ★   D: ★★★   I: ★

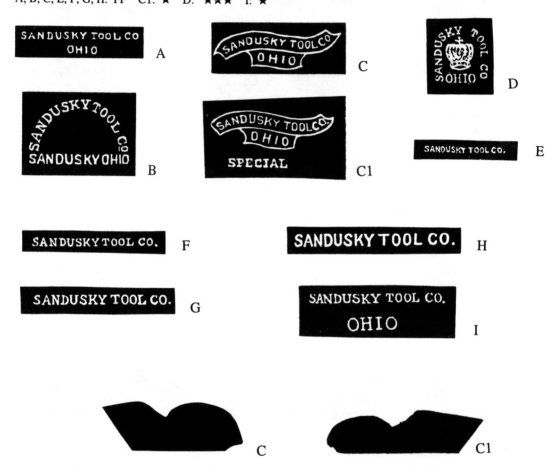

E. SANFORD & CO.

A hardware dealer —1857-71 in Fort Demoin, IA (which became Des Moines in 1857).

L. SANFORDS PATENT

This imprint appears on a 26" long, closed handle jointer. The inscription L. SANFORD/PATENT/1844 also appears on the adjusting screw which feeds into a cast steel bed plate rabbeted into the plane's throat. This patent (Patent No. 3838 dated Nov. 26, 1844) for the purpose of holding and adjusting the cutter, was issued to Levi Sanford of East Solon, NY. The example shown in *Patented and Transitional Planes in America Vol. I* appears on a jointer imprinted A. & E. BALDWIN/ NEW YORK. This example is imprinted by N. WRIGHT/KEENE of whom nothing is presently known.

J. SANGER

This imprint was reported on a smoothing plane.

C. SAPP

Conrad Sapp was listed in the 1850 census as a carpenter, born in Ohio, age 35, and living in Ravenna, Ohio. A history of Portage County, OH, mentions that he was apprenticed as a planemaker at age 21 (ca.1836) and worked at the trade for 10 years. He may have trained under Fitch Collins (see Collins). ★★★

D. SARGENT

Dana Sargent (1818-1884) worked as a planemaker in Nashua, NH, and then in Manchester, NH, where he was also in the hardware business during the 1840's. He returned to Nashua ca.1860 and became a merchant and later mayor of the city.   A:★★   B: ★   C: ★★

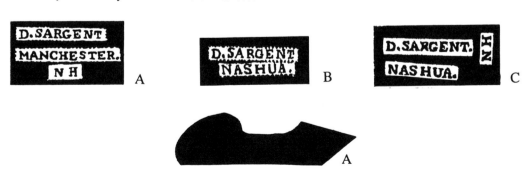

E. SARGENT

An ogee cornice plane with a 3" iron has been reported with the additional location stamp CONCORD N.H. A 9⅜" beech skewed rabbet with ⅜" flat chamfers without the above location imprint has also been reported. Appearance is ca.1800. (see P. Sargent)

P. SARGENT

Philip Sargent (1790-1858) made planes in Concord, NH. He came to Concord ca.1827 and was listed in the 1830 directory as a house carpenter, in the 1834 directory as a joiner, and between 1844 and 1856 as a planemaker. He produced a number of coachmaker's planes, reflecting Concord's importance as a coachmaking center. (see E. Sargent)   A & B: ★★

 A

 B

 B

SARGENT & CO.

One of the oldest, and at one time largest, hardware manufacturers and distributors in the U.S., with major manufacturing facilities in New Haven, CT. Beginning in 1871, Sargent started to offer wooden planes, first selling planes manufactured by H. Chapin/Union Factory (w.s.), and later adding a Sandusky Tool Co. line, first as Sandusky planes and later under the Sargent A and A1 imprints, which were apparently derived from the Sandusky C imprint. There is an example of a Sandusky tongue plane overprinted Sargent & Co. (see Kenewa Tool Co.) Sargent was also a major manufacturer of metal planes, many under Sargent patents. The A1 imprint appears on a 12" long nosing plane.   A: FF   A1: ★

 A

 A1

JOHN SAUNDERSOD

Listed in the 1839-40 Cincinnati, OH, directory as a planemaker. No example of his imprint has been reported. Possibly the same person as John Sunsersond (w.s.).

CHRISTIAN SAUNDERSOUS

Listed in the 1834 Cincinnati, OH, directory as a planemaker. No example of his imprint has been reported.

SAVAGE & CARTER

Made planes in Middletown, CT —1849—. No example of this imprint has been reported.

GEORGE SAVILLE

A shield-shaped label reading "GEORGE SAVILLE/ HARDWARE DEALER/ ELM STREET/ GLOUCESTER/ MASS" has been reported on a 16" long razeed beech jack made by P.A. Gladwin & Co. (w.s.) with a Moulson Bros. iron. *The Massachusetts Register and Business Directory* of 1874 listed Saville as a hardware dealer.

SAWHEAG WORKS

Made planes and sold tools and hardware in Wallingford, CT, —1850—. Joel Fenn (w.s.) was agent. The 1850 Industrial census showed 10 employees producing $15,000 worth of planes for the year. Since the arrow, name, and location imprints are separate die stamps, various combinations and placements are found, as shown in A and A1.   A & A1: ★

A

A1

J. SAWYER

John Sawyer (1823 - 1894) of Moravia, NY, who was granted a patent (#60265, December 4, 1866) for a miter plane, no example of which is known. There do exist a number of bench planes bearing his imprint, and one toted boxwood plow plane. He is noted in local histories as having been an excellent craftsman, active in the 1850's and 1860's, who had built several structures in Moravia.   A & A1: ★★

A

A1

A. SAYLES

This name has been reported on a group of birch planes with relieved wedges, 9¾" to 9⅞" long. Two of the planes also bear the imprint HENRY WETHEREL IN NORTON (w.s.).

C.B. SCHAEFER & CO.

Charles B. Schaefer and Henry McKinnell who made planes and edge tools and dealt in hardware in Cincinnati, Ohio, 1850-52. No example of an imprint has been reported. (see Schaefer & Cobb)

SCHAEFER & COBB

Charles B. Schaefer and Joseph E. Cobb who made planes and edge tools and dealt in hardware in Cincinnati, Ohio, 1853-55. (see C.B. Schaefer & Co.)   A, A1, & B: ★

A

A1

B

I. SCHAUER

Probably John Schauer (b.1776), who made planes in eastern Pennsylvania in the early 19c. He was working in East Petersburg, PA, in 1824 when he sent Oglesby & Pool (Harrisburg hardware dealers who later became Kelker & Co. and then Kelker & Bro.) a list of planes he could provide them with. Included were "sash gittics and ovlows @ $2.00, felisters @ 1.37, screw arm plows with brass stops @ 3.50, single iron foreplanes eighty cents, dubble iron 1.20, beads and astragals .45." (see N. Schauer and also J. Schauer) ★

J. SCHAUER
Possibly Joehanes Schauer (b.1800), a member of the Schauer family which made planes in eastern Pennsylvania. (see I. Schauer and also N. Schauer) ★★

N. SCHAUER
Nicklaus Schauer (1755-1829), an eastern Pennsylvania planemaker —1800—. The N. Shovar imprint (w.s.) is probably an early variant for N. Schauer, based on the stylistic similarities and probable location. (see I. Schauer and also J. Schauer) ★★

P.A. SCHLAPP AGT.
This imprint appears on a boxed molding plane with an Ohio Tool Co. iron and #137, the Ohio Tool Co. style number for boxed table plane sets, imprinted on its toe.

F.E. SCHMIEDING & CO.
Retail and wholesale hardware dealers in St. Louis, MO, 1857-73. In 1864 the principals of Schmieding were F. Wiebusch and Frederick A. Witte. ★

SCHMIEDING & WOLFING
An applewood toted plow plane with screw arms has been reported. Appearance is ca.1850.

H. SCHMITT
Believed to have been a Newark, NJ, hardware dealer and/or importer. Among the planes reported with this imprint are a Joh. Weiss "Austria" horned plane, two other horned planes, and a European fore plane. ★★★

F.W. SCHNEIDER

This imprint appears on the side of a plane imprinted SARGENT & CO. (w.s.) and also on the wedge. A probable hardware dealer.   ★★

D.A. SCHUTTE

A Chillicothe, Ohio, hardware dealer —1850-55.   ★★

D.A.SCHUTTE

SCIOTO WORKS

An Ohio Tool Co. (w.s.) imprint for its second-grade line of beechwood planes 1893-1907. It seems ironical that the phrase "extra quality" that appears on the E imprint was used to describe "second grade" planes. The name may have originated from the fact that the Ohio Tool Co. was located near the Scioto River in Columbus, Ohio.   A, B, C, C1, & D: FF   E: ★★

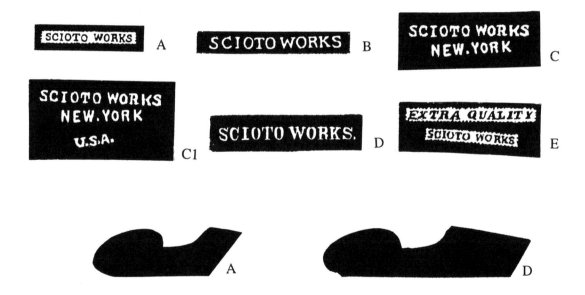

W. SCOTT

William Scott was one of the earliest Pittsburgh, PA, planemakers. He was identified as a planemaker in an 1812 property purchase and was listed as a planemaker in the 1813 city directory and as late as the 1839 directory. Sometime between 1826 and 1837 he moved from Pittsburg City across the Allegheny River to "Allegheny Town" (now known as Pittsburgh's North Side), giving rise to the B imprint.   A: ★★   B: ★★★

(see next page)

333

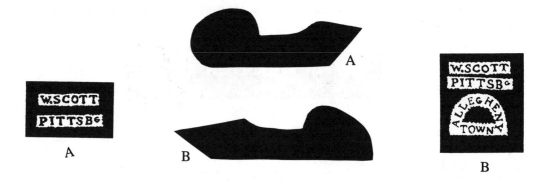

A

B

A

B

L. SCOVIL (also sometimes spelled SCOVILL)

Lyman Scovil (1781-1840), father of J. Scovill (w.s.), was born in Connecticut. He was a carpenter, builder and made planes in Johnstown, NY. An 1837 statement of account submitted by Lyman Scovill to Lawrence Marcellus, a carpenter. for planes made was signed as paid in 1838 by Scovill, using two l's in his signature. Also of interest is the fact that prices were still expressed in English shillings, as well as in dollars. The C imprint may have been used by either the father or son, or perhaps both.   A & A1: ★★   B: ★★★★   C: ★★

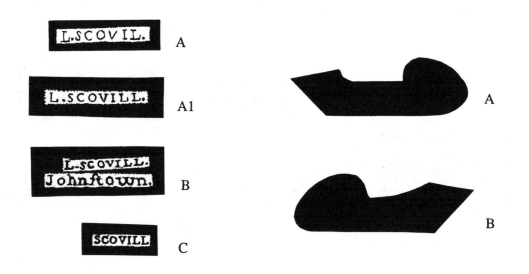

A

A1

B

C

A

B

J. SCOVILL

John Scovill (1804-62), son of Lyman Scovil (w.s.), made planes in Johnstown, NY, as early as 1827 and probably worked until ca.1830 when he joined the ministry, becoming an Episcopal priest in 1838.   A: ★

A.M. SEAMAN

Abram M. Seamn (1826-92) was a carpenter and woodworker and made planes in Ithaca, NY 1872-91.
A & B: ★

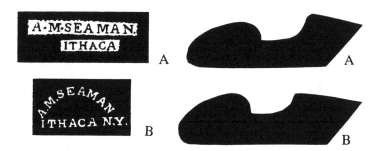

J. SEARING

This imprint was probably used by both James Searing and John D. Searing, who may have been father and son, and who made planes in Newark, NJ —1821-49. James Searing (b.1783) was one of the representatives of the planemakers in the 1821 Fourth of July pageant in Newark. The first Newark city directory (1835-36) lists only John D. Searing as a planemaker. In the 1850 census John Searing is listed as a sash and blindmaker, age 37, born in NJ. ★

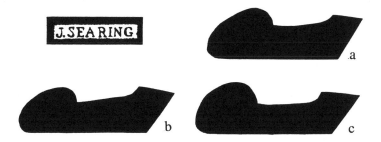

A. SEARL

Ashbel Searl (also spelled Searle) ran a hardware store in New York City 1849-53. During 1852-53 he occupied the premises just previously used by Way & Sherman (w.s.). ★★★

SEARS, ROEBUCK

This retailing and mail order giant sold wooden planes, presumably made by others, from the late 1800's to around 1930 as part of its hardware department. A: ★ B: FF

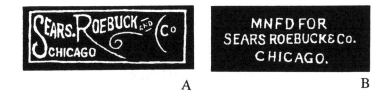

C.S. SEE

Cornelius S. See made planes in New York City 1829-46, and also in Watertown, NY, dates not known.

A: ★★   A1 & A2: ★★★   B: ★★   C, C1, C2, C3: ★★★   D: ★★★

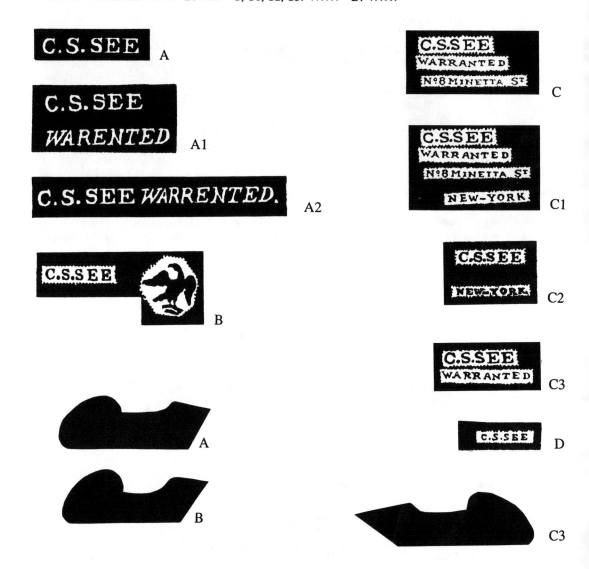

A.B. SEIDENSTRICKER

Albert B. Seidenstricker made and/or sold planes under this imprint in Baltimore, MD, 1870-72. (see also A. B. Seidenstricker & Co. and Young & Seidenstricker)   ★★★

A.B. SEIDENSTRICKER & CO.

Planemaker and tool dealer in Baltimore, MD, 1856-66, that described itself as successor to Philip Chapin. (see Yount & Seidenstricker, A.B. Seidenstricker, P. Chapin, and also Wm. C. Ross/A.B. Seidenstricker & Co.)

A, A1, & B: ★★★   C: ★★

 A

 A1

B

C

A.B. SEMPLE & BRO.

Louisville, KY, hardware dealers 1838-59.   ★★★

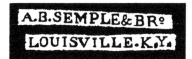

L. SENTER

A 30" jointer has been reported with this imprint. Appearance is mid-19c.

AUSTIN W. SEWARD

Austin Seward (1797-1874) was variously a blacksmith, gunsmith, threshing machine manufacturer, plow maker, and foundry operator in Bloomington, IN, ca.1830-70. He made edge tools and planes during his early working years. No example of his imprint has been reported.

J.A. SEX & CO.

This name has been reported with a location imprint AUBURN, and has appeared on a plane also imprinted CHAS. ASHLEY/OGDENSBURG (w.s.), a New York hardware dealer.

C. SEYBOLD

Catherine, the widow of E.F. Seybold (w.s.), continued his hardware business in Cincinnati, Ohio 1853-55. No example of an imprint has been reported.

E.F. SEYBOLD

Emanuel F. Seybold was listed in the Cincinnati, OH, directories as a planemaker 1836-44 (in the Western Address Directory of 1837 as a "Wholesale and Retail Plane Manufacturer and Tool Store") and a hardware merchant in 1849-52, though he was reported in the 1850 Products of Industry census as employing 12 hands and manufacturing $12,000 worth of planes. The D imprint may have occurred from Seybold buying some of Creagh's closing inventory. (see J. Creagh, F. Lender, C. Seybold, Seybold & Smith, and Seybold & Spencer)
A: ★   B: ★   C: FF   D: ★★★

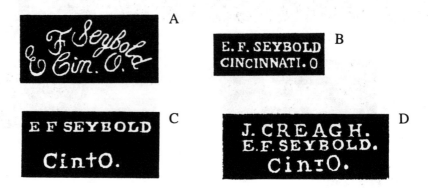

SEYBOLD & SMITH

Emanuel F. Seybold and John H. Smith were partners in a hardware business in Cincinnati, OH, in 1846. No example of an imprint has been reported. (see E.F. Seybold, J.H. Smith, and J. & C. Smith)

SEYBOLD & SPENCER

This imprint has been reported on a 14" screw-arm plank grooving plane.

W.N. SEYMOUR

This imprint appears on a Greenfield Tool Co. #707 two-iron sash plane. Probably a New York hardware dealer.

JACOB SHANNON - see J.B. Shannon

J.B. SHANNON

A Philadelphia, PA, hardware dealer —1873—, whose imprint has appeared on an A. Kelly & Co. plane (w.s.). An imprint MADE FOR JACOB SHANNON PHILA. has also appeared on a Chapin plane. (see J. Jacob Shannon)   *(see next page)*

338

J. JACOB SHANNON

This imprint appears on a double iron nosing plane made by Union Factory/H. Chapin (style no. 133).

SHAPLEIGH & CO.

A large St. Louis, MO, hardware firm that was organized in 1863 by A.F. Shapleigh (1810-1902) as successor to Shapleigh, Day & Co. (w.s.), one of a series of companies that culminated in the acquisition of E.C. Simmons Co. and the Keen Kutter line in 1940. The "D-E" or Diamond Edge trademark was adopted in 1864 and is still in use, having been purchased by the Imperial Knife Co. in 1961, around the time Shapleigh & Co. went out of business. (see Keen Kutter)

SHAPLEIGH, DAY & CO.

A St. Louis, MO, hardware firm that operated 1847-63. (see Shapleigh & Co.)   A & B: FF

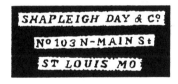

A

B

I.E. SHATTUCK

Ira E. Shattuck, a wholesale and retail hardware dealer, whose imprint has been reported on A. Howland & Co. and Greenfield Tool Co. planes (both w.s.).

339

SHELTON & OSBORNE MFG. CO.
This imprint has been reported on a screw-armed, toted plow plane made of cocobola wood with boxwood fence, and on an ebony plow with boxwood fence. The location stamp reads BIRMINGHAM CT. Appearance is mid-19c.

B. SHENEMAN
Benjamin Sheneman, was a prolific Philadelphia, PA, planemaker 1846-67. (see D. Colton & B. Sheneman and also B. Sheneman & Bro.)   A & B: FF   C: ★   D: ★★★

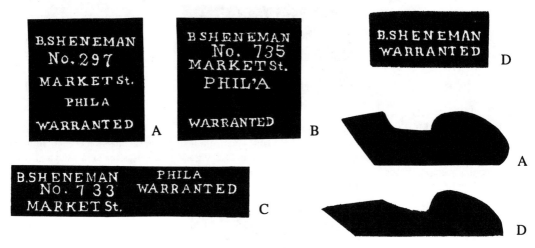

B. SHENEMAN & BRO.
Benjamin and Thomas Sheneman made planes in Philadelphia, PA, —1856-60. (see B. Sheneman)
A, A1 & B: ★

EDWARD SHENEMAN
Listed in the 1863 Philadelphia, PA, directory as a planemaker. No example of an imprint is known.

HENRY SHENEMAN
Listed as a Philadelphia planemaker in the 1850 census, age 20, and born in PA. No example of an imprint has been reported.

D.M. SHEPARD
Daniel M. Shepard made planes in Albany, NY, 1827-28 under these imprints. (see Randall & Shepard)
A & A1: ★★★   *(see next page)*

340

A

A1

A1

S. SHEPARD

The A imprint appears on a boxed bead of mid-19c appearance, the B imprint on a 22" fore plane. Possibly a hardware dealer. (see J. Sanderson)

A

B

S. SHEPARD & CO./J. SANDERSON   see J. Sanderson and S. Shepard

SHEPHERD & BUFFUM

This imprint appears on a 9" miter plane.

SHERMAN BARNES

Reported on a #6 hollow and on three rounds (#2, 4, and 6) made by J. KILLAM. Probably a hardware dealer.

SHERMAN BROS.

Bryon and Porter Sherman were New York City hardware merchants 1853-73. (see Barry, Way & Sherman and also Way & Sherman)   ★★

SHIVERICK

David Shiverick made planes in Brooklyn, NY, under these imprints 1865-67—. (see D. Shiverick & Co., Shiverick & Malcolm, and Wing H. Taber)   A: FF   B: ★★   *(see next page)*

 A  B  B

D. SHIVERICK & CO.

This stamp has been reported on a plane with the additional location imprint BROOKLYN. (see Shiverick and also Shiverick & Malcolm) ★★

SHIVERICK & MALCOLM

David Shiverick and Frederick S. Malcolm dealt in tools and made planes in Brooklyn, NY, 1853-64. Frederick Malcolm was listed earlier (in 1846) as a planemaker in New Haven, CT. The 134 GREENWICH AVE., N.Y. referred to a Manhattan address and was listed in the NYC directories 1854-56. Shiverick lived and worked in Brooklyn; Malcolm worked in Brooklyn but lived in Manhattan. The Greenwich Avenue address was probably a sales outlet. (see Shiverick, D. Shiverick & Co. and also Pond, Malcolm & Welles)
A: ★★   B & C: ★★★

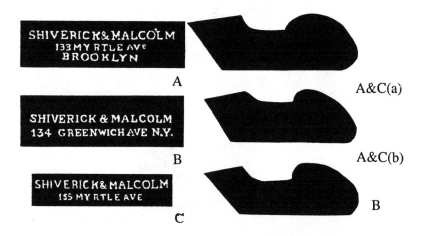

N. SHOVAR

Various planes have been reported. Appearance is 18c. Based on the area in which the planes have been found, the stylistic similarities, the lack of any records on any Shovar, the common use of Newbould irons, and the fact that "V" was frequently used for "U" giving us Shouar, it is probable that N. Shovar was the early variant of N. Schauer (w.s.). ★★★★

B. SHUMAN & BRO.

This company was listed in the Philadelphia Merchants and Manufacturers Business Directory of 1856 as a plane manufacturer at 297 Market Street, the same address as B. Sheneman (w.s.). Possibly a typographical error by the publisher. No example of an imprint has been reported. (see B. Sheneman & Bro.)

SICKELS, SWEET & LYON

Robert Sickels, Edwin S. Sweet and Henry M. Lyon were partners in a New York City hardware firm 1890-97. The imprint shown below is incuse. (see Gilbert, Sweet & Lyon)   ★★

SICKELS SWEET &LYON

C.G. SIEWERS

Charles G. Siewers, a son-in-law of E.W. Carpenter (w.s.) was listed as a planemaker in Cincinnati, OH, 1839-40, and as maker of various carpenter's tools, saws and marking gauges between 1842-66.   A & B: ★★

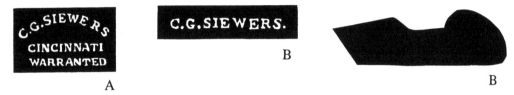

A

B

B

ARAD:SIMONS

Arad Simons (1754-1836) was trained as a joiner in Connecticut and came to Lebanon, NH, at the end of the Revolutionary War, in which he served. He was a joiner and a planemaker and made clock cases for Jedediah Baldwin between 1795 and 1796. He appeared in a number of land transactions between 1795 and 1831, often described either as a gentlemen or a captain. His molding planes vary in length from 9¾" to 10", with some made of beech and others of yellow birch, and some having the Sleeper-style wedge B.   ★★★★

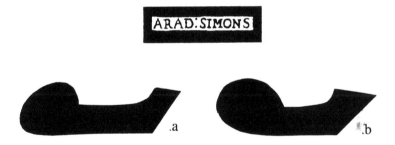

.a

.b

C.J. SINTON & CO.

A Richmond, VA, hardware firm —1850-88.

SLARK, DAY, STAUFFER & CO.

A New Orleans, LA, hardware firm ca.1841-55, formed after Augustus Whiting withdrew from Whiting & Slark (w.s.) and his former partner, Robert Slark, a native of Sheffield, England, formed a partnership with James I. Day and Isaac H. Stauffer.

343

J.M. SLATER

James M. Slater was a planemaker in Detroit, MI —1850-51— and previously was a partner in Slater & Byram (w.s.). He was listed in the 1850 Federal census as a 38 year old planemaker, born in England. He apparently lived in Michigan as early as 1839.

SLATER & BYRAM

James M. Slater and Ebenezer Byram were plane manufacturers in Detroit, MI, listed in the 1845 and 1846 city directories. No example of an imprint has been reported. (see J.M. Slater)

SLAUGHTER

James B. Slaughter, a Louisville, KY, hardware merchant 1832-43. In 1844, the firm name was changed to James B. Slaughter & Brother. Successor firms included Slaughter & Miles (1848-49) and Slaughter, Honore & Carpenter (1851-52). No example of an imprint has been reported. (also see Slaughter C & C)

SLAUGHTER C & C

Slaughter, Carpenter & Co. was a Louisville, KY, hardware merchant listed in the 1848, 1855-56, and 1858-59 city directories, with James B. Slaughter (see Slaughter) shown as a partner. ★★

I. SLEEPER

John Sleeper (1754-1834) was a cabinetmaker and planemaker who was born and worked in Newburyport, MA. He was the youngest son of Henry Sleeper, a renowned Newburyport cabinetmaker, and brother of Moses Sleeper (w.s.). John, who never married, was appointed guardian of his brother's children in Newburyport in 1792. In an 1813 house transfer to his sister Mary in Newburyport, he described himself as a tool maker. In 1814 he was noted as living with his brother-in-law, Nathaniel Brown, in Chester, NH. In his will, dated November 2, 1825, at Chester, he described himself as a planemaker.

There is an interesting entry written by Benjamin Chase in his book *History Of Chester*: "SLEEPER John, b. Aug.2, 1754, d. unm. June 27, 1834. He was in the Battle of Bunker Hill; also in the expedition under Montgomery, which went up through the woods to Quebec, suffering severely. Upon the death of Montgomery he was taken prisoner, and lay in prison nine months. He went on a voyage as carpenter in the frigate Boston, and several in privateers. He had quite a mechanical genius. I think that he once told me that he made the first joiners' moulding tools made in this country. He came to Chester with his brother-in-law Nathl. Brown in 1814."

Sleeper was one of the most prolific of the early planemakers, and his long planemaking career is reflected in the transition in the length of his molding planes from 10" to 9½". His molding planes are made of beech and have a distinctive wedge style and bold, flat chamfers. They frequently have irons signed by 18c Sheffield (England) makers and occasionally use lignum boxing.

His early cornice planes have offset handles and two separated irons for convenience in honing and setting. An interesting feature of his sash planes is the separated ovolo and rabbet irons, sawed from a single Sheffield iron and secured with a single flat wedge. Sleeper's moving filletsters have a wooden depth stop (instead of a purchased brass stop) and this is held in a dovetailed slot. His plow planes, which are rare, are also of beech;

the stocks are 8½" long, the fences 9½", extending forward of the toe. Several examples have been reported of what may be a later Sleeper plane style. They have tight round chamfers and the B wedge.   FF

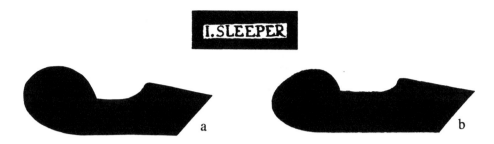

I.SLEEPER

a   b

M. SLEEPER
Moses Sleeper (b.1752) was a cabinet- and planemaker in Newburyport, MA. He was the son of Henry Sleeper and the older brother of I. Sleeper (w.s.). His last known location was Newburyport in 1789. His planes have the same characteristics as those of his brother but are much rarer.   ★★★★

M·SLEEPER

S. SLEEPER
Sherburn Sleeper was listed as a planemaker in Dover, NH, in 1830. Some time before, he had moved to Somersworth, NH, and in the 1850 Federal census he was listed as a 50 year old machinist, born in Vermont. The B imprint may or may not have been used by Sherburn Sleeper. Was the "e" omitted because of a lack of space, bad spelling, or was the name really SLEEPR? The imprint was stamped five times on the toe and heel of a well-made single iron 11¾" long beech sash with narrow round chamfers and an unmarked iron. There are no owners' stamps.   A: ★★★

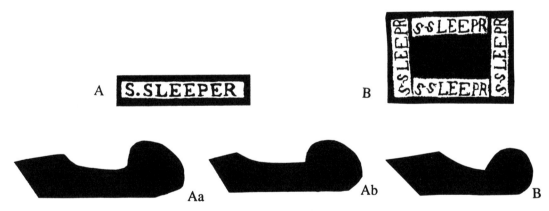

A S.SLEEPER   B S·SLEEPR / S·SLEEPR / S·SLEEPR / S·SLEEPR

Aa   Ab   B

C.H. SLOCOMB & CO.
In 1859 Cuthbert H. Slocomb became a partner in this New Orleans hardware firm founded in 1821 by his father, Samuel B. Slocomb, and now renamed. In 1867 Albert Baldwin joined as a partner and the firm was once again renamed, this time as Slocomb, Baldwin & Co. A "zb" imprint C.H. SLOCOMB/ NEW ORLEANS has been reported on a 28" long jointer.

S. SLOOP

Samuel Sloop was born in Pennsylvania and made planes in Cincinnati, Ohio, 1829-40. He advertised in the 1837 Western address directory as a "Wood Screw and Plane Manufacturer." ★

JACOB SMALL

Jacob Small (or Schmall) did carpentry work in 1798-99 on the German Reformed Church in York, PA, along with Peter Small (see P. Small) and his brother, Henry. Jacob Small molding planes have been reported $9\frac{7}{16}$" long with $\frac{1}{4}$" flat chamfers and with the A wedge, and one example $10\frac{1}{8}$" long with the A1 wedge. ★★★★

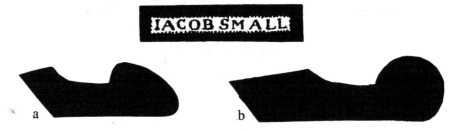

P. SMALL

Peter Small was a carpenter and housewright in York, PA, —1798-1815—. One group of his molding planes was reported, the planes ranging in length from $9\frac{7}{16}$" to $9\frac{11}{16}$". (see Jacob Small) ★★★

JOHN SMILEY

Listed in the 1850 census as a Lawrence, MA, carpenter, age 40.

A. SMITH

Aaron Smith (1769-1822) was born in Swansea, MA. His first record in Rehoboth, MA, was on a land transaction in 1791, his occupation given as housewright. In 1803 he was listed a a shop joiner, in 1806 as a tool maker and in 1816 as a planemaker, although his planemaking is believed to extend well back into the 18c. He also owned a blacksmith shop. Three sons, among his nine children, became planemakers: Ezekiel Smith (see E. Smith), Aaron Mason Smith (see A.M. Smith) and Jarvis Brown Smith, who in 1823 was referred to as a journeyman planemaker.

Aaron Smith, like his contemporary Jo. Fuller (w.s.) of nearby Providence, used the relieved wedge and decorative fluting on his early planes. They were made of birch and were 9¾" - 10" long. As with Fuller during this transitional period in planemaking, the later planes became the standard 9½", the wedge unrelieved, the fluting was omitted, and beech was used. In general his planes show a marked resemblance to those of Jo. Fuller, and like Fuller, he was a prolific producer and was apparently active right up until his death.

His early period imprint was distinctly longer than that used later. The imprints shown in A, A1, B and C are arranged in what we believe to be their chronological order. A & A1: ★★ B & C: ★

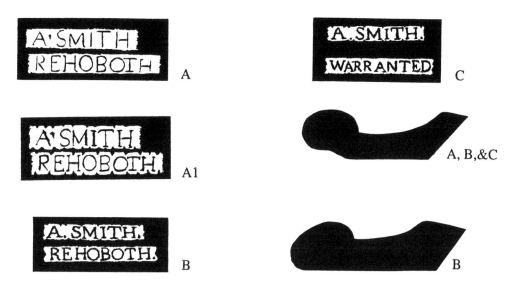

A

A1

B

C

A, B,&C

B

A. SMITH

Alpheus Smith, of Lowell, MA, was a drygoods and hardware merchant 1832-37. In the 1832 Lowell directory he advertised that he made all kinds of carpenter's planes. In 1835 only, the firm was called Smith & Burbank (Alpheus Smith and Samuel Burbank). ★

A.M. SMITH

Aaron Mason Smith (1805-34) was a son of Aaron Smith (w.s.). He made planes in New Bedford, MA, and in 1832 was listed as a machinist. ★★

C.F. SMITH

Two plow planes bearing this imprint have been reported. Appearance is mid-19c.

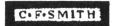

347

C.J. SMITH & CO.

Charles J. Smith was a Cincinnati, OH, hardware dealer 1853-58. This imprint has been reported overstamped on a Roseboom & Magill, and on a T. Rickards, plane (w.s. - see also Heim & Smith and J. & C. Smith) A & B: ★★

E. SMITH

Ezekiel Smith II (1799-1880), the oldest son of Aaron Smith (w.s.), inherited his father's workshop in 1823 and was listed as a planemaker in Rehoboth, MA, through the 1820's. An advertisement in several issues of the *Providence Daily Advertiser* had Benjamin Allen & Co. offering "An assortment of molding tools of Smith's make." He appeared in Smithfield, RI, in the 1850 census, and in the Worcester, MA, directories during most of the 1857-73 period as a patternmaker, carpenter, and planemaker. He was succeeded by Edward H. Smith & Co. (w.s.) in 1874.   A & B: ★   B1: ★★   C: ★   D, E, & F: ★★★

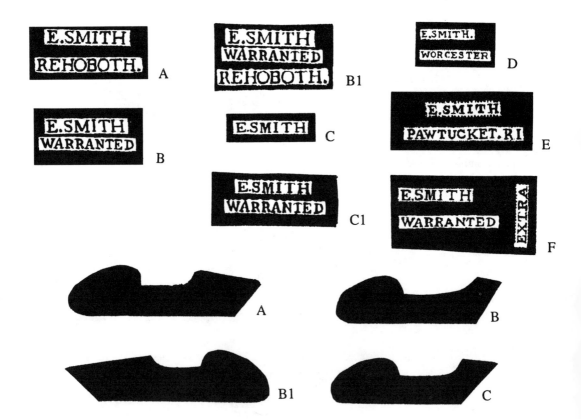

E.H. SMITH & CO.

E.H. Smith & Co. succeeded E. Smith (w.s.), Worcester, MA, in 1874 and appeared that year only. The firm consisted of Edward H. Smith and A.N. Learned. They advertised as manufacturers and retail dealers for carpenter's and joiner's planes. No example of an imprint has been reported.

ELI SMITH

Several examples have been reported, all molding planes; one with ¼" flat chamfers, a relieved wedge and made of birch; another 9½", beech, with a relieved wedge, rounded chamfers, and iron marked "I. Parks" (Birmingham, England, —1800—).

I. SMITH

Several planes have been reported, all made of beech, including a rabbet, a molder, and a crown molder. Appearance is early 19c.

I.E. SMITH

A planemaker and/or dealer in Pawtucket, RI. His working dates are not known but the appearance of the planes is ca.1850.   A & B: ★★

 A    B

J.B. SMITH

Jarvis Brown Smith (1801-1894), one of the three planemaking sons of Aaron Smith (see A. Smith), was a farmer in Rehoboth, RI, who, in 1823, was referred to as a journeyman planemaker. The "Warranted" in the B imprint seems identical to that in the E. Smith (w.s.) B imprint. (also see A.M. Smith)   A & B: ★★★

 A    B

J.H. SMITH

John H. Smith was a Cincinnati, OH, hardware dealer. (see J. & C. Smith)   ★★

J.W. SMITH

John W. Smith made planes in New Bedford, MA, 1856-89.   ★★

349

J. & C. SMITH

John H. and Charles J. Smith were wholesale hardware dealers in Cincinnati, OH, 1851-52. (see Heim & Smith; C.J. Smith & Co.; Lockwood, Lyons & Smith; and E.F. Seybold & Co.) ★★★

O.H. SMITH

This name has been reported on a pair of handled tongue and groove planes and on a jointer. The jointer has a decorative eagle stamp, similar to that of other Northampton makers.

PHINEAS SMITH

A New York City planemaker and hardware dealer 1855-96. A 6¾" long coffin smoother has been reported with the incised imprint PHINEAS SMITH/ NEW YORK. Also imprinted on the toe of the plane is JOHN HILLS TOOL STORE (w.s.) B1 imprint.

S. SMITH

Reported on a beech bead with full lignum boxing. While Natchez, Mississippi, is a logical possibility, there is a Natchez that became part of Zanesville, OH, and was located in an active planemaking region.

SAMUEL SMITH

SAMUEL SMITH HARDWARE/ NEW HAVEN appears on a paper label affixed to a double beader.

W. SMITH

This imprint has been reported on various planes, all of a mid-19c appearance.

SMITH BIGELOW & CO.

Smith Bigelow was listed in the 1852 Massachusetts Register as a tool factory. Apparently not a very large or active one as far as planemaking is concerned, since very few examples have been reported. ★★★

SMITH & BURBANK   see A. Smith

SMITH, COHU & CO.

Henry S. Cohu and Thomas Smith were listed as cutlery dealers in the NYC 1871-72 directory. They apparently also carried some tools since the imprint has been reported on several bench planes.

SMITH, LYON & FIELD

William T. Smith, Judson A. Lyon, and Richard T. Field were partners in a New York City hardware firm 1884-1895. The imprint shown below is incuse.   ★

SMITH & ROBERTS

Smith & Roberts was a hardware dealer in Richmond, VA, —1850-55.

SMITH & STEWART

A hardware company —1873-75— in Springfield, MA. Some planes bear the additional stamp 488 MAIN/SPRINGFIELD MASS (designated as the B imprint).

SMITH, WINCHESTER & CO.

This imprint was reported on a Greenfield Tool Co. molding plane.

C.T. SNOWDEAL

Reported on a 9⅜" long beech spar plane with the additional location imprint THOMASTON ME. all arranged in a semi-circle.

SOEDING BROS.

Casper and Charles Soeding were hardware dealers in St. Louis, MO, 1854-63—. In 1863, the firm became Soeding & Brother and from 1870 to 1883 was called Casper Soeding.

W.M. SOUDER

William M. Souder (b.PA ca.1799) was a Philadelphia, PA, planemaker 1823-53. A W.M. Souder hollow has been reported overstamped A. WALLACE/DUNDEE. Alexander Wallace made planes in Dundee, Scotland —1824-1837 and in Montreal, Canada —1843-1858—. The A imprint has been reported with the addition of the eagle in imprint B, and is designated as A1. (see Souder & Summers)   A: ★   B: ★★★

 A

B

SOUDER & SUMMERS

Probably W.M. Souder and Martin Summers, listed as a planemaker in the 1837 Philadelphia directory. Summers was listed as a planemaker in the 1840 Philadelphia directory at a different location from Souder. (see W.M. Souder)   ★★★★

L.S. SOULE

Believed to be Lewis S. Soule (b.1813) of Waldoboro, ME, who was also a joiner and made doors, sash and blinds, 1849-54.   A & B: ★★★

 A

B

SOULE, WHITE & SPEAR

A planemaking firm in Warren, OH, ca.1845, probably comprising Josiah Soule Jr., who was listed in the 1850 census as a carpenter, age 31, born in Ohio, and/or Josiah Soule Sr., who arrived in Ohio in 1817; Charles White, a Yankee mechanic (w.s.); and Edward Spear, a woodworker who came to Ohio in 1818 from Pennsylvania (see White & Spear).   ★★★

SOUTHWORTH & NOYES

This name was reported on a nosing plane. The 1867 Plymouth County, MA, directory carried an advertisement by Southworth & Noyes stating that they were dealers in "Groceries, Flour, and Hardware" at 447 Main St. in North Bridgewater.

W.H. SPALDING

William H. Spaulding (the "u" is omitted in the imprint), (1822-1897), son of N. Spaulding (w.s.), who made planes in Elmira, NY, ca.1850. The 1850 census reported him employing two men.   A & B: ★★

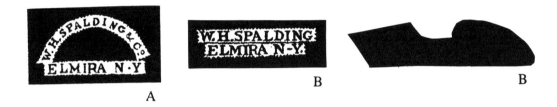

A   B   B

W.H. SPALDING CO.   see W.H. Spalding

N. SPAULDING

Nathaniel Spaulding (1795-1871), father of W.H. Spaulding (w.s.), who made planes in McLean, NY (Tompkins County) —1824-50— and in Ithaca, NY, —1869-70. The 1850 census listed him employing three men, producing 2000 joiner's planes worth $1500.   A & B: ★

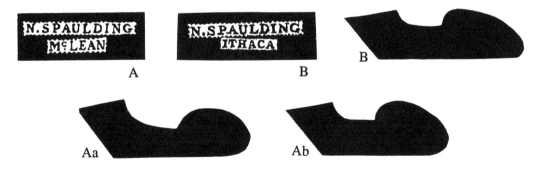

A   B   B

Aa   Ab

JOHN E. SPAYD

Listed as a planemaker in the 1831 and 1833 Philadelphia directories and earlier (in 1819) as a carpenter. (see Spayd & Bell and Spayd & Wheeler)   ★★★★

SPAYD & BELL

John Spayd and John Bell made planes in Philadelphia, PA, ca. 1830-40. (see John Spayd, Spayd & Wheeler, and also John Bell)   A & B: ★★★★

 A    B    A

SPAYD & WHEELER

This name has been reported on a foreplane with an offset handle. (see John E. Spayd and Spayd & Bell)

HOWARD W. SPEAR

Listed in the Chelsea, MA, 1874 and 1876 directories as a planemaker. (see Spear & Wood)

SPEAR & WOOD

A bead plane has been reported with the Spear & Wood imprint and an additional location stamp CHELSEA (designated imprint B). Below it is a LEWIS HUNT/CHARLESTOWN MASS. (w.s.) imprint, indicating a Massachusetts location for Spear & Wood and the likelihood that at least one or the other was a hardware dealer. Both Charlestown and Chelsea are part of the Boston environs. (see Howard W. Spear)

SPENCER

A number of planes have been reported. Some Spencer planes also appear in the inventory of the Duncan Phyfe tool chest. Appearance is early 19c. The firm of E. & B. SPENCER (w.s.) of New Haven, CT, was listed as a planemaker in 1831. The B. Spencer was probably Benjamin Spencer, who lived in Saybrook, CT (1810-30) and who was listed in the 1850 census at age 71 and a planemaker in New Haven, CT. Patten's 1840 New Haven city directory listed Benjamin Spencer as a planemaker at 27 Brewery, home at 25 Brewery. It seems likely that the Spencer imprint was used by Benjamin Spencer and/or E. & B. Spencer.   ★★

SPENCER/NEW YORK

Franklin G. Spencer operated a hardware store in New York City 1866-67 and was joined by Oscar A. Spencer in 1869. They subsequently ran separate establishments from 1870 to 1875. Oscar only is listed in the directories during the 1878-84 period.   A, B, & C: ★★   (*see next page*)

354

 A  B  C

A.F. SPENCER

This name has been reported on an ebony plow plane with boxwood arms and nuts and the location imprint WINSTED, CT.

E. & B. SPENCER

The American Advertising Directory of Manufacturers and Dealers in America for the Year 1831 lists E. & B. Spencer of New Haven, CT, as planemakers. B. Spencer was probably Benjamin Spencer, who lived in Saybrook, CT, 1810-30 and was listed in the 1850 census as age 71 and a planemaker in New Haven, CT. (see Spencer)

F.G. SPENSER   see Spencer/New York

A. SPICER

Amos Spicer (1762-1822) made planes in North Groton, CT. (see A.C. Spicer, O. Spicer, & S. Spicer) ★★★

A.C. SPICER

Thought to be Abel Chapman Spicer (1796-1859) of Groton, Plainfield, and Norwich, CT, who was a cabinetmaker, carpenter, and mechanic, and who drowned while oystering. Various planes have been reported, including a rosewood jointer with a closed offset tote, and a rosewood rabbet. Appearance is early 19c.   ★★★

O. SPICER

There were two Oliver Spicers in North Groton, CT, one (1726-1804) who was a carpenter and joiner, the other (1766-1839); one or both of them may have made planes. The planes reported are made of fruitwood as well as birch, and the molding planes are generally between 9¼" and 9½" long. (see S. Spicer) ★★★

355

P. SPICER

Possibly Peter Spicer, who was born in Preston, CT, and was shown as a carpenter, age 58, living in Canterbury, CT, in the 1850 census. A 10" birch molding plane has been reported that has rounded chamfers and is boxed, possibly with ebony.

S. SPICER

May be Silas Spicer; the 1790 census showed him living next to O. Spicer (w.s.) in North Groton, CT. The stamp has been found on an ovolo made of yellow birch, 9⅞" long, with flat chamfers, in the collection of the Farmers Museum at Cooperstown, NY. Appearance is 18c.

I. STALL

John Stall appeared in the 1797 Philadelphia, PA, directory as a planemaker. The 1802 directory listed his wife as a widow. (see Stall & Massey)   A & A1: ★★★

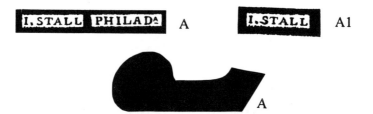

STALL & MASSEY

This name has appeared on a wedge-arm plow and on a molding plane, and overprinting a molding plane made by W. Brooks (w.s.). Appearance is ca.1800. (see I. Stall and also J.W. Massey)   ★★★★

J. STAMM

Joseph Stamm made planes in Mount Joy, Lancaster County, PA, and earlier, before 1850, in Hinkletown ("Chickentown" in Pennsylvania Dutch), PA. His imprint has also appeared on marking gauges, from which the Hinkletown imprint shown below has been taken. The wedge outline was taken from a plane with no location imprint. A jack plane with the B imprint has been reported with the same 1849 patented double wedge found on E.W. Carpenter and Samuel Auxer (both w.s.) planes. An imprint has beeb reported with the J. Stamm name only and has been designated B1.   A: ★★★   B: ★★

L.G. STARKEY

This name has been reported stamped on a plane with the additional location imprint DEARBORN.

JOHN STAR

The 1818 tax list of Pittsburgh, PA, listed John Star as a "plainmaker." No example of an imprint has been reported.

J. STARR

James Starr (1795-1872) was a carpenter and planemaker in New Lisbon (now Lisbon), Ohio, ca.1850. He was listed as a plane and churn manufacturer in the 1853-54 directory. Additionally he held a patent (#3258 Sept. 9, 1843) for an improved grain winnower, and was also a brickmaker, wood turner, bee keeper, and maker of cider presses. The cause of death, as shown on his death certificate, read simply "worn out." His estate inventory, dated 1872, included a number of planemaking tools and supplies. ★★★

R.C. STARR

Probably Reverend Robert C. Starr (1779-1862) of Thomaston, ME, born in Massachusetts and a joiner before becoming a Baptist minister. His imprint reads R.C. STARR and is embossed.

A. STEAD

This name has appeared on a 10" birch molder, a 9$^{15}\!/_{16}$" long birch bead, a rabbet, and at least two Yankee-style birch plow planes. Appearance is ca.1800.

GEORGE STEDMAN

George Stedman (b.1828) made planes in Rome, NY, —1859-70—, apparently as a secondary occupation to woodworking and cabinetmaking. No example of an imprint has been reported.

STEDMAN & CO.

Probably a hardware dealer. The imprint was reported on a Sandusky Tool Co. (w.s.) #124 screw arm plow (Sandusky imprint C).

357

ALEX STEEL

Probably a Rock Island, IL, hardware company. A hollow bearing this imprint is also imprinted "#72", which is the Ohio Tool Co.'s catalog number for hollows and rounds. (see Harper & Steel)

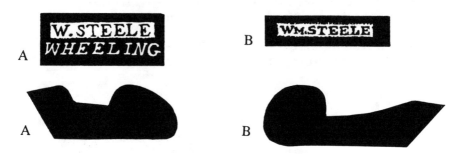

W. STEELE

William Steele was a planemaker in Wheeling, VA (now WV), —1839-51—. The B imprint appears on a 9½" long molding plane of different appearance from those with the A imprint. A: ★★

W. STEELE & CO.

This imprint was reported on a 14" long 4¾" wide panel raiser. It is also imprinted by Logan & Kennedy, a Pittsburgh, PA, hardware dealer (w.s.).

J.G. STEIGER

Made planes in Cleveland, Ohio, —1863-64—. No example has been reported.

STEINMAN & CO.

A Lancaster, PA, hardware company that was founded in 1744 by John Frederick Steinman, stepson of Johann Christopher Heyne (one of America's leading early pewterers), to sell hardware to westward-bound settlers. It went out of business in the 1960's. Examples of the Steinman imprint have been reported on an E.W. Carpenter jointer (John F. Steinman was sole agent for Carpenter for a period of time), and on a Sandusky Tool Co. plow plane. A & B: ★★

 A  B

L. STEPHENSON

Levi Stephenson (also spelled Stepenson) was listed in the 1860 census for Johnstown, NY, as a planemaker, age 31, born in MA, and owning real estate worth $1000. The *History of Johnstown, N.Y.* (1878) states "In 1855 Levi Stephenson opened a manufactory of carpenters tools, the first of its kind in the county. It closed in 1861 and in 1871 he opened a lumber yard." ★★

(see next page)

358

STERLING   see Logan & Gregg

B. STERN & TOLLNER

The A imprint was reported on a toothing plane and a hollow. Another imprint, designated B carries the additional location imprint "221 Bowery." Very probably related to C. Tollner and also C. Tollner & Hammacher (both w.s.).

STETSON   see Ionah Stetson

IONAH STETSON

Possibly one or both: Jonah Stetson (1721-83) a housewright, and his son Jonah (1761-1825) shipwright, both born in Scituate, MA, the son later working in Charlestown, MA. The Stetson B imprint planes vary in style from the A imprint ones, suggesting that there was more than one maker.   A & B: ★★★★

                  A   B

STEVENS

The A imprint appears on a 9⅜" boxed complex molding plane with spring marks. Appearance is ca.1830.
A & B: ★★★★

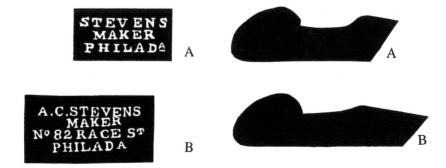

A.C. STEVENS   see Stevens

359

H. STEVENS

This name has been reported stamped on a slide arm plow plane with thumbscrews and brass tips on the arms, with the additional location imprint BOSTON.

J. STEVENS

James Stevens was a tool, plane, and rulemaker in Boston, MA. He made planes at Court Street 1821-22, and Merrimac Street 1823-60 and appeared in the 1861 Boston Almanac under "Planes" at 32 Sudbury St. ★

J. STILES

James Stiles was born in England in 1743 and probably apprenticed there. He worked in New York City as a carpenter, toolmaker, and planemaker 1768-75—. There is a record of his having bought from Thomas Napier (w.s.) in 1774 "sundry plans" for one pound one shilling. He fought with the colonists in the American Revolution and then settled in Kingston, NY. He turned his tools and shop over to his grandson, J.J. Styles (w.s.) in 1823 though he apparently remained semi-active. He died in 1830.

There are several versions of the Stiles' stamp. Those marked NEW YORK (A) are pre-revolution (1775). There are a number of J. STILES (B) with date imprints (he was one of the very few American planemakers who dated his planes); the earliest we know of is 1778 (B imprint), the latest 1830 on planes bearing the D imprint. (The earliest presently known date on that imprint is 1812) It is likely that the dated planes were made in Kingston, since NYC remained under British occupation until 1783 and Stiles, as a Continental soldier, would not have found himself welcome there. The upper and lower case "J. Stiles" C imprint has been reported several times and both imprint and wedge are stylistically very different from the other Stiles' planes. Appearance would date it ca.1800. The D wedge appears with the later dated Stiles planes and with the last imprint, the D.

A: ★★★★ B dated before 1800: ★★★★ B dated after 1800: ★★ C: ★★★★ D: ★

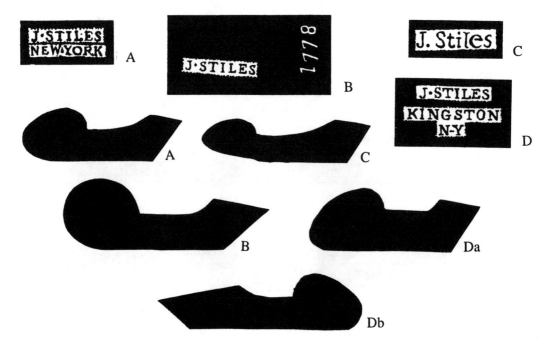

360

H.G. STILLEY

Henry Gunn Stilley (1827-1913) was a carpenter, joiner, ship carpenter and ship joiner, and a part time planemaker. Most of his planes are made of rosewood or other exotic woods, and are bench planes and molders. He was born in Delaware, moved to Cincinnati, OH, in 1833 or '34, and was noted in the 1850 census as "gone to California." His brother John, or possibly his father James (see J. Stilley) was listed in the 1860 census in Cincinnati as a planemaker. Henry Stilley first appeared in California in the San Francisco directory of 1864 as a carpenter; in 1877 he moved to Oakland.   A & B: ★★★

 A
 B

J. STILLEY

Probably John Stilley, brother of H.G. Stilley (w.s.), who was listed in the 1860 census in Cincinnati, OH, as a planemaker, age 30. It was during 1860-61 that his brother returned briefly to Cincinnati before going back to California. Also possibly James Stilley, father of H.G. and John, who was a carpenter in Cincinnati 1834-75. ★★★★

F.L. STODDARD

This imprint was reported on an Ohio Tool Co. (w.s.) closed handle 10⅓" long smoother.

G.L. STORER

Various planes have been reported with the G.L. Storer imprint, most showing multiple name strikes. Most are made of lignum and are typical of northern New England seacoast planemaking. (see J.P. Storer)

J.P. STORER

Joshua P. Storer was a sparmaker and carpenter who made planes in Brunswick, ME, 1854-73. In 1860, he was reported producing 500 planes valued at $750, made out of both lignum and beech. (see G.L. Storer)
A: ★★ B: ★★★

 A

 B

M. STOUT

Moses Stout made planes under his own name in St. Louis, MO, 1836-38 and with his son (see M. & N.H. Stout) 1838-49. He was listed as a hardware merchant in the 1857 Memphis directory.   A & B: ★★

 A

A

 B

M. & N.H. STOUT

Moses and Nathaniel H. Stout, father and son, made planes and cooper's tools —1838-49 and were also hardware dealers 1847-54 in St. Louis, MO. (see M. Stout and also N.H. Stout)   ★★

N.H. STOUT

Probably Nathaniel H. Stout, son of Moses Stout. (see M. & N.H. Stout, N.H. Stout/W.W. Richey, N.H. Stout Bro. & Co., and T.J. Rickard)   A: ★★ B: ★★★

 A

A

 B

N.H. STOUT BRO. & CO.

Nathaniel H. Stout, Moses Stout and W.W. Richey, who advertised in the 1859 and 1869 Memphis, TN, city directories as dealers in Hardware, Cutlery, and Mechanics Tools. N.H's brother, Isaac, was a salesman in the firm. (see N.H. Stout, W.W. Richey; N.H. Stout; M. Stout; and M. & N.H. Stout) ★★★

N.H. STOUT/ W.W. RICHEY

Believed to be Nathaniel H. Stout (see N.H. Stout) and W.W. Richey (w.s.), hardware merchants in Louisville, KY, 1836-38, who were listed in the city directory as Stout & Richey. In 1837 they advertised as "Wholesale & Retail Plane Manufacturers and Tool Store." A & B: ★★★

B

A

T. STOUT

Theodore Stout (b.1824), son of Moses Stout (see M. Stout) and brother of Nathaniel H. Stout (see N.H. Stout), was listed as a journeyman planemaker in 1842 in St. Louis, MO, and as working for M. & N.H. Stout (w.s.) in 1844. In 1850 he was a planemaker in New Albany, IN, where he remained until about 1855. ★★★

T.H. STRANGE

This name has been reported on a hollow, with the location imprint PROV/R.I. In the 1862 Providence directory Thomas H. Strange advertised as a sash, blind, and door manufacturer, "moldings of all sorts."

STRAUB & SON

This imprint has appeared on an early Ohio Tool Co. ogee. A probable hardware dealer.

C.A. STRELINGER & CO.

A large Detroit, MI, hardware and tool dealer begun by Charles A. Strelinger in 1885. Formerly he had been a clerk at T.B. Rayl & Co. (w.s.). The company's 1897 Woodworkers Tool Catalog has been reprinted (see Bibliography).

J. STRODE

This imprint has been reported on various beech planes. A Joshua Strode was listed in the 1840 census as residing in E. Fallowfield Twp., Clinton County, PA, with one person in the household, engaged in manufacturing or trades.

STRONG H'DW'E CO.

This imprint has been reported on several planes including an H. Chapin/Union Factory plane. The company was first organized as Strong Brothers Hardware Co. in 1852, and incorporated in 1867. The Strong Hardware Co. name was adopted some time after 1867 and the company finally ceased business in 1971.

S. STUBBS

Samuel Stubbs was born in Georgia in 1790 and was listed as a mill mechanic as late as 1860. His imprint has been reported on a plank plane. P.C. is believed to be Preble County (Ohio).

J.J. STYLES

James J. Styles (1800-94) was the grandson of J. Stiles (w.s.) and inherited his grandfather's books, his tools, his stock of planes, and the use of his workshop. He made planes in Kingston, NY, from ca.1820 to 1876. The 1850 census reported $600 worth of planes produced. He also made stone rules, did clock repair, and scissor and saw sharpening. ★ *(see next page)*

SUDDING & RUSSELL
This imprint has been reported on an Auburn Tool Co. bead. Probably a hardware dealer.

MARTIN SUMMERS   see Souder & Summers

JOHN SUNSERSOND
Listed as a planemaker in the 1836-37 Cincinnati, OH, directory. No example of his imprint has been reported. Possibly the same person as John Saundersod (w.s.).

B. SWAIN
This name has been reported on a rabbet.

R. SWAIN
Various planes have been reported, including two complex molders, one 9½" long, and a waterpipe plane, all with flat chamfers.

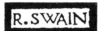

WM. D. SWAIN
Made planes in Rowe, MA, ca.1856.   ★★

H. SWEET & CO.
This name appears on two fore planes and two smoothing planes of mid-19c appearance. Stephentown N.Y. is near the Massachusetts border and about 10 miles from Pittsfield, MA, where M. Sweet (w.s.) was located. H. Sweet's shop appears in Rogerson's 1854 map of Rensselaer County in Stephentown on the Black River where there were a number of mills and water wheels.   *(see next page)*

M. SWEET

J.E.A. Smith in his *History of Pittsfield, Mass.* says "About the year 1820 a small building was erected on or near the site of the Rufus Allen iron forge on Onota Brook and from that date until 1843 was occupied as a manufactory of carpenter tools by Moses Sweet." (We think the beginning date was sometime after 1820 since Sweet would have been only 15 then). He was listed in the 1850 census as a carpenter, age 45, born in MA. In 1840 he lived four houses from J. Webb (w.s.). Sweet was one of the few planemakers who apparently dated some of his planes (J. Stiles was another). (see H. Sweet & Co.)   A, B, & B1: ★★

A

B

B1

SWETMAN

James Swetman was listed in the 1819 Pittsburgh, PA, directory as a planemaker and was also a partner in Swetman, Hughes & Co. (w.s.). In the next directory (1826) there was no listing of Swetman.   ★★★★

SWETMAN, HUGHES & CO.

A planemaking firm consisting of James Swetman and William P. Hughes, who were listed in the 1819 Pittsburgh, PA, directory. Among their employees listed in the directory were Thomas Clark (see T. Clark) and Benjamin King (see B. King), who later became planemakers in their own right. The next directory, which was published in 1826, had no listing for the firm. (see James Swetman)   ★★★★

T.D. & CO.

The mark of Tyler Davidson & Co., hardware dealers in Cincinnati, OH, 1843-65. Tyler Davidson, a Cincinnati hardware merchant 1836-42 was the predecessor firm.

T.S. & CLARK

There have been a number of reports on this imprint. Appearance is mid-19c. There has been no information as to who they are.

EDWARD P. TABB & CO.

Edward P. Tabb was a hardware dealer in Norfolk, VA, —1851-76. By 1872 the firm also included E.W. Moore, Pendleton Moore and William B. Tufts. A variant stamp EDWARD TABB/NORFOLK VA., which we are designating B, has been reported.

ALLEN TABER

Allen Taber was born in 1800 and died in 1882. His obituary in the *Kennebec Journal* of May 1882 said, "He moved to Augusta [Maine] in 1844 and consequently has been a resident of the city for some 38 years. He was a very quiet, industrious man and highly esteemed by all those who had the pleasure of his acquaintance. Until enfeebled by ill health, he was a manufacturer of bench planes and all the carpenters far and near sought for Taber's planes."

He was the son of Nicholas Taber (see N. Taber) and the brother of John Marshall Taber (see J.M. Taber). His father, in a will dated 1844, left him "all of my shop tools." Taber came to Augusta from Fairhaven, MA, where he was listed in the 1830 and 1840 censuses. In the 1850 census he was cited as a farmer. In 1855 he bought a house in Augusta, having previously owned a farm some six miles from town. The 1870 and 1880 censuses listed him as a planemaker. No examples of his imprint have been reported.

J. TABER

Various examples have been reported, including a 14" long crown molder with a 2⅝" iron, an offset handle and a rounded wedge; also a 9½" beech molder with a relieved wedge and broad flat chamfers. Appearance is 18c. ★★★

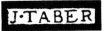

J.M. TABER

John Marshall Taber (1796-1873) was an active planemaker 1820-72 in New Bedford, MA. He was the son of Nicholas Taber (see N. Taber), whose business he took over ca.1820, and the brother of Allen Taber (w.s.). The 1870 census listed seven men who worked in "John M. Taber's plane factory": Clarence Pearce 27 (sic. - see Clarence A. Bearse), John Hussey 26 (see J. Hussey), Arnold Townsend 20, Charles H. Sherman 23, John S. Southwick 26, Henry E. Howard 19, and Henry A. Bodman 38. (see Bodman & Hussey, Bodman & Bearse, and Bodman, Bearse & Hussey)   A, B, C, C1, D: ★

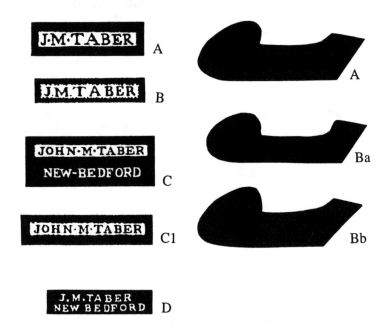

JOHN M. TABER   see J.M. Taber

L.H. TABER

Leander H. Taber (b.ca.1819 in Tiverton, RI) was listed in the New Bedford, MA, directories 1838-52 as a planemaker in connection with J.M. Taber (w.s.). The relationship is not known nor is the precise period in which he made under his own label. ★★

N. TABER

Nicholas Taber (1761-1849) made planes in New Bedford and Fairhaven, MA,—-1785-1820—. In his will dated 1844, he left his workshop to his son J.M. Taber (w.s.) and all his shop tools to his son Allen Taber (w.s.). A: (earlier) ★★   B (later) ★★

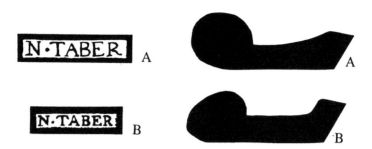

V. TABER

This imprint appears on a 7⁷⁄₁₆" long beech ⁵⁄₁₆" side bead. It was found together with a J.M. TABER and an N. TABER plane.

W. TABER   see Wing H. Taber

W.H. TABER   see Wing H. Taber

WING H. TABER

Wing Howland Taber (b.1809) made planes in Fairhaven, MA, —1833, New York City 1836-43, and Lowell, MA, 1844-66. The 1860 Massachusetts Industrial census showed him having one employee and producing $800 worth of planes. In 1865 he received a patent (No. 46614, Feb. 28, 1865) on a method of holding the iron in a bench plane by means of a metal frog. Planes using this patent were manufactured by the Taber Plane Co. (w.s.). Various imprints, not shown here, were used on the patented planes. See *Patented and Transitional Metallic Planes in America, Vol II* (listed in the Bibliography) for details and illustrations.

Earlier, Wing H. Taber, together with John H. Currier of Fairhaven, MA, received patent 1224 dated July 8, 1839, for a "new and useful machine for drilling iron, steel, brass, and the like substances. . .The nature of our invention consists in combining the powers of the lever and screw so as to force forward the chuck and drill while it is turned by a crank." One of the witnesses to Wing H. Taber's signature was a David Shiverick (see Shiverick).   A: ★   B, & C: ★★   D & E: ★★★

(see next page)

TABER & ABBOTT

This imprint appears on smooth planes with varying types of cap screws that were made under Patent No. 46614, dated February 28, 1865, issued to Wing H. Taber (w.s.) and assigned to him and Thomas H. Abbott. It was a precursor of the successful Bailey lever cap.   ★★★★

TABER PLANE CO.

Incorporated in 1866 and made planes in New Bedford, MA. 1866-72—. In 1869 W.G. Lamb (w.s.) and J.H. Lamb (w.s.) were officers of the company. The Taber Plane Co. manufactured planes using Wing H. Taber's (w.s.) 1865 patent. It ceased operations in 1872 and was succeeded by the New Bedford Tool Co. (w.s.).
A: ★   B: ★★

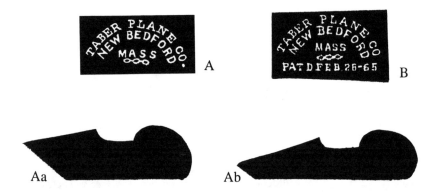

E. TAFT

The 1790 Federal census listed three E. Tafts in Mendon, MA: Enos, Elibah and Ebenezer. Mendon is very close to both Wrentham and Norton, where some of the earliest planemakers lived. The planes' appearance indicate they were made ca.1750. (see also S. Partridge)   ★★★★★

F. TARBOX

Made planes in Calais, ME, 1871-80. No example of an imprint has been reported.

FREDERICK TAYLOR
This imprint has been reported on a lignum fore plane whose appearance is ca.1850.

H. TAYLOR
Hiram Taylor made planes in Cincinnati, OH, 1839-40, as an employee of E.F. Seybold (w.s.); and was listed as a planemaker in the city directories of 1842-43, 1844 (planemaker store), 1846, as a partner in H. & J.C. Taylor (w.s.) 1850-59, and as a planemaker again in 1867.   ★★

H. & J.C. TAYLOR
Hiram and John C. Taylor made and retailed planes in Cincinnati, OH, 1850-59. The 1850 census showed them employing six hands and producing planes worth $2500. They also held patent no. 13626 (Oct. 2, 1855) for a cast iron cooper's crozing plane. (see H. Taylor and J.C. Taylor, and also C. Eyman) A: ★★★   B: ★★

J. TAYLOR   see J.C. Taylor

J.C. TAYLOR
John C. Taylor was listed as a planemaker in the Cincinnati, OH, directories of 1842-44 and 1868-69. During the period 1850-59 he was a partner with Hiram Taylor in H. & J.C. Taylor (w.s.).   A, A1, B, C, D, E, E1: ★★

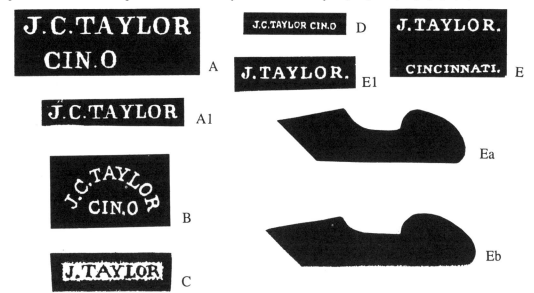

371

I. TEAL

John Teal (1765-1827) was born in England and made planes in Leeds before coming to the U.S. some time before 1811. In 1811 he appeared on a deed as a carpenter's tool maker in Hubbardstown, Worcester County, MA. In the 1820 census he was listed as a planemaker in Princeton, Worcester County, MA, with annual sales of $300, his age given as "over 45." His probate inventory included 10 new planes and a box of plane irons. His estate was declared insolvent. *British Planemakers, 3rd edition,* shows the A and B imprints, used by Teal in England. Apparently he brought his die stamps to America and used them here, since they appear, one or the other, on all of the examples found in the U.S. Only the I. TEAL/LEEDS English imprint offers a certainty of time and location. A & B: ★★★ C: ★★★★

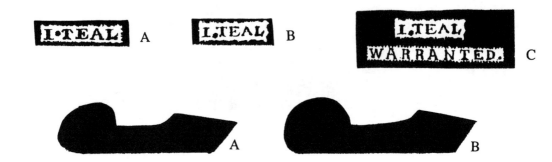

JOHN TEASMAN

Listed in the 1835-37 Newark, NJ, directories as a planemaker, "colored," and in the 1850 census as age 56, born in NJ, and a planemaker. No example of an imprint has been reported.

R. THAYER

Various examples have been reported, an 11½" handled tongue plane and four molding planes, all with flat chamfers and made of birch. Appearance is late 18c.

E. THIESING

Ernest Thiesing was a hardware dealer 1839-46 and a partner in THIESING & EVENS [FRANCIS], Hardware and Edge Tools 1849-51.

THOMAS THOMAS

Thomas Thomas was listed as a planemaker in Baltimore, MD, —1842. No example of an imprint has been reported.

WILLIAM THOMAS

William Thomas was listed as a planemaker in Baltimore, MD, —1835-75. A bead bearing the imprint Wm. THOMAS/BALTIMORE was sold at auction in 1992.

THOMPSON

William Thompson of Steubenville, OH, whose name appears on several molding planes and on a wedge-arm plow that originally belonged to a Columbus, OH, cabinetmaker (R.R. Ritchie 1843-1938).

Wm. A. THOMSON

William A. Thomson, who was born in Scotland, operated a hardware store in Buffalo, NY. 1839-46. (see also Thomson Brothers)

THOMSON BROTHERS

Robert H. and Thomas M. Thomson, who were born in Scotland and were sons of Wm. A. Thomson (w.s.), succeeded their father in his hardware store in Buffalo, NY, which they operated under this name 1847-59.

WILLIS THRALL & SON

Hardware dealers in Hartford, CT. 1860-95. ★★

M.B. TIDEY

M.B. Tidey is best known for his patented double beveling plane (pat. no. 11235, July 4, 1854) and his less successful patented beech smoothing plane (patent no. 16889, March 24, 1857) that Roger Smith has called the inspiration for the subsequent designs by Bridges and Gage.

The 1850 Federal census listed a Marcus Tidey, age 20, born in Canada and living in the village of Starkey, Yates County, NY, the same county as Penn Yan and Dundee, and not far from Ithaca. On March 10, 1857, Tidey was granted a patent for a sawing machine table gauge (no. 16812). The 1870 Products of Industry census for NJ listed M.B. Tidey as employing 10 men, building 75 machines and 20 dozen saw gauges in Newark, NJ. Tidey-imprinted non-patent planes are seldom found, suggesting that although he used four different imprints, planemaking was apparently not his major occupation.   A & A1: ★★★   B & C: ★★★★   D: ★★★

(see next page)

A

B

373

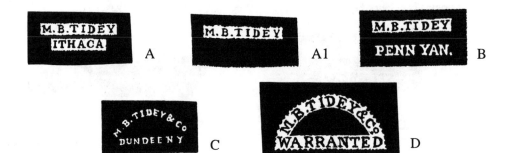

A   A1   B   C   D

M.B. TIDEY & CO.   see M.B. Tidey

J. TILBURN
   Listed as a planemaker in the 1837 Philadelphia directory.

R.M. TILBURN
   Richard Mayer Tilburn was married in Newbury, MA, November 29, 1806, and appeared in the 1810 Federal census in Newbury, MA. In the 1820 New Jersey Federal Industrial census he was listed as a journeyman planemaker in New Brunswick, NJ. A Richard H. Tilburn was listed as a planemaker in the 1837 city directory.
   Tilburn's earlier molding planes are $9\frac{3}{4}$" long, have a Sleeper-style wedge (A), and flat chamfers. The later planes are $9\frac{1}{2}$", have round chamfers and a typical early-19c wedge (B). It is likely that the A wedge represents his Newbury period and B his work in New Brunswick and perhaps Philadelphia.
with A wedge: ★★   with B wedge: ★★★

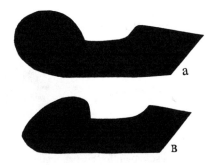

a

B

H. TILESTON
   Harvey Tileston, brother of Timothy Tileston, was listed as a planemaker in the Boston, MA, directories of 1810-16.   ★★★

T. TILESTON

(d.1866) Timothy Tileston Jr.'s birthdate and birthplace are unrecorded, though he was listed in the 1850 census as a planemaker age 67. His first planemaking location was at 55 Orange Street, Boston, the same premises as Levi Little's last listed address. (see L. Little). Tileston's name appears several times in the accounting of Levi Little's estate and it is probable that Timothy Jr. worked for Little and took over after Little's death in 1802.

Tileston's early planes are beech, 9½" long, with broad flat chamfers and round wedge finials. He used the same "Bofton" stamp and boxed his planes with rosewood, as did Levi Little.

Other Tilestons, all related to Timothy Jr., are listed as journeymen or planemakers in the Boston directories. The planemaker's father, Timothy Tileston (laborer and well-digger), lived on Pleasant Street and had two other sons, Harvey and Charles (a hatter). Harvey worked as a planemaker from 1810 to 1816 and lived with his father. (see H. Tileston)

Timothy Tileston, the planemaker, dropped the Jr. and his son, Timothy Tileston Jr., a planemaker, is shown residing at 16 Ash Street from 1834 to 1840. This was a property owned by Timothy Tileston in 1824 and still owned by him at his death.

Another son, Benjamin L. Tileston, was a planemaker working for, and residing with, his father on Front Street from 1841-1857. He was listed in the 1850 census as a planemaker, age 39. No plane marked B. Tileston has been reported. Apparently all journeymen's planes were signed T. Tileston.

In the 1860 Massachusetts Industrial census, Timothy Tileston was listed as a planemaker with one employee and producing plane stocks worth $700; indicating that his planemaking had become rather inactive, not surprising since he was then 77 and apparently well-to-do. The estate of Timothy Tileston was appraised at $49,202.51, an unusually large amount for a planemaker, or anyone, in that period. Of this $389.25 was stock and tools.

The Tileston imprints are shown chronologically. The "Bofton" stamps A and B, 1802-08, when he worked at 55 and then 41 Orange Street. The "Front St" without "Bofton" E was used 1809—. The "Boston/Front St" F was used —1840. The last, the Harrison Ave. address G, was used 1841-66, when Front Street's name was changed to Harrison Avenue. Imprint B is zb with the name slanted slightly. Imprint C is lb with the name upright. Imprint D is zb with the name upright.   A, B, C, D, E: ★★   F: ★   F1: ★★   G: ★

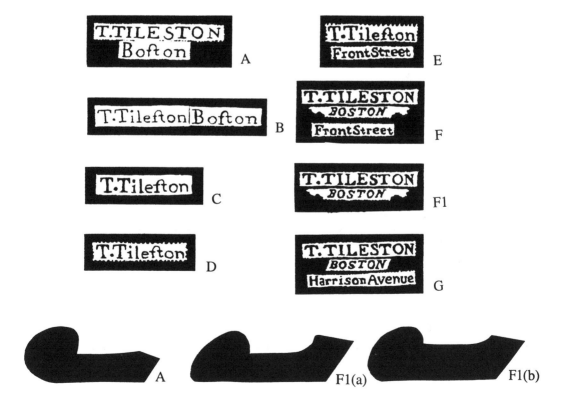

375

TINKHAM see J. Tinkham

J. TINKHAM

The 1850 census listed a Jesse Tinkham, age 65, machinist, in Enfield, MA. Enfield was one of four towns inundated when the Quebbin Reservoir was created in the 1930's to supply water to metropolitan Boston.

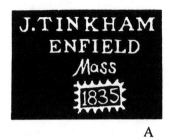

A

B

A

L. TINKHAM

Thought to be Levi Tinkham (1766-1857) of Middleboro, MA, who was a "mechanic in wood" and a farmer. Examples have been reported, some of birch, some of beech, the molding planes varying from 9½" to 9¾"; one bench plane with an offset tote, another with a centered tote, suggesting a transitional maker, working in the late 18c and beginning 19c. The early Levi Tinkham planes (A) bear a striking resemblance to those of E. Clark (w.s.) also of Middleboro. A: ★★★★ A1: ★★★★★ B: ★★★★

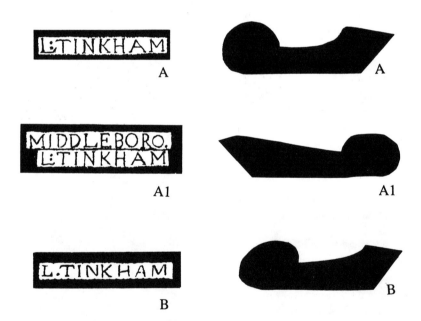

S. TINKHAM

A group of 11 planes, including 7 molding, 2 beading planes, and a rabbet, all 9" long, and a 9½" adjustable-screw, double-iron sash plane have been reported. They are made of beech, have relieved wedges, round chamfers and a name stamp similar to that of J. Tinkham (w.s.). Appearance is early 19c. A Samuel Tinkham of Enfield, MA, was listed in the 1850 census as a cabinetmaker, age 57. *(see next page)*

I. TITCOMB   see Joseph Titcomb

I.C. TITCOMB
Isaac Cummings Titcomb (b.1813) was a Newburyport, MA, cabinetmaker —1840—. His imprints appear on various examples, indicating some planemaking activity. The N.P. on the B imprint is believed to stand for his location, Newburyport.   ★★★

 A    B

JOSEPH TITCOMB
Joseph Titcomb (1770-1850), of Newbury, MA, was described as a joiner on an 1805 surety and as a toolmaker in his probate documents. His estate inventory included 26 jointers, 12 fore planes, "2 ploughs [planes], three pairs of match plains, 42 crease tools [molding planes]" and 20 plane irons, among other items. A number of his planes have been reported with Sleeper-style wedges and narrow flat chamfers. The I. TITCOMB imprints are believed to be those of Joseph, although Joseph also had a son named Isaac.   A & B: ★★★

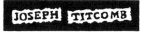
A
B

S. TITCOMB
Possibly Solomon Titcomb (1803-87), the son of Joseph Titcomb (w.s.), who was born and died in Newbury, MA. A grooving plane has been reported with a rosewood skate and a non-Sleeper-type wedge, also a beech molding plane and a beech gutter plane; all with wide flat chamfers.

D.B. TITUS
Daniel Butters Titus (b.1829 in Union, ME) was noted as a carpenter in 1850 and in —1880— was a maker of mast and truss hoops and cooper's tools. A cooper's croze has been reported bearing a paper label with a circular imprint that reads "D.B. TITUS/ MANUFACTURERS OF/ MAST HOOPS, TRUSS/ HOOPS AND CROZES/ EAST UNION ME." Also stamped on the top edge was H.H. CRIE & CO. (w.s.), a hardware dealer in Rockland, ME.

C. TOBEY
Probably Cornelius Tobey of Hudson, NY, who was a builder —1792—. The A1 wedge comes from a 9⅞" long yellow birch complex molder, the A2 wedge from a 9¾" long beech astragal. (see J.I. Tobey)
A: ★★★   B: ★★   *(see next page)*

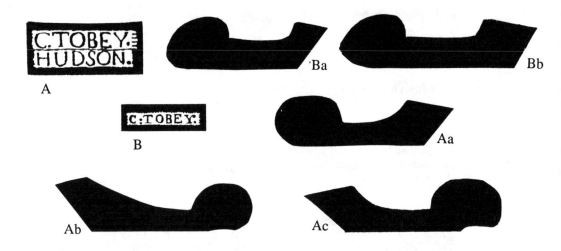

A Ba Bb

B Aa

Ab Ac

C. TOBEY/S. TOBEY

This dual imprint appears in the planemaker's slot on a 9¼" long beech round. (see C. Tobey)

J.I. TOBEY

Probably John I. Tobey, son of C. Tobey (w.s.) of Hudson, NY, who was an assistant alderman in 1827-28.
★★★

C. TOLLNER

Charles Tollner ran a hardware and tool store in New York City 1851-61. During 1862-63 he was in partnership with Albert Hammacher as C. Tollner & Hammacher. (see C. Tollner & Hammacher, Stern & Tollner, and also H. Hammacher & Co.)   A, B & B1: ★★

A B B1

C. TOLLNER & HAMMACHER

A New York City hardware and tool dealer 1862-63. Partners were Charles Tollner and Albert Hammacher. The firm was the predecessor of A. Hammacher & Co. (w.s.). No example of an imprint has been reported. (see also C. Tollner)

J.R. TOLMAN

Joseph Robinson Tolman (1787-1864), the father of T.J. Tolman (w.s.), probably first made planes in South Scituate, MA, in the 1820's. He is listed in Boston, MA, in 1841 and worked in Hanover, MA, —1849—. He is notable for the large number of spar and other shipbuilders' planes he made, as well as the high quality of his workmanship. He also tended to use double irons in many of his planes. In the 1860 Massachusetts Industrial census he was shown employing three hands and producing $3000 worth of planes. In imprint A the ends of the first two lines are zb and not indented (also in A1, the name imprint). In B the ends of the first two lines *are* indented. In B1, B2, and B3 only the first line in indented. In B2 both lines 2 and 3 (Hanover and Mass.) are larger than in B1. (see James Merritt)

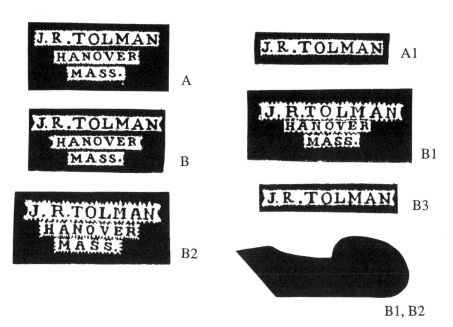

T.J. TOLMAN

Thomas J. Tolman (b.1819), the son of J.R. Tolman (w.s.) was a planemaker in Hanover and South Scituate, MA. —1850-80—. Tolman also received Patent No. 16,412 on Jan. 13, 1857, covering a method for adjusting the mouth size of a plane. A 9½" smoothing plane with such an adjustable rosewood mouth, and a beech miter plane with an adjustable boxwood mouth have been reported. (see Tolman & Merritt)   A: ★ B: ★★★★

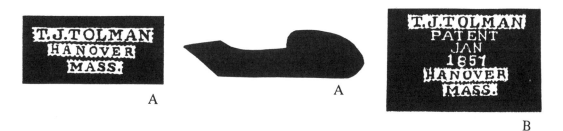

TOLMAN & MERRITT

Thomas J. Tolman and Charles H. Merritt, partners in South Scituate, MA. 1864-80. It is believed that Merritt continued the firm alone from 1881-93. Charles H. Merritt was listed as a planemaker, age 23, in the 1850 census, as a carpenter in the 1860 census, as a planemaker in the 1870 census, and as a plane manufacturer in the 1880 census. Since there has been no report of a Tolman & Merritt imprint, the T.J. Tolman stamp may have been used. (see T.J. Tolman and J. Merritt)

S. TOPPAN
Probably Stephen Toppan, housewright, of Newburyport, MA, who was born in 1756 and died in Newbury, MA, in 1839. Planes reported include a birch Yankee plow and various molding planes, made of beech, and usually 9½" long with flat chamfers and Sleeper-style wedges. A Sleeper plane, also imprinted by Toppan, has been reported. Toppan was also involved in furniture manufacturing. An 1830 ad in the Dover, NH, *Inquirer* offered Cabinet Furniture manufactured "in the latest and most improved patterns." His estate inventory included 6 beds, 6 desks, 11 tables, and 27 chairs, plus other items of furniture. ★★★

TOPPING & BRO.
Erastus D. Topping, Marcus H. Topping, John S. Topping, and Lucas Topping, trading as Topping & Bro., were hardware dealers in Alton, IL. 1849-1884.

Jn. TOWER
Jonathan Tower was born in Sudbury, MA, in 1758 and later settled in Rutland, MA. (near Worcester), where he made carpenter's and cabinetmaker's tools, and died in 1846. ★★

Aa   Ab

S. TOWER & CO.
Listed in the 1856 directory as a planemaker in Chesterfield, MA. No example of an imprint has been reported.

TREMAN & BROTHERS
A hardware firm in Ithaca, NY, consisting of Leonard (1819-88) and Lafayette L. (1821-1900) Treman, that succeeded Edward G. Pelton. In 1849 a third brother, Elias (1822-98), joined the company. The firm then added an iron foundry and a plane factory. In 1857 the firm became Treman, King & Co., when Leander Rutherford King joined, and continued in business until 1944. No planes have been reported with a Treman, King imprint. A & B: ★★

A   B

J.S. TRIPP
Possibly Jonathan S. Tripp, who lived in Union Vale, Dutchess County, NY, from 1830-50 and was listed in the 1850 census as a carpenter, age 67. This imprint has been reported on a 9½" long moving filletster, two rabbets, and a round.

P x TRIPP

Very similar in appearance to the imprint of J.S. Tripp (w.s.). Probably Philip Tripp (1784-1868) who worked as a mill carpenter and contractor in Fall River, MA, and in 1835 bought a farm in Freetown, farming the rest of his life. The imprint appears on a group of 10 molding planes, each 9½" long, made of beech, and with ⅜" wide flat chamfers. Included are two boxed beads, a double boxed complex molder, and a moving filletster.

PRESTON TROW

(1810-1879) Came to Montpelier, VT, in 1830. He was listed as a planemaker 1842-43, as a joiner age 39, born in NH in the 1850 census, and later as a house builder. His imprint has been reported on a jointer.

TROY TOOL CO.

This name has appeared on a jack plane of mid-19c appearance, which has an AUBURN TOOL CO/THISTLE BRAND iron.

S.W. & H. TUCKER

The 1860 census for Keokuk, Iowa, listed Samuel W. Tucker, age 40, as a hardware merchant. Howard Tucker was a younger brother of Samuel and probably his partner. By 1870 both brothers had entered the insurance business.

TUCKER & CO.

Possibly Charles E. Tucker, partner in Tucker & Appleton (w.s.), or Isaac F. Tucker, who was listed under hardware in the 1870 Boston directory, or perhaps both.

 A    B

TUCKER & APPLETON

A hardware dealer in Boston, MA. 1868-71, consisting of Thomas L. Appleton and Charles E. Tucker. (see Tucker & Co. and Thomas L. Appleton) ★★

381

A. TULLOCH (or TULLOCK)

Alexander Tulloch was listed in the 1830 NYC directory as a planemaker at 194 Grand St. Two Tullock planes were sold at auction in England in 1988, suggesting that Tullock might be another of those who apprenticed and began making planes in England or Scotland before emigrating to the U.S.   A & B: ★★★

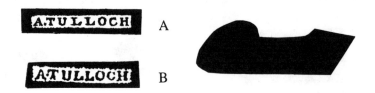

A

B

TUTTLE, HIBBARD & CO.

Frederick Tuttle and William Hibbard, Chicago, IL, hardware dealers 1856-65, who became Hibbard, Spencer & Co., when Franklin F. Spencer joined the firm. (see Hibbard, Spencer, Bartlett & Co.)   ★★

P. TYLER

Various examples have been reported. Possibly Putnam Tyler, born in Marlow, NH, in 1793, and still living in 1888. Appearance of planes is early 19c.

382

U

UNDERHILL, CLINCH & CO.

This name has been reported on several planes. Appearance is mid 19c. Very possibly a hardware dealer.

F. UNDERWOOD

Frank Underwood, who was a partner in F. UNDERWOOD/C.B. SCHAEFFER (w.s.), apparently also made planes under his own name. This imprint appears on a $9\frac{1}{2}$" long $\frac{1}{4}$" single boxed center bead.

F. UNDERWOOD/C.B. SCHAEFFER

Frank Underwood and Charles B. Schaeffer made planes in Cincinnati, Ohio, 1854-57. (see C.B. Schaeffer)
A & B: ★★

A

B

UNION FACTORY   see H. Chapin and also M. & A. Copeland

UNION TOOL CO.

Made planes in Goshen, MA, 1852-54, using a millsite and machinery bought from Abner C. More. Among those involved were Hiram Barrus, Caleb C. Dresser and ? Washburn. One of the early users of both water and steam power in the manufacturing process, the company employed 20 hands and went bankrupt after two years. (see H. Barrus & Co., C.C. Dresser, and A.C. More)   ★

W. UPTHEGROVE

This name has appeared on a molding plane made by Reed (w.s.).

USON & CO.

Has been reported with an additional location mark HAMILTON.

RALPH UTLEY

A planemaker in Goshen, MA, in 1845. No example of his imprint has been reported.

J.H. VAJEN

John H. Vajen was a hardware dealer in Indianapolis, IN. 1857-66—. A plane has been reported with a C.J. SMITH & CO. (w.s.) imprint overprinted by J.H. VAJEN.   A & B: ★★

F.W. v.A.

Believed to be F.W. van Allen, a planemaker in Delhi, NY. A rabbet has been reported branded F.W.v.A. on the side with the year 1861 carved. His father, Orran van Allen, is also believed to have been a planemaker.

VAN BAUN

Believed to be William D. Van Baun, who was listed as a planemaker in the 1818 Philadelphia directory. ★★★

VAN LEW & MORTON

Probably a hardware merchant in Petersburg, VA, ca.1850.

VAN LEW SMITH & CO.

A Richmond, VA, hardware firm, 1845-46—.   *(see next page)*

385

A

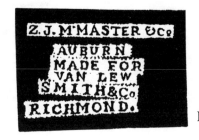

B

S.D. VANSANDS

A planemaker in Middletown, CT. —1849—. No example of his imprint has been reported.

I. VAN ZANT

Made planes in Georgetown, KY; the appearance of the planes reported is early 19c.   ★★★

W. VANCE

William Vance was one of the early Baltimore, MD, planemakers. In 1806 he advertised the receipt of a complete assortment of edged tools, and that he "manufactures all kinds of planes in the neatest manner and of the best seasoned timber, which enables him to supply mechanics in the wood way in a superior manner. Moulding plane irons warranted." His working dates are estimated to be —1799-1833. The script imprint E is the one most often found.   A, A1, & B: ★★★★   C & D: ★★★   E: ★

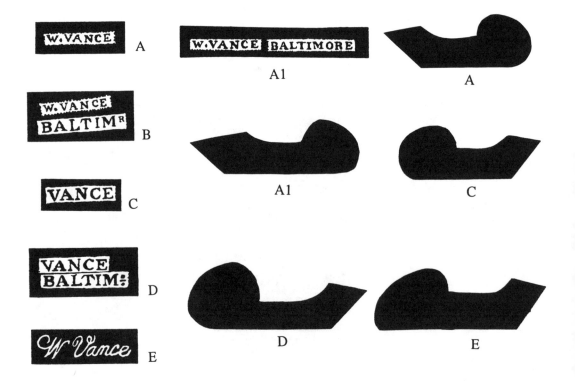

VANCE & MOORE
This imprint was reported on a 9¼" long beech round. (see W. Vance, Theophilus Moore, Thomas Moore, and William H. Moore)

C.L. VARNEY
This name has been reported with the additional location imprint HANOVER/MASS.

THOMAS VAUGHN
A Chelsca (Boston) MA, plane manufacturer, listed in the 1874 directory. No example of an imprint has been reported.

JOHN VEIT
A prolific planemaker in Philadelphia, Pa. 1857-99, whose imprint has also appeared on a workbench, a wooden compass, and various cooper's tools. FF

J.H. VERBRYCK
A planemaker in Mason, Ohio —1853—. No example of his imprint is known.

VERMONT STATE PRISON
A beech jointer has been reported with this imprint. (see also Vermont S.P.)

VERMONT S.P.
A 12⅝" skewed, handled, rabbet has been reported. (see Vermont State Prison)

J. VINALL   see J.J. Vinall

J.J. VINALL

John J. Vinall was listed as a planemaker in the Cleveland, Ohio, directories 1845-53. He advertised that he made cooper's tools, "did job work such as sawing, turning or anything that steam can be applied to" and sold wholesale and retail. The 1850 census listed him as a planemaker in Cleveland, age 32, born in England, owning real estate worth $1000. He had been in Ohio at least since 1843. In 1850-51 he apparently was associated with F.B. Marble (w.s.).   A & B: ★★

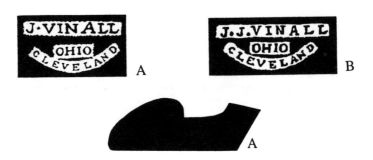

SIMEON VIRGIN

(1781-1838) A carpenter and furniture maker in Concord, NH, 1803-37, who is also known to have made planes.

C.L. VOLCKHAUSEN & CO.

This imprint has been reported on a toothing plane. A probable hardware dealer.

I. WAIN

Various examples have been reported, the molding planes 9¾" to 10" long, beech, with wide flat chamfers, some with Newbould irons. Provenance of the planes reported suggest a Pennsylvania origin. Appearance is ca.1800.

 A    B

J. WAIT J.

Probably J. Wait Jr. whose name has been reported several times on crisply made beech molding planes with flat chamfers. Two examples have owner's marks, each different. One plane is boxed; all are 9½" long. Appearance is ca.1800.

B. WALBMIEIER

This imprint was reported on an Arrowmammett (w.s.) handled plane. Probably a hardware dealer.

D. WALKER

David Walker was a Cincinnati, OH, planemaker —1829—. (see Walker & Hall)   ★★

ESTHER WALKER

Widow of Jesse Walker, she was listed as a plane manufacturer in Cincinnati, OH, in 1829 and as keeping a boarding house in 1831. No example of her imprint has been reported. (see J. Walker)

GUS WALKER

Reported on a 9" long shipbuilder's type smoother of late 19c appearance. Gustavus Walker (1830-1902) was a hardware dealer in Concord, NH, 1855-83.

J. WALKER

Thought to be Jesse Walker, a Cincinnati, OH, planemaker 1825—. A panel raiser and a sash plane have been reported with the iron imprinted J. WALKER. The J. Walker imprint appears both with and without an eagle. (see Esther Walker, and B.King/J. Walker)

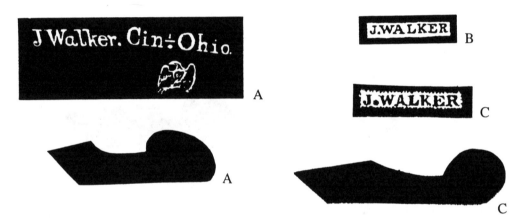

R.W. WALKER & CO.

This name has been reported on a sun plane.

WALKER & HALL

David Walker and John H. Hall, Cincinnati, OH, planemakers listed in 1831. No example of an imprint has been reported. (see D. Walker and Hall & Lyon)

N.N. WALLACE

This name has been reported on various planes. Possible location is northern NY state. Appearance is mid-19c.

B. WALTON

Benjamin Walton (1750-1824), housewright, in that part of Reading, MA, which is now Wakefield. He was the younger son of John Walton (see I. Walton) and was probably the co-maker of planes signed I:B:Waltons (w.s.), the "I" probably being his older brother John. His "B:Walton" name stamp was made from the "I:B:" stamp with the first and last letters ground off.

Benjamin was a Minuteman during the alarms, and was elected a lieutenant in the militia and served throughout the Revolutionary War. He married Sarah Boardman in 1780. An interesting item appears in the *Genealogical History of the Town of Reading*: "Timothy Bryant, the father of Joseph, had occupied the same tenement and died there, and at his funeral one of the bearers (Benjamin Walton) became intoxicated, and while carrying the body to the grave stumbled and fell, and the coffin came to the ground and burst open."

For characteristics of his planes see I. Walton. The "B. Walton" planes would date after 1771, the year his brother moved to Cambridge. He used his father's "IN READING" stamp. ★★★★

I:B: WALTONS

John Walton (1744-1823) of Reading, MA, until 1771 and Cambridge, MA, thereafter; and Benjamin Walton, his brother, (see B. Walton).

Planes signed I:B:Waltons were probably made before 1771, when John Walton moved to Cambridge to work as a housewright. Some of the brothers' planes are fruitwood, others birch. Though they had their own name stamp, they used their father's location stamp IN READING. It should be noted that there never was a "Waltons" family in Reading or Wakefield and the letter "s" was therefore used to indicate a plurality. The planes' details are described under I. Walton (w.s.). ★★★★

I. WALTON

John Walton, Jr. (1710-1785) was listed as a joiner and housewright in Reading, MA, in 1754, served as a lumber surveyor, a tax assessor, and on several parish committees, and attained the rank of captain during the French and Indian Wars. Records indicate that he was still working in 1776 at age 66. He was the father of Benjamin and John Walton, both planemakers.

His planes are of birch and are 10" or longer, low in height and typically have a very small wedge finial. The chamfers are flat and narrow. His cornice planes have offset totes. An example of one of Walton's cornice planes is pictured in Kenneth Roberts' *Wooden Planes In 19th Century America* on p. 192.

John Walton died intestate in 1785 and his son Benjamin was appointed administrator. His estate inventory, real and personal, came to 492 pounds sterling, of which lumber and joiner's and carpenter's tools were 34 £. The joiner's shop was additionally valued at $7\frac{1}{2}$ £.

In Benjamin's accounting of the estate, dated November 6, 1786, an entry reads "to sundry tools sold out of the shop before the appraisal 3 pounds 14 shillings, 4 pence." The sale of tools, or anything else, before an appraisal would not be permissible unless the items were normally for sale at the same price prior to the owner's decease, indicating that tools were being sold by the shop up to the time of Walton's death. A plane has been reported dated 1764 in ink, under an apparent owner's name. The monogrammed imprint "I.W." shown below has been reported on several examples, which are identical in style to those planes bearing the full imprint I. WALTON/IN READING. (see B. Walton and I:B:Waltons)   A: ★★★   B: ★★★★★

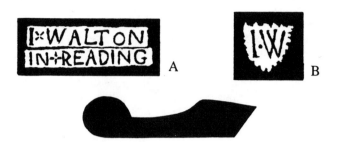

G.C. WARD

A G.C. Ward was noted as having agreed to work for the Union Factory (see H. Chapin) in April 1835. Po'kepsie is an abbreviation for Poughkeepsie, NY.   A & B: ★★★

G. & H.J. WARD

George and Horace J. Ward made planes, gauges, handscrews, bench screws and levels in Riverton (New Hartford), CT, 1870-73.   ★★

J.G. WARD

A molding plane has been reported with the location stamp NEW HARTFORD CONN.

R.A. WARD

Robert Ward was listed in 1836-37 Cincinnati, OH, directories as a planemaker with E.F. Seybold (w.s.), but apparently also made planes under his own name, both in Cincinnati and in Madison, Indiana, which is just down river from Cincinnati.   A, A1, & B: ★★★

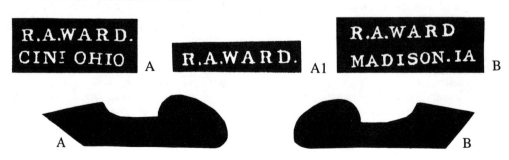

S^L. WARD

Various planes have been reported, 9½" long, birch, with flat chamfers. Appearance is ca.1800, location probably southeastern New England.

W.J.C. WARD

William J.C. Ward (1821-1891) was born in Sheffield, England, and came to the U.S. in 1846, settling in New York City. There he made planes under his own name at various addresses: 1850-51 and 1853-68 at 513 Eighth Avenue, 1868-73 at 549 Eighth Avenue, and 1873-74 at 307 W. 37th St. An exception to this was during 1852-53 when he was a partner in Ward & Fletcher (w.s.). He subsequently moved to Saddle River, NJ, where he established an edge tool factory and sawmill, producing planes and other products until his death.

Ward planes are not as numerous as his variety of name stamps and long working period would suggest. Among the examples that survive are some unusual types, including a three-arm plow quite similar to those made by Mockridge & Francis (w.s.) and probably a precursor to the Rust-Chapin patent of 1868. There are also examples of a screw arm sash filletster, possibly reflecting his English background, as well as a handsome handled applewood moving filletster.   A, B, C, E, F, G: ★★   D: ★★★

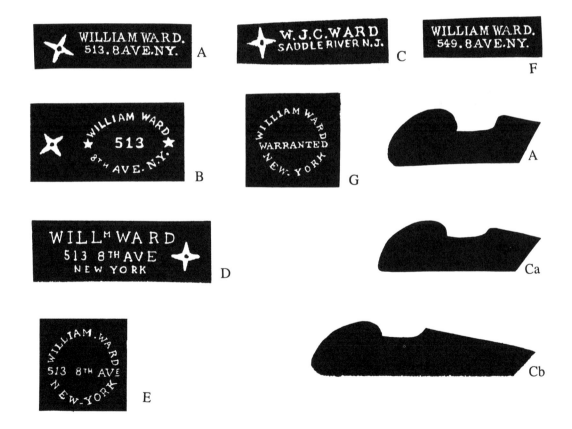

393

WILLIAM WARD   see W.J.C. Ward

WARD CARTER
   This imprint has been reported on a Chapin-Stephens rabbet; probably a hardware dealer.

WARD & CHAPIN
   ? Ward and Philip Chapin made planes in Baltimore, MD, —1831—. (see P. Chapin)   ★★

WARD & FLETCHER
   John R. Fletcher and William J. C. Ward made planes and other tools in New York City 1852-53. (see W.J.C. Ward)   A, A1, B: ★★★

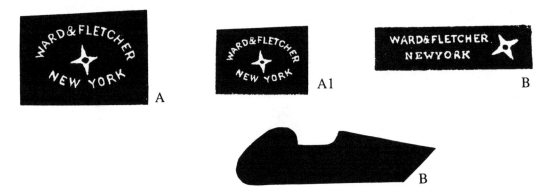

WARDE HUMPHREY & CO.
   This imprint appears on planes made by the Greenfield Tool Co., E & T. Ring & Co., and Lamb & Brownell (all w.s.). Warde, Humphrey & Dodge, a partnership consisting of David A. Warde, Stillman Humphrey, and Howard A. Dodge were hardware dealers in Concord, NH, 1870-74.

N.H. WARDWELL & CO.
A Rome, NY, hardware store that began in 1851 and was still in business in 1970. This imprint appears on a Bensen & Crannell (w.s.) round.

WARING & STANTIAL
Daniel H. Waring and John W. Stantial were NYC hardware dealers 1875-77. ★★★

W.A. WARNER
A paper label reading W.A. WARNER, 13 E. GRAND COR. N. FRONT ST. NEW HAVEN, HARDWARE was reported affixed to a Thos. L. Appleton plane. Probably a hardware dealer.

W. WARNER
William Warner made planes under this imprint in New Hartford, CT, —1849-51—. Earlier (1831-35) he worked for Hermon Chapin (see H. Chapin). He was listed in the 1850 census as a toolmaker, age 41, born in CT, with real estate worth $3000, having five employees and producing $2500 worth of planes annually. (see Warner & Driggs) ★★

WARNER & DRIGGS
William Warner and Hiram B. Driggs made planes in New Hartford, CT. 1852-53—. Driggs was listed as a New Hartford planemaker, age 25, and working for H. Chapin (w.s.) in the 1850 census,. (see Wm. Warner)
A: ★★   A1: ★★★

 A  A1  A

C. WARREN

Cyrus Warren (1804-1888), a prolific New Hampshire planemaker who may have taught the art to his brother William (see W. Warren), to his son George Henry (see G.H. Warren), to Dana Sargent (see D. Sargent), and to Addison Heald (w.s.). Trained earlier as a carpenter, he came to NH in 1837, opening a planemaking shop in Hudson. His brother William joined him in partnership in 1853. The partnership was later dissolved and Cyrus moved to nearby Nashua in 1857. He retired from planemaking in 1875. He was probably the Warren of WARREN & HEALD (w.s.). A beech miter plane has been reported carrying both a C.Warren and a Warren & Heald imprint. Some examples exist bearing the location imprint LOWELL. These may date before his coming to New Hampshire (1837) when he lived in the Lowell, MA, area where he is believed to have acquired his training in planemaking. It is believed that all planes made by the Warrens in Hudson were imprinted Nashua, which was nearby and had much better public recognition.   A: ★★★   B: ★   C: ★

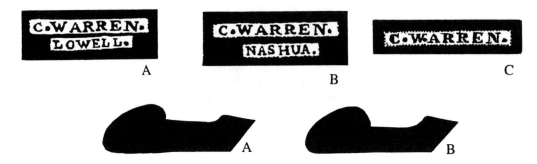

G.H. WARREN

George Henry Warren (1829-1900), son of C. Warren (w.s.), who was a planemaker in Hudson, NH, both alone and with his uncle William Warren (w.s.) until 1857 when he became a tailor. His location imprint is NASHUA, although the planes were actually made in nearby Hudson.   A & A1: ★★

JOHN WARREN

A Louisville, KY, planemaker who appeared in the city directories 1832-48.   ★★

W. WARREN

William Warren (1818-1861), brother of C. Warren (w.s.) made planes in partnership with his nephew G.H. Warren (w.s.) in Hudson, NH, from 1853 until ca.1857, when he built his own plane shop nearby. He was a member of the state legislature in 1852 and 1853. An example exists of a W. Warren smoothing plane incorporating Bailey's patented lever plane iron cap (pat'd. Aug. 31, 1858).   A: ★   B: ★★

396

J.M. WARREN & CO.
Joseph M. Warren operated a hardware store in Troy, NY, starting in 1845. The business continued into the 20th century.   A & B: ★

   A      B

WARREN & HEALD
A planemaking partnership of Addison Heald (w.s.) and probably C. Warren (w.s.) ca.1860.   ★★

O. WASHBURN
Oscar Washburn made planes in Goshen, MA, ca.1845. The imprint shown, carrying a Portland location, appears on a 9½" long grooving plane, whose appearance is ca.1840.

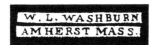

W.L. WASHBURN
William Lyman Washburn made planes in Amherst, MA, 1835-40.   ★

WASHINGTON FACTORY   see J. Coates

J. WATERMAN & CO.
A hardware firm listed in city directories of New Orleans, LA, from 1843 until 1852. This partnership included Jedediah Waterman, his brother Charles Marshall Waterman, and their father Captain Robert Waterman, all of New York. From 1853 to 1860, the firm was known as J. Waterman & Brother. In 1856, C.M. Waterman, a member of the Know Nothing Party, became the first merchant to be elected mayor of the city of New Orleans. His election as mayor was marked by violence, as was his term, which ended in 1858, when he was impeached while armed mobs gathered in the city. In 1860, he disappeared after leaving his house and was believed to have committed suicide by drowning in the Mississippi River. His succession record notes that he was $20,000 in debt to the firm at the time of his apparent death. The firm lasted several more years under the name J. Waterman, ending sometime during the Civil War or Reconstruction.

T. WATERMAN

Thomas Waterman (b. ca.1775) was the son of Abijah Waterman (d.1782), a merchant in Waldoborough (then Massachusetts, now Maine). Thomas, "a minor above the age of 14 years" was made the ward of Charles Samson on October 7, 1794. He is listed as head of the family in Waldoborough in the censuses of 1800, 1810, 1830, 1840 and 1850. In the 1850 census he is listed as a farmer, age 75, owning real estate valued at $1200. His planes are 9½" long, birch, have relieved wedges, broad flat chamfers, and appear to be professionally made. ★★★★

R. WATROUS

Riggs Watrous was a hardware dealer in Elmira, NY. His advertisement in the Elmira *Gazette* of December 21, 1843, offered all types of hardware and "also connected with the above establishment, a plane factory." The connection was probably William H. Spaulding. (see W.H. Spalding)   ★★★

WATROUS & OSBORNE

John L. Watrous & Joseph Osborne ran a hardware store in Auburn, NY, ca.1850. In the 1850 census, Joseph Osborne was listed as age 30, a merchant, born in England and John L. Watrous was listed as age 49, a merchant, born in CT. By 1857 both men were in other occupations.   ★★

H.H. WATTS

The imprint H.H. WATTS/85 AV. D/N.Y. appears on a J.W. Farr & Co. (see J.W. Farr) adjustable sash plane. Presumably a hardware dealer. (see L.H. Watts)

L.H. WATTS

Lewis H. Watts, who earlier was a New York City edge tool maker and who became a NYC tool dealer in the 1860's. A boxed bead has been reported with the imprint FROM L.H. WATTS/85 AVE D/N.Y. (see H.H. Watts)

WILLIAM WAY

Operated his own hardware store in New York City in 1848 under this imprint. He was a member of the Way family of Hartford, CT, who were hardware dealers. Between 1841 and 1859 he was a partner in the following

firms (w.s.): Kennedy, Barry & Way; Barry & Way; Barry, Way & Sherman; Way & Sherman; and Way & Co.
★★

WILLIAM WAY & CO.   see Way & Co.

WAY & CO.
A hardware firm operated by William Way (w.s.) in NYC 1853-59 that was the successor to Way & Sherman
(w.s.).   A & B: ★★★

WAY & SHERMAN
William Way and Byron Sherman operated a hardware store in New York City 1849-52. (see William Way
and Way & Co.)   ★★

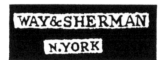

J.L. WAYNE & SON
Jacob L. Wayne, Sr. and Jr., were hardware dealers in Cincinnati, OH, 1857-77.

J.W. WAYNE & CO.
Joseph W. Wayne & Co. were hardware merchants at 196 Main Street, Cincinnati, OH, 1846-50. Between
1850-65 it was called Joseph W. Wayne & Co., with T. Pickering as a partner. (see T. & A. Pickering)

J. WEBB
John Webb made planes in Pittsfield, MA. —1837-49—. Smith's *The History of Pittsfield Mass.* says: "The
fulling mill was succeeded in 1816 by a Wooden Factory forty feet by thirty feet in size. John Webb occupied
most of the upper story for the manufacture of carpenter's planes from 1837 to Sept. 27, 1849, when the building
was destroyed by fire." Field's *A History of the Town of Pittsfield* (1844) relates: "The factory is now a plane

and planing factory. Ten hands on an average are employed." In 1840 Webb lived four houses from M. Sweet (w.s.). The 1850 census listed him as a planemaker, age 35, and born in England. He was probably a brother of William Webb. (see J. & W. Webb, Webb & Baker, and Webb & Gamwell) ★

J. & W. WEBB

Probably John, and his brother William, Webb, both of whom also made planes separately in Pittsfield, MA, then briefly together there and in New York City. (see J. Webb and also W. Webb) A, B, & C: ★★

A   B   C

W. WEBB

William Webb was listed in the 1850 census as a planemaker in Pittsfield, MA, age 33, and born in England. He was probably a brother of John Webb. (see J. Webb, J. & W. Webb, Webb & Baker, and Webb & Gamwell) A: ★★   B: ★★★★

A   B

Wm. P. WEBB

Listed as a planemaker in the 1855 Washington, DC, directory. In the 1860 census he was listed as a woodturner, age 40, born in Maryland. He probably came to Washington from Maryland ca.1852. A 22" long beech fore plane with the A imprint is also imprinted "Patented/Feb. 28, 1856." There is no record of a patent under Webb's name nor does the plane seem to incorporate any patent features. A: ★★★   B: ★★★★

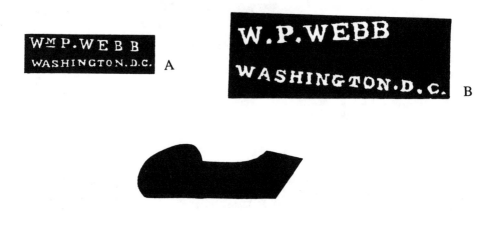

A   B

WEBB & BAKER

A Pittsfield, MA, plane manufacturing partnership probably consisting of Isaac Baker, who was listed in the 1850 census as a Pittsfield planemaker, age 29, born in MA; and John and/or William Webb (see J. Webb and also W. Webb). The 1860 Massachusetts Industrial census showed the firm employing six hands, using steam power, and producing $10,000 worth of planes. A complex molder with this name has a 1:12 (see below) imprinted on the heel, presumably the "suggested retail price." Normally one finds inked price notations made by the dealer, often employing his own special code.   ★★

WEBB & GAMWELL

A Pittsfield, MA, plane manufacturing partnership, probably consisting of Marcus Gamwell who was listed in the 1850 census as a Pittsfield planemaker, age 23, born in MA; and John and/or William Webb. (see J. Webb and also W. Webb)   ★★

WEBB'S

A plane has been reported with the location imprint PITTSFIELD. Probably Massachusetts and possibly related to J.& W. Webb (w.s.).

P. WEBER & CO.

Made planes in Milwaukee, WI; dates not known. No example of an imprint has been reported.

M.H. WEBSTER

M. Howard Webster was a hardware dealer in Detroit, MI, 1837-58—.   A: ★★   B: ★★★

 A　 B　 A

STEPHEN C. WEBSTER

Stephen C. Webster (1779-1850) was a joiner in Salisbury, NH (1804-43), who is known to have made planes and other tools.

J. WEEDEN

A number of examples have been reported; all beech, with the molding planes 9½" long. Almost certainly a planemaker, possibly from the NY-PA region. Appearance is early 19c; the workmanship is rather crude.
A: ★★★   B: ★★★★

 A    B

WELCH

This name has been reported on a W. CUDDY/N.YORK (w.s.) plane. Probably a hardware dealer.

C.R. WELLS

Chester Robbins Wells (1799-1867), brother of Elisha G. Wells and first cousin of R. Wells, was born in Hartford, CT, raised in Holland Patent, NY, and shortly after his marriage in 1827 moved to New Haven, NY, near Oswego, where he spent the rest of his life, primarily as a farmer. However, an account ledger has survived, listing many entries for planemaking and repair between 1828 and 1856. (see *A Planemaker's Account Ledger* by Patrick M Kelly in the Bibliography. Also see E.G. Wells, E. G. & R. Wells, and R. Wells)   ★★

C.S. WELLS

Charles S. Wells (d.1863) was an Evansville, IN, hardware dealer —1857-63.

E.G. WELLS

Elisha Griswold Wells (1788-1858), the brother of C.R. Wells and first cousin of R. Wells (both w.s.) was born in Hartford, CT, and was raised in Holland Patent, NY, near Oswego. He spent most of his life as a farmer and acquired some wealth as a land speculator. There is no indication in the records that he engaged in planemaking and, based on the scarcity of his surviving planes, it was not a major or long term occupation. (see E. G. & R. Wells and C.R. Wells)   ★★★

E.G. & R. WELLS
Almost certainly Elisha Griswold Wells and Robert Wells, first cousins, the location being Trenton, NY, close by to Holland Patent where they both lived. (see E. G. Wells and R. Wells)   ★★★

H. WELLS
Henry Wells made planes in both Northampton and Williamsburg, MA (the towns were adjacent), —1847-56. He was listed in the 1850 census as a tool maker, age 33, born in CT; and in the 1860 Massachusetts Industrial census as employing 12 hands and producing 31,000 planes (in Williamsburg). A Henry Wells, minor, worked for H. Chapin (w.s.) as an apprentice planemaker 1836-40. The eagle imprint appearing on some H. Wells' planes also appears on planes made by J.D. Kellogg, Arnold & Crouch, and Peck & Crouch, all of Northampton, MA (all w.s.).   A (without eagle), B, & C: FF   A (with eagle): ★★★

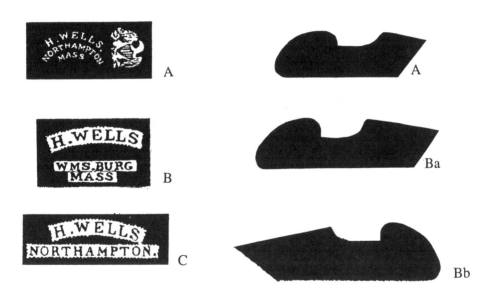

JAMES H. WELLS
A hardware dealer in Hartford, CT. —1798-1820—. No example of an imprint has been reported.

R. WELLS
Robert Wells (1792-1862) was a first cousin of Elisha G. Wells and Chester R. Wells. He was born in Wethersfield, CT, and moved to Holland Patent, NY, near Oswego, in 1815. He probably was involved in planemaking by 1820, and in the 1840 census was shown as having two members of his household in manufacturing. The 1855 NY census and the 1860 U.S. census both listed his occupation as a planemaker. (see C.R. Wells, E.G. Wells, and E.G. & R. Wells)   A: ★   A1 & B: ★★★   *(see next page)*

 A

 B

 A1

A

B

WELLS & ALLING

Wm. W. Wells and John Alling were hardware dealers in Madison, IN, 1852-57, and were succeeded by McKinney & Alling (w.s.). No example of an imprint has been reported.

WELLS & REED

This imprint has been reported on two beech jointers. (see H. Wells)

H. WENTZ

Various examples have been reported, including a pump log plane, a molding plane and a 13½" grooving plane, all with 18c characteristics. A Henry Wentz was listed in the 1850 census for the town of Jackson, Perry County, PA, as a cabinetmaker, age 84 (b. ca.1766). In 1800 he was living in York, Lancaster County, in 1810 in Tyrone, Cumberland County, and in 1820 and 1830 in Toboyne, Cumberland County, all in eastern PA.

JOHN T. WEST

Listed as a planemaker in the 1874 Baltimore, MD, directory. No example of his imprint has been reported.

H. WETHEREL

Henry Wetherel (one "l") (ca.1729-1797) was a farmer, a blacksmith, a toolmaker, and a planemaker, and the father of Henry Wetherell (w.s.). His earlier planes are imprinted IN NORTON [MA], where he was married in 1760. In 1773 he was listed as a shop joiner and in 1776 he served in the Revolutionary War. His later planes are marked CHATHAM [CT] on the Connecticut River, 15 miles from Hartford, where he moved in 1779 and appeared in the 1790 census. His will was dated December 20, 1793, and his estate inventory December 24, 1797. Shown below with his two imprints is a cartouche that occasionally appears in part or whole as a decoration alongside the name stamp.   A: ★★★   B: ★★   *(see next page)*

A

A

B

B

H. WETHERELL

Henry Wetherell (two "l's"; 1764-1840) was the son of Henry Wetherel (w.s.) and inherited his father's blacksmith shop and stock of tools. Location imprints exist for Glastonbury, Chatham, and Middletown, CT (all in the Connecticut River valley), as well as his name alone. Wetherell lived in Chatham until 1808, when he moved to adjoining Glastonbury, and in 1809 returned to Chatham. From 1824 to 1827 he lived in Middletown (adjacent to Chatham) and by 1830 was back in Chatham. Wetherell advertised in 1808 and 1809 in the Hartford, CT, *Courant* "Joiners Tools, all kinds of Joiners moulding tools made and kept constantly for sale." In his later years he became a successful investor and left an estate valued at $24,000 when he died in 1840.

A double crown imprint (fleur de lis) frequently appears by the maker imprint. Occasionally a single crown will appear. The earlier planes are of birch, 9¾" long, with flat chamfers. The later ones are beech, 9½" long, with rounded chamfers. A plow plane with both Glastonbury and Chatham imprints and an 1811 date has been reported, as well as a Yankee plow dated 1790, with the CHATHAM imprint. There are two CHATHAM imprint stamps; the slightly larger A and A1 seeming to be the earlier. Though the Glastonbury location imprint appears on the aforementioned plow plane, there has been no report of it appearing alone on any H. Wetherell imprint. From the appearance of Wetherell's planes, his father's will of 1793 naming him as heir to the shop and tools, and the dates on the two plow planes, we estimate his working dates at —1790-1830—. A & A1: ★★★ B & B1: ★ C: ★★★ D: ★★★★★ E: ★★★★ F: ★★★★★ *(continued on next page)*

A

C

F

A1

D

B

B1

E

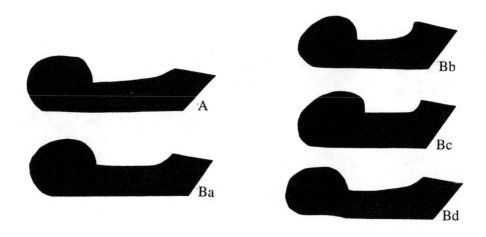

WHEATCROFT & SIEWERS
Cincinnati, OH, planemakers ca.1840. No example of an imprint has been reported.

A. WHEATON
Amos Wheaton Jr., one of the early Philadelphia, PA, planemakers, who first appeared in the directories in
1793 and again in 1796.   A & B: ★★★

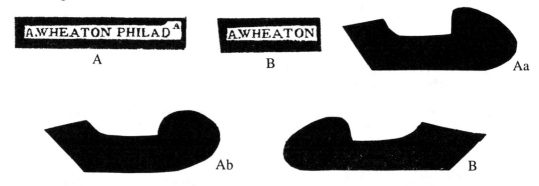

S. & J.H. WHITAKER
This name has been reported on Ohio Tool Co. planes. The 1850 census listed S. Whitaker, age 28, and J.
Whitaker, age 40, as hardware merchants in Toledo, OH.

CATHERINE WHITE   see G. White

CHARLES WHITE
Listed in the in the 1850 census as a mechanic in Warren OH, age 55, born in CT. The 1850 Census of
Industry listed him in tool- and cabinetmaking, employing three hands, who made 1200 planes, cabinets worth

$2000 and job work valued at $1000. His older brother Dyer White (1788-1852) was a partner in Kennedy & White (w.s.) and may have joined Charles when he moved to Warren, OH, some time after 1840. (see Soule, and White & Spear) ★★

CHARLOTTE WHITE

Charlotte White (1804-1884), the widow of Israel White (w.s.), ran his plane manufactory and general tool store from 1839 (when Israel died) to 1845, when she was listed in the city directory under her remarried name, Charlotte Burnett. Planes made during this period presumably carried the Israel White imprints.

G. WHITE

George White (1791-1824), son of Jacob White, brother of Israel White, and father of Henry G. White (all w.s.). He was operating a plane shop in Philadelphia, PA, in 1824, when he died at the age of 33. Earlier, in 1818-19, he was associated with his father and William Grinnel in White & Grinnel (w.s.). His widow, Catherine, succeeded him for a short time until her death in November 1825. She was listed as a planemaker in the 1825 city directory. No planes have been reported bearing her name and it is presumed that all planes made in the shop carried the G. White imprint.

The C imprint is particularly interesting because of the initials I.W. in its center, indicating that Israel White most probably worked for his brother and father. Israel was first listed as a planemaker in the city directory in 1831, seven years after his brother George's death. We believe that George White's shop was run by his father, Jacob White, from 1825, after his daughter-in-law's death, to 1831, although continuing to use the G. WHITE imprint. The use of the I.W. initials is similar to the use of journeymen's initials seen later on the Israel White imprints, initials such as T.D. for Thomas Donoho, N.N. for Nathan Norton, etc. The I.W. initials would imply that Israel White had a journeyman status during this interim period (1825-31). A: FF B: ★ B1: ★★ C: ★★★★★

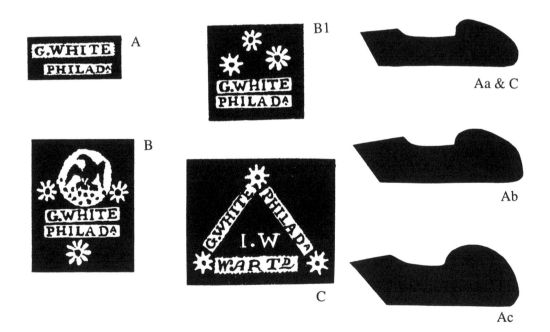

H. WHITE

Hiram W. White was a gunsmith and owned a hardware store in Jackson, OH, in 1855. He was listed in the 1850 census as a gunsmith, age 32, from NY state.

 A   B

H.W. WHITE   see H. White

HENRY G. WHITE

The orphaned son of George and Catherine White, who was probably raised by Israel and Charlotte White, and who ran the White's plane shop from 1846 to 1858. He used some of Israel White's imprint stamps, substituting his own name. (see H. White and also Israel White)   A: FF,   B: ★★★   C: ★★   D & E: ★★

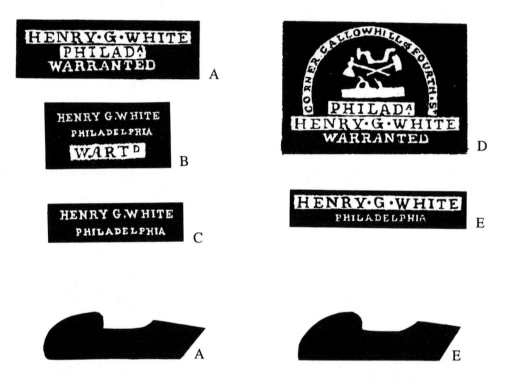

ISRAEL WHITE

Israel White (1804-1839) was a member of the prolific White family of planemakers; son of Jacob White, brother of George White, and uncle of Henry G. White (all w.s.). He operated one of the largest planemaking shops in Philadelphia and was listed in the Philadelphia directories as a planemaker from 1831 until his death in 1839. His widow Charlotte (1805-84) continued running the shop from 1839 until 1845. She was succeeded by Henry G. White.

Israel White made a wide variety of planes, some of exotic woods, but the most famous was a three-arm plow plane (patent no. 7951X, Jan.9, 1834). Only ten of these plows are presently known to have survived, eight imprinted by Israel and two by Henry G. White. Imprint D was used on the patent plows. They were numbered consecutively with the imprint shown being number 123 and the J.S. standing for James Silcock, the journeyman

408

who made them. The lowest number reported is 26, the highest 187. The patent plow was made in two basic models. One is similar to that depicted on the patent paper: numbers 26, 31, 138, 169, 183, and 187 are of this type. The other model has a bridge on the fence for the adjustment knob: numbers 39, 160, and the two by Henry G. White are of this type.

In addition, one example of a three-arm filletster has been found. It was reported in Volume 18 (1834) p.109 of *The Franklin Journal,* published by the Franklin Institute, along with Israel White's three-arm plow.

Israel White probably did not imprint his own name on the planes that he produced until after his father's death in 1833. His imprints appear in many varieties. They are among the largest and most striking examples of the planemakers' marks. Several of the large imprints include initials, which have been identified as those of his bench hands, some of whom went on to become planemakers in their own right: e.g., T.D. (Thomas Donoho), N.N. (Nathan Norton), and E.W.P. (Edward W. Pennell) (see T. Donoho, N. Norton, and E.W. Pennell). Others who apparently remained journeymen were A.M. (Adam Miller), D.H. (David Hanley), W.M.D. (William McDaniel), F.M. (Frederick Miller), T.B. (Thomas Beckman), and W.F. (William Fennell).

Imprint I-2, with the "I" missing from I. White (the period remaining), may have been used by Henry G. White, or simply damaged. A: ★★ B: ★ C: FF D: ★★★★ E: ★★ F: ★★★ F1: ★★★★ G: ★ G1: ★★ H: FF I: FF I-1: ★★★ I-2: ★★★★ J: ★ K: ★★ L: ★★★★ M: ★★ N: ★★★★ O: ★★★★ *(continued on next two pages)*

F1

G

G1

H

I

I-1

I-2

J

K

L

H & I

M

N

O

L

M

N

O

J. WHITE

Jacob White was listed as a planemaker in Camden for 1844-45 at the same address as his father Lemuel G. White, an elocutionist who was the second son of Jacob White, the father of Henry G. and Israel White. Later, Jacob White was listed at the same address as his cousin Henry G. White, and may have been working for him. A & A1: ★★★★

A

J.WHITE A1

A

JACOB WHITE

Jacob White (1760-1833) the father of Israel and George White. He first appeared as a planemaker in the Philadelphia, PA, directories in 1818 (when he was 58) working in the same location as his son George and William Grinnel, the planes being marked WHITE & GRINNEL.

From 1818 he appeared in the directories as a planemaker intermittently until his death in 1833: in 1823 as planemaker, 1825 hardware merchant, 1828 planemaker, 1830 planemaker. He displayed his planes at the Franklin Institute fairs of 1830 and 1831, in which year he received an honorary mention. At his death his estate inventory listed 3000 finished planes and cut billets for over 9000 more. No planes exist with his imprint and it is assumed that he used his son's G. WHITE imprints, both during the period they worked together and after George's death in 1824, until 1831, when his son Israel White apparently took over the business. (see G. White and Israel White)

J.D. WHITE

This imprint, with the location stamp WILLIAMSTOWN/VT., was reported on a 15½" long fore plane with a Moulson iron.

L. & I.J. WHITE

Leonard (1810-1893) and Ichabod Jewett White (d.1880) were brothers, born in Connecticut. They, and their successors, made planes and edge tools 1837-1928; first (1837-44) in Monroe, MI, and then in Buffalo, NY. The Whites and D.R. Barton of Rochester were the largest edge tool makers of their period in New York state. Imprint B shown below is incuse.   A, B, & C: ★

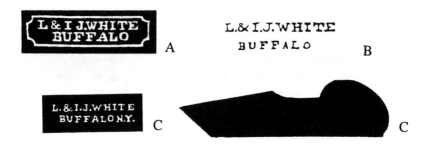

N. WHITE

This name appears on a 9½" beech screw top dado with #177 imprinted on the heel. This is the Auburn Tool Co. style number for a screw top dado. Meadville is in northwestern Pennsylvania, south of Erie. A probable hardware dealer.

T.W. WHITE

A lignum boxed molding plane has been reported with the additional imprint PHILA. He may be Thomas White, son of Henry G. White (w.s.).

W.H.H. WHITE

W.H.H. White (b. 1815) was listed as a carpenter in New Brunswick, NJ, in the 1850 census, age 35. His planes appear professionally made.   ★★★★

WHITE & CONANT

A Worcester, MA, hardware firm, listed in the directories for 1880 and 1893. The 1907 directory lists a Worcester Hardware, H.J. Conant Prop. A pair of matched tongue and groove planes made by J.F. & G.M. Lindsey have been reported with the White & Conant imprint.   *(see next page)*

WHITE & GRINNEL

A partnership consisting of George White, Jacob White and William Grinnel who were listed in the 1818 Philadelphia, PA, directory as planemakers. (see G. White, Jacob White, and W. Grinel) ★★★★

WHITE & SPEAR

A planemaking firm in Warren, OH, ca.1840, probably consisting of Charles White (w.s.) and Edward Spear, who was listed in the 1850 census as a sash maker, age 55, born in PA. Spear was in Warren in 1818, started his sash shop in 1848 and sold it in 1862. (see Soule, White & Spear) ★★

Aa

Ab

WHITE RIVER WORKS

Four examples have been reported. Appearance is mid-19c.

WHITE VAN GLAHN & CO.

White Van Glahn & Co. was a New York City hardware dealer, established in 1816, listed in the 1889-90 city directory, and advertising as late as 1910. Its stamp appears as an overprint on a center bead made by Marten Doscher (w.s.).

WHITING & SLARK

A New Orleans, LA, hardware firm listed in the city directories 1832-38 whose partners were Augustus Whiting and Robert Slark. Whiting founded the original store, which was in business by 1824. (see Slark, Day, Stauffer & Co.)

413

A. WHITMARSH

Possibly Abial Whitmarsh (1731-1816) of Dighton, MA (southeastern Massachusetts), who was called a joiner and whose probate inventory and probate sale included many tools, including planes. It could also be Asa Whitmarsh (1764-1808) of East Bridgewater, MA, who was described as a housewright in deeds from 1797 to 1805.

WHITMORE & WOLFF

This firm was a Pittsburgh, PA, hardware dealer and wholesaler, founded by M. Whitmore and C.H. Wolff in the 1840s. No example of an imprint has been reported. (see Whitmore, Wolff, Duff & Co.)

WHITMORE, WOLFF, DUFF & CO.

A Pittsburgh, PA, hardware company whose principals were Michael Whitmore, Christian H. Wolff, and George H. Duff. It was successor to a company also operated by these same men and began operations under the new name in 1858. In 1872 the name was changed to Whitmore, Wolff, Lane & Co. when Thomas H. Lane became one of the principals. (see Whitmore & Wolff)

WHITMORE, WOLFF, LANE & CO.

A Pittsburgh, PA, hardware dealer that succeeded Whitmore, Wolff, Duff & Co. (w.s.) in 1874. No example of an imprint has been reported.

WHITTIER & SPEAR

Four examples have been reported, all 16" jack planes; one with an iron imprinted MIDDLESEX MFG CO/MIDDLETOWN CONN/USA/BALDWIN WTD, another imprinted NEW HAVEN EDGE TOOL, and one with an Auburn Thistle Brand iron. Appearance is mid-19c.

ARNOLD WICKES

Arnold's Vital Records for the town of Coventry, RI, (southwest of Providence) lists an Arnold Wickes, born 1779, died in 1816. The 1810 Rhode Island census lists an Arnold Wickes living in Coventry. The few examples reported appear to fit into this time frame and location.

E. WIGHTMAN

This stamp has been reported on a 9½" beech molder, a boxed double bead plane, and a 9⁷⁄₁₆" long boxed beech complex molder.

JO:WILBUR

This stamp has been reported on molding planes having flat chamfers, a relieved wedge, and a 10" length. Also reported is a 9½" sash plane with flat chamfers. Appearance is late 18c. The NEWPt imprint A probably refers to Newport, RI.   A: ★★★★★   B: ★★★★

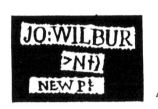  

A   B   B

C.H. WILCOX

The 1850 census listed Chauncy Wilcox as a planemaker, age 30, born in NY state, and living in Kingsville, Ashtabula County, Ohio.   ★★★

G.S. WILDER

George Sheldon Wilder (1828-1900) appeared in the directories of 1860, 1865, and 1875 as a planemaker in Hinsdale, NH. He also worked with his uncle Pliny Merrill and in Merrill & Wilder, Wilder & Thompson, and probably Wilder & Hopkins, making edge tools and carpenters' tools. No example of his imprint has been reported.

I. WILDER

Various planes have been reported, including a 9½" birch thumb molding plane, a 9⁷⁄₁₆" tongue plane, and a 14½" birch panel raiser. Appearance is ca.1800.

A.J. WILKINSON & CO.

A Boston, MA, hardware dealer 1842-1973.   A & B: ★   C: ★★

A

B

C

W. WILLIAMS

William Williams (1807-48) made planes in New York City 1843-47.   A: ★   B: ★★   B1: ★

A

B

A

B1

B1

WILLIAMSON

David Williamson was listed as an edge tool maker in Cincinnati, OH, 1839-40. He apparently made or dealt in planes at some time as well.

A

B

D. WILLIAMSON   see Williamson

WILLIAMS RICH & CO.

A hardware dealer that operated in Worcester, MA. The imprint has been reported on a H. Wells (w.s.) hollow.

M.P. WILMARTH
Various molding planes of mid-19c style have been reported. Central Falls, RI, is just north of Providence.

 A

 A1

DAVID WILLS
Listed as a planemaker in the 1837 Newark, NJ, directory, but no example of an imprint has been reported.

C. WILLSON
A Clark Willson was listed in the 1830 and 1840 Federal censuses for Worcester, MA, but with no indication of occupation. The imprint appears on a 23" fore plane, appearance ca.1840-50.

WILSON/NEW YORK
Henry Wilson made planes, 1852-54, having previously been a sawmaker, and was a tool dealer, 1855-56, all in New York City. (see H. Wilson)   A & B: ★★★

 A

 B

WILSON [PITTSBURGH]
William Wilson, who was listed as a planemaker in the 1847 and 1850 Pittsburgh, PA, directories. The imprint name WILSON is preceded by a heart, the same as used by another early maker, W. EVENS (w.s.), between the first initial and the last name EVENS.

C. WILSON
Several planes have been reported, two with James Cam irons. Appearance is ca.1820-40. The location is probably Dracut, MA, about 25 miles northwest of Boston. A Cyrus Wilson lived in the town 1810-20. The 1830 census noted two Charles Wilsons.

H. WILSON   see Wilson/New York

WILSON & BROTHER

A St. Louis, MO, hardware firm —1842—, comprising William K. and Samuel K. Wilson. It was succeeded by Wilson & Bros. (w.s.) in 1847.

WILSON & BROS.

A St. Louis, MO, hardware firm that succeeded Wilson & Brother (w.s.) in 1847. The firm consisted of William K., Samuel K., and LaFayette N. Wilson. It became Wilson Bros. & Co. sometime between 1854-57 and Wilson Brother & Co. in 1859-60.

 A  B

WILSON, LEVERING & WATERS

A probable hardware dealer whose imprint has appeared on several Scioto Works (w.s.) planes.

J.H. WINSLOW

James H. Winslow (b.1817 in Noblesboro, ME), was a carpenter and probably also a planemaker in Thomaston, ME. He married in 1842, and worked in Thomaston —1842-65.   ★★

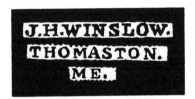

WINSTED PLANE CO.

Winsted's certificate of incorporation, which is dated Dec. 23, 1837 (though a Winchester, CT, town history has the company organized in 1851), states as the corporate purpose "to manufacture and deal in all kinds of Joiners tools, sash blinds, Doors, and all kinds of lumber." Directories list the company as a maker of joiner's tools from 1851 to 1856. The B imprint, which is probably another stamp used by Winsted, bears the additional "& L Co." This may refer to levels though no levels so marked have been reported. Examples to date have been bench planes.   A: ★   B: ★★★

 A    B

W. WINTKLE

This name has appeared on several examples, including a boxed bead with wide round chamfers. Appearance is ca.1840. A probable Cincinnati, OH, planemaker who did not appear in the city directories.

WISEMAN & ROSS

Made planes in Baltimore, MD. 1842-43—. (see Wm. C. Ross)   ★★

G. WOLCOTT

Gideon Wolcott (1805-1867), born in CT and died in NY. He made planes under his own imprint in New Haven, CT, —1828. He moved to Utica, NY, where he made planes for L. Kennedy (w.s.) 1828-29, and then for himself —1832—. No example of a Utica location imprint has been reported.   ★★

WOLFE DASH & FISHER

This imprint was reported on a tongue plane whose appearance is ca.1850. (see Wolfe, Gillespie & Co.)

WOLFE, GILLESPIE & CO.

This name has been reported on a beech jointer with the additional location imprint NEW YORK. Appearance is mid-19c. (see Wolfe Dash & Fisher)

B. WOLFF, JR.

A Pittsburgh, PA, hardware merchant 1858-70—, successor to Wolff & Lane (w.s.), and succeeded by Lane Brothers.

B. WOLFF JR. & CO.   see B. Wolff, Jr.

WOLFF & LANE

A Pittsburgh, PA, hardware company founded ca.1850 by Bernhard Wolff Jr. and A.H. Lane. In 1858 the name was changed to B. Wolff Jr. & Co. In 1878 the name was revived with different family members involved, and used until the company's demise in 1912. (see B. Wolff, Jr.)

A.D. WOOD

Augustus D. Wood was a hardware merchant in Indianapolis, IN, 1858-66—, and apparently also in Lafayette, IN. The A imprint appears on a plow plane with a ca.1850 style. (see Wood & Co.)

 A    B

I. WOOD

Four examples have been reported, all complex molding planes, 9½" long, beech, with Sleeper-style wedges. (see I. Sleeper)

J. WOOD

Various examples have been reported, including a fruitwood jack and a beech skewed rabbet with heavy flat chamfers, a complex molder, and a birch tongue plane. Appearance is late 18c.

J. WOOD/WATERTOWN

Probably a Watertown, NY, planemaker ca.1850. (see W.W. Wood & Co.)

    B

A

T.J. WOOD   see Wood's Tool Store

W.W. WOOD   see W.W. Wood & Co.

W.W. WOOD & CO.

William W. Wood was listed as a joiner in Watertown, NY. 1855-59, and as a partner with Albert L. Gleason in Gleason & Wood (w.s.). In 1863 he formed a partnership with Stewart Smith, as Wood & Smith (w.s.). From 1865-70 he was listed as a tool manufacturer under the names Wm. W. Wood, Wm. W. Wood & Co., and then Wm. W. Wood & Bro. Wood died ca.1875. A William Wood was listed as a planemaker in the 1850 census in the town of Pamelia (a few miles north of Watertown), age 22, and born in NY. Albert Gleason was also listed as a tool maker in 1850, same location, age 21, also born in NY. (see A.L. Gleason, J. Wood, and Wood & Smith)   A & B: ★★

A

B

C

WOOD & SMITH

A Watertown, NY, partnership 1863-65, between William W. Wood (w.s.) and Stewart Smith, who were carpenters and tool makers. No imprint is known. (see W.W. Wood & Co.)

E.C. WOODBRIDGE

Edwin C. Woodbridge made planes in Boston, MA, 1851-52. (see Montgomery & Woodbridge)   ★★

R. WOODFORD & CO.

Romeo and Bissell Woodford were hardware dealers and tinsmiths in Owego, NY. 1839-55.   ★★

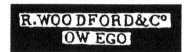

B.F. WOODMAN

A carpenter in Fremont, NH (1872-82).

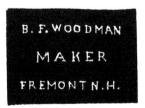

ALEX S. WOODRUFF

Alexander S. Woodruff was a hardware dealer and plane manufacturer in Louisville, KY. 1844-46. No example of an imprint has been reported. (see Woodruff & McBride)

C. WOODRUFF
Charles Woodruff advertised as a planemaker in New Albany, IN, in 1820 and 1821, and appeared as a hardware dealer in the 1856-57 New Albany city directory.

C.P. WOODRUFF
This imprint was reported on a 9½" long skewed rabbet plane.

S.P. WOODRUFF
Probably Stephen P. Woodruff (b.1824 in NJ), who was listed as a carpenter in New Albany, IN, in the 1850 census.

T. WOODRUFF
This name has been reported with the additional imprint HARTFORD.

WOODRUFF & McBRIDE
Alexander S. Woodruff and Alexander McBride, hardware dealers and plane manufacturers in Louisville, KY, 1848-49. (see A. McBride, Alex S. Woodruff, Hulings, and S. Cook) ★★

WOOD'S TOOL STORE
Thomas J. Wood operated a tool store in New York City under this name 1831-55: 1831-42 on Chambers Street and 1843-55 on Chatham Street. A, B, & C: ★★★ *(see next page)*

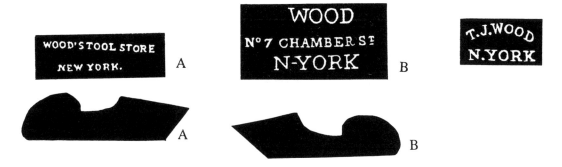

J. WOODS

A number of examples have been reported. Most are 9½" long, made of beech, with flat chamfers and a Sleeper-type wedge. Three planes, however, are reported as 10" long, beech, one with a Sleeper-type wedge, one with a relieved wedge, and one with a rounded wedge finial and rounded chamfers.

A. WOODWARD

A 9⅝" birch plane with ⁵⁄₁₆" flat chamfers has been reported. It was found with some Wm. Woodward (w.s.) planes. He may be Abishai Woodward (1752-1809) of Preston and New London, CT, who was a joiner and married Mary Spicer (1774) daughter of Capt. Oliver Spicer (see O. Spicer). His inventory included 122 planes, as well as 109 unfinished molding stocks, 16 new plane irons and a steel stamp with his name.   ★★★★

WM. WOODWARD

William Woodward made planes in Taunton, MA, where he was born in 1782. He married Betsy Dean in 1807 and last appeared in the 1850 census. He was variously listed as a house carpenter, "mechanist", housewright and yeoman. The 1823 accounting of Aaron Smith's estate shows "of William Woodward $5.31." An adjustable screw sash plane has been reported with the date 1839 imprinted on it.   (see Aaron Smith and also A. Woodward)   ★

JOSEPH WOODWELL & CO.

A Pittsburgh, PA, company founded in 1847 which became one of the city's largest wholesale hardware establishments, remaining in business under this name until 1954 when it was merged with another company. In the 1850's its trade sign was a four foot long fore plane that hung over the main entrance to its building.   ★★

WORDEN, COLE & GIOR

This name has been reported on a cooper's head jointer. An Eli Gior was listed in the 1861 Rochester, NY, city directory as an edge tool maker at "Gregg's shop." Mahlon Gregg (see M. Gregg) was an edge tool maker 1861-65 who also advertised cooper's tools. A Christopher Worden appeared as a blacksmith in 1844 and again as an edge tool maker for D.R. Barton 1855-59.

G. WORTHINGTON & CO.

Hardware dealer in Cleveland, OH, founded in 1823 and still operating today. It discontinued wooden planes sometime before 1880. ★★

N. WRIGHT

Various examples have been reported. Two are hollows, heavily chamfered, made of birch, one $9\frac{7}{8}$" long, the other $9\frac{3}{4}$". Appearance is 18c.

N. WRIGHT/KEENE

This imprint appears on a 26" long, closed handle jointer with a double $2\frac{3}{4}$" wide iron. The inscription L. SANFORDS/PATENT/1844 also appears on the adjusting screw which feeds into a cast steel bed plate rabbeted into the plane's throat. This patent (Patent No. 3838 dated Nov. 26, 1844) was issued to Levi Sanford of East Solon, NY, for the purpose of holding and adjusting the cutter. The example shown in *Patented Transitional and Metallic Planes in America Vol. I* (see Bibliography) appears on a jointer imprinted A. & E. BALD-WIN/NEW YORK (w.s.). This example is imprinted by N. WRIGHT/KEENE of whom nothing is presently known.

R. WRIGHT
One of the early Philadelphia, PA, planemakers who appeared in the 1793-97 city directories. ★★★

a   b

A. WYCKOFF
This imprint has been reported on a plow plane and several complex molders.

425

YARNELL & McCLURE

A Philadelphia, PA, hardware and tool dealer, that appeared in the 1840 Philadelphia directory. The imprint has been reported on several E.W. Carpenter (w.s.) planes, including the patented plow. (see W.M. McClure) ★★★

H. YOST

Reported on a 14½" long panel raiser with an adjustable fence and a 2⅜" wide W. Butcher iron.

GEO. W. YOUNG JR. & CO.

George W. Young made planes in Baltimore, MD, —1870. (see Young & Seidenstricker) ★★

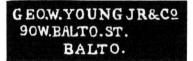

YOUNG & McMASTER

A planemaking partnership comprising Alonzo D. McMaster (b. 1811) and Jacob Young, respectively assistant superintendent and superintendent of Truman McMaster's planemaking shop at Auburn Prison, NY, 1829-38. They succeeded to the convict labor tool contract held by T.J. McMaster (w.s.) in 1838 and continued until 1843. Their five-year contract called for the employment of 30 to 40 convicts at 37½¢ per day per convict. Alonzo D. McMaster was later employed, in 1849, as a planemaker at D.R. Barton (w.s.). The A imprint shown below is embossed. (also see Z.J. M'Master & Co.) A: ★ B: ★★ C: ★★★ *(see next page)*

 A

 B

 A

 C

YOUNG & SEIDENSTRICKER

Baltimore, MD, planemakers and probably hardware dealers 1868—. Principals were George W. Young, Jr. and Albert B. Seidenstricker. No example of an imprint has been reported. (see A.B. Seidenstricker and George W. Young, Jr.)

J. ZIMMERMAN

John Zimmerman was a cabinetmaker and undertaker who also made wooden planes in Kingston, Ross County, OH. He was listed in the 1850 census as a cabinetmaker, age 48, born in OH. He was shown in the 1851 Columbus, OH, directory as a planemaker.

(P) means probable location

CALIFORNIA

OAKLAND
H. G. Stilley

SAN FRANCISCO
P. Quigley
H.C. Stilley

COLORADO

DENVER
Harper & Housman

CONNECTICUT

BIRMINGHAM (now DERBY)
L. DeForest
L. & C.H. DeForest
Simeon DeForest
Shelton & Osborne Mfg. Co.

BRIDGEPORT
Elias Francis
J.T. Platt

CANTERBURY
P. Spicer (P)

CHATHAM
H. Wetherel
H. Wetherell

CORNWALL
Charles Gardner

DERBY (formerly BIRMINGHAM)
L. DeForest
L. & C.H. DeForest
Simeon DeForest
A. Gilbert & Sons
W.F. Gilbert
Shelton & Osborne Mfg. Co.

EAST HARTFORD
L.B. Bidwell
J.J. Bowles
Brooks & Bowles
F. Brooks & Co.
Burnham & Brothers
H. Crane
E. Moses

GLASTONBURY
O. Andrus
G.A. Benton (P)
J. Killam
Lyman Killam
H. Wetherell

GRANBY
J. Church

GROTON
E. Gere (P)
A.C. Spicer (P)

HARTFORD
Bragaw & Blake
E. Clark
David Collins
R.J. Collins
Copeland & Chapin
D. Copeland
D. & M. Copeland
M. Copeland
M. & A. Copeland
Crane & Way
Giddings & Meek
J. Gilbert (P)
L. Kennedy (Leonard Jr.)
L Kennedy (Leonard Sr.)
Kennedy & Co.
L. Kennedy & Co.
Kennedy & Bragaw
Kennedy & Collins
Kennedy & Way
J.T. Loomis
L. Parkhurst (P)
Willis Thrall & Son
James H. Wells

HITCHCOCKVILLE (now RIVERTON)
Phoenix Company
Alfred Alford Plane Co.

LEBANON
I. Fitch

LISBON
S. Branch (P)

MERIDEN
N.E. Hart & Co.

MIDDLETOWN
Arrowmammett
Baldwin Tool Co.
N.H. Closson
Stephen H. Crane
Savage & Carter
S.D. Vansands
H. Wetherell

NEW HARTFORD
H. Chapin & Sons
H. Chapin's Son
H. Chapin's Son & Co.
H. Chapin's Sons
N. Chapin & Co./ Eagle Factory
J.G. Ward
Warner & Driggs
W. Warner

NEW HAVEN
C.W. Addis
J.E. Bassett & Co.
Beacher & Addis
E.S. Bradley & Co.
C.P. Brown
J.G. & F.H. Brown (P)
Brown Bros.
N.T. Bushnell
M.A. Carrington
Clark & Wiswall
English & Mix
J. Gilbert (P)
Hudson Hale
I. Hammond
E. Hoadley
Kimberly & Rowe
Matthewman & Co.
C. Morehouse
New Haven Plane Co.
W. & E. Perry
J.T. Platt
David Pond

W.H. Pond
Pond & Briggs
Pond & Welles
Pond, Malcolm & Welles
Porter & Sperry
Sargent & Co.
Sherman Barnes
Spencer
E. & B. Spencer
G. Wolcott

NEW LONDON
Harris & Ames

NORTH GROTON
A. Spicer (P)
O. Spicer
S. Spicer (P)

NORWALK
E.V.A. Chichester

NORWICH
A. Hide
C.W. Holden
A.C. Spicer (P)

PINE MEADOW
H. Chapin
Chapin-Stephens Co.
Copeland & Chapin

PLAINFIELD
A.C. Spicer (P)

RIVERTON
(formerly HITCHCOCKVILLE)
Alfred Alford Plane Co.
Phoenix Company
G. & H.J. Ward

SAUGATUCK (now WESTPORT)
Doscher Plane & Tool Co.

SAYBROOK
C. & S. Bulkley
J. Denison
J. & L. Denison
J. Gladding, Jr.
James W. Mason

SOUTH WINDHAM
Smith Winchester & Co.

WALLINGFORD
Joel Fenn & Co.
P.A. Gladwin & Co.
Gladwin & Fenn
Gladwin & Platts
Sawheag Works

WEST HAVEN
W. & E. Perry

WESTPORT (formerly SAUGATUCK)
Doscher Plane & Tool Co.

WINCHESTER
Winsted Plane Co.

WINDSOR LOCKS
Wm. Muir & Co.

WINSTED
A.F. Spencer

WINTHROP
G.W. Denison & Co.

DELAWARE

WILMINGTON
Samuel Dickson (P)
Hammitt & Bro.
Thos. Napier (P)
S. Niles

DISTRICT OF COLUMBIA

WASHINGTON
Barber & Ross
Bridge
Brumley
Wm. B. Davis
H.L. Kendall
Wm. P. Webb

ILLINOIS

ALTON
Dant & Ryan
Nelson & Hayner
Root & Platt
Ryan & Bro.
Topping & Bro.

BELLEVILLE
Goedeking & Newhoff
BLOOMINGTON
C.W. Holder & Co.

CANTON
McQuaid & Co.

CHICAGO
A.C. Bartlett
W. Blair & Co.
Rudolph Born
S. Deschauer
W.F. Dominick & Co.
F. Elkins, Runyon & Bartlett
J. & A. Fish
Hibbard, Spencer, Bartlett & Co.
E. Hunt
J. Mattison
A.R. & G.H. Miller
Sears, Roebuck & Co.
Tuttle, Hibbard & Co.

EAST ST. LOUIS
Benj. F. Horne

JACKSONVILLE
Ayers & Co.
H. & J. Hoghenhull

QUINCY
L. & C.H. Bull
L. & C. Hill

ROCK ISLAND
Harper & Steel
Alex Steel

SPRINGFIELD
B.F. Fox
E.B. Pease & Co.

INDIANA

BLOOMINGTON
Austin W. Seward

BROWNSVILLE
Joseph Gribble
B. Lape

CAMBRIDGE CITY
H.S. Kellogg
N.H. & C.H. Raymond

EVANSVILLE
Babcock Brothers
C.M. Griffith
Straub & Son
C.S. Wells

FORT WAYNE
H. Durrie
Oakley & French
B.W. Oakley & Son

INDIANAPOLIS
S. Cook
C. Frese & Co.
Frese & Kropf
H.S. Kellogg
J.H. Vanjen
A.D. Wood

JACKSONVILLE
Ayers & Co.

JEFFERSONVILLE
S. Cook

LAFAYETTE
B. Coddington
A.D. Wood
Wood & Co.

MADISON
George Albert
J. Burke
J.S. & B. Lape
G.W. Leonard & Son
McKinnel & R.A. Ward
McKinney & Alling
R.A. Ward
Wells & Alling

NEW ALBANY
S. Cook (P)
S. Cook & J. Gilmer
Christopher Duffey
J. Gilmer
T. Stout
C. Woodruff
S.P. Woodruff

RICHMOND
S.F. Fletcher
Fletcher & Benton
William Fulghum
J. Hughes
J. Hughes/H.M. Park

J. Moseley
Edwin C. Park
H.M. Park
Peters & Trimble

TERRE HAUTE
Bebee Booth
J. Cook & Co.
S.N. Fonder (P)
S.H. Potter
Potwins

VALPARAISO
Bidwell & Bickford

VINCENNES
D.D. Johnson

IOWA

BURLINGTON
Walter F. Jones & Co.

DES MOINES (formerly FORT DEMOIN)
Sanford & Co.

DUBUQUE
Farley Christman & Co.

FORT DEMOIN (now DES MOINES)
L.E. Sanford & Co.

KEOKUK
S.W. & H. Tucker

MUSCATINE
Geo. C. Mahan

WINTERSET
Eli Odell

KENTUCKY

GEORGETOWN
I. Van Zant

LOUISVILLE
T. Atkinson
J.M. Babbit
W. Baum & Co.
O.T. Bull & Co.
A. Caughter & Co.
John Conover

S. Cook & Co.
W.L. Epperson
T. Fugate & J.D. Conover
Lewis-Wilkes & Co.
Thomas Littell
T. Littell/T. Atkinson
A. McBride
Ormsby-Blair & Co.
Ormsby & Owen
E. Parsons/J.M. Babbit
Potter & Richey
W. Richards & Co.
W.W. Richey
A.B. Semple & Bro.
Slaughter
Slaughter C & C
N.H. Stout
N.H. Stout/W.W. Richey
John Warren
Alex S. Woodruff
Woodruff & McBridge

RICHMOND
W. Richards & Co. (P)

LOUISIANA

NEW ORLEANS
William Armstrong
J.M. Ellis & Co.
C.C. Gaines & Co.
Kellogg & Co.
A. Kirkman & Co.
P.A. Lanauze
Priestley & Bein
Ries & Schuber
Slark, Day, Stauffer & Co.
C.H. Slocomb & Co.
J. Waterman & Co.
Whiting & Slark

MAINE

AUBURN
H. Lovejoy (P)

AUGUSTA
Allen Taber

BANGOR
M. Moriarty
B. Morrill

P.B. Rider

BATH
George Chick
J. Foster

BERWICK
I.P. Holmes

BRUNSWICK
J.P. Storer

CALAIS
F. Tarbox

EAST UNION
D.B. Titus

FREEPORT
C.H. Dennison

LISBON FALLS
S. Plummer

OTISFIELD
N. Nutting

PORTLAND
J. Bradford
E.T. Burrowes Co.
G. Chase
G. Chase & Co.
George Chick
Emery, Waterhouse & Co.
J. L. Hersey
A. Sampson
Oscar Washburn

ROCKLAND
H.H. Crie & Co.

THOMASTON
G.G. Merrick
T.J. Rider (P)
C.T. Snowdeal
R.C. Starr
J.H. Winslow

VASSEL BOROUGH
L.M. Barrows

WALDBORO
L.S. Soule

WALDOBOROUGH
T. Waterman

WATERVILLE
J.C. Jewett (P)

WAYNE
H. Lovejoy (P)

WEST GARDINER
D. Fuller

MARYLAND

BALTIMORE
Atkinson
Atkinson & Chapin
Atkinson & Co.
Baltimore Plane Co.
Jno. M. Barkley
Barkley & Hughes
J.S. Brown
J.T. Brown
E. Caldwell
N. Camper
Carlin & Fulton
E.W. Carpenter
P. Chapin
Chapin & Kendall
Wm. Crook & Son
G. Freburger, Jr.
B. Huff
I. Keller
Kendall
H.L. Kendall
H.L. Kendall & Co.
Kendall & M'Cubbin
Kendall & Schroeder
R.W. Maccubbin
E.L. Matthews
Theophilus Moore
Thomas Moore
William H. Moore
Norris & Brother
Wm. C. Ross
A.B. Seidenstricker
A.B. Seidenstricker & Co.
Thomas Thomas
William Thomas
W. Vance
Vance & Moore
Ward & Chapin
John T. West
Wiseman & Ross
Geo. W. Young Jr. & Co.
Young & Seidenstricker

FREDERICKTOWN
Samuel Dickson

MASSACHUSETTS

ADAMS
James A. Eldridge

AMHERST
Amherst Tool Co.
Geo. Burnham, Jr.
Burnham, Fox & Co.
Horace Church
Charles Copeland
E.P. Dickinson
G. Fox
Hiram Fox
Luther Fox
L. Fox & Son
Fox & Washburn
Fox, Nutting & Washburn
J.W. Goodale
S. Hastings
Hills & Wolcott
S. & H. Hills
W.S. Howland
J. Kellogg
 William Kellogg
J. Kellogg & Co.
J. Kellogg & Son
Kellogg & Fox
Kellogg, Fox & Washburn
E. Nutting
E.P. Nutting
J.H. Nutting (P)
T. Nutting
Nutting & Fox
C.W. Rhoades
William Rich & Co.
J. Sanderson
W.L. Washburn

ASHFIELD
A. Kelly & Co.

ATTLEBORO
S. Cumings

BERKELEY
S.M. Burt

BEVERLEY
E. Berry
B. Raymond

W. Raymond

BOSTON
Allen & Noble
Thos. L. Appleton
T.P. Barnes
G.A. Benton
Bogman & Vinal
Boston Factory (P)
John E. Bowker
Brown & Pike
B. Callender & Co.
W. Cooley
Cooley & Montgomery
Corey, Brooks & Co.
J. Crehore
A. Cumings
S. & R. Cummings
E. Curtis
N. Curtis
J.L. Foster
C. Fuller
Charles H. Fuller
L. Gardner
S. Gardner & Co. (P)
Gardner & Appleton
Gardner & Brazer
Gardner & Murdock
Gladwin & Appleton
P.A. Gladwin & Co.
Albert S. Haven
Homer, Bishop & Co.
W. Hull
Hull & Montgomery
C. Jensen
A. Lincoln
L. Little
Lovell & Co.
Macomber, Bigelow & Dowse
Montgomery
Montgomery & Woodbridge
A.S. Morss
C.W. Morss
Multi-Form Molding Plane Co.
A. Murdock
J. Myers II
J. Perry
N. Phillips
L.T. Pope
M. Read
M. Read & Co.
Read & Cumings
James Rumrell
H.M. Sanders & Co.
H. Stevens

J. Stevens
H. Tileston
T. Tileston
J.R. Tolman
Tucker & Co.
Tucker & Appleton
Thomas Vaughn
E. Wightman
A.J. Wilkinson
A.J. Wilkinson & Co.
E.C. Woodbridge

BROCKTON
E.O. Noyes (P)

CAMBRIDGEPORT
James H. Fuller

CHARLESTOWN
Lewis Hunt

CHARLTON
I. Comins

CHELSEA
Thos. L. Appleton
G.A. Benton
Gladwin & Appleton
John Lester
Multi-Form Molding Plane Co.
Howard W. Spear
Spear & Wood

CHESTER
J.F. & G.M. Lindsey

CHESTERFIELD
Gideon W. Rhoades
S. Tower & Co.

CONWAY
Conway Tool Co.
S. Eldridge
Parker, Hubbard & Co.
Smith, Bigelow & Co.

CUMBERLAND
David Clark
I. Nicholson

CUMMINGTON
William A. Barrus
J. Hussey
J. Lovell
H.L. Narramore

A.C. Parsons

DEDHAM
S. Dean
I. Doggett
S. Doggett
I. Pike

DIGHTON
A. Whitmarsh

DRACUT
C. Wilson (P)

EAST SUDBURY
S. Noyes

ENFIELD
Enfield Tool Co. (P)
J. Tinkham
S. Tinkham (P)

FAIRHAVEN
L. Sampson
Allen Taber (P)
N. Taber
Wing H. Taber

FALL RIVER
Joseph B. Field
J.W. Pearce
P.M. Peckham
P. Tripp

GARDNER
U. Clap (P)

GLOUCESTER
I. Day (P)
George Saville

GOSHEN
H. Barrus & Co.
C.C. Dresser
W.E. Johnson & Co.
H.L. Narramore
Union Tool Co.
Ralph Utley
Oscar Washburn

GREENFIELD
Greenfield Tool Co.
S. Phillips Works

GROTON
D.B. Lewis

HANOVER
J. Merritt
J.R. Tolman
T.J. Tolman
C.I. Varney

HARVARD
Hosea Edson

HAVERHILL
Chase Brothers (P)

HINGHAM
Benjamin Parker

HOLLISTON
M. Adams (P)
I. Iones

HOLYOKE
Farrington & Burditt
J. Russell & Co.

HOPKINTON
H. Adams
William Adams

HUBBARDSTOWN
I. Teal

HUNTINGTON
Copeland & Co.
M. Copeland
Hosea Hunt
J.F. & G.M. Lindsey

IPSWICH
A. Lord (P)

KINGSTON
Jer. Samson

LANESBORO
E. Newell

LAWRENCE
Wm. L. Dustin
W.A. Kimball & Co.
C. R. Mason & Co.

LEVERETT
E. Nutting

LOWELL

Adams Hardware & Paint
Samuel L. Benson
Brazer
Chase, Sargent & Shattuck
Fielding & Bartlett
A. Fish
G.C. Hanes
L.W. Hapgood
C.E. Harrington
D. Lovejoy
John Pettingell
C. Prescott
D. Rogers (P)
Jacob Rogers & Co.
Rogers, Taylor & Co.
John Smiley
A. Smith (Alpheus)
Wing H. Taber
Frederick Taylor
C. Warren

LYNN

N. Potter

MEDWAY

I. Iones

MENDON

S. Partridge
E. Taft

MIDDLEBORO

E. Clark
S. Doggett
L. Sampson
L. Tinkham

MILTON

B. Crehore

NEW BEDFORD

Acushnet
Clarence Bearse
Charles H. Lamb
J.H. Lamb
Lamb & Brownell
W.G. Lamb
J. & W. Lamb
New Bedford Tool
A.M. Smith
J.W. Smith
J.M. Taber
L.H. Taber
N. Taber

Taber Plane Co.

NEWBURY

N. Little
R.M. Tilburn
J. Titcomb
S. Titcomb (P)

NEWBURYPORT

J. Jewet (P)
I. Sleeper
M. Sleeper
I.C. Titcomb
S. Toppan (P)

NEWTON

B. Piper

NORTH BRIDGEWATER

Southworth & Noyes

NORTHAMPTON

Arnold & Crouch
Julius Barnard
B.A. Edwards
J.D. Kellogg
N. Nutting & H.C. Smith (P)
Peck & Crouch
S. Pomeroy
O.H. Smith
H. Wells
Wells & Reed

NORTON

Iohn Basset
N. Briggs (P)
Hussey, Bodman & Co.
C.D. & O.H. Lord
S. Presbrey
H. Wetherel

NORWICH

Hills & Richard

PITTSFIELD

Baker & Gamwell
P. Brooks & Co.
James A. Eldridge
W.E. Johnson & Co.
M. Sweet
J. Webb
J & W. Webb
W. Webb
Webb's
Webb & Baker

Webb & Gamwell

PRINCETON
I. Teal

RAYNHAM
B. Dean

READING
B. Walton
I. Walton
I:B Waltons

REHOBOTH
A. Smith (Aaron)
E. Smith
J.B. Smith

RINGVILLE
E.C. Ring

ROWE
H. Browning
Wm. D. Swain

ROYALSTON
D. Hubbard

RUTLAND
Jn. Tower

SALEM
Charles Odell
Shepherd & Buffum

SALESBURY
T. Fowler

SOUTH ORANGE
A. Barnes
R. Barnes

SOUTH SCITUATE
J.R. Tolman
T.J. Tolman
Tolman & Merritt

SOUTH WILLIAMSTOWN
P. Brooks & Co.

SOUTHAMPTON
Davis & Lester

SPRINGFIELD
H. Crane
Gouch & Demond

Griswold & Dickinson
Hill, Swinselle
H. Hills
S. Hills
S. & H. Hills
Hills & Winship
F. Richards & Co.
Smith & Stewart

TAUNTON
Iohn Basset (P)
E. Bassett (P)
D. Presbrey
Wm. Woodward

TOWNSEND
R.A. Lancey

WALPOLE
Charles Dupee

WATERTOWN
Alfred Howes (P)
J. Sanger

WESTFIELD
P. Brooks & Co.
N. Chapin & Co./Eagle Factory
Marshall & Brown

WILLIAMSBURG
Eagle Mng. Co.
H.L. James
James Mfg. Co.
R.L. Jones
H. Wells

WILLIAMSTOWN
Allen & Eldridge
P. Brooks & Co.
H.N. Raze

WINCHESTER
Winsted Plane Co.

WORCESTER
Brown & Wood
E.J. Gouch
Hosea Hunt
William Rich & Co.
D.P. Sanborn
Sanborn & Co.
Sanborn & Gouch
E. Smith
E.H. Smith & Co.

White & Conant
Williams, Rich & Co.
C. Willson (P)

WORTHINGTON
Benjamin F. Rhoades
Gideon W. Rhoades
E.C. Ring
E. & T. Ring & Co.
J. Sanderson & Co.
J.E. Sanderson

WRENTHAM
Ce. Chelor
Sam'l. Druce (P)
Charles Dupee
G. Hawes
F. Nicholson
I. Nicholson
H. Pratt

MICHIGAN

ADRIAN
G. L. Bidwell

COLDWATER
A.F. Bidwell
L.F. Bidwell

DETROIT
J.P. Cook
H.V. Deming
Ducharme Fletcher & Co.
Gooderich, Andrews & Co.
Hamlin (P)
C.B. James
H.H. Knapp (P)
A.H. Newbould
B.B. & W.R. Noyes
T.B. Rayl & Co.
J.M. Slater
Slater & Byram
C.A. Strelinger & Co.
M.H. Webster
C.P. Woodruff (P)

MONROE
L. & I.J. White

MISSISSIPPI

NATCHEZ
Cavanach & Miller
Jno. P. Quegles

VICKSBURG
J.A. Peale & Co.

WORTHINGTON
Benjamin F. Rhoades

MISSOURI

CAPE GIRARDEAU
Reily (P)

HANNIBAL
J.P. Richards

ST. LOUIS
Bailey & Richardson
William K. Bogges
G. Bremerman
G. Bremermann & Co.
Bremermann Raschoe & Co.
Bridge Tool Co.
Child, Farr & Co.
Child, Pratt & Co.
Child, Pratt & Fox
L.G. Conklin
J. Donaldson/J.H. Hall
A.R. Earl
Wm. Enders
Isaac Goslin
J.W. Gosnell
J.W. Gosnell/W. Hall
W. Hall
Hall & Hynson
Benj. F. Horn
Hunt & Wiseman
S.C. Hunt
Hynson
Hynson & Coleman
Hynson Tool & Supply Co.
E.F. Kraft & Co.
A. Meier & Co.
Herman H. Meier
Meyer & Schulze
Henry Miller
J. Miller & Bro.
W.W. Miller
Julius Morisse

Pratt & Fox
Rickard
Chas. Rogers
Geo. A. Rubelmann Hdw. Co.
F.E. Schmieding & Co.
Shapleigh & Co.
Shapleigh, Day & Co.
Soeding Bros.
M. Stout
T. Stout
M. & N.H. Stout
Wilson & Bros.
Wilson & Brother

NEW HAMPSHIRE

AMHERST
C.W. Rhoads

BEDFORD
John Dunlap
Samuel Dunlap
Matthew Patten

BENNINGTON
J. Lock (P)

CANAAN
J. Milton
M.H. Milton

CHESTER
I. Sleeper

CONCORD
James Moore & Sons
E. Sargent
P. Sargent
Simeon Virgin
Gus Walker
Warde Humphrey & Co.

CONWAY
J.M. Allard

DOVER
D. Durgin
S. Sleeper

DUBLIN
E. Pasquarelli
R. Piper

EPPING
T.E. Burley

EXETER
E. Clifford

FREMONT
B.F. Woodman

GILFORD (formerly GILMANTIN)
J. Chase

GILMANTIN (now GILFORD)
J. Chase

GOFFSTOWN
John Dunlap
Samuel Dunlap

HAMPTON FALLS
T.B. Gove (P)

HENNIKER
Samuel Dunlap

HINSDALE
G.S. Wilder

HOLLIS
B. Farley
G.W. Manning

HOPKINTON
I. Long
J. Morse, Jr.

HUDSON
L. Senter
C. Warren
G.H. Warren (marked Nashua; made in Hudson)
W. Warren (marked Nashua; made in Hudson)

KEENE
E. Briggs
N. Briggs
Knowlton & Stone
E. Rugg
N. Wright (P)

KENSINGTON
E. Clifford

LEBANON
D. Amsden
Arad Simons

LITTLETON
J. Dow
D.P. Sanborn
Sanborn & Weeks

MANCHESTER
D. Sargent

MARLOW
P. Tyler (P)

MILFORD
Addison Heald
A. Heald & Son

NASHUA
M. Barr & Co.
Eayrs & Co.
Addison Heald
D. Sargent
C. Warren
G.H. Warren (marked Nashua; made in Hudson)
W. Warren (marked Nashua; made in Hudson)
Warren & Heald

NEW BOSTON
J.H. Gregg

PETERBOROUGH
E. Puffer (P)

PLYMOUTH
I. Merrill

PORTSMOUTH
Tho. Foss
I. Hill (P)
I. Nutter (P)

SALISBURY
Samuel Dunlap
Stephen C. Webster

SANDWICH
Dearborn & Skinner
Warren Dearborn

WOLFEBORO
A.M. Piper

NEW JERSEY

BURLINGTON
T. Aikman

CAMDEN
N. Norton
J. White

EAST ORANGE
H.L. James

JERSEY CITY
H. Luttgen

MT. HOLLY
Brumley

NEW BRUNSWICK
S.C. Cook
E. Danberry
Eastburn (R. Eastburn)
Joseph Eastburn
B. Norman
R.M. Tilburn
W.H.H. White

NEWARK
Andruss
J. Andruss
Thomas Burns
J. Doremus (P)
S.E. Farrand
I. King
J.A. King
Market Hardware Co.
E.W. & L.R. Miller
A. Mockridge
Mockridge & Francis
Mockridge & Son
Newark Plane Rule & Level Co.
Timothy B. Noe
C. Parkhurst
J. Parkhurst
Parkhurst & Coe
P. Quigley
H. Schmitt Co.
J. Searing
John Teasman
B. Walbmieier
David Wills

NEWTON
John Frace

SADDLE RIVER
W.J.C. Ward

SPRINGFIELD
J. Parkhurst

TRENTON
Brumley (P)

WESTFIELD
W.B. Chamberlin

NEW YORK

ALBANY
Albany Tool Co. (P)
E. Baldwin
David Bensen
Bensen & Crannell
Bensen & M'Call
Bensen & Munsell
Bensen & Parry
Benson & Mockridge
J. Coughtry
M. Crannell
J. Gibson
J. & J. Gibson
Joseph Gibson
Jones
L. Kenney
Thomas J. McCall
Parry
S. Randall
Randall & Co.
Randall & Bensen
Randall & Cook
Randall & Shepard
S. Rowell
Rowell & Gibson
Rowell & Kenney
E. Safford
D.M. Shepard

ASHFORD
E. Moses

AUBURN
Auburn Tool Co.
Barker & Baldwin
C. Carter
Casey & Co.
Casey, Clark & Co.
Casey, Kitchel & Co.
Dunham & M'Master
Easterly & Co.
A. Howland & Co.
Lockport Edge Tool Co.
T.J. M'Master
Z.J. M'Master & Co.

J.A. Sex & Co.
Watrous & Osborne
Young & McMaster

BINGHAMTON
G.W. Gregory

BROOKLYN
J.C. Duryea
J.W. Farr
Fowler Bros.
P. McCuen
Parry
Shiverick
D. Shiverick & Co.
Shiverick & Malcolm

BUFFALO
G. Axe
Beak & Lang
Robert Bingham
Bond & Sargeant
Buffalo Tool Co. (P)
Edgerton
Edgerton, Reed & Co.
Edward F. Folger
E.F. Folger & Co.
Horton & Crane
M. Lang
Lang & Co.
Matteson & Sully
J.A. & F.W. Newbould
Geo. Parr
Pratt & Co.
S.F. Pratt & Co.
Sanderson & Warren (P)
J. Sanderson/S. Shepard
S. Shepard
Thomson Brothers
Wm. A. Thomson
L. & I. J. White

CONCORD
J. Sanderson

DELHI
A. Inglis
F.W.V.A. (F.W. Van Allen)

DEPOSIT
E. Moses

De RUYTER
W.H. Blye

DUNDEE
  A.L. Raplee
  G.W. Rogers
  M.B. Tidey
EAST HAMPTON
  Dominy

ELMIRA
  W.H. Spalding
  R. Watrous
  A. Wyckoff

HASTINGS
  E. Moses

HUDSON
  C. Tobey
  J.I. Tobey

HYDE PARK
  I.M. Carter

ITHACA
  E.D. Milliken
  T.P. Piper
  A.M. Seaman
  N. Spaulding
  M.B. Tidey
  Treman & Brothers

JOHNSTOWN
  L. Scovil
  J. Scovill
  I. Stephenson

KINGSTON
  J. Stiles
  J.J. Styles

LANSINGBURGH (now TROY)
  C. Allen
  S.E. Jones

LITTLE FALLS
  G. Ashley
  A. Cumings
  Harris & Shepard

LOCKPORT
  H. Flagler & Co.
  Lockport Edge Tool Co.

McLEAN
  J.T. & R.G. Davidson
  N. Spaulding

MEDINA
  C.T. Anthony

MIDDLETOWN
  Israel O. Beattie
  J. Hannan (P)

MOORES FORKS
  L. Bundy

MORAVIA
  A. Howland
  J. Sawyer

MT. VERNON
  H.A. Kammerer

N. LEBANON
  J. Kendall (P)

NEW BERLIN
  A. Cumings

NEW HAVEN
  C.R. Wells

NEW YORK
  H. Adams & Co. (P)
  Alford
  American Plane Co. (P)
  Antarctic Co. (P)
  A. & E. Baldwin
  E. Baldwin
  George Ball
  S.S. Barry
  Barry & Way
  Barry, Way & Sherman
  W.B. Belch
  Bewley
  John Boernhoeft
  J. Bogert
  N.J. Boyd
  Bruff Brother & Seaver
  W. Bryce & Co.
  C.T. & Co.
  Cassebeer Reed & Co.
  Cation
  Columbia Tool Co.
  E.L. Cooper
  J. Coughtry
  Stephen H. Crane
  W. Cuddy
  Davis & King
  Moses H. Davis
  L. DeForest

W.J. Demott
Demott & DeVoys
DeValcourt
Marten Doscher
Douglass
P. Duryee
Eagle (P)
Eclipse Tool Co.
H. Eyre
J.W. Farr
J. Fish (P)
Fletcher
A. & E. Fox (P)
J.W. Gibbs
Gibbs & Cation
Gilbert, Sweet & Lyon
Gillespie (P)
Gottfried Goebbel
Tho. Grant
J. Green
Griffin (P)
A. Hammacher & Co.
Hammacher, Schlemmer & Co.
J. Hannan
J.W. Harron
R. Harron
Hegny & Bollermann (P)
J. Heisser
R.W. Hendrickson
John Hill's Tool Store
R. Hoey
Hoey & Taber
W. Hoffmann
Hubbell & Lunnagan
Henry A. James
C.E. Jennings & Co.
Jordan Hardware Corp.
Kennedy (Samuel L.)
Kennedy, Barry & Way
Kennedy & White
H. & J.W. King
Josiah King
Josiah N. King
Josiah King & Son
Josiah King Sons
Wm. King
E.R. Krum
C.S. Little & Co.
Wm. H. Livingston & Co.
John S. Lunnagan
Mannebach
Marley
Martin & Corey
James W. Mason
Merritt & Co.

J. Miller (P)
M. Miller (P)
A.G. Moore
William H. Moore
Nathusius, Kugler & Morrison
A. Newell
Osborn & Little
John Parr
Parry
J.H. Perry
J.S. Pruden Sons
J.E. Quackenbush & Son
Quackenbush Townsend Co.
C. Recht (P)
Reed & Auerbacher
Richards & Fleury
J.H. Rigby's Tool Store
F.W. Schneider
A. Searl
C.S. See
W.N. Seymour & Co.
Sherman Bros.
Shiverick & Malcolm
Sickels, Sweet & Lyon
Phineas Smith
Smith, Cohu & Co.]
Smith, Lyon & Field
Spencer
B. Stern & Tollner
J. Stiles
T.S. & Clark (P)
Wing H. Taber
C. Tollner
C. Tollner & Hammacher
A. Tulloch
C.L. Volckhausen & Co.
W.J.C. Ward
Ward & Fletcher
Waring & Stantial
H.H. Watts
L.H. Watts
William Way
Way & Co.
Way & Sherman
J. & W. Webb
Welch (P)
White Van Glahn & Co.
W. Williams
Wilson (Henry)
Wolfe, Dash & Fisher
Wolfe, Gillespie & Co. (P)
Wood
T.J. Wood
Wood's Tool Store

NEWPORT
E. Robbins

OGDENSBURG
Chas. Ashley
R.C. Bailey

OSWEGO
Huntington (P)
E.S. Leroy
Wheeler & Allen

OTSEGO
B.S. Howe

OWEGO
E.S. Leroy
R. Woodford & Co.

PAMELIA
B.F. Perry
A.L. Gleason

PENN YAN
Charles V. Bush (P)
M.B. Tidey

POUGHKEEPSIE
A. Albertson & Co.
Allen & Storm
C. Donat
Ellsworth & Dudley
J.F. MacNeil
T. Palmer
J.G. Sandkuhl
G.C. Ward

ROCHESTER
D.R. Barton & Co.
D.R. Barton Tool Co.
Barton & Babcock
Barton & Belden
Barton & Milliner
Barton & Smith
Benton, Evans & Co.
Robert Bingham
W.W. Bryan
Bush & Bryan
H. Bush
H. Cassebeer
R.J. Collins
S.G. Crane
Crane & Scott
Louis Ernst
E. Evans

E. & J. Evans
M. Gregg
Gregg & Hamilton
H. Haight & Co. (P)
Kennedy (Leonard, Jr.)
H.H. Knapp
Mack & Co.
Worden, Cole & Gior

ROME
H.W. Pell
Pell & Wright
George Stedman
Wardwell & Co.

SALINA
Lyman Nolton

SCHENECTADY
H.S. Edwards & Bro.

SING SING
T.J. M'Master
Z.J. M'Master & Co.

STATEN ISLAND
D. Richardson

STEPHENTOWN
H.S. Sweet & Co.

SYRACUSE
C. Carter
D.S. & S.P. Geer
Hayden
E.T. Hayden
Hayden & Nolton

TRENTON
E.G. Wells
E.G. & R. Wells
R. Wells

TROY (formerly LANSINGBURGH)
C. Allen
L.C. Ashley
C. Carter
Edward Carter
E. & C. Carter
R. Carter
R. & C. Carter
R. & L. Carter
Carter's Tool Store
S.E. Jones
C.S. Rowell

S. Rowell
Ward Carter
J.M. Warren & Co.

UTICA
B.F. Berry
C. Carter
H. Clark (P)
Collins (Fitch K.)
R.J. Collins
Collins & Robins
D.O. Crane
Kennedy (Leonard, Jr.)
Reed
E. Robbins

WATERTOWN
B.F. Berry
L. Case
A.L. Gleason
Gleason & Wood
J. Lord
Lord & Ransom
J.F. Ransom
J. Wood (P)
W.W. Wood & Co.
Wood & Smith

WINDSOR
J. Kent (P)

OHIO

BROOKLYN
P.S. Francisco
Asa Hicks

CHILLICOTHE
Denning & Campbell
J. Morrison
D.A. Schutte

CINCINNATI
W. Baum & Co.
William K. Boggus
R.W. Booth
R.W. Booth & Co.
L.R. Carter
Carter, Donaldson & Co.
John Conover
S. Cook
George Copeland
J. Creagh
J. Creagh/J.W. Lyon
J. Creagh/J.W. Lyon/McKinnel

J. Creagh/E.F. Seybold
J. Creagh/W. Wintkle
Creagh & Rickard
Creagh & Williams
Cunningham & Co.
Daggett & Walker
J. Donaldson
J. Donaldson/L.R. Carter
J. Donaldson/J. Creagh/J.H. Hall
J. Donaldson/J.H. Hall
J. Donaldson & T. Fugate
C. Eyman
William Franklin
T. Fugate
James Galbreath
G.W. Glaescher
Glaescher & Co.
J. Hall
J.H. Hall/J.W. Lyon
W. Hall
N. Harris
Heather & Wellman
Heim & Smith
G. Herder
Thomas Holliday & Co.
Holliday & Smith
J.H. Huepel & Co.
Hulings
Hulings & Kemper
Samuel Kemper
B. King
B. King/J. Walker
L. Kruse
Kuhlman Hdwe. Co.
R. Lang
H.A. Langhorst
B. Lape
Jacob S. Lape
J. Lawton & Co.
F. Lender
J.H. Lohr
J.W. Lyon
J.W. Lyon/McKinnell
Lyon, McKinnell & Co.
Lyon & Kellogg
Lyon & Smith
James McGennis
McKinnell & Co.
Mead, Selden & Co.
Miller & Probasco
John P. Miller
Moon & Laby
William Mosey
Peter Neff & Sons
B. Phillips

T. & A. Pickering
P. Probasco
Queen City Tool Co.
W. Richards & Co.
Rickard
H. Rohrkasse & Co.
G. Roseboom
G. & W.H. Roseboom
Roseboom & Magill
Roseboom & Roe
John Saundersod
Christian Saundersous
C.B. Schaefer & Co.
Schaefer & Cobb
C. Seybold
E.F. Seybold
Seybold & Smith
Seybold & Spencer
C.G. Siewers
S. Sloop
C.J. Smith & Co.
J. & C. Smith
J.H. Smith
J. Stilley
John Sunsersond
T.D. & Co. (Tyler, Davidson & Co.)
H. Taylor
H. & J.C. Taylor
J.C. Taylor
F. Underwood/C.B. Schaeffer
David Walker
Esther Walker
J. Walker
Walker & Hall
R.A. Ward
J.L. Wayne & Son
J.W. Wayne & Co.
Wheatcroft & Siewers
Williamson
W. Wintkle

CLEVELAND (includes OHIO CITY)
James Cain
Colwell & Co.
Cutler & Co.
P.S. Francisco
G. Hastings & Co.
A.G. Hicks
M.E. Higley
Higley & Hicks
J. Kellogg
Kellogg & Hastings
F.B. Marble
Marble & Smith
A. & W. Marsh

A. Morton & Co. (P)
W. Pawlett & Co.
J.G. Steiger
J.J. Vinall
G. Worthington & Co.

COLUMBUS
Buttles & Runyon
E.W. Case
A. Copeland
George Copeland
Gere, Abbott & Co.
Hall, Case & Co.
Hall Stone & Co.
P. Hayden & Co.
Kilbourne Kuhns & Co.
J.M. McCune & Co.
F.B. Marble
Ohio Tool Co.
J. Zimmerman

DAYTON
J. Bracelin
D.N. Garrison
D.N. Garrison/T.A. Heim
P.C. Hathaway
Holcomb & Slentz
Isaac D. Mitchell
J. Richmond
Rogers & Fowler

DELAWARE
C.D. Potter & Co.

GRANVILLE
G.P. Bancroft (P)

JACKSON
H. White

KINGSTON
J. Zimmerman

KINGSTON CENTER
John Lindenberger (Jr.)

KINGSVILLE
C.H. Wilcox

LEBANON
J.M. Babbit
H.B. Miller
P. Probasco

LISBON
J. Starr
MASON
J.M. Babbit
S. Hastings
J.H. Verbryck

NEW LISBON (Now LISBON)
J. Starr

OHIO CITY (now CLEVELAND)
P.S. Francisco
Higley & Hicks
M.E. Higley

PORTER TWP.
C. Lindenberger
John Lindenberger (Jr.)

PREBLE COUNTY
S. Stubbs (P)

RAVENNA
T.C. Cain
Collins (Fitch K.)
R.J. Collins
Griffin
C. Sapp

SANDUSKY
A.C. Bartlett's Ohio Planes
Sandusky Tool Co.

SPRINGFIELD
John L. Berry
Runyon & King

STEUBENVILLE
Thompson (P)

TIFFIN CITY
J.M. Naylor & Co.

TOLEDO
J.F. Card
S. & J.H. Whitaker

TROY
J. Donaldson
J. Donaldson/J.H. Hall
J. Richmond

VERNON
J.S. Allen

WARREN
A. Low
Warren Packard
Soule, White & Spear
Charles White
White & Spear

WOOSTER
Wm. Henry Jr.
Henry Hiser

XENIA
H. & W.T. Carey (P)

ZANESVILLE
E.E. Fillmore
J. Harrison & Co.

PENNSYLVANIA

AARONSBURG
F. Reager (P)

ALLEGHENY CITY (now PITTSBURGH)
J. Lautner
W. Scott

BERLIN
G. Mundorfff

BETHEL
M. Daub (P)

BETHLEHEM
Brunner

BROOKLYN TWP.
C. Gere
C.M. Gere
E. Gere
J. Kent (P)
A.W. Mack
J.B. Mack

DOUGLAS
F. Dallicker
H.J. Harpel

EAST PETERSBURG
I. Schauer

FRANKFORD (now PHILADELPHIA)
R. Keen

HANOVER
Adam Ault

HARRISBURG
H. Gilbert (P)
W.O. Hickok (P)
Kelker

HINKLETOWN
J. Stamm

JACKSON
H. Wentz (P)

KANE
Kane Mfg. Co.

LANCASTER
Samuel Auxer
Auxer & Remly
J.F. Bauder
E.W. Carpenter
I. Carpenter
S. Carpenter
W. Carpenter
Iohn Heiss
D. Heiss (Heis)
Iacob Heiss
Kieffer & Auxer
G. Mayer
Steinman & Co.

LEBANON
W.F. Achenbach

LEWISBURG
H. Yoɛt (P)

MANHEIM
J.F. Bauder

MEADVILLE
N. White

MERCER
H.H. Clark

MOUNT JOY
J. Stamm

MUNCY
Herman & Mohr (P)

PHILADELPHIA
(includes FRANKFORD)
T. Aikman

H. Albert & Co.
B. Armitage
Barry & Co.
W.J. Barton
J.F. Bauder
John Bell
S.H. Bibighaus
Biddle & Co.
R. & W.C. Biddle & Co.
D. Brooks
W. Brooks
Bunting & Middleton
Bushnell
Butler (George)
Butler (John)
Andrew Butler
Frederick Butler
S. Caruthers
A.J. Colton
D. Colton
D. Colton & J. Colton
D. Colton & B. Sheneman
J. Colton
M. Deter
Dillworth Branson & Co.
T. Donoho
T. Duke
Elder & Son
G. & S. Elfrey
Field & Hardie
Glenn & Duke
Eli Goldsmith
George Goldsmith
T. Goldsmith
Wm. Goldsmith
Jn. Gordon
W. Grinel
B. Hannis
Benjamin Harris
Hazlet
D. Heis (Heiss)
Horner & Son
J.F. Jones
J.T. Jones
John C. Keen
R. Keen
C.F. Kellner
Kneass
Kneass & Co.
W.M. McClure
William McDaniels
Mander & Dillin
M. Martien
Martin
W. Martin

448

J.W. Massey
Samuel Massey
A. Miller
F. Miller
Thos. Napier
N. Norton
Parrish
R.A. Parrish
Parrish & Barry
Parrish & Massey
John Passcul
E.W. Pennell
Pennell & Miller
Philada. Works (P)
John Pickering
T. Poultney & Sons
Powel
P. Probasco
Richards
Sandoe & Edelen
J.B. Shannon
B. Sheneman
B. Sheneman & Bro.
Edward Sheneman
Henry Sheneman
B. Shuman & Bro.
W.M. Souder
Souder & Summers
John E. Spayd
Spayd & Bell
Spayd & Wheeler (P)
I. Stall
Stall & Massey
Stevens
A.C. Stevens
J. Tilburn
Van Baun
John Veit
A. Wheaton
Catherine White
Charlotte White
G. White
Henry G. White
Israel White
Jacob White
R. White
T.W. White (P)
White & Grinnel
R. Wright
Yarnell & McClure

PITTSBURGH
John Barclay
A. Bright & J. Chappell
J. Chappell

T. Clarke
W. Evens
W.H. Fahnstock
W.C. Hopper
Wm. P. Hughes
P.H. Laufman
J. Lautner
Lautner Hardware Co.
Llithgow
Logan, Gregg & Co.
Logan, Wilson & Co.
Logan & Kennedy
J. M'Cully
A.D. McGrew
Samuel H. Richmond
W. Scott
John Star
Swetman
Swetman & Hughes
Whitmore & Wolff
Whitmorem, Wolf, Duff & Co.
Whitmore, Wolff, Lane & Co.
Wilson (William)
B. Wolff, Jr.
Wolff & Lane & Co.
Joseph Woodwell & Co.

POTTSVILLE
Bright & Co.

READING
W. & J.H. Keim
M. Long

UPPER MAHANTONGO TWP.
J. Haas

WASHINGTON
J. Coates

YORK
Jacob Small
P. Small

RHODE ISLAND

CENTRAL FALLS
M.P. Wilmarth

COVENTRY
Arnold Wickes (P)

CUMBERLAND
David Clark

I. Nicholson
NEWPORT
Jo. Wilbur

PAWTUCKET
Bodman & Bearse
Bodman & Hussey
Bodman, Bearse & Hussey
E. Smith
I .E. Smith & Co.

PROVIDENCE
Ion Ballou
I.S. Battey
Battey & Eddy
Belcher Bros.
L.B. Bigelow
J.E. Child
S. Cumings
Cumings & Gale
James A. Eddy
Isaac Field
Rich'd M. Field (P)
Jo. Fuller
Fuller & Field
J.R. Gale
R. Hazard
I. Lindenberger
P.H. Manchester
Miller
I. Miller (P)
Olney
J.W. Pearce
T.H. Strange

SMITHFIELD
E. Smith (P)

WARREN
N.L. Barrus

WOONSOCKET
G. Darling & Co.

SOUTH CAROLINA

CHARLESTON
Wm. Adger
Roosevelt, Hyde & Clark

CHESTER
Ja. McKee

COLUMBIA

Fisher & Agnew

TENNESSEE

MARYVILLE
John Cummings

MEMPHIS
S. Cook
Holyoake-Lownes & Co.
R.T. Lamb & Co.
Lownes & Co.
Orgill Bros. & Co.
N.H. Stout

NASHVILLE
Alex Fall
Fall & Cunningham
Gray & Kirkman
J.W. Horton & Co.
Macey & Hamilton

VERMONT

BARNARD
S. Culver

BELLOWS FALLS
Dewey Brown

BETHEL
H.S. Dewey/L.W. Newton

BRANDON
J. Conant

BURLINGTON
J. Herrick
I..E. Shattuck
Strong H'dwe Co.

CABOT
H. Perkins
H. Russell

EAST CORINTH
L.F. Hale

HYDE PARK
S.A. Harris

JAMAICA
E.G. Pierce Jr.

MONTPELIER
Preston Trow
NORTH DANVILLE
J.F. Bachelder

ST. JOHNSBURY
A. Kasson
Wm. Renfrew

VERGENNES
S.J. Gage (P)

WILLIAMSTOWN
J.D. White (P)

WILLISTON
I. Chapman

WILMINGTON
H.H. Read

VIRGINIA

FAIRMONT (now WV)
Joseph Nuzum

LYNCHBURGH
H.B. Richards

MARTINSBURG (now WV)
William Evans

NEWARK
Bidwell & Hale

NORFOLK
E.P. Tabb & Co.

PETERSBURG
Davis, Lamb & Co.
Dunn & Spencer
Q. & W.L. Morton
Van Lew & Morton

RICHMOND
T. Moore
C.J. Sinton & Co.
Smith & Roberts
Van Lew & Smith

STAUNTON
George E. Price

WHEELING (now WV)
Anderson & Laing
Christopher Bonnell
Greer & Laing
Samuel Neel
Ott & Greer
W. Steele
W. Steele & Co.

WINCHESTER
Crum & Schultz

WEST VIRGINIA

FAIRMONT (formerly VA)
Joseph Nuzum

MARTINSBURG (formerly VA)
William Evans

WHEELING (formerly VA)
Anderson & Laing
Christopher Bonnell
Greer & Laing
Samuel Neel
Ott & Greer
W. Steele
W. Steele & Co.

WISCONSIN

MILWAUKEE
T.C.G. Allen
Jonathan Beiley
W.H. Byron
E. Clark (Edwin)
E. & H. Clark
H. Clark
J.B. Danner
L.J. Farwell & Co.
Haney & Debow
W.J. Hunt (P)
Geo. W. Kelley
L. Kennedy (Leonard Jr.)
Otto Kleist
Henry J. Nazro
H.J. Nazro & Co.
J. Nazro & Co.
Nazro & King
P. Weber & Co.

For a much more detailed and complete view of planes and other tools, we suggest that the reader refer to John Whelan's *The Wooden Plane* and R.A. Salaman's *Dictionary of Tools*. (see Bibliography)

ASTRAGAL A molding comprised of a bead (approximately half-circle) set in some distance from the edge of the work; also the plane that makes such a molding.

BEAD, also BEADING PLANE A small half-circle ornament repeated in a straight line to form a molding; also the plane that makes such a molding.

BENCH PLANES A series of flat-soled planes used on the workbench to smooth the surfaces of boards. Ranging in size from smallest to largest, they include the smoother, or smooth plane (6½" to 10½" long), the jack (14" to 16" long), the fore plane (18" to 22" long), and the jointer (24" to 36" long).

BEVEL A section of a molding profile consisting of a sloping straight line.

BELECTION, BILECTION, or BOLECTION MOLDING A molding with a rabbet cut into it so that it will fit over the edge of the surface or panel on which it is used.

BOXING Inserts in the sole of a plane to resist wear; usually of boxwood, but can be lignum, ebony etc.

CABINETMAKER Furniture maker.

CHAMFERS, also CHAMFER PLANE Flat surface made by planing off the right angle at the top and sides of a plane (or other woodwork); also a plane to make such flat surfaces.

COMPLEX MOLDER A plane that cuts compound curves, usually for decorative purposes.

COOPERS' PLANES Planes used by a barrel maker, e.g. howel, croze, sun plane etc.

CORNICE PLANE Planes used to make a wide complex molding; sometimes called crown molders because the moldings were often used at the top, or crown, of a room.

CROWN MOLDER See cornice plane.

CROWNED INITIALS Imprints found on some early planes, consisting of a letter topped by a fleur-de-lis-type crown; initial and crown are not separate stamps but parts of the same stamp. Found frequently on planes of Thomas Grant (and thought to be owned by the Grant family) and Robert Eastburn, as well as on a few other American and English planes. Believed to have been used by Grant, as seller of the planes, to imprint the buyer's initials.

DADO PLANE A plane made to cut a groove across the grain without tearing the wood. The iron is skewed and is preceded by a vertical iron (nicker) that scores the edges of the cut.

DEPTH STOP Device used on many planes (particularly grooving-type planes) to limit the depth of the cut. Usually controlled by a screw.

DIRECTORY A book published annually in many cities, listing the residents by address and occupation.

DOUBLE–IRONED Refers to the use of a smaller cap iron placed in front of the cutting iron and usually affixed to it, to provide stability and prevent tearing. Can also refer to a plane that uses two separate cutting irons.

DRAW KNIFE Consisting of a flat or curved blade with tangs at either end at right (or slightly larger) angles to the blade; the tangs fitted with wooden handles. Draw knives are used in place of planes to remove unwanted wood.

EDGE TOOL Any tool with a sharpened blade. Can include planes, chisels, draw knives, axes, adzes, etc.

EMBOSSED STAMP A planemaker's imprint in which the background is depressed and the name is thereby raised above the surrounding wood.

FENCE A vertical guide used on many planes (notably plow planes and filletsters). It is held against one edge of the workpiece and therefore controls the placing of the cut.

FILLET A small horizontal straight section of a molding.

FILLETSTER (in England FILLISTER) A plane that does the same job as a rabbet, i.e. cuts a rectangular step on the edge of a piece of wood, except that the filletster has a fence and also has a small mouth like a molding plane and unlike the open, curved mouth of the rabbet. (see rabbet)

FINIAL The rounded top part of a plane wedge.

FLOAT A coarse rasp with parallel teeth, 4 or 5 to the inch.

FLUTING Carved out curve at the place where the upper stock of the molding plane meets the lower stock.

FORE PLANE The third in size of the bench planes, about 18" to 24" long and used to smooth the work after using the jack plane.

GROOVE (OR GROOVING) PLANE Plane used to make the groove into which the tongue fits when joining the edges of two pieces of wood by this method. Together the groove-making plane plus the tongue-making plane are called "match planes." The term grooving plane can also be used generically to refer to any plane that makes a groove, including groove planes, dado planes, and plow planes.

GUTTER PLANE A jack-type plane, except with a convex, rounded bottom, used to hollow out wood to make gutters. Usually about 15"-16" long.

HEEL The back end of a plane.

HOLLOW PLANE A simple molding plane with a shallowly concave sole (makes a convex molding). Together with its opposite, the round plane, it is the most common of the molding planes.

HOWEL A cooper's plane used to cut a shallow indentation (a howel) on the inside of the barrel at both ends. The croze (plane) was then used to cut a sharp groove in the howel into which the tops and bottoms (heads) of the barrel were fitted.

IMPRINT The planemaker's name (and sometimes address) stamped onto the toe of a plane.

INCISED STAMP A planemaker's imprint in which the name is cut into, engraved, or carved into the wood.

INCUSE STAMP A planemaker's imprint in which the name is hammered, stamped, or pressed into the wood.

IRON The cutting blade of the plane.

JACK (PLANE) The second from the smallest of the bench planes, approximately 14"-16" in length and used for rough work and rapid wood removal.

JOINER A finishing carpenter.

JOINTER Longest of the bench planes, about 24"-36" in length, used to finish off the edges of the wood before they are joined.

LIGNUM Lignum vitae ("wood of life"); a very hard, extremely heavy, waxy wood, native to the Caribbean. Deep brown in color. Brought into seaports during the 19c; often used on wear surfaces and soles of planes for boxing. Occasionally the whole plane was made of lignum, but this was quite costly.

MARKING GAUGE Used for marking lines parallel to the edge of the wood. Consists of a fence that slides on a 9" or 10" long stem and is fixed in place by a wedge or thumbscrew. The stem has a metal spur on one end that marks the wood as the fence is pushed along the edge of the wood.

MAST PLANE Used by shipwrights to smooth masts and spars. About the size of a smooth plane, with a shallow hollow-curving sole and iron.

MATCH PLANES Matching tongue and groove planes; sometimes both incorporated in the same plane. (see tongue plane and groove plane)

MITER PLANE Like a smooth plane except that the iron is set at a 35° rather than a 45° angle from the stock. Used to trim the ends of boards.

MOLDING PLANE -also **MOLDER** A wide variety of different planes used to make decorative wood work.

MORTISING Joining two boards by fitting a rectangular tenon (or tongue) on one into a rectangular hole (mortise) in the other.

NOSING PLANE Plane with large semi-circular molding profile, used to round the front edge of a stair tread.

OFFSET HANDLE A term used to designate the placing of a plane's handle off to one side, rather than exactly in the center of the stock.

OGEE A molding plane that cuts an S-shaped curve; also the name of the curve that is cut.

OVOLO A molding plane that cuts a convex curve, round or elliptical; also the name of the curve that is cut.

PANEL RAISER - also RAISING PLANE A plane used to cut the wide beveled rabbet around the sides of a panel (e.g. a door panel), so that the panel stands out in relief. A rather wide, flat-soled plane, with the iron skewed, and generally a movable fence.

PLANK PLANES Match (tongue and groove) planes, about 14"-15" long, for use in planks of thickness $1\frac{1}{4}$" to $1\frac{1}{2}$". Compare with "board" match planes, which were used on boards 3/8" to 1" thick.

PLOW PLANE An intricate, often beautiful, plane used to cut a groove parallel with the edge of the wood. Consists of two major sections: the plane stock (usually about 8" to 10" long) which came with a set of irons of varying widths; and the fence, whose attached arms fit through the stock and are fixed in place by wedges or by screw nuts. (Continental European planes have the arms attached to the stock and fitting through the fence). Usually the plow is fitted with a depth stop also.

P–TAMPIA Commonly used abbreviation for Roger Smith's book *Patented Transitional & Metallic Planes in America 1827-1927 Vols. I and II* (see Bibliography).

QUARTER ROUND Common convex molding consisting of one quarter of the arc of a circle; also the plane that makes such a molding.

QUIRK Generally a small angle or turning between one part of a molding and another.

RABBET – in England, REBATE A rectangle, or step, cut out along the edge of a piece of wood. Used for joining two pieces of wood, with rabbets cut in the edges of each. The rabbet plane has a flat sole, with either a straight or skewed iron, and is distinguished by a wide, curved mouth for shavings escape, often in a extremely graceful, lovely curve. (see filletster)

RAISING PLANE See panel raiser.

RAZEE A plane on which the rear end of the stock is partially cut down so that the handle is seated lower than it ordinarily would be. The front end of the plane can also be razeed, though this is not so common.

RELIEVED WEDGE A wedge in which a small part of the finial (the back part, resting against the iron shank) is cut away, so that the wedge can be more easily removed. Generally used only on 18c and early 19c planes.

ROUND PLANE A simple molding plane whose sole and iron are shallowly convex-shaped and therefore cut a concave molding. Together with its opposite, the hollow, it is the most common of the molding planes.

ROUTERS Any plane or other tool that routs out waste from a groove or carved recess in wood. Generally speaking, it has a single cutter, either in a plane or in a holder with handles on either side.

SASH PLANE A combination rabbet and molding plane used in making window frames. The rabbet side cuts the groove for the glass to fit into and the molding side cuts the decorative inside molding. Both cuts are made at the same time.

SCOTIA Simple molding, concave in shape, and unsymmetrical; also the plane that cuts such a molding. Also sometimes called a "cove".

SIDE RABBET Plane with the cutting edge on the side of the stock. Used to clean the side of a rabbet cut. Sold in right and left side pairs.

SIDE BEAD Molding plane used to cut a bead on the edge of the wood.

SKATE The metal plate found on grooving planes (plows, grooves) which serves as a bed for the iron and a sole for the plane.

SKEW Refers to a plane in which the iron is set at an angle to the length of the stock, rather than squarely at right angles.

SMOOTH PLANE - or SMOOTHER The smallest of the bench planes, about 7" to 10".

SNIPE BILL A plane used to clean up the cuts made by other molding planes. Sold as a right and left pair.

SPAR PLANE See mast plane.

SPILL PLANE A plane used to make a curled shaving that was lit from the fire and then used to light a pipe or cigar.

STAVE Each of the wooden sections used to form the body of a barrel.

STOCK The main part of the plane, into which the iron is fitted.

STOP See depth stop.

STUFF The wood that is being worked on.

SUN PLANE A cooper's plane, 10" to 14" long, with the stock shaped in a curve. Used to even up the outer edge of the stave ends.

TENON See mortising.

THROAT Opening at the top of the plane for the escape of shavings.

TOE The front end of a plane.

TONGUE PLANE Plane used to make the tongue that fits into the groove, when joining the edges of two pieces of wood by this method. Together the tongue-making plane plus the groove-making plane are called match planes.

TOOTHING PLANE Used to ridge the wood so that veneers can be glued to it. Similar to a smooth plane, except that the iron is serrated and is set almost perpendicular to the stock.

TOPPING PLANE Another name for cooper's sun plane (which see).

TORUS BEAD A molding similar to an astragal, but usually of an elliptical shape and set off from the rest of the molding by a quirk and a fillet.

TOTE The handle on a plane. In a closed tote the wood completely encircles the finger opening; an open tote lacks the front part that completes the circle.

TURNING Fixing the wood between two spindles on a lathe, then turning it while shaping it with gouges, chisels. etc.

WEAR PLATE The inside facing of a fence on a plow plane.

WEDGE Piece of wood or metal that fits in front of the iron of a plane and holds it in place. Other movable parts of a plane may also be wedged, e.g. fence arms and depth stops.

W.S. Abbreviation for "which see":refer to that entry in the directory.

YANKEE PLOW PLANE 18c or early 19c plow plane usually made in New England. It is almost always oversized ($9\frac{7}{8}$" to 10"), made of yellow birch, with a plain unadorned fence the same length as the body of the plane, and square fence arms. The arms are fixed by wedges or wooden thumbscrews or both.

ZB The zigzag border often found around planemakers' stamps. The zb differentiates the stamp from those with no border or with straight-line borders (lb) or decorative borders.

BIBLIOGRAPHY

We have listed below a number of books, pamphlets, catalogs and articles that we felt would be helpful to readers who might wish to delve more deeply.

We have divided the bibliography into three categories: 1) general background information, 2) regional studies of planemaking and planemakers, and 3) studies of individual planemakers and dealers.

We will be referring to these sources in the following listings:

- **THE CHRONICLE** is the quarterly journal published by the Early American Industries Association (EAIA) for its members (see chapter on clubs).

- **PLANE TALK** was a quarterly journal that provided information of interest to plane collectors. Though it is no longer being published, back issues are available from The Astragal Press. (P.O. Box 239, Mendham, NJ 07945)

- **THE MECHANICK'S WORKBENCH** was a catalog issued periodically by Anne and Donald Wing that offered tools for sale as well as articles of interest to collectors. (P.O. Box 544, Marion, MA 02738).

- **THE CATALOG OF AMERICAN WOODEN PLANES,** is a quarterly journal available from Bacon Street Press, 46 Western Ave., Sherborn, MA 01770.

Ken Roberts Publishing Co., Box 151, Fitzwilliam, NH 03447 and Roger K. Smith, Box 177, Athol, MA 01331, both publish books of interest to tool collectors as well as reprints of old catalogs.

GENERAL BACKGROUND INFORMATION

THE WOODEN PLANE: Its History, Form, and Function by John M. Whelan. The Astragal Press.
WOODEN PLANES IN 19th CENTURY AMERICA, Volume I 1978, Volume II (abbrev. WPINCA) by Kenneth D. Roberts 1983, Ken Roberts Publishing Co., Box 151, Fitzwilliam, NH, 03447
PATENTED TRANSITIONAL & METALLIC PLANES IN AMERICA 1827-1927, Vols. I & II, (abbrev. P-TAMPIA) by Roger K. Smith, 1981, Box 177, Athol, MA 01331.
DICTIONARY OF TOOLS by R.A. Salaman. Available from The Astragal Press.
BRITISH PLANEMAKERS FROM 1700, 3rd ed., by W.L. Goodman, Revised by Jane and Mark Rees. Available from The Astragal Press.
COLLECTING ANTIQUE TOOLS by Herbert P. Kean and Emil S. Pollak, 1990, The Astragal Press.
A PRICE GUIDE TO ANTIQUE TOOLS by Herbert P. Kean and Emil S. Pollak, 1992, The Astragal Press.
PRICES REALIZED ON RARE IMPRINTED AMERICAN WOOD PLANES 1979-1992, by E. & M. Pollak, The Astragal Press. This book, together with *A PRICE GUIDE* (above) will provide useful pricing information for the majority of planes.

REGIONAL STUDIES OF PLANEMAKING AND PLANEMAKERS

DIRECTORY OF BALTIMORE PLANE & EDGE TOOL MAKERS by Richard E. Hay ($9.75 postpaid from the author, at 1809 Midlothian Ct., Vienna, VA 22180 or from Fromer's Antiques, Box 224, New Market, MD 21774).

A CHECKLIST OF BOSTON PLANEMAKERS by William B. Hilton, *The Chronicle* June 1974.

CINCINNATI PLANE, EDGETOOL MAKERS AND DEALERS, 2nd ed., by Gil and Mary Gandenberger, published by the authors, 5171 Willnet Drive, Cincinnati, OH 45235.

DOWN EAST (MAINE) PLANEMAKERS by Larry Brundage, *Plane Talk* VII-1-20.

THE PLANES OF MAINE by Larry Brundage, *The Chronicle* June 1984.

PLANEMAKING IN THE VALLEY OF THE CONNECTICUT RIVER & HILLS OF WESTERN MASSACHUSETTS by Elliot Sayward and William Streeter, *The Chronicle* July 1975.

CHRONOLOGY OF 18th CENTURY PLANEMAKERS IN SOUTHEASTERN NEW ENGLAND by Anne and Donald Wing, *The Mechanick's Workbench,* Autumn/Winter 1984

INSTRUMENTS OF CHANGE:NEW HAMPSHIRE HAND TOOLS AND THEIR MAKERS 1800-1900 by James and Donna-Belle Garvin, New Hampshire Historical Society, 30 Park Street, Concord NH 03301.

EARLY TOOLS OF NEW JERSEY AND THE MEN WHO MADE THEM by Alexander Farnham, 1985, 78 Tumble Falls Rd., Stockton, NJ 08559.

SEARCH FOR EARLY NEW JERSEY TOOLMAKERS by Alexander Farnham, 1992, address above.

SHAVINGS FROM THE PAST: The Wooden Plane Collections of the Chemung County Historical Society and the DeWitt Historical Society of Tompkins County (a study of planes from upstate NY) 1983. Available through the EAIA.

PLANES IN CENTRAL NEW YORK by Seth W. Burchard, *The Chronicle* December 1975.

PLANEMAKERS & OTHER EDGE TOOL ENTERPRISES IN NEW YORK STATE IN THE NINETEENTH CENTURY by Kenneth & Jane Roberts, Ken Roberts Publishing Co. 1971

PLANEMAKERS OF 18th CENTURY PROVIDENCE, RHODE ISLAND by Anne and Donald Wing, *The Mechanick's Workbench* July 1978.

DATING OF ST. LOUIS PLANES by George E. Murphy M.D., *The Chronicle,* Part I June 1980, Part II September 1980.

ARTICLES ON PLANEMAKERS AND DEALERS, AND TOOL CATALOG REPRINTS

THOMAS AIKMAN by Kenneth K. Hopfel, *Plane Talk,* Vol. XIV, No. 3 1990.

AUBURN TOOL CO.: 1869 Price List and Catalog, The Astragal Press.

JONATHAN BALLOU by Anne & Donald Wing, *Plane Talk,* Vol. XV, No. 2, 1991.

BARNES by Roger K. Smith, *Plane Talk* III-4-14.

D.R. BARTON: 1873 Catalog, The Astragal Press.

D.R. BARTON IMPRINTS ON PLANES by Robert D. Graham Jr., *The Chronicle* September 1973.

J.F. BAUDER: TWO LANCASTER COUNTY PLANEMAKERS by Richard Peiffer, *The Chronicle* June 1984.

J.F. BAUDER, *Plane Talk,* Vol. XII, No. 3, 1988.

E. BRIGGS by John S. Kebabian, *Plane Talk* II-12.

S.M. BURT—Turner, Wheelwright, & Planemaker? by Richard T. DeAvila, *The Chronicle* June 1989.

THE CHAPIN-STEPHENS CO. 1914 catalog, The Astragal Press.

H. CHAPIN'S SON: 1890 Price List and Illustrated Catalogue, reprinted by The Mid-West Tool Collectors Assn., August 1986.

CESAR CHELOR: A Study of Planes Made by Francis and John Nicholson and Cesar Chelor, by Emil and Martyl Pollak, *The Chronicle* June 1985.

CESAR CHELOR AND THE WORLD HE LIVED IN by Richard T. DeAvila, *The Chronicle*, Part I: June 1993; Part II: December 1993.

G.W. DENISON & CO. by Robert H. Carlson, *The Chronicle* December 1973.

DEWEY & NEWTON by Paul B. Kebabian, *Plane Talk*, Vol. XIV, No. 3 1990.

S. DOGGETT: THE DOGGETTS OF DEDHAM by Richard T. DeAvila, *Plane Talk* V-1-7.

DOMINY: WITH HAMMER IN HAND by Charles F. Hummel, University Press of Virginia 1968.

ROBERT EASTBURN by Emil & Martyl Pollak, *The Chronicle* June 1982.

HOSEA EDSON by Roger K. Smith, *The Chronicle* December 1979.

B.A. EDWARDS by John S. Kebabian, *The Chronicle* March 1976.

S. FISK by Richard T. DeAvila, *Plane Talk* IX-1-6.

ISAAC FITCH OF LEBANON CONNECTICUT, MASTER JOINER 1734-91 by William L. Warren, 1978, The Antiquarian and Landmarks Society of Connecticut, 394 Main Street, Hartford, CT 06103.

DAVID FULLER: Rural Planemaker of West Gardiner, Maine by Dale J. Butterworth & Bennett Blumenberg, *The Chronicle*, Part I: September 1991; Part II: December 1991.

JOSEPH FULLER OF PROVIDENCE: An Update by Anne & Donald Wing, *Plane Talk*, Vol. XV, No. 3, 1991.

PORTER A. GLADWIN by William B. Hilton, *The Chronicle* March 1975.

THOMAS GRANT - IRONMONGER by Daniel M. Semel, published by the EAIA. Also see ROBERT EASTBURN by Emil and Martyl Pollak, *The Chronicle* June 1982.

GREENFIELD TOOL CO. by Anne and Donald Wing, *The Mechanick's Workbench*, August 1980.

GREENFIELD TOOL CO. 1872 Catalog, The Astragal Press

HAMMACHER, SCHLEMMER: The Country's Largest Tool Store at the Turn of the Century, by James Aber, *The Chronicle* September 1971.

HAMMACHER, SCHLEMMER & CO. 1896 Catalog, reprinted by the EAIA and the Mid-West Tool Collectors Assn.

THE HEALDS by William B. Hilton, *The Chronicle* April 1974.

THE PLANEMAKERS HEISS by Alan G. Bates, *The Chronicle* September 1978.

PLANEMAKERS J. SAWYER & A. HOWLAND by Bruce E. Bradley, *The Catalog of American Wooden Planes*, No. 6, March 1993.

THE JETHRO JONES - CESAR CHELOR CONNECTION by Richard T. DeAvila, *The Chronicle*, December 1989.

THE H.L. KENDALL PATENT, *Plane Talk*, Vol. XIV, No. 2, 1990.

THE KENNEDYS: Planemaking in Early Hartford by Anne & Donald Wing, *Plane Talk*, Vol. XIV, No. 4, 1990.

LINDENBERGERS, *The Mechanick's Workbench*, Winter 1983-84.

JOHN LINDENBERGER, by Anne & Donald Wing, *Plane Talk*, Vol. XIII, No. 3 1989.

ASA LOW by Larry Brundage, *Plane Talk* Vol. XIII, No. 1, 1989.

ASA LOW, A Follow-Up by Larry Brundage, *Plane Talk*, Vol. XIV, No. 2, 1990.

GEORGE W. MANNING — Cooper's Toolmaker by Roger K. Smith, *Plane Talk*, Vol. XI, No. 2, 1987.

LUTHER AND JOSEPH METCALF: Two Cabinetmakers/Planemakers of New England by Bennett Blumenberg & Dale J. Butterworth, *The Chronicle,* June 1991.

MATTHEW MORIARTY—Cooper and Tool Maker by Larry Brundage, *Plane Talk,* Vol. XI, No. 3, 1987.

THOMAS NAPIER: The Scottish Connection by Alan G. Bates, 1986, published by The Early American Industries Assn. and The Mid-West Tool Collectors Assn. and available from them.

THOMAS NAPIER by Joseph T. Stakes, *The Chronicle* March 1977.

THE NICHOLSON FAMILY by Anne and Donald Wing, *The Mechanicks Workbench* Autumn 1981.

THE NICHOLSON FAMILY: JOINERS AND TOOL MAKERS by Anne Wing, *The Chronicle* June 1983.

FRANCIS AND JOHN NICHOLSON: A Study of Planes Made by Francis and John Nicholson and Cesar Chelor, by Emil and Martyl Pollak, *The Chronicle* June 1985.

THE LIFE & TIMES OF TRUMAN NUTTING, by Michael R. Humphrey, *Plane Talk,* Vol. XIII, No. 2, 1989.

OHIO TOOL CO.: Catalog #23, reprinted by Roger K. Smith.

NATHANIEL POTTER by Robert Wheeler, *The Chronicle,* March 1993.

THE PRESBREY FAMILY by Richard T. DeAvila, *Plane Talk* V-2-4.

JOHN F. RANSOM by Larry Brundage, *Plane Talk,* Vol. XV, No. 1, 1991.

RAYL'S CATALOG: #21 (ca.1905), reprinted by Roger K. Smith.

WILLIAM RAYMOND by Herman Freedman, *The Chronicle* March 1981.

THE SAMSONS (SAMPSONS) and STETSON by Michael R. Humphrey, *Plane Talk,* Vol. XV, No. 2, 1991.

ABEL SAMPSON: Maine Privateer Turned Planemaker by Dale Butterworth & Bennett Blumenberg, *The Chronicle,* June 1992.

SANDUSKY by Thomas N. Tully, *The Chronicle* September 1977.

SANDUSKY TOOL CO.: 1877 Catalog, The Astragal Press.

THE SANDUSKY TOOL CO. STORY by W.G. Schwer, *The Chronicle,* September 1993.

PLANEMAKERS J. SAWYER & A. HOWLAND, by Bruce EE. Bradley, *The Catalog of American Wooden Planes,* No. 6, March 1993.

SCHAUERS: TWO LANCASTER COUNTY PLANEMAKERS by Richard Peiffer, *The Chronicle* June 1984.

JOHN SLEEPER by Herman Freedman with Anne and Donald Wing, *The Mechanick's Workbench* Summer 1983.

AARON SMITH OF REHOBOTH by Anne & Donald Wing, *Plane Talk,* Vol. XV, No. 4, 1991.

THE SMITH FAMILY - PLANEMAKERS OF REHOBOTH by Anne & Donald Wing, *The Mechanick's Workbench* October 1979.

JAMES STARR by Richard F.S. Starr, *The Chronicle* December 1980.

H.G. STILLEY by Kendall Bassett, *Plane Talk* II-2-11.

THE LIFE AND TIMES OF JAMES & J.J. STYLES, *Plane Talk,* Vol. XII, No. 1, 1988.

JOHN TEAL. "D'ye ken John Teal? Carpenter's Tool Maker, Leeds, England—Princeton, Massachusetts" by Larry Brundage, *The Chronicle* September 1988.

MARCUS B. TIDEY by Larry Brundage, *Plane Talk,* Vol. XIV, No. 3, 1990.

LEVI TINKHAM by Richard T. DeAvila, *Plane Talk* VII-2- 14.

D.B. TITUS by Clarence Blanchard, *Plane Talk,* Vol. XIV, No. 4, 1990.

J.R. TOLMAN by Larry N. Brundage, *The Chronicle* December 1976.

TREMAN & BROS. by Seth Burchard, *Plane Talk,* Vol. XIV, No. 2.

THE WELLS FAMILY PLANEMAKERS by Patrick M. Kelly, *The Chronicle,* March 1991.

CHESTER R. WELLS—A Planemaker's Account Ledger by Patrick M. Kelly, *The Chronicle,* Part I: March 1992; Part II: June 1992; Part III: September 1992.

HENRY WETHEREL by Anne and Donald Wing, *Plane Talk* I-4- 3.

THE WETHEREL(L)S, FATHER & SON, by Anne & Donald Wing, *Plane Talk,* Vol. XIV, No. 1 1990.

THE WHITE FAMILY OF PHILADELPHIA, by Carl E. Bopp, *Plane Talk,* Vol. XI, No. 3 1987.

NOTES

NOTES

NOTES

NOTES